Contemporary Literary Hermeneutics
and
Interpretation of Classical Texts

Herméneutique littéraire contemporaine
et
interprétation des textes classiques

Reprinted from The University of Ottawa Quarterly
Extrait de la Revue de l'Université d'Ottawa
Vol. 50, Nᵒˢ 3-4, p. 325-642

Contemporary Literary Hermeneutics
and
Interpretation of Classical Texts

* * *

Herméneutique littéraire contemporaine
et
interprétation des textes classiques

Edidit, praefatione introductioneque instruxit

STEPHANUS KRESIC
Universitatis Ottaviensis Professor Emeritus

Éditions de l'Université d'Ottawa
Ottawa University Press

Ottawa 1981

Avant-Propos

La nouvelle herméneutique (l'art de comprendre et la théorie de l'interprétation des textes) a accompli dans les dernières décennies des progrès énormes. La philologie aurait grand avantage à profiter de ces résultats pour élargir son champs d'activité, renforcer ses fondements intellectuels et accroître son rayonnement.

Désireux d'amorcer ce rapprochement nécessaire, nous avons organisé les 9, 10 et 11 novembre 1978, à l'Université d'Ottawa, un Symposium international sur l'herméneutique littéraire contemporaine et l'interprétation des textes classiques. Philosophes-herméneuticiens et philologues classiques ont discuté ensemble des problèmes théoriques et pratiques que pose le rapprochement souhaité.

Nous publions ici, en anglais et en français, les fruits de leurs labeurs. Nous y avons ajouté des contributions des meilleurs experts au monde dans le domaine des principes herméneutiques de la compréhension et de l'interprétation des textes littéraires. Plusieurs philologues classiques — promoteurs de nouvelles voies dans l'interprétation des textes — qui n'avaient pu assister à notre Symposium, ont bien voulu s'associer dans cette discussion nouvelle.

* * *

Nous tenons à exprimer ici notre gratitude à tous ceux qui ont collaboré à la réalisation de ce projet.

Nous remercions d'abord tous les herméneuticiens et philologues qui ont enrichi ce volume d'idées neuves susceptibles de profiter aux études classiques.

Notre gratitude va ensuite au Conseil de recherches en sciences humaines du Canada et à l'Université d'Ottawa qui nous ont aidé matériellement, et aux Éditions de l'Université d'Ottawa qui ont assumé la tâche de la publication.

Nous tenons à remercier particulièrement le Comité des publications de la Faculté des Arts et son président, le vice-doyen Norman Pagé, qui a si promptement et chaleureusement recommandé la publication du volume aux Éditions de l'Université.

Nous n'apprécierons jamais assez la sollicitude, le dévouement et la compétence du Père Léopold Lanctôt, directeur des Éditions et de M. P. Savard, président du Comité directeur de la *Revue de l'Université d'Ottawa*.

En achevant ce travail, notre gratitude va aussi à nos collègues de l'Université qui ont bien voulu, malgré leurs nombreuses occupations, nous aider de différentes façons: en traduisant des manuscrits (M. B. Plaskacz), en revisant le français de certains manuscrits (M. P. Brind'-Amour, E. Gareau, Y. LePage) ou l'anglais (M. F. M. Tierney), ou en nous prodiguant des suggestions utiles (particulièrement M. John Thorp). Nos étudiants (Mme Bonnie Ward et M. David Conrad), *semper fideles*, nous ont aussi rendu avec amabilité et bienveillance mille petits services d'un très grand prix.

Que tous veuillent bien trouver ici l'expression de notre sincère et profonde gratitude.

S. KRESIC, rédacteur du volume,
Université d'Ottawa.

TABLE OF CONTENTS / TABLE DES MATIÈRES

Editor's Introduction

Nam gaudere novis rebus debere videtur
Cui veteres obsunt.
(Lucretius V. 170-1)
He who is bored by the old should rejoice in the new.

Literature is reproved for uselessness and irrelevance in our technological age. But reproved literature proves itself: mankind immemorially craves the knowledge and the satisfaction which literature gives. The poet existed among the cave men, and he will exist until the last ding-dong of doom is clanged, for he is an inherent part of man's desire for truth and beauty. Although literature has many functions, they can be reduced to the basic one: through its significantly patterned language, in an organic and dramatic way, literature tells us the truth about ourselves and about the world in which we live. It is a kind of truth not usually found in other forms of discourse: a revelation of our own feelings, emotions, sensibilities and their hidden relationships, of other people's hardships and joys, and of social life, all from an unexpected angle which only the writer is able to reveal. Literature has always refused to divorce art from life; it has ever been carved upon the bedrock of humanity. Hölderlin affirmed that a man dwells poetically upon the earth, and Rilke added that song is our existence. Literature cannot be replaced or supplanted by any positive utilitarian science because besides its own poetic truth, it allies itself with beauty. Science, with its aggressiveness and so-called neutrality has made man rootless and alienated. Nietzsche was right in saying: "The purpose of art is to shelter us from the truth" (Wir haben die Kunst, damit wir nicht in der Wahrheit zugrunde gehen). We are convinced that the enigmatic phrase of Dostoevsky "Beauty will save the world" is a true prophecy. Poetry alone transcends the scientific reduction of everything human to calculation and mechanics. Jean-Paul Sartre, with his usual irony, remarks: "Le monde peut fort bien se passer de la littérature. Mais il peut se passer de l'homme encore mieux."

The literature of classical antiquity is the mother of our Western literature. Without her heritage we would sever the Medieval and Modern literature of the Western world from its source and its point of reference, and we would exclude all serious study of the seminal influences that have molded our letters. The long receding corridor of almost three millennia would no longer be illuminated. The noble line of European cultural succession would be broken. "Where men have dug for so long, there must be gold," said Nietzsche with his usual pregnancy. The culture of the West must faithfully bear its debt to its spiritual ancestors. Without Greek or Roman literary forms, stylistic devices, literary artistry and mythological lore, we would be utterly impoverished in our esthetic pleasure. Renan said that to break our contact with Greek or Roman antiquity would be to make of us "le vase vide, dont on respire encore le parfum." Bergson added: "Mais on ne respire pas indéfiniment le parfum d'un vase vide."

But it is not *only* because of this inherited life, *survie, Nachleben*, that we read and study the literary works of Greece and Rome. After almost three thousand years they are worth reading *for their own sake*, for their permanently attractive sobriety of form and for their universally meaningful human content, which are amalgamated into one artistic excellence.

It might be argued that the human content of classical Greek and Roman works is radically different from ours today — and as such an irrelevant one — because of the different historical, cultural and social contexts. But even conceding this argument, we can affirm that it is enormously valuable to compare our own human experience with that of previous epochs, for only thus may we assess ourselves with objective detachment and so widen our own horizons.

We think with Croce that "all true history is contemporary history" and with Ortega y Gasset that "the past is not there, at that date, but here, in me, in my life." We deem that the human condition is essentially a continuing and perennial problem, common to all mankind in all civilizations and epochs. Of course, each epoch rediscovers part of itself differently in the ancient Mediterranean world.

There is the paradox that literature which tells us more about the human condition it its depth, breadth and length than any other discipline, which gives us the untechnical, homely fullness of life, is of necessity a technical act of extreme difficulty. Gerard Manley Hopkins drew the distinction between a poet's *overthought* — explicit meaning — and his *underthought* — real poetic meaning. Since in every poetic work there are overt and covert experiences, outward actions and inward reflections, denotative and connotative meanings, conscious, subconscious and unconscious ingredients, allusive and elliptical techniques, revelations and concealments, more suggestions than statements, it is the task of the learned interpreter by severe, rigorous and methodical procedures, and using all the relevant knowledge that is available, to help the readers of literary works to understand them thoroughly in their varied facets, to appreciate them properly in the dynamics of their esthetic purpose, and to enjoy them with plenitude in their organic totality.

The ancient world laid such stress on literary artistry that it would be wrong to disregard this element in Greek and Roman literature. But Classical scholars have shown a limited ability to interpret literature *as literature*. They have often used Classical literary texts as pretexts to discuss minutiae of sclerotic grammar and unintegrated *realia*.

How many times we have heard the illuminating story of the Classics master who introduced to his class one of the greatest Greek tragedies with the following words: "Boys, this term you are to have the privilege of reading the *Oedipus Coloneus* of Sophocles — a veritable treasure-house of grammatical peculiarities"!

Alfred Edward Housman, the foremost English Latinist of the twentieth century and an authoritative textual critic, in his *Cambridge Inaugural* delivered in 1911 and never printed in its author's lifetime (the first unexpurgated printing appeared in 1969), affirmed that Classical scholarship is not literary criticism, and that it was not a scholar's business to communicate the appreciation of literature to his audience. In his words (p. 38): "The criticism and interpretation of Classical texts is not an exact science; and to treat it as if it were is falsification... (p. 39) The laws of criticism are nothing but a string of generalizations, necessarily inaccurate, which have been framed by the benevolent for the guidance, the support and the restraint of three classes of persons. They are leading strings for infants, they are crutches for cripples, and they are straight-waistcoats for maniacs." Since Housman pronounced these words, literary scholarship has become conscious of its scope and methods, it has become an autonomous professional science, although not an "exact" science in the nineteenth century meaning of this term. Literary criticism and literary scholarship are *not* now each other's antithesis.

Let us now quote what the *poet* Housman thought about *poetry*:

> Poetry indeed seems to me more physical than intellectual. A year or two ago, in common with others, I received from America a request that I would define poetry. I replied that I could no more define poetry than a terrier can define a rat, but that I thought we both recognised the object by the symptoms which it provokes in us. One of these symptoms was described in connexion with another object by Eliphaz the Temanite: 'A spirit passed before my face: the hair of my flesh stood up.' Experience has taught me, when I am shaving of a morning, to keep watch over my thoughts, because, if a line of poetry strays into my memory, my skin bristles so that the razor ceases to act. This particular symptom is accompanied by a shiver down the spine; there is another which consists in a constriction of the throat and a precipitation of water to the eyes; and there is a third which I can only describe by borrowing a phrase from one of Keat's last letters, where he says, speaking of Fanny Brawne, 'everything that reminds me of her goes through me like a spear'. The seat of this sensation is the pit of the stomach. ("The Name and Nature of Poetry", in the Leslie Stephen Lecture for 1933, delivered at Cambridge, on the 9th of May of that year, in A.E. HOUSMAN, *Selected Prose*, edited by John Carter, C.U.P., 1961, p. 193.)

We regret the limitations of Housman's theory of literary criticism and interpretation and can only imagine how a scholar of his intellectual calibre who possessed refined organs of appreciation, a great amount of taste and judgement, minute and profound learning, could have contributed to the interpretation of Latin authors had he but understood this endeavour as we understand it today: to draw the ancient text out of its historical remoteness and make it understandably present, thus abolishing the historical distance between past text and present reader.

If we examine the other side of the coin, we find that G.S. Kirk complains bitterly about the Classical scholars who have "a very limited ability to criticize and discuss Classical literature as literature... the perceptive and expressive criticism of literature does not seem to be a gift that goes frequently with the gift for language in its philological sense... Really impressive exponents of Classical literary criticism are rare indeed; I can hardly think of more than two, whether here or in America." (*Didaskalos*, Vol. III, 3, 1971, pp. 612-13).

This lamentation is continued by the eight contributors to the book *Quality and Pleasure in Latin Poetry* (C.U.P., 1974). These practising Latinists affirm in the epilogue (p. 129) that they have now "no specialist knowledge of the recent history of literary criticism. The twentieth century has seen an explosion of theories, methods and controversies in this field... We have heard the rumblings of the great critical storms of the century, and the waves have beaten on our shores. But have they re-shaped the coastline?"

In recent years, Classical scholarship has tried an increasing emphasis on the literary study of literary Classical texts, a serious concern with literature in itself. Charles Segal synthesizes these tendencies in his excellent article "Ancient Texts and Modern Literary Criticism" (*Arethusa* I, 1968, 1-25). He shows how Classical literature has become increasingly accepted in its own terms in spite of the remains of nineteenth century historicism, antiquarian literalism, and exaggerated 'scientism' (by which he means emulation of the 'objectivity' of natural sciences). Segal mentions however that cautious Classical critics have not of late been pioneers of new approaches. Speaking of the influence of (once) 'New Criticism', he points out its often inaccurate, unimaginative and pedantic application in the interpretation of Classics. He condemns *furorem arithmeticum*, the finding of exaggerated analytic patterns and numerologies which often led further and further from the primary experience of the work as poetry. He shows how symbolic and mythical allusions are put to profitable use in the modern interpretation of Classical texts. He ends his criticism of criticism with the encouraging note that modern interpretation of Classical texts shows "a serious concern with literature in itself; a greater openness to new approaches; a leaning to more critical rigour, discipline, and intellectual order."

L.P. Wilkinson, in his President's Address, "Ancient Literature and Modern Literary Criticism" (*Proceedings of the Classical Association*, Vol. 59, 1972, pp. 13-26), follows Segal's path, and surveys critically certain tendencies in new poetry in the past fifty years and the criticism it has fathered. He shows what effects these modern trends in literature have had on the study of Classical literature. He deals also with some of the problems in interpreting the poetry: writers' intention, the "intentional fallacy," symbolism, metaphor, simile, biographical irrelevancies, the shift in modern taste for poetic language, poetic word-order, reaction to rhetorics etc. He touches the crucial question "to what extent are we entitled, in interpreting Classical literature, to by-pass literal meaning, to disregard the ostensible intentions of authors, and to seek below the surface for allegory, symbolism, hidden meanings, ambiguities, and patterns of imagery?'' At the end, Professor Wilkinson draws up a rough balance sheet of Classical interpretation for the period of the past fifty years, saying "Within that period, Classical studies have greatly expanded in breadth by calling in other disciplines... 'close reading' has sharprened discrimination. There has been increased awareness of the possible existence of undertones beneath literal meaning.'' In brief he shows how interpretation and literary appreciation are gaining the upper hand in Classical studies.

There is another recent survey about new tendencies in the interpretation of Classical texts, this time limited only to Latin studies, to the period of the last ten years and to the European, especially the Italian, scene. Fabio Cupaiuolo, in his survey "A Proposito di Alcuni Recenti Studi Latini" (*BSL*, IX, 1979, pp. 93-125), embraces the period from 1969-1978. He emphasizes how the new tendencies have, for various reasons, come into prominence only since 1960, through the seeds are much older. As a main characteristic of interpretation, he mentions the procedure of dismantling the text and the identification of its immanency through the literary decoding. This new approach is a reaction against idealistic aesthetics which often consumed itself in a kind of commentary on literary artifact, kind of paraphrasis with emotional overtones. The new approach tries to unfold the literary text, to find out its different layers, to assemble its constitutive forces and concealed purposes, to discover the work's centre, the jugular vein which justifies not only the totality of the art-work but also its different levels and aspects, its life in all its parts.

Cupaiuolo advocates a plurality of approaches in interpretation. It is our opinion also that all approaches which honestly try to penetrate into the author's text, so that the reader might come into a more active connection with what he has read, are valid and useful on the condition that they do not pretend to be exclusive, doctrinal, normative, prescriptive, dogmatic and canonical, provided they are coherent and that they clearly state their premises.

Some modern interpreters of literary works of art, by an extremist zeal, often attack and reject the traditional approaches: historical-biographical, moral-philosophical, genetic and generic.

The use and abuse of the *historical-biographical* approach we shall discuss at appropriate points in our interpretation of *Miser Catulle*. Obviously, no literary work exist in a historical vacuum, and without an author's motivation. We cannot divorce it completely from its human and historical context. Even the representatives of the so-called autonomous immanence of a literary work cannot, in practice, avoid using biographical and historical documentation, although they pretend that the life of a poet is outside the poetry and that the poem should be explained purely *per se,* in terms of itself. The complete separation of subject and object, agent and act, the artist and the art, the poet and the poem, cannot, in our opinion, become the philosophical foundation and framework for literary interpretation because "the words of a poem come out of a head, not out of a hat", and the writer, in writing of himself, writes of his time. But, the 'biographical fallacy' begins when one approaches a literary art-work *only* in biographical and historical terms, pretending that poetry is autobiography or autobiography poetry, and that a literary work is *nothing more* than a mirror of an historical epoch or a bundle of historical facts ("the historical fallacy").

The *moral-philosophical* approach is as old as Classical Greek and Roman critics. On the one hand, we cannot deny that one of the functions of serious literature is to deal with the moral core of a given society. To be sure, man has never at any time attained a stable utopia in which moral concerns could be ignored. Every artist is necessarily a moralist. On the other hand, we cannot share the opinion of those who think that the larger function of literature is to teach morality, to preach to people what to do.

Source-hunting (which eventually can become *source-haunting*), has surely done much harm to Classical studies when it has become an aim in itself and when an indication of the source was believed by the critic to be a "proof" of the imitator's artistic impotence. Gide once said that the only authors are those who have been influenced. Imitation was the main artistic principle in Greco-Roman aesthetics. What is of the utmost importance is how an ancient author challenged his predecessors, and how he excelled in his emulation. What matters is not where he quarried his stone, but what he made with it.

The *generic* approach is more effective, with certain limitations, in Classical than in modern literature. It is by being aware of the conventions of a certain genre that we can fully appreciate the originality of the poets who created within that genre.

So much for the *traditional* approaches in the interpretation of Classical texts, and the justification of their eclectic application.

As to *modern* approaches, one of the characteristics of some modern Classical scholars has been, and remains, a disinclination to admit such approaches into their arcana; so they work in self-imposed isolation from other disciplines. It is our opinion that the texts from the past cannot be properly understood by modern readers and cannot have a living appeal for them, unless they are interpreted in the idiom of the present day. To ignore or to evade these approaches is to miss the significance and relevance of Classical authors for modern man. Gadamer rightly insists that a vital, contemporary understanding of the past is the only understanding worth having. As Odysseus in the underworld had to give the ghosts blood before they could speak to him, so the philologist has to give fresh blood to the spirits of the past — his own new blood — before they will reveal their mysteries. A historical gap between an ancient text and a modern reader does not lead at all to the text losing its innovative, contemporary character. It is a distinct property of literary texts that they never lose their ability to communicate.

All modern approaches: formalistic, structuralist, stylistic, psychological, psychoanalytical, sociological, mythological, anthropological, archetypal and others, may validly be applied to a Classical text if they are consistent with it. Each of them has also its own limits, for no single one can exhaust the manifold interpreting potentialities of a great literary work. There is never such a thing as definitive, complete interpretation of a polyphonic and polysemous literary work, because the human experience is too dynamic to be contained by such fixity and too diverse to answer such uniformity. The multiple frameworks handle its different aspects and they are complementary in results.

Let us conclude this first part of our introduction with T.S. Elliot's words from his essay "Tradition and the Individual Talent": "The historical sense involves a perception, *not only of the pastness of the past but of its presence* [italics mine]; the historical sense compels a man to write not merely with his own generation in his bones, but with a feeling that the whole of the literature of Europe from Homer and within it the whole of the literature of his own country has a simultaneous existence and composes a simultaneous order. This historical sense, which is a sense of the timeless as well as of the temporal, and of the timeless and of temporal together, is what makes a writer traditional. And it is at the same time what makes a writer most acutely conscious of his place in time, of his own contemporaneity." (T.S. Elliot, *Select Essays*, London, Faber, 1976, p. 14.)

*   *   *

Recent developments in scholarship outside the field of literature have profoundly affected the relationship of a contemporary reader to any text, ancient or modern. There has been much conscious and stubborn resistance to these new influences, not only by Classicists but also by scholars of modern literatures who have clung to the traditional criteria of literary appreciation and interpretation. Advances in linguistics and philosophy, combined with the development of the social sciences, have shown these traditional approaches to literary studies to be unacceptably limited and for the contemporary public, poverty-stricken.

Many Classicists now recognize the changed nature of literary studies and the need for the development of new skills and perspectives by literary scholars. The majority of these same scholars, however, are at something of a loss over what to do about these new necessities. Competent knowledge of two difficult Classical languages, is the *conditio sine qua non* of Classicists worthy of this name, and to this condition we can add that of a working knowledge of the several European languages in which much important research in classics is published. It requires also at least the basic knowledge of the various other disciplines that have become intertwined in the science of antiquity. Without this all-embracing knowledge a Classicist is not able to maintain a sense of common interrelation, he is a stranger in his own land. All of these leave the professional Classicist little opportunity for investigating the panoramic perspectives of the interdisciplinary visionaries, but it is precisely this investigation which Classics now needs in order to broaden its scope and strengthen its intellectual foundations.

New Literary hermeneutics, the art of understanding and the theory of interpretation of literary works, is of paramount importance to the contemporary interpreter of Classical and modern works. In this area, Classicists are practically non-existent, notwithstanding the tremendous development of contemporary literary hermeneutics in recent decades. (See Norbert Henrichs *Bibliographie der Hermenentik und ihrer Anwendungsbereiche seit Schleiermacher*, Düsseldorf, Philosophia Verlag, 1972).

Conscious of this changed nature of literary studies and of this need for the development of new skills and new perspectives by Classical literary scholars, I organized on Nov. 9-11, 1978, at the University of Ottawa, with the financial help of the Social Sciences and Humanities Council of Canada, as well as of the University of Ottawa, an International Symposium on Contemporary Literary Hermeneutics and Interpretation of Classical Authors, the first of this kind in the world. At this conference some prominent scholars of hermeneutics on this side of the Atlantic (R.E. Palmer, M. Murray, and P. McCormick) together with some innovative Classicists (V. Pöschl, P. Colaclides, Kenneth Quinn, Charles Segal, G.P. Sullivan) tried to establish a creative and critical dialogue between philosophical understanding of what interpretation should do and literary interpretation by Classical scholars. The learned public, consisting of some 100 professors and students from various disciplines, especially literature (and not only *Classical* literature) listened attentively and gave vigorous challenge to this interdisciplinary investigation. Both theoretical and practical problems in the contemporary approach to interpretation were discussed in papers, panels, and question periods. The conference was of considerable significance both to modern and to Classical literary scholars who confront the same problems concerning the interpretation of literary texts.

In response to the urging of the participants in the Symposium and of the learned public who wished to have access to the material presented, I proposed to the University of Ottawa Press that it publish the written versions of the papers presented at the Symposium and also some additional contributions from scholars of international repute on the same theme, so that we might have in one volume a comprehensive treatment of these problems. The University of Ottawa Press approved our plan.

In addition to the papers from the participants we solicited and received contributions from these following hermeneuticists: H.-G. Gadamer, P. Ricoeur and D.C. Hoy, and from the following philologists: B. Gentile, A. Tovar, J.-P. Chausserie-Laprée, F. Cupaiuolo, G.A. Privitera, A.L.T. Bergren, C. Salerme, and F.I. Zeitlin.

The papers and discussions in the volume are in French or English. This reflects the bilingual character of the University of Ottawa. The

German, Italian and Spanish contributions were translated into one of these two languages. The articles from the Symposium are in the language in which the paper was given.

The papers of the five hermeneuticists in the first part of the volume discuss both general and particular issues in contemporary literary hermeneutics which are of utmost importance for our understanding of literary texts and for an interpretive encounter with them. These hermeneuticists urge us to think about our thinking while interpreting literary texts, and about deepening of our understanding of works of literary art by synthesizing form and content in a single interpretive act to attain an authentic apprehension of human reality and culture. The conquest of the literary text is an ardouous march, interrupted by long silences, accompanied by exacting attention to details, reflective gazings and ponderings, and issuing in very cautious conclusions.

In the second section philologists discuss theoretical and practical problems of interpretation in Greek and Latin texts, some in traditional but most of them in a relatively innovative way. Their elucidations do not always illustrate the doctrines of the hermeneuticists in an exact way. That is understandable if we take into consideration the newness of this direction for them.

In contemporary literary hermeneutics there is a violent upsetting of traditional historical philology which was confident that it knew the past and its meaning. This historical basis of meaning in literary texts is now challenged by the hermeneuticians who follow Hegel, Heidegger and Gamader and who assert the futility of objective and accurate historical reconstruction. Even among contemporary hermeneuticians a polarity is clear. Emilio Betti, E.D. Hirsch Jr., Jürgen Habermas and their followers do not agree with the stated position. "Is it the destiny of those who practice interpretation never to achieve oecumenical harmony of theoretical principles?" asks Hirsch ("Three Dimensions of Hermeneutics", *New Literary History* 3, 1972, p. 245).

Hirsch, for example, seeks unique, determinate, permanent, unchanging and reproducible author's meaning represented by the author's final intention in the use of his particular sequence of linguistic signs. He argues that the object of interpretation is to discover the textual author's meaning in and for itself. He distinguishes between the verbal *meaning* of the text *(Bedeutung)* and its *significance (Bedeutsamkeit)*. The meaning of the text does not change, but its significance — our relationship to author's meaning, response to the text — varies significantly with different men and different times. Interpretation, Hirsch believes, deals with meaning, and criticism is concerned with significance. The two functions are distinct. The fact that understanding, interpretation, judgement and criticism are in practice entangled and interdependent does not represent a denial that all these functions are distinct, with distinct aims and requirements (*Validity in Interpretation*, New Haven and London,

Y.U.P. 1967, *passim*, and *The Aims of Interpretation*, Chicago and London, Ch.U.P., 1976, *passim*).

The focus of Gadamer's criticism is methodological alienation of the knower from his own historicity. He takes the knower's bondness to his present horizons and the temporal gulf separating him from his object to be the productive ground of all understanding. Gadamer affirms that understanding is not a repetition, duplication or reproduction of a past intention (the *mens auctoris*) but rather a genuinely productive procedure that involves the interpreter's own hermeneutical situation in communication with the author. For Gadamer, understanding is not reconstruction of the past but mediation, transmission, translation of past meaning into the present situation, the so-called "fusion of horizons" (*Wahrheit un Methode*, Tübingen, Mohr,[2] 1965. This seminal work of the most outstanding modern hermeneutician is translated into English, French and Italian).

Wolfgang Iser, professor of English and comparative literature at the University of Constance, in his book *The Act of Reading* (The John Hopkins University Press, Baltimore, 1978) does not believe in the archeological approach: digging for the hidden treasure of meaning through interpretation. First, he does not believe in a *single* hidden referential meaning. Second, he thinks that the potential meanings of a text are the product of a dynamic interaction between the external signals and the reader's act of comprehension. As reader and text merge into a single situation, meaning is no more an object to be defined, but an effect to be experienced. Iser affirms that the establishment of consistency is essential to all comprehension of a literary work. The consistency-building that takes place during the reading process is a product of the interaction between text and reader, dependent on "Gestalt"-groupings (= correlation of textual signs). For Iser the literary work has two poles: the artistic pole (=the author's text) and the aesthetic pole (=the realisation accomplished by the reader). The interpreter's task is to elucidate the potential meanings of a given text, and not to restrict himself to just one.

The philologists still adhere to the traditional virtues of Classical scholarship: concern for linguistic accurary, respect for the author and his work, and for the knowledge of the past. But they ought to be conscious of the contemporary theoretical principles of understanding and interpretation of literary texts: we feel the fresh air streaming through this volume. Both hermeneuticists and Classicists, with their intelligence, knowledge and desire for harmonious interaction are seeking to establish a fusion of horizons between contemporary literary hermeneutics and traditional philological hermeneutics. This fusion is directed to expanding the context of interpretation, not to cutting philology out.

To make a meaningful interlocking visible in a practical way, and with less esoterism, we arranged during the Symposium an evening of interpretation of Horace's Soracte Ode (*C*. 1.9). Five Classical philologists, in succession interpreted the ode, each in his own manner, with fine feeling for poetry and a sensitive understanding of the ancient intellectual world.

A trio of hermeneuticists gave their philosophical reappraisal of the interpretations from the standpoint of hermeneutical theory, and finally the
Classicists gave their *responsio*.

It was really an intellectual feast, made the more memorable by the
interfusion of Apollonian and Dionysian elements. Despite the fittingness
of these remarks for that convivial occasion, we could not print them as
they were *inter pocula* orally performed. So the two philologists (J.P.
Sullivan and Ch. Segal) and two hermeneuticists (M. Murray and R. Palmer) made a synthesis of this significant discussion from the transcript
of tapes which was sent to them.

To foster the same dynamic interaction between hermeneutic thinkers
and classical philologists we have added our own poetical, philologico-
aesthetic interpretation of *Miser Catulle,* to which hermeneuticists P.
McCormick and A.G. Gadamer have responded.

We hope that this interdisciplinary marriage (to use Martianus Capel-
la's phrase) between philology and philosophy will encourage a further
exploration of these problems and will provide a fresh avenue for subsequent research in the elucidation of Classical texts. Participation in an
on-going dialogue remains open and without end.

Stephen KRESIC, editor,
University of Ottawa.

I. — Literary Interpretation:
Philosophical Groundings
Interprétation littéraire :
fondements philosophiques

Allegorical, Philological, and Philosophical Hermeneutics: Three Modes in a Complex Heritage

I. — INTRODUCTION TO HERMENEUTICS

Hermeneutics, as a body of methods, theory, and philosophizing focussed on the problem of understanding texts, dates back to antiquity — to the earliest time a "text" became puzzling and problematic, and thus had to be explained, excused, translated, or somehow "interpreted" in order to be intelligible. The objects of hermeneutical methods and theory need not be specifically literary but rather include every kind of text that requires interpretation: dreams, oracles, laws, sacred scripture, and literary works insofar as they require interpretation in order to be rightly understood. Of course, since sacred texts do tend to be preserved in a fairly exact way over long periods of time, and since a good deal of importance attaches to the interpretation of such texts, the longest unbroken hermeneutical tradition in the West is that associated with the sacred scriptures in the Hebrew and Christian tradition. Nevertheless, hermeneutics as such is not restricted to the interpretation of sacred texts but in principle includes within its scope any text that requires explication.

Hermeneutics should be clearly distinguished from textual criticism on the one hand and literary criticism on the other. Textual criticism is directed to establishing the most correct form of the text, but hermeneutics takes up the problem of how that text is to be understood once it is established. (Needless to say, textual criticism requires hermeneutics and hermeneutics would be lost without the work of textual criticism). Hermeneutics has in common with textual criticism the fact that it is not necessarily literary: the methods of textual criticism apply in principle to the establishment of any kind of text. On the other hand, literary criticism does direct itself exclusively to literary texts. Furthermore, it goes beyond the processes of textual exegesis which are central to hermeneutics to take up considerations of the literary merit of the text in itself, in comparison with other works by the author and in the same genre. Literary criticism may also deal with the text with the purpose of showing things extrinsic to the particular meaning of the text, such as its place in the development of an author's throught, its place in a genre as part of an historical development. Hermeneutics does not exclude matters of literary criticism or literary history, but they are taken up only to the extent that they enable the interpreter to unfold more fully the sense in which a particular text is to be understood.

Both in its methods and in its theoretical formulations, hermeneutics in modern times is inseparably connected to the development of both classical and sacred philology. Insofar as hermeneutics may be said to have a central tradition in modern times, it would be found within philology. While it is true that the patient work of codifying and classifying the available works of antiquity in order to have access to the many uses of the same word in ancient documents gave to the discipline the reputation of plodding pedantry and lack of imagination, it also enabled the interpreter to explicate texts with unprecedented thoroughness and sensitivity to trope, etymology, genre, grammatical convention and shades of meaning in different contexts. What is involved here is not just establishing a text but understanding its intended sense from a full consideration of its grammatical, historical, and generic contexts. In the hands of such creative scholars as Ernst Robert Curtius, Leo Spitzer, or Erich Auerbach for instance, these methods show that philological grounding need not lead to dry pedantry but can creatively enhance exegesis.

The term "hermeneutics" was used in nineteenth century philology in basically the sense we have described above: the theory of the understanding of texts. The great philologist, August Boeckh, in a section entitled "Theory of Hermeneutics" prefacing his *Encyclopaedie und Methodologie der philologischen Wissenschaften* (1877), presents four different kinds of interpretation that comprise hermeneutics:

1. Understanding from the objective conditions of the thing communicated:
    a. from the literal meaning of the words — *grammatical interpretation* ;
    b. from the meaning of the words in reference to the material relations and context of the work — *historical interpretation.*
2. Understanding from the subjective conditions of the thing communicated:
    a. from the subject itself — *individual interpretation* ;
    b. from the subject in refenrece to subjective relations which lie in the aim and direction of the work — *generic interpretation.* [1]

These four kinds of interpretation, according to Boeckh, although seperate in theory do intermingle in practice:

---

[1]   August BOECKH, *On Interpretation and Criticism,* trans. John Paul PRITCHARD (Norman: University of Oklahoma Press, 1968), p. 51. The German original was published posthumously in 1877, a product of some forty years of lecturing on the subject of philology at the University of Berlin.

> Without individual interpretation the literal meaning is unintelligible, for each word spoken by anyone is drawn from the common vocabulary but invested with an additional peculiar meaning. To obtain this latter meaning, one must know the individuality of the speaker. Likewise the general sense of words is modified by their actual relations in discourse and by the kinds of discourse. To interpret these modification, one needs historical and generic interpretation, the bases of which are in turn to be found only through grammatical interpretation, from which all interpretation starts.[2]

While we might go into an explanation of each of these four dimensions of interpretation, it is enough for our purposes to note that such interpretation requires broad historical knowledge and linguistic competence as well as understanding of conditions of genre. Yet such interpretation stops short of relating the text to something else so as to judge or evaluate it. Such would be criticism, in which there are, for Boeckh, the same four subdivisions, but for a different purpose than merely understanding the text.[3]

Although Boeckh's theory of hermeneutics excludes criticism, it includes texts other than literary, and it does not allow a distinction between sacred and secular texte. He argues that "As the actions of the understanding, or the principles according to which one will understand, are everywhere the same, no specific distinctions of interpretation can be made with respect to the subject to be interpreted. Such distinctions as sacred and secular interpretation are accordingly untenable. If a sacred book is of human origin, it must be understood according to human rules in the usual treatment applied to books."[4] So hermeneutics is first distinguished from criticism — either text criticism or literary criticism — by its restriction to the specific task of understanding the text, and then it is universalized (and here Boeckh follows his teacher, Friedrich Schleiermacher) to apply to any text, whether literary or not, so long as it is historical and requires the tools of philology to render its meaning intelligible. The differentia for forms of hermeneutical activity do not lie in the objects of interpretation so much as in the forms of activity in interpretation: "Effective divisions of interpretation may be drawn only from the essential nature of interpretive activity."[5] Already in Boeckh one sees the trend toward the philosophical and general: hermeneutics deals with "the essential nature of the interpretive activity."

Hermeneutics, understood as a universal discipline concerned with the understanding of texts, has been taken up by a number of philosophers since the death of Boeckh about a hundred years ago such as Dilthey, Heidegger, Emilio Betti; and among the still living, hermeneutics is ably represented by three philosophers of first rank: Hans-Georg Gadamer, Paul Ricoeur, and Jacques Derrida. In their hands, hermeneutics becomes philosophical hermeneutics. Its purpose is no longer that of easing the problem

---

[2] *Loc. cit.*
[3] *Ibid.*, pp. 121-22.
[4] *Ibid.*, p. 48.
[5] *Ibid.*, p. 49.

of interpreting difficult texts; it is directed toward unfolding the problematic, and the problematical character, of interpretation itself.

In the century since the death of Boeckh, the issue of positivism in intrepretation has increasingly come to the fore. As a recent article by Günther Buck has made clear, the philosophical foundations of the humane sciences tended to take over the methods and conceptualities of the natrual sciences, and thus the hermeneutical experience was increasingly dealt with in scientific terms inherited from the positive sciences.[6] It is from the aporiae created by this procedure (which also applies to philology) that contemporary hermeneutical reflection attemps to retrieve hermeneutical experience in order to account for it in quite different terms. One may see the present symposium as a chapter in effort at some kind of diffusion of hermeneutical reflection from the philosophical side back to the more practical and specific activity of interpreting texts. In this movement one may see a return of hermeneutics to its earlier strong connection with the philological problematic of understanding texts.

II. — NEEDED: A COMPREHENSIVE VIEW
OF HERMENEUTICS

There is today a veritable ferment in philosophical hermeneutics. Fundamental questions are raised as to the nature of language, textuality and intertextuality, speech as act and artifact, the meaning of metaphor, subjectivity and nonsubjectivity in interpretation, logocentrism and the question of origins, and so on. To grasp the full dimensions of these questions and the context from which they spring, one needs a grounding in phenomenology. For it so happens that the three major living theorists in philosophical hermeneutics mentioned above came to their present positions through study first of Husserlian phenomenology and then of the Heideggerian critique and modification of phenomenology. Gadamer, Ricoeur, and Derrida have all written penetrating commentary on the contributions of Husserl and Heidegger.[7] The phenomenological method of turning back on oneself in the very act of interpretation is, in a sense, the essence of philosophical hermeneutics.

---

[6] Günther BUCK, "The Structure of Hermeneutic Experience and the Problem of Tradition," trans. Peter HEATH, *New Literary History*, X (Autumn 1978), 31-47. Issue is devoted to the theme of "Literary Hermeneutics".

[7] See Hans-Georg GADAMER, *Truth and Method* (New York: Seabury Press, 1975), pp. 214-24, and his essay, "The Phenomenological Movement," in *Philosophical Hermeneutics*, ed. David LINGE (Berkeley: University of California Press, 1976). Ricœur and Derrida were translators of Husserl, Ricœur of the *Ideas* during his period of confinement as a prisoner of the Germans in World War II, and Derrida of "The Origin of Geometry," to which he supplied a lengthy critical introduction, and which figures importantly in his theoretical formulations. Derrida's second book, *Voice and Phenomenon*, is dedicated to Husserl. RICOEUR's book, *Husserl: An Analysis of His Phenomenology*, has been translated into English by Edward G. Ballard and Lester Embree (Evanston: Northwestern University Press, 1967).

A lengthy account could be given of the appropriation of phenomenological hermeneutics by contemporary theologians and by literary critics. Among the leading names associated with hermeneutics in theology are James M. Robinson, Robert Funk, Ray Hart, and David Tracy. Of course, the theoretical implications of phenomenology for literature were grasped more quickly in Germany and France than in the English-speaking world, and certain German critics, such as Emil Staiger and Beda Alleman, engaged Heidegger in dialogue or tried to see what more "hermeneutical" form of interpretation would be like.[8] In Germany, a working group of scholars as early as 1962 began meeting every two years to discuss themes of interpretation — the "Poetik und Hermeneutik" Research Group — and continue to meet, with the papers presented there later published as a volume.[9] The late Peter Szondi was an occasional member of this group, and a series of his lectures from the lates sixties has recently been published as *Einführung in die literarische Hermeneutik.*[10] These contain valuable lectures on the historical development of hermeneutics in the eighteenth and nineteenth centuries.

But the reception of hermeneutical theory in relation to literature has not been limited to the Franco-German sphere. For instance, over a decade ago, Sarah Lawall contributed a valuable account of phenomenological forms of literary criticism in her book on the Geneva critics,[11] and major articles on these critics were written by J. Hillis Miller,[12] among others. More recently Robert Magliola and Michael Murray have contributed books on the subject of phenomenology and literary criticism.[13] Edward Said's recent book *Beginnings* is a treatise in literary hermeneutics, with heavy debts to contemporary French thought.[14] And matters have reached the point that one finds references to the "hermeneutical mafia" at Yale.[15] The term refers primarily Geoffrey Hartmann, Harold Bloom, J. Hillis

---

[8]   See James M. ROBINSON and John COBB, eds., *The Later Heidegger and Theology* (New York: Harper & Row, 1962) and *The New Hermeneutic* (New York: Harper & Row, 1964); Robert FUNK, *Language, Hermeneutic, and Word of God* (New York: Harper & Row, 1966); Ray HART, *Unfinished Man and the Imagination* (New York: Herder & Herder, 1968); Stanley Romaine HOPPER and David L. MILLER, eds., *Interpretation: The Poetry of Meaning* (New York: Harcourt, Brace and World, 1967); Emil STAIGER, *Grundbegriffe der Poetik*. Zurich: Atlantis, 1963; David TRACY, *Blessed Rage for Order* (New York: Seabury Press, 1975).

[9]   Some half-dozen volumes have appeared in the past decade: *Nachahmung und Illusion, Immanente Aesthetik, Die nicht mehr schönen Künste, Terror und Spiel, Geschichte: Ereignis und Erzählung, Positionen der Negativität* (Munich: Wilhelm Fink, 1964-78).

[10]   "Studienausgabe der Vorlesungen" Band 5, ed. Jean BOLLACK and Helen STIERLIN (Frankfurt: Suhrkamp, 1975). Edited from notes from his lectures. Very helpful on hermeneutics before Schleiermacher; second half offers perceptive interpretations of Hölderlin.

[11]   *Critics of Consciousness* (Cambridge: Harvard University Press, 1968).

[12]   "The Geneva School," *Virginia Quarterly Review*, XIII (Summer 1967), 465-88.

[13]   Robert MAGLIOLA, *Phenomenology and Literature: An Introduction* (West Lafayette, Indiana: Purdue University Press, 1977), and Michael MURRAY, *Modern Critical Theory: A Phenomenological Introduction* (The Hague: Martinus Nijhoff, 1975).

[14]   New York: Basic Books, 1975.

[15]   William H. PRITCHARD, "The Hermeneutical Mafia or, After Strange Gods at Yale," *Hudson Review*, 28(Winter, 1975-76), 601-10.

Miller, and Paul deMan — to make a "hermeneutical quartet" at Yale, as I have elsewhere more complimentarily designated them.[16]

For this symposium, however, I do not propose to undertake a sketch of the diverse contemporary contemporary developments in philosophical hermeneutics,[17] nor of the appropriation of phenomenology and hermeneutics by literary critics and theorists — as important and interesting as these may be. Rather, I propose to deal with the problem of obtaining a more adequate and comprehensive view of hermeneutics as such.

There is, today, a critical need for a view of hermeneutics that will encompass both philosophical hermeneutics and the hermeneutical tradition since antiquity. In the vogue that the term "hermeneutics" is enjoying, one often hears the word used merely as a fashionable synonym for interpretation. In more knowledgeable use, it refers to a fairly specific tradition of philosophical reflection whose principals are Schleiermacher, Dilthey, Heidegger, Gadamer, Ricoeur, and most recently, Derrida. Yet both of these uses neglect what I consider very important for hermeneutics: the tradition of theories of textual exegesis that stretches back through the renaissance to ancient times. Hermeneutics is not just a synonym for interpretation, nor is it simply philosophical reflection on language and textual encounter; it is a discipline on the order of literary criticism, but more encompassing, that stretches back to antiquity — a discipline that richly repays study by enabling us to grasp more clearly the character of our interpretive encounter with texts.

To illustrate what I mean, I should like to do two things in this paper: first, to set in relief three quite distinctive modes of hermeneutics: the allegorical, the philological, and the philosophical; second, to place before you in concrete detail an outline of the development of hermeneutics and the major works that comprise it. For the first I will limit myself to a few general remarks without going into analysis of specific works. For the second, I will simply present a table of contents for a hypothetical six-volume collection of essays in hermeneutics, with appropriate headings. As you will see, there is a rough correspondence between the three forms of hermeneutics I will discuss and the three major periods into which the *Hermeneutics Compendium* I propose is divided. While these forms do not exhaust the possibilities for hermeneutics in the three eras, they do in a certain way typify what is most characteristic of premodern, modern, and contemporary hermeneutics.

An historical collection or anthology of works in the history of hermeneutics would be particularly useful today for several reasons. As have mentioned above, the vogue of philosophical hermeneutics may lead to a

---

[16] "Toward Postmodern Hermeneutics," unpublished paper presented at Memphis State University, April 6, 1978, symposium on literary theory.

[17] See my article "Hermeneutics" in *Contemporary Philosophy: A Survey*, 3rd edition, Vol. II, for a chronicle of developments between 1966-76 (Florence: La Nuova Italia Editrice, ca. 1980), and Gadamer's chronicle of 1955-65 in the 1969 edition of this collection.

conception of hermeneutics that omits its rich heritage in premodern and modern times. Furthermore, the tendency of discrete disciplines to learn only the history of their own textual methods has a narrowing effect on one's view of what constitutes the task of interpretation, so such an anthology would place such disciplinary hermeneutics within the horizon of all other methods of textual exegesis, as well as in the critical light of philosophical hermeneutics.

Regrettably, Boeckh's vision of hermeneutics as the general art of textual understanding did not, historically, result in the kind of comprehensive and inclusive approach to hermeneutics in philology that it would seem to imply. Rather, it was one or two philosophers who took up the project of a general hermeneutics, and general hermeneutics evolved into philosophical hermeneutics. Consequently, there do not exist today comprehensive interdisciplinary accounts of the development of textual exegesis from antiquity to the present. A helpful survey of exegesis in antiquity is found in the article *"Exegese"* in the *Reallexikon für Antike und Christentum* edited by Theodor Klauser. One can look forward to the appearance of the article on *"Hermeneutik"* in *RAC* which should appear within the next few years. A few attempts at tracing the development of hermeneutics since the renaissance do exist. There is Dilthey's history of hermeneutics from the reformation to Schleiermacher, which only became available when unpublished portions of Schleiemacher's *Leben* appeared in 1966,[18] but this offers no account of hermeneutics prior to modern times. Joachim Wach has contributed a valuable account of hermeneutics in the early nineteenth century, but since Wach was writing in the twenties, the standpoint of contemporary philosophical hermeneutics is missing.[19] Hans-Georg Gadamer provides the clearest account of the philosophical issues and development of hermeneutics in the period since the enlightenment, but the form of hermeneutics is already philosophical: *Truth and Method* is already a treatise in philosophical hermeneutics.[20] Emilio Betti's proposed "theory of interpretation" approaches the subject systematically rather than historically, so it to does not supply an historical account of hermeneutics.[21]

Given this lack of historical accounts, either in article or book form, in French, German, or English, it becomes exceedingly difficult to get hold

---

[18]   *Das Leben Schleiermachers*, ed. Martin Redeker, *Gesammelte Schriften*, Vol. 14 (Berlin: de Gruyter, 1966), pp. 597-787. Rudolf Makkreel has proposed to translate major portions of this and other works of Dilthey in a six-volume set of selections from Dilthey; the proposal is presently under consideration by a major university press.

[19]   Joachim WACH, *Das Verstehen*, 3 vols. (Tübingen: J.C.B. Mohr, 1926, 1929, 1933). Wach was professor for a number of years at the University of Chicago but this early work was never translated.

[20]   Published in German as *Wahrheit und Methode: Grundzüge einer philosophischen Hermeneutik* (1st ed., Tübingen: J.C.B. Mohr, 1960), this major work has gone through several editions.

[21]   Emilio BETTI, *Teoria generale della interpretazione*, 2 vols. (Milan; Giuffrè, 1955). Translated by its author into German as *Allgemeine Auslegungslehre als Methodik der Geisteswissenschaften* (Tübingen: J.C.B. Mohr, 1967).

of the subject of hermeneutics in a comprehensive way — that is, in a way that transcends the limits of such disciplines as theology, literary criticism, legal hermeneutics, or myth and dream interpretation, and (1) sees what they have in common, (2) sees their historical development, and (3) see them in relation to each other. Of course, to see interpretation as the act of the interpreting subject, as Boeckh does, is already taking a certain view of hermeneutics — a subjectivistic hermeneutics. It is not at all my purpose to try to unify hermeneutics on the basis of what has already become a philosophically questionable position. Rather, I have in mind basing such a collection as I propose on a more broadly critical and self-reflective question: What is it that interpretation *does* in examples A, B, and C? What view of the text, of language, of truth, of reading-event, is presupposed by the method of text interpretation in question?

It seems to me that philosophical hermeneutics as we have it today opens the way for a critical review of the whole history of textual exegesis in all its forms and in the range of disciplines in which such interpretation takes place. But such a review is hampered by the lack of a sufficiently comprehensive view of the history of textual interpretation. The student of hermeneutics finds it difficult to compare various modes of textual interpretation and to evaluate the presuppositions of his own contemporary modes in the light of an inclusive historical context. Furthermore, hermeneutics does not wear one label but many, so its source materials are scattered all over the library. Often out of print, presenting itself in a variety of languages, hermeneutics constitutes a frustratingly amorphous and elusive body of materials.

In light of this, the need for some kind of key to the materials of hermeneutics becomes critical. For even the main periods and categories that comprise hermeneutics are not altogether clear. The *Hermeneutics Compendium* here suggested as a multivolume historical nathology of texts in hermeneutics, would help to alleviate the pressing problem of inaccessibility of materials and amorphousness of field that now hamper the practical study of hermeneutics. Because of its complexity, length, and the amount of translation required, as well as the problem of use of copyright materials, the proposed *Hermeneutics Compendium* will require a publisher of courage, patience, and foresight.

It may be some time before the *Compendium* sees the light of day. In the meantime, it may be helpful to lay before you the categories presently contemplated and the works probably to be included in each category. The periodization of hermeneutics in the *Compendium* would be into premodern, modern, and contemporary — two volumes each. As a preface to the tables of contents for the *Compendium*, I venture to discuss briefly three modes of hermeneutics that typify, though not exhaustively, the three periods.

III. — THREE MODES OF HERMENEUTICS

In even the briefest survey of the history of hermeneutics, one senses the decisiveness of developments that took place in the renaissance. At this time, there arose the beginnings of scientific and philological approach to texts that we now take for granted. This was a turn in text interpretation so decisive as to divide hermeneutics into two great periods: the premodern and the modern. The contrast is not just in method but in the very status of the text. It is impossible to discuss this contrast without taking into account the differences between a premodern worldview and that which prevails in modernity; for, as philosophical hermeneutics has shown, interpretation is guided by presuppositions, and presuppositions with regard to texts stand within a view of the world. [22] For example, premodern interpretation stands in a certain constellation of assumptions about the status of "scripture" and the relation of "reason" to it. [23] This also involves a view of the figural use of language which contrasts with the modern view of such uses.

Something happened in the renaissance, a spiritual change of the first magnitude, which is in part reflected in the fortunes of allegorical interpretation. Regrettably, a history of allegorical interpretation also does not exist, although there are some recent articles and encyclopedia accounts that are very helpful. [24] Certainly a critical history of allegorical interpretation (not allegory, which is something else) is not available, which is to be lamented the more in view of its obvious relation to the historical development of hermeneutical methods and theories. In any case, the allegorical method, for certain reasons, enjoyed a tremendous popularity in antiquity and the middle ages, but has suffered an eclipse in modern times. Joseph Mazzeo has recently lamented the death of allegorical interpretation, assigning it something of the status of a fossil we may find interesting but no longer of any value in the light of our historical consciousness. [25] We may go so far as to say that the premodern era in hermeneutics is the "golden age of allegorical interpretation" and that the modern era is something like the "golden age of literalism."

Now the word "literalism" has certain unfortunate associations, so I have chosen the term "philological", but it is true to say that since the renaissance, interpretation of texts focusses, almost exclusively, on the surface verbal meaning. Is it accidental that the modern era is also an age

---

[22]   Cf. GADAMER, *Truth and Method, passim;* also see my articles "Toward a Postmodern Hermeneutics of Performance," in *Performance in Postmodern Culture,* ed. Michel BENAMOU and Charles CRAMELLO, (Madison, Wisconsin: Coda Press, 1977), and "Postmodernity and Hermeneutics," *Boundary 2,* V (Winter 1977), 363-91.

[23]   See Harry A. WOLFSON, *Philo: Foundations of Religious Philosophy in Judaism, Christianity, and Islam,* 2 vols. (Cambridge: Harvard University Press, 1948).

[24]   See Joseph MAZZEO, "Allegorical Interpretation and History," *Comparative Literature,* XXX (Winter 78), 1-21; the article by J. GEFFCKEN, "Allegory," in HASTINGS' *Encyclopedia for Religion and Ethics;* or "Allegorese," in the *Reallexikon für Antike und Christentum* (ca. 1970)

[25]   MAZZEO, cited above, p. 21.

of what Blake called "single vision" and that we now refer to "one-dimensional man"? I think not. Rather, since the renaissance we have a new consciousness of the world of space in which we find ourselves. The Swiss art historian Jean Gebser has called it a "mensural" and a perspectival cousciousness. I have elsewhere argued on the basis of Gebser's analysis, that the rise of single-point perspective in art is not an isolated and unimportant development in aesthetics but introduces a perspectival consciousness that conditions the modern way of seeing the world. [26] This has its effects in modern philosophy, say, in Cartesian dualism, in the desacralization of nature, and thus the rise of nominalism, and so on. [27]

In relation to the interpretation of texts, one finds an increasingly scientific, detached, and historical way of relating to texts and objects. The interpretive task is refered in terms of the quest for the intended meaning of the presumed historical author. This effort, on the basis of careful grammatical and historical analysis of text, marks the beginning of modern philology, and thus of philological hermeneutics as the guide to our understanding of the task of interpreting texts. Thus, I would say that the modern era is "the golden age of philological hermeneutics." In a sense, this term, in its positive meaning, sums up what the modern age has held dear in the interpretation of texts: grammar, history, genre, and the psychology of the author. Even when these elements are departed from in recent interpretation, they are generally presupposed as the context for interpretation. A formalist may reject "biographical criticism" but he will not turn to allegorical interpretation; rather, he will generally argue that the author's intended meaning is contained fully in the text and not in some combination of the text and the author's life. On the other hand, recent claims for the autonomy of the poetic text do have a parallel to the premodern view of the sacred text as above and outside historical conditions. The philosophical basis for such claims to autonomy could be made much more coherent and compelling. In order to make good these claims, however, it is necessary for literary critics — in the case of poetic texts — to grapple with the philosophical issues involved — i.e., to have recourse to philosophical hermeneutics.

Garamer's most recent work, on the seeming specialness of literary and religious language, addresses this problem, as does Ricoeur's work on religious language.

Yet this indicates one of the limitations of a philological hermeneutics that unconsciously adopts the philosophical position of positivism instead of taking a resolutely self-critical position such as that of phenomenology. A positivistic philological hermeneutics cannot account adequately for the

---

[26] See my article in *Performance and Postmodern Culture*, cited in #22 above. The collected works of Gebser are now being published, of which *Ursprung und Gegenwart*, his masterwork, is vols. II and III (Schaffhausen, Switzerland: Novalis, 1978, after the enlarged 1973 edition by DTV, Munich).

[27] See James Hillman's similar arguments on nominalism, literalism, personification, and scientific abstraction, in *Re-Visioning Psychology* (New York: Harper & Row, 1975). Hillman's remarks on personification are relevant to the decline of allegory in modern times.

hermeneutical experience because of its unhistorical premises, even while professing a commitment to the historical context. As we shall see, a major contribution of philosophical hermeneutics has been to show the limits of a philological hermeneutics bogged down in positivism. [28]

Another way of gaining a clear sense of the nature of philological hermeneutics in all its modernity is to place it in contrast with allegorical hermeneutics. This also allows us to perceive some of the characteristic traits and limits of the "modern" perspective. So let us recall briefly how allegorical hermeneutics arises and what problems it characteristically proposes to solve.

Allegorical hermeneutics represents a certain kind of solution to an interpretive dilemma. The need for it arises when a text like Homer's *Iliad* or the first five books of the Old Testament become an embarrassment to enlightened intelligence. Thus, it became necessary for Greek interpreters of Homer to explain away why gods were fighting in the Trojan war; how a human being, Diomedes, could wound Aphrodite and Ares; and how Aphrodite and Ares could be wounded at all — the ichor flowing painfully out, Ares taking to his heels, etc. [29] And Philo of Alexandria found his cultured Greek friends laughing at the Hebrew story of the Garden of Eden, of God walking in the garden, of God sewing clothes for Adam and Eve. Not for a minute relinquishing his faith in the God-given scriptures, Philo explained that God did not really walk in the garden; rather, this was a figure of speech, an allegorical story that conveyed a deeper meaning. [30] Likewise, the Greek defenders of Homer said that the strife of the gods was really an allegory for the strife of the physical elements. [31]

Just from these two examples several things may be observed about allegorical interpretation. First, the text has such an exalted status that the issue is not whether to discard it as irrelevant but how to find a hidden relevance and meaning behind the surface meaning. The surface meaning is not taken as problematical or difficult to construe; the meaning is plain. The interpretive problem is one of *accomodation* — how to reconstrue the import of the plain meaning so that it is not offensive to the hearer's conception of the gods or of God. One might call this an early form of "demythologizing" — to use a term from twentieth century protestant theology, in which Rudolf Bultmann attempted to save the New Testament message from being rejected by cultured despisers who rejected a triple-

---

[28] See Peter Szondi's article on philological knowledge, "Über philologische Erkenntnis," in his *Hölderlin-Studien* (Frankfurt: Insel, 1967; also later a Suhrkamp paperback, pp. 9-30), forthcoming in the collection of essays from Yale University Press. Also relevant is the article by Günther Buck cited in #6 above.

[29] Regarding the many allegorical interpretations of Homer see Pierre LEVEQUE, *Aurea Catena Homeri: Une étude sur l'allégorie grecque* (Paris: Les Belles Lettres, 1959), and also Jean PÉPIN, *Mythe et allégorie: les origines grecques et les contestations Judéo-Chrétiennes* (Paris: Aubier, 1958).

[30] *Quaestiones et Solutiones in Genesin.*

[31] See LEVEQUE, cited above.

decker universe of heaven, earth, and hell, along with Satan and all the powers and principalities of the middle air. Bultmann argued that the message, though couched in an antiquated world-picture, was not oustdated because the New Testament was not a lesson in natural science but an admonishment to receive "new being," to be "born again." Like the Homeric text, the Biblical text is accomodated to the worldpicture of its hearers and its relevance shown in contemporary terms. Its meaning has to be restated in "existential" terms. [32]

The allegorical interpretation which is found in the Greeks (and Romans, such as Cicero in *De natura deorum*), in Philo, and in the early Fathers (like Clement of Alexandria, and Origen) right through the Middle Ages and into Luther, where we may observe the turn against it, constitutes a contrast to the treatment of texts in the modern period from Erasmus to the present. For Erasmus, the prerequisite of all interpretation is source-criticism. [33] The interpreter must know Greek, Latin, and Hebrew; he must compare sources and arrive as the best available text; and he must see the text in its historical context. In his *Ratio seu Methodus Compendio Perveniendi ad Veram Theologiam*, Erasmus says, for instance, that "There is also some light added to our understanding of the sense of the scripture if we not only consider what is said but by whom it is said, but for whom and in what words, at what time, on what occasion, what came before, what followed." [34] Unlike the allegorical interpreter, for whom the text's clear sense is generally unproblematical, and who takes the text as it is given, sometimes even though in a translated form (Philo using the Septuagint, the Fathers using the Vulgate), the philological interpreter minutely questions the transmitted text itself. Each word must be confirmed and tested for its proper sense, listened to in the original language, compared with other uses of the same word, tested for the possibility of copyists's errors, and interrogated historically: who was the author of the text? In what context was he speaking? On what occasion, in what historical time, before and after what? All this sheds light on the *sense* of the scripture as something not allegorically pointed to somewhere outside the obvious meaning but rather as something present in the overt sense which is illuminated. In the words of Erasmus, "Accedet hinc quoque lucis nonnihil ad intelligendum scripturae sensum, si perpendamus..." [35] The process of interpretation increases the light of our understanding of the sense, then, in somewhat the may one increasingly knows an object better by seeing it from all sides, learning more and more about it as an object. One is not seeking a hermeneutical "key" that will unlock a secret meaning hidden (often purposely) from the multitude; rather one is, through patient and unglamorous philological consideration of gram-

---

[32]   Rudolf BULTMANN, *Jesus Christ and Mythology* (New York: Scribner's, 1958).

[33]   See John William ALDRIDGE, *The Hermeneutic of Erasmus* (Richmond, Virginia: John Knox Press, 1966, and in Switzerland, Zurich; EVZ, 1966), see ch. I, "Ad Fontes."

[34]   Desiderius ERASMUS, *Ausgewählte Schriften*, translated into German, with facing Latin original, by Gerhard B. WINKLER (Darmstadt: Wissenschaftliches Buchgesellschaft, 1967), Vol. 3, p. 178. Cited in Aldridge, p. 62.

[35]   *Ibid.*

matical, etymological, lexical, and historical facts, arriving at what must have been the originally intended meaning in the original context of its utterance. This may not necessarily be its literal meaning if one has reason to believe that the author was speaking in figurative language. But the philological interpreter does not feel he has the license to assume that God is the true author of the text and He has inserted His meaning in some kind of secret code.

Luther, too, insisted on the clear sense of Scripture. His famous commentaries display a thorough knowledge of the tradition of interpretation in the Church, so he is able to enter into dialogue with the Fathers of the Church all the way back to Clement. In fact he knew the tradition better and was less condescending than Erasmus, who laughed patronizingly at the numerous errors the Fathers had made through linguistic ignorance. Yet Luther extricates himself from the fanciful constructions of allegorical interpretation and insists on the power of the text to speak in its now voice: salvation comes through the ears. The Scripture *interprets itself* to the hearer, but not in a way that accomodates the text to the worldpicture of the hearer and the conception he already has of God through philosophical reflection and common sense; rather, the text demands that the reader accomodate himself to the meaning of the text. Luther perceived the way in which allegorical interpretation diluted the claim of the text by removing the stumbling blocks — but precisely this leaves the hearer untransformed by the message. [36]

The development of hermeneutics in the modern era continues the philological focus of this Renaissance-Reformation return to the open sense of the text, a sense determined in the light of historical knowledge of the conditions of its production. In Spinoza the issue of the status of revealed truth in contradiction to reason comes to a head, and the modern conclusion is reached that reason is the guide to the truth of revelation. The era of Scriptural absolute priority was over, as Harry Wolfson makes clear in his study of Philo and his comparison of Philo with Spinoza. [37] The rise of Enlightenment scholarship and "historical consciousness" in the ensuing centuries only intensified the tendency to define the meaning of a text as a combination of philological factors: the grammatical sense, illuminated by historical knowledge, knowledge of other works by the author, and the conventions of the medium.

It is not our purpose here to trace the development of modern hermeneutics in detail but to suggest that we find in philological hermeneutics much that typifies modernity, both in its strengths and its limitations, just as we find in allegorical interpretation much that typifies the premodern approach to texts. It also should be clear that "philological" is not

---

[36]   See Karl HOLL, "Luthers Bedeutung für den Fortschritt der Auslegungskunst," in his *Gesammelte Aufsätze zur Kirchengeschichte,* I (*Luther*), 544-82. See also Gerhard EBELING, *Luther: An Introduction to his Thought,* trans. R.A. Wilson (London: Collins, 1970).

[37]   See WOLFSON, above.

being defined narrowly but in a very broad sense. I realize that the term has, for some scholars, the connotation of a hidebound narrowness in interpretation, of a determination to live only in the horizon of nineteenth century German scholarship, a fusty lack of interest in learning about such new-fangled developments as "New Criticism." One classicist at this symposium told me that the connotations of the term were such that he never referred to himself as a philologist but as an interpreter of texts. The philologist apparently has the image of being one who is only interested in the words for their own sake and not in the larger meaning of the text. I do not have in mind this uncomplimentary conception, but rather philology as a radically more comprehensive and systematic approach to texts than that to be found in such movements as the New Criticism, myth criticism, or psycho-analytic criticism. The tradition of philology is rich, and its resources are varied. In fact, the lack of awarness of the heritage of philology in such courses as "literary criticism" taught in university English Departments is greatly to be lamented. It is but another symptom of the current lack of competency in foreign, and especially in ancient, languages.

Far from scorning philology, I hold that some of the best textual interpretation in the twentieth century is by persons grounded in the philological traditions of German nineteenth century scholarship.[38] There are the parallel and intertwined streams of Biblical interpretation and classical philology, along with the rise of comparative linguistics and romance philology. Far from implying a shallow and empty objectivism, the term "philology" should suggest the loving treatment of texts in the full dimensions of their possible meaning.

It is true that the late Peter Szondi attacked the objectivist pretensions of philology,[39] and that Hans-Robert Jauss has called for a new literary history that takes into account the reader's reception of literary works[40] — but both of these manifestos are also in reaction against any narrowly rhetorical approach to textual interpretation. They do not render the heritage of philology obsolete; rather, they attempt to revitalize a basically philological-hermeneutical mode of relating to texts. In any case, "hermeneutics," insofar as it is identified with any tradition of interpretation, has its roots in philology and philological speculation on understanding and textual interpretation; any historical account of hermeneutics in modernity would have to have the development of philology at its center.

The contrast between philological and allegorical hermeneutics, then, is a fundamental one. While it is true that anticipations of a philological approach to texts are to be found in antiquity, philological hermeneutics comes into its own with the Renaissance and Reformation scholarly interest in ancient texts. And while it is true that some forms of

---

[38] In fact, Aldridge above distinguished philological from historical interpretation with regard to the passage cited in #34 above, but I include both historical and grammatical in the sense of the term philological.

[39] See citation in note 28 above.

allegorical interpretation persist in the modern era, it is in the two thousand years between sixth-century Athens (in fact before this) and fifteenth century Europe that allegorical interpretation was the logical recourse within historical context, accepts it as a "given" and stands above the conditions of its historical production. One might call this the contrast between an "open-meaning" hermeneutics and a "hidden-meaning" hermeneutics, and one could see this as a fundamental distinction in all hermeneutics.

For reasons that are not quite clear initially, one form predominates in one period and the other in another, although both forms are found in antiquity and both in the modern era. Philological hermeneutics is interpretation of the "open meaning" and predominates in the modern era, while allegorical hermeneutics is interpretation of a "hidden meaning" and predominates in antiquity. It would seem that the historical methods of textual interpretation rather inhibit allegorical interpretation. The factors at work here are complex and one has to bear in mind both the problem that interpretation is attempting to solve and the assumptions regarding the text that prevail in the era. As we stated earlier, allegorical interpretation arose in antiquity when interpreters of Homer or interpreters of the Torah were confronted with texts that were an embarrassment to philosophical reason but which held a high place in the tradition. As Joseph Mazzeo notes, allegorical interpretation seems to have been a casualty of modern historical consciousness; it no longer appeals to the contemporary interpreter as a viable mode of relating to texts.[41] A more detailed examination would be required in order to show the causes for the modern rejection of allegorical interpretation. This is an interesting problem; in fact, it is fair to say that both allegorical and philological hermeneutics deserve a great deal more study than they are now receiving, and a comparative examination would illuminate the presuppositions of both forms of hermeneutics.

The third mode of hermeneutics is the philosophical. Hermeneutics in this mode comprises an impressive body of recent philosophical reflection on the matrix of factors that condition interpretation. Philosophical hermeneutics in its earlier nineteenth century form follows a "subjective" orientation — the processes of understanding in the perceiving subject become the focus of much theory in Schleiermacher, Boeckh, Dilthey, and more recently Betti. Contemporary hermeneutics, however, tends to reflect the contemporary rejection of subject-centered thinking. Thus, Ricoeur, in his recent *Interpretation Theory* lectures, dissociates himself from the tradition of Scheiermacher's hermeneutics in order to speak of hermeneutical processes not as subjective processes but as "discourse" and "events of language."[42] Foucault and Derrida share this rejection of man-centered

---

[40]   See his *Literaturgeschichte als Provokation der Literaturwissenschaft* (Frankfurt: Suhrkamp, 1974), especially the title essay, which was translated into English earlier, *New Literary History*, II, No. 1 (1970).

[41]   See note 24.

[42]   *Interpretation Theory* (Fort Worth: Texas Christian University Press, 1978).

thinking of the "human sciences," and Derrida asserts the priority of written language over language thought of as lodged in the speaking subject. [43] Philosophical hermeneutics, then, is not necessarily a continuation of the subject-centered philosophical tradition of Schleiermacher and Dilthey.

Indeed, one can trace philosophical reflection on the nature of language, on understanding, text, and interpretation, back to ancient times — for instance, into Plato and Aristotle. Two popular recent anthologies of philosophical hermeneutics emphasize it as a recent development however, dating especially from Dilthey at the turn of our century. [44] It is fair to say that the sudden unfolding of philosophical hermeneutics as the focus of thought by many different scholars — orchestrating, as it were, the dimensions of textual encounter — is a phenomenon of the past two decades. Philosophically, four thinkers are central to any discussion of contemporary hermeneutics: Martin Heidegger, Hans-Georg Gadamer, Paul Ricoeur, and Jacques Derrida. All four are philosophers of major importance in their own right, not just in connection with hermeneutics, and through them hermeneutics moves into the very center of current philosophical thought.

Hermeneutics has thus become a major focus of French and German philosophy of the past twenty years. In fact, it is perhaps fair to see its present form as the child of phenomenology — both Husserlian and Heideggerian. To understand its major assertions presupposes a background in the development of phenomenology in this century; and also the post-phenomenological tradition if one wishes to see the later Heidegger and Derrida in these terms. Nevertheless, it is *through* phenomenology that all four of the major thinkers we have mentioned have come to the issues of hermeneutics. All four have written important critical commentary on Husserl and on Heidegger. So just as modern method-oriented hermeneutics is inconceivable without philological methods and approaches to exegesis, so philosophical hermeneutics is inconceivable without its roots in phenomenology, even when it rebels against certain aspects or forms of phenomenology.

Regrettably, it is beyond the scope of the present paper to go into the fascinating complex of problems that occupy contemporary philosophical hermeneutics, and how the four philosophers we have mentioned might differ or agree on such issues as subject-centered thinking, meta-

---

[43] See Michel FOUCAULT, *The Order of Things: An Archaeology of the Human Sciences* (New York: Pantheon, 1970), and Jacques DERRIDA, *Of Grammatology,* trans. Gayatri C. SPIVAK (Baltimore: Johns Hopkins University Press, 1976) and *Writing and Difference,* trans. Alan BASS (Chicago; University of Chicago Press, 1978).

[44] Otto PÖGGELER, *Hermeneutische Philosophie: Zehn Aufsätze* (Munich: Nymphenburger Verlagshandlung, 1972), and Erwin Hufnagel, *Einführung in die Hermeneutik* (Stuttgart: Kohlhammer, 1976). A more balanced collection of essays is *Seminar: Philosophische Hermeneutik,* ed. Hans-Georg GADAMER and Gottfried BOEHM (Frankfurt: Suhrkamp, 1976); it includes nine selections from the heritage of hermeneutics between Flacius and Schleiermacher, six more before Heidegger, and only four in the final section.

physics, ontology, philosophies of consciousness, textuality, language, discourse, metaphor, mediation, the status of the text, writtenness, eminent texts, history, poetry, psychoanalysis, and so on. We will merely mention a point or two about the relation of philosophical hermeneutics to the other two modes.

First, philosophical hermeneutics does not displace philological hermeneutics. Rather, it is on a different level altogether. As reflection on the conditions of interpretation, it does not suggest specific methods nor invalidate the traditional tools of philological work with texts. It does offer a critique of the illusions of objectivity cherished by unphilosophical philologists. To this extent, yes, it does threaten the philologist. Yet it does not explicitly offer him an *alternative* set of methods because it is not a competing methodology but rather philosophical reflection on all text interpretation.[45]. It does, because of its roots in phenomenology, offer a critique of objectivity, of the determinability of authorial intention, and so on. But its criticism of modern philological hermeneutics as a limited view of interpretation proceeds from a larger criticism of the modern epoch's view of man, of history, of language, of person. In this regard, I have elsewhere argued that there is a "postmodern" dimension in contemporary philosophical hermeneutics.[46]

For instance, Heidegger criticizes the cartesianism of the modern world-picture in *Holzwege*,[47] and Gadamer shows that the redefinitions of truth, man, being, language, and history simply redefine the whole context of interpretation.[48] The lesson of their thinking for hermeneutics is that philological hermeneutics does have limitations, but these are the consequence of the kinds of assumptions about reality that have guided thought in the modern era. And these assumptions have now become questionable. But, like Einstein, Heidegger introduces a critique of modern thinking that is so radical that its significance can only gradually be absorbed into our thinking.

Nevertheless, it is the illusions of the philologist that are the object of philosophical critique, not the value of lexicographical work, of grammatical interpretation, or of historical factors in interpretation. In fact, philosophical hermeneutics would criticize every form of reductionist approach to the hermeneutical event, including structuralist strategies.

---

[45]   This does not meant that philosophical hermeneutics might not result in a change in methods of interpreting literature. In German circles, it very much does affect method, as indicated by the manifestos by Szondi and by Jauss cited in 28 and 40 above, as well as in the section on hermeneutics by Jürgen HAUFF, in *Methodediskussion: Arbeitsbuch zur Literaturwissenschaft*, ed. J. Hauff, et al. (Frankfurt: Athenäum, 1971), II, 1-75. This latter collection illustrates the problems that do arise when one tries to reduce hermeneutics to methodological terms.

[46]   See the articles cited in note 22 above.

[47]   "Die Zeit des Weltbildes, in *Holzwege*, and on this same theme essays in *The End of Philosophy* (New York: Harper & Row, 1973) and *Basic Writings*, ed. David F. KRELL (New York: Harper & Row, 1977).

[48]   See *Truth and Method*, cited above, and my article in *Performance in Postmodern Culture*.

Philosophical hermeneutics inquires into such matters as the structure of interrogation itself; the status and nature of the event of disclosure in various common forms of texts; the problem of overcoming of temporal distance and other forms of alienation; and into what kind of "use" the text has. It may try to put the text back into its performative context to see what it *does*. [49]

So philosophical hermeneutics is not a competing form of methodological hermeneutics — a superior *method* of exegesis — but a body of critical reflection about the event of understanding. It is directed to expanding the *context* of interpretation, not cutting old-fashioned philology out. It asks the interpreter to turn on himself and ask resolutely whether his understanding of interpretation is not itself narrowing and reducing the richness of the text. The possible contribution of philosophical hermeneutics is to lay open the presuppositions of *both* philological and allegorical hermeneutics, not with a view to displacing or disqualifying either but to reclaim elements that a limited view of text-interpretation may have caused us to lose sight of. Thus the great importance of maintaining an historical sense of the heritage of premodern and modern forms of hermeneutics.

IV.   A HERMENEUTICS COMPENDIUM

As the final section of this paper, I offer the general outlines of a proposed six-volume set of essays in hermeneutics. Each volume would run about 650 pages and the total set would be about 3300 pages. Even so, most selections would be only the hermeneutically relevant portions of larger works. The outline generally does not indicate which portion is to be selected, or even that only a section is to be used. Although these matters have been left indefinite, enough detail has been included to give the reader a good picture of the basic categories and the major works selected. In some sections where the contents are still being planned, the detail is fragmentary. Of course, many selections are in other languages and would have to be translated or retained in the original. Obviously another volume might have taken been proposed which would deal with hermeneutics in contemporary literacy criticism, but such would involve easily available materials and extensive copyright fees, and furthermore the basic purpose of this anthology is an historical, rather than a contemporary, collection of essays in hermeneutics.

Richard E. PALMER,
MacMurray College.

---

[49]   See *Performance in Postmodern Culture*, cited in 22 above.

Proposal

A HERMENEUTICS COMPENDIUM: AN HISTORICAL ANTHOLOGY IN SIX VOLUMES

Each volume is separately titled and may be published and sold separately.

Vol. I: PREMODERN ALLEGORICAL AND ESOTERIC HERMENEUTICS: *An Historical Anthology on the Exegesis of Dreams and Oracles, Sacred Texts, and Homer*

Section I: Dreams and Oracles
> The Egyptian Dreambook (2000BC); Greek oracles; Joseph interprets Pharaoh's dream; Philo, *On Dreams;* Artemidorus, *Oneirocritica;* Macrobius, *On the Dream of Scipio;* St. Synesios, *On Dreams;* Talmud, *Berakoth* IX; Cicero, *On Dreams;* Added section on modern dream interpretation: selections from Freud, Jung, Campbell, Hillman.

Section II: The Rise of Allegorical Interpretation in Greece
> Pépin, *Mythe et Allégorie;* Diels, *Fragmenten;* Arnim, *Stoicorum veterum Fragmenta;* Leveque, *Aurea Catena Homeri;* Diogenes Laertius and Sextus Empiricus; Cornutus, *Theologiae Graecae Comp.;* Heraclitus, *Allégories d'Homère;* ps. Plutarch, *De vita et poesi Homeri;* Cicero, *De natura deorum;* Hersman, *Studies in Greek Allegorical Interpretation;* Tate, art. *Classical Q;* Geffken, *ERE* article

Section III: Allegorical and Mystical Interpretation in Philo of Alexandria (plus)
> *Letter of Aristobulus; Letter of Aristeas;* sels. from Philo; Wolfson, "What's New in Philo?"; Christiansen, *Die technik der alleg. Auslegungsw, bei Philon;* Kelly, "Techniques of Composition in Philo"; Stokes, sections from unpublished dissertation on "Schools of Allegorical Interpretation in Hellenistic Judaism"

Section IV: Gnostic Exegesis
> Jonas, *The Gnostic Religion; The Nag Hammadi Library; Corpus Hermeticum,* I; Heracleon (from Origen, *Comm. on John*); Pagels, *The Johannine Gospel in Gnostic Exegesis;* sels. from International Conference on Gnosticism, Yale, 1978.

Section V: Neoplatonism
> Plotinus, *Enneads;* Porphyry, *De Antro Nympharum;* Prophyry, *The Life of Pythagoras;* Iamblichus, *In Timaeum;* Ficino, *Commentary on Philebus.*

Section VI: Hermeneutics of the Kabbalah
> Scholem, *The Kabbalah and its Symbolism;* Scholem, *Major Trends in Jewish Mysticism; Zohar;* Cordovero, *The Palm Tree of Deborah;* Suarès, *The Cipher of Genesis* and *The Song of Songs;* Jacobs, *Jewish Mystical Testimonies* and *Jewish Biblical Exegesis;* Wiener, "How to Read a Hasidic Text" from 9½ *Mystics.*

Section VII: Esoteric Exegesis in the Middle Ages and Renaissance
> (See vol. 2 for Biblical exegesis within the Church tradition, including mystical.) Corbin, *Creative Imagination in the Sufism of Ibn Arabi;* Burckhardt, *Alchemy; Bibliothèque des philosophes chimiques;* F. Yates, from two articles in *JCWI;* Pico della Mirandola, *Conclusiones;* Blau, or Allen, on Christian Kabbalah.

VOLUME II: PREMODERN HERMENEUTICS IN THE JEWISH AND CHRISTIAN TRADITIONS: *Major Hermeneutical Statements and Types of Exegesis*

Section I: Introduction to Talmud and Midrash
> Goldin, *The Living Talmud* (Introduction); *Berakoth I;* Goldin trans. of *Pirkê Abot* and *Abot Rabbi Nathan;* Bab. *Hagigah* 3a-b "The Words of the Torah Grow and Increase"; eg. of Gemara, *Berakoth* IX, 31a-32b; eg. of Aggadic Midrash from Blau, *Judaism;* eg. from Mishnah, *Nezikim,* Sanhedrin 4:5; Midrashim in poetic trans. by Glatzer, *Hammer on the Rock,* ch. 2; Uffenheimer, "The Consecration of Isaiah in Rabbinic Exegesis" (Targum, Aggadic Midrash, and mystical exegesis); Goldin, *The Shirta,* chs, 3 & 6; and S. Spiegel, *The Last Trial.*

Section II: Jewish Hermeneutics Proper: The Rules of Exegesis
> *The Seven Rules of Hillel; The 13 Rules of Ishmael* (from *Sifra* to *Leviticus*); *The Baraita of 32 Rules;* Jacobs, *Jewish Biblical Exegesis;* Bacher, *Die Aggada der Tan-*

naiten, vol. 2, ch. 8; Lieberman, *Hellenism in Jewish Palestine;* Mielziner, Introduction to the Talmud; Rosenblatt, *The Interpretation of the Bible in the Mishnah;* Strack, egs. from his book; Bonsirvin, *Exégèse Rabbinique et Exégèse Paulinienne.*

Section III: The Dead Sea Scrolls — Three Forms of Exegesis
Vermes, *The Dead Sea Scrolls;* Dupont-Sommer, "The Habbakuk Commentary"(?); Russell, *The Method and Message of Jewish Apocalyptic;* Brownlee, "Biblical Interpretation in the Dead Sea Scrolls."

Section IV: Maimonides — Philosophical Exegete in the Middle Ages
Guide of the Perplexed; Introduction to the Talmud; Letter to Samuel Ibn Tibbon on translation.

— The Christian Tradition —

Section V: Modes of Scriptural Exegesis in the New Testament
Jesus interprets himself to the disciples; the use of typological exegesis of OT; the use of parables; references to riddles and secret meaning in *John;* Rabbinical methods of exegesis in NT; allegorical interpretation in NT (other than typological); Doeve, *Jewish Hermeneutics in the Synoptic Gospels and Acts;* Longenecker, *Biblical Exegesis in the Apostolic Period;* von Rad on typological interpretation of the OT; Pagels, *Gnostic Exegesis in the Johannine Gospel.*

Section VI: Early Patristic Biblical Exegesis (to Gregory)
The Epistle of Barnabas; The Apology of Aristides; Justin Martyr, *Apology;* Irenaeus, *Against Heresies;* Clement of Alexandria, *Stromata;* Origen, *De principiis* and *Contra Celsum;* Eusebius, *Preparatio Evangelica;* perhaps some of Tertullian and Theodore of Mopsuestia; Eustathius, *Engastrimytho contra Origenem;* Cassian, *Conf. of Abbot Nesteros;* St. Jerome, on Job; St. Basil, "Address to Young Men on Greek Literature"; Augustine, *De doctrina Christiana,* III; article "Exegese" from *Realencyclopadie der Antike und Christentum,* 1975 ed., dealing with *NT und alte Kirche;* Pépin, "Allégorisme grec et Chrétien" from *Mythe et Allégorie;* James Barr, "Typlogy and Allegory," in *Old and New in Interpretation;* Hanson, *The Spirit and the Letter* (on Origen); Gruber, *Die pneumatische Exegese bei den Alexandrinen.*

Section VII: Exegesis in the Middle Ages
Hugh of St. Victor, *Didascalion;* Richard of St. Victor; Rabani Mauri, *Allegoriae in Universam Sacram Scripturam;* Aquinas, *Summa,* I,i,19,10; Nicholas of Lyra; deLubac, *Exégèse médiévale* (analytic table of contents only); Dobschütz, "Vom vierfachen Schriftsinns"; Smalley, *The Study of the Bible in the Middle Ages;* Leclercq, "From Gregory the Great to St. Bernard."

Section VIII: Mystical Exegesis in the Christian Tradition
(In addition to Gnosticism in Vol. I, see V-VII above.) In this section: Pseudo-Dionysius, *The Divine Names* and *Mystical Theology;* Richard of St. Victor, *Benjamin major;* St. Anselm, *Meditations;* Bernard of Clairvaux, *On the Love of God;* St. Bonaventura, *Théologie Séraphique;* Ramon Lull, *The Art of Contemplation;* Meister Eckhardt, *Sermons;* Ruysboeckh, *A. of Spiritual Marriage;* Gerson, *De mystica theologica speculativa;* Julia of Norwich, *The Shewings of Divine Love; Theologia Germania* (1350); Jakob Boehme, sels.; Loyola, *Spiritual Exercises;* Underhill, "Historical Sketch of European Mysticism from the Beginning of the Christian Era to the Death of Blake" (to Boehme only); Besant, *Esoteric Christianity;* Osment, Introduction to his *Mysticism & Dissent.*

Volume 3: THE RISE OF MODERN PHILOLOGICAL AND THEOLOGICAL HERMENEUTICS: *A Reader of Major Texts from Erasmus to Schleiermacher, plus Certain Forerunners in Antiquity*

Section I: Forerunners in Antiquity
Dionysius Thrax, *Grammatike technê;* Aristarchus, *Scholia* on Homer; Gellius, I, 17, exegesis of a sentence of Varro; Mette, *Parateresis* (on Crates of Pergamon); Gudeman, *Grundriss der Geschichte der klassischen Philologie* (sels.); Müller, "Galen als Philologe," *Verhandlungen der 41. Versammlung deutscher Philogen und Schulmeistern;* Plato, *Cratylos, Protagoros;* Aristotle, *Poetics* 1460-, 6-13, 1461a, 9-16; Longinus, *On the Sublime* (on rules); Horace *Ars Poetica* (on rules); Plotinus, *Enneads;* Porphyry, *Commentary on the Timaeus;* Jewish Targum, pesher, Karaite

interpretation; Dobschütz, *Die einfache Bibelexegese der Tannaiten;* Theodore of Mopsuestia (against allegorical interpretation); Tertullian; Origen (re: his *Hexapla* and *Scholia*); Dio Chrysostom, *Homily* on Ps. 64; St. Jerome.

Section II: Erasmus, Luther, Calvin, and Flacius
> Valla, *Adnotations;* Erasmus, *Ratio seu methodus compendio;* Erasmus, Apologia to *In Novum Testamentum Praefationes;* Aldridge, *The Hermeneutic of Erasmus;* sels. from Luther in Ebeling, *Evangelische Evangelienauslegung;* Holl, "Luthers Bedeutung für den Fortschritt der Auslegungskunst," *Ges. Aufsaetze;* Ebeling, *Luther,* ch. 6; Ebeling, comparison of Luther with early Fathers, in *Evang. Ev.;* Calvin, *Institutes,* chs. X, XI in Book I; Calvin, *Commentaries;* Kraus, "Calvin's Exegetical Principles"; Flacius, secs. 1-4 of *Clavis Scripturae I;* Schwartz, *Die theologische Hermeneutik des Matt. Falcius Illyricus* (1933); Preger, *Flacius* vol. 2, final chapter: "Die hermeneutischen und exegetischen Arbeiten d. Flacius."

Section III: Spinoza and the Rise of Rationalist and Critical-Historical Exegesis
> Spinoza, *Tractatus Theologico-Politicus,* VII; Wolfson, "Spinoza"; Wolle, *Regulae XXX hermeneuticae* (1722); Rambach, *Institutiones hermeneuticae sacrae* (1723), and Erläuterung über seine IHS; Baumgarten, *Biblische Hermeneutik;* Semler, *Vorbereitung zur theologischen Hermeneutik* (or *Abhandlungen von freier Untersuchung des Kanon,* 4 vols.); Ernesti, *Principles of Interpretation* (1762); Herder, *Theologische Werke:* Morus, *On Translating the Scriptures;* Beck, *Rules of Higher and Lower Criticism;* Keil, *Elementa Hermeneutica.*

Section IV: 18th Century Philological Hermeneutics: Forerunners of Schleiermacher
> Winkelmann, sels.; Herder, *Kritische Wälder;* Schlegel, *Lessings Geist* and *Charakteristik Wilhelm Meisters;* Wolf, *Vorlesungen über die Enzyklopädie der Altertumswissenschaften;* Ast, *Grundlinien der Grammatik, Hermeneutik und Kritik;* Szondi on Ast in Szondi's *Einführung in die literarische Hermeneutik;* also perhaps some of Dilthey on forerunners of Schleiermacher in *Leben Schleiermachers.*

Section V: Schleiermacher and the Uniting of Sacred and Secular Hermeneutics
> *Aphorisms;* The *Compendienartige Darstellung* of 1819; Kimmerle, Introduction to his edition, and also 1968 postscript.

Volume 4: PHILOLOGICAL   AND   THEOLOGICAL   HERMENEUTICS   SINCE SCHLEIERMACHER: *Major Texts*

Section I: The Rise of Comparative Linguistics in the Romantic Period
> Schlegel, *Über die Sprache und Weisheit der Inder;* Bopp on Sanscrit; Humboldt;

Section II: Mid-Nineteenth Century Altertumswissenschaft and the "Historical School"
> Boeckh, introduction to *Enzyklopädie und Methodologie der philologischen Wissenschaften;* Blass, *Hermeneutik und Kritik;* Steinthal, *Die Arten und Formen der Interpretation;* Droysen, *Historik.*

Section III: The Flowering of Romance Philology in the Nineteenth Century
> Diez, Gröber, and Meyer-Lübke; articles on these by Curtius in his *Ges. Aufs.*

Section IV: Three Great 20th Century Romance Philologists (Inheritors of the 19th century tradition of Diez, Gröber, Meyer-Lubke). E.R. Curtius, on his method of working, in "Marcel Proust," *Französischer Geist im 20. Jahrhundert* and *ELLMA;* Spitzer, *Linguistics and Literary History;* Auerbach, on figural interpretation.

Section V: Twentieth Century German Classical Philology
> (Part II of Vol. 4 takes up "The Impact of Historical and Scientific Consciousness on 19th and 20th Century Theological Hermeneutics" — secs. VI-XVI as follows:)

Part II

Section VI: The Quest for the Historical Jesus
> Strauss, *The Life of Christ,* intro; Renan, *Vie de Jesus;* Schweitzer, *The Quest for the Historical Jesus.*

Section VII: The History of Religions School and the Dialectical Theology
> Kamlah, Troelsch, and Harnak; Barth, *Epistle to the Romans* (foreword); Brunner, *Wahrheit als Begegnung;* Bultman, intro to Jesus, Jesus Christ and Mythology, and "The Problem of Hermeneutics"; Buber, "On the Interpretation of the Bible".

Section VIII: The "New Hermeneutic" and Language-Event Theology
> Ebeling, policy statement on taking over *ZThK;* Fuchs, *Hermeneutik;* Heidegger,

Toward a Nonobjectifying Thinking in Theology''; Ebeling, ''The Significance of the Critical Historical Method in Protestantism'' (abridged); Ebeling, ''Word of God and Hermeneutics''.

Section IX: The New Quest for the Historical Jesus — James M. Robinson

Section X: The Death of God Theology and Hermeneutics — Vahanian, Altizer, Hamilton

Section XI: Narrativity and Hermeneutics — Frei and others

Section XII: The Hermeneutics of Parable

Perrin, *Rediscovering the Teaching of Jesus;* Funk, *Language, Hermeneutic and Word of God*; Via, *The Parables;* Crossan, *In Parables;* Teselle, *Speaking in Parables.*

Section XIII: Hermeneutics and God-Talk

Hart, *Unfinished Man and the Imagination;* Gilkey, *Naming the Whirlwind.*

Section XIV: Hermeneutics and Process Theology; The New Metaphysics?

Schubert Ogden, *The Reality of God;* L. Ford, *The Lure of God;* Russel Pregeant, Christology Beyond Dogma; David Lull, ''What is the Task of Hermeneutics?''

Section XV: Hermeneutics and Revisionist Theology

Tracy, *Blessed Rage for Order,* ''Five Theses'' and ''Interpretation Theory''

Section XVI: Hermeneutics and Rhetoric (Theology and Literary Criticism)

Crossan, *Raid on the Articulate;* Via; etc.

(sections and selections above are tentative, illustrative)

Volume 5: ''GENERAL HERMENEUTICS'' FROM CHLADENIUS TO BETTI: *A Collection of Major Texts*

Section I: Johann Martin Chladenius (1710-1759)

Einleitung zur richtigen Auslegung vernünftiger Reden und Schriften (1742); Müller, *Johann Martin Chladenius;* Szondi, on Chladenius in *Einführung in die literarische Hermeneutik* (1975).

Section II: Georg Friedrich Meier (1718-1777)

Versuch einer allgemeinen Auslegungskunst (1757); Geldsetzer, Intro. to 1965 ed.; Szondi, ELHermeneutik, chs. 6, 7.

Section III: Friedrich Schleiermacher (1768-1834)

Sels. from *Notes,* 1805-11; (note that Schleiermacacher appears in vol. 3, already); Szondi, chs. on Schleiermacher's hermeneutics (pp. 155-91).

Section IV: Wilhelm Dilthey (1833-1911)

''The Rise of Hermeneutics'' (1900); selections from *Preisschrift* on the early development of hermeneutics: Flacius, Wolff, Chladenius, Baumgarten; portions of *Leben Schleiermacher,* not in the *Preisschrift* early essay; on Michaelis, Semler, Ernesti, Kant, Ast, Schelling, Fichte, Schlegel, and Schleiermacher.

Section V: ''General Hermeneutics'' after Dilthey (except Betti)

Spranger, *Zur Theorie des Verstehens und geisteswissenschaftliche Psychologie;* Bollnow, *Zum Begriff der hermeneutischen Logik,* or *Das Verstehen;* Rothacker, *Logik und Systematik der Geisteswissenschaften* (1927); Bubner, ''Transcendentale Hermeneutik?''

Section VI: Emilio Betti (d. 1973 or so)

Allgemeine Auslegungslehre als Methodik der Geisteswissenschaften (1967); *Die Hermeneutik als allgemeine Methodik der Geisteswissenschaften* (1962).

Section VII: E. D. Hirsch, Jr.

Validity in Interpretation (1967); *The Aims of Interpretation* (1976).

Volume 6: PHILOSOPHICAL HERMENEUTICS: *A Collection of Texts from Plato to Derrida*

Section I: Ten Thinkers from Plato to Wittgenstein

    1. *Plato:* On dialectic, words and language, knowing and perceiving, the weakness of writing, on love and the levels of understanding.

    2. *Aristotle:* On appropriate exactness, practical wisdom, enunciation.

    3. *Vico:* from *De nostri temporis studiorum ratione*

    4. *Schleiermacher:* On understanding as reconstruction; on understanding an author better than he understood himself; on divinatory understanding.

5. *Hegel:* On experience, on dialectic, on the speculative sentence, and on desire and self-consciousness.
6. *Kierkegaard:* On indirect communication.
7. *Nietzsche:* "On Truth and Lying in the Extramoral Sense"; on scholars and objectivity; on several themes in *The Will to Power*.
8. *Dilthey:* On *Geschichtlichkeit;* on the historical character of self-understanding; on life speaking to life in all the deeper forms of understanding; on *Erlebnis-Ausdrück-Verstehen;* on *Verstehen and Erklären*.
9. *Husserl:* On the intentionality of consciousness; overcoming the subject-object dichotomy; on the lifeworld.
10. *Wittgenstein:* On the nature of language; on language game and family resemblances; on understanding as "being able to go on."

Part II: Four Major Figures: Heidegger, Gadamer, Ricœur, Derrida

Section II: Heidegger

Selections from *Being and Time;* selections from that later Heidegger, including the discussion of hermeneutics in "Dialogue with a Japanese".

Section III: Gadamer

"Hermeneutics and Historicism"; selections from *Wahrheit und Methode;* Replik in *Hermeneutik und Ideologiekritik;* others to be selected.

Section IV: Ricœur

"The Hermeneutiks of Symbols and Philosophical Reflection"; "Existence and Hermeneutics"; "Explanation and Understanding"; portion of the introduction to *Freud;* portions of *Interpretation Theory* indicating rejection of Schleiermacher's hermeneutics; autobiographical sketch of problems dealt with, appendix to *The Rule of Metaphor*.

Section V: Derrida

Voice and Phenomenon; On Grammatology; Glas, first two pages, with article by Geoffrey Hartman; "White Mythology".

Explanation and Understanding

What is it to understand a discourse when that discourse is a text or a literary work? How do we make sense of written discourse?

BEYOND ROMANTICIST HERMENEUTICS

With the dialectic of explanation and understanding, I hope to provide my interpretation theory with an analysis of writing, which will be the counterpart of that of the text as a work of discourse. To the extent that the act of reading is the counterpart of the act of writing, the dialectic of event and meaning, so essential to the structure of discourse generates a correlative dialectic in reading between understanding or comprehension (the *verstehen* of the German hermeneutical tradition) and explanation (the *erklären* of that same tradition). Without imposing too mechanical a correspondence between the inner structure of the text as the discourse of the writer and the process of interpretation as the discourse of the reader on our discussion, it may be said, at least in an introductory fashion, that understanding is to reading what the event of discourse is to the utterance of discourse and that explanation is to reading what the verbal and textual autonomy is to the objective meaning of discourse. A dialectical structure of reading therefore corresponds to the dialectical structure of discourse. This correspondence confirms that the theory of discourse presented elsewhere governs all the subsequent developments of my interpretation theory.

Just as the dialectic of event and meaning remains implicit and difficult to recognize in oral discourse, that of explanation and understanding is quite impossible to identify in the dialogical situation that we call conversation. We explain something to someone else in order that he can understand. And what he has understood, he can in turn explain to a third party. Thus understanding and explanation tend to overlap and to pass over into each other. Il will surmise, however, that in explanation we ex-plicate or unfold the range of propositions and meanings, whereas in understanding we comprehend or grasp as a whole the chain of partial meanings in one act of synthesis.

This nascent, inchoative polarity between explanation and understanding as it is dimly perceived in the communication process of conversa-

---

* Reprinted with permission from Paul RICOEUR, *Interpretation Theory* (Fort Worth, Texas: Texas Christian University, 1976), pp. 71-88. The Texas Christian University Press retains all rights to further reproduction or publication of this essay.

tion becomes a clearly contrasting duality in Romanticist hermeneutics. Each term of the pair there represents a distinct and irreducible mode of intelligibility.

Explanation finds its paradigmatic field of application in the natural sciences. When there are external facts to observe, hypotheses to be submitted to empirical verification, general laws for covering such facts, theories to encompass the scattered laws in a systematic whole, and subordination of empirical generalizations to hypothetic-deductive procedures, then we may say that we "explain." And the appropriate correlate of explanation is nature understood as the common horizon of facts, laws and theories, hypotheses, verifications, and deductions.

Understanding, in contrast, finds its originary field of application in the human sciences (the German *Geisteswissenchaften*), where science has to do with the experience of other subjects or other minds similar to our own. It relies on the meaningfulness of such forms of expression as physiognomic, gestural, vocal, or written signs, and upon documents and monuments, which share with writing the general character of inscription. The immediate types of expression are meaningful because they refer directly to the experience of the other mind which they convey. The other, less direct sources such as written signs, documents, and monuments are no less significant, except that they convey the other mind's experiences indirectly, not directly, to us. The necessity of interpreting these signs proceeds precisely from the indirectness of the way in which they convey such experiences. But there would be no problem of interpretation, taken as a derivative of understanding, if the indirect sources were not indirect expressions of a psychic life, homogenous to the immediate expressions of a foreign psychic life. This continuity between direct and indirect signs explains why "empathy" as the transference of ourselves into another's psychic life is the principle common to every kind of understanding, whether direct or indirect.

The dichotomy between understanding and explanation in Romanticist hermeneutics is both epistemological and ontological. It opposes two methodologies and two spheres of reality, nature and mind. Interpretation is not a third term, nor, as I shall attempt to demonstrate, the name of the dialectic between explanation and understanding. Interpretation is a particular case of understanding. It is understanding applied to the written expressions of life. In a theory of signs that de-emphasizes the difference between speaking and writing, and above all that does not stress the dialectic of event and meaning, it can be expected that interpretation only appears as one province within the empire of comprehension or understanding.

A different distribution of the concepts of understanding, explanation, and interpretation is suggested, however, by the maxim derived from my analysis that if discourse is produced as an event, it is understood as meaning. Here mutual understanding relies on sharing in the same sphere of meaning. Already in oral conversation, for example, the transfer into a foreign psychic life finds support in the sameness of the shared sphere of meaning. The dialectic of explanation and understanding has already begun. To understand the utterer's meaning and to understand the utterance meaning constitute a circular process. The development of explanation as an autonomous process proceeds from the exteriorization of the event in the meaning, which is made complete by writing and the generative codes of literature. Then understanding, which is more directed towards the intentional unity of discourse, and explanation, which is more directed towards the analytic structure of the text, tend to become the distinct poles of a developed dichotomy. But this dichotomy does not go so far as to destroy the initial dialectic of the utterer's and the utterance meaning. This dialectic is mediated by more and more intermediary terms, but never canceled. In the same way the polarity between explanation and understanding in reading must not be treated in dualistic terms, but as a complex and highly mediated dialectic. Then the term interpretation may be applied, not to a particular case of understanding, that of the written expressions of life, but to the whole process that encompasses explanation and understanding. Interpretation as the dialectic of explanation and understanding . Interpretation as the dialectic of explanation and understanding or comprehension may then be traced back to the initial stages of interpretative behavior already at work in conversation. And while it is true that only writing and literary composition provide a full development of this dialectic, interpretation must not be referred to as a province of understanding. It is not defined by a kind of object — "inscribed" signs in the most general sense of the term — but by a kind of process: the dynamic of interpretative reading.

For the sake of a didactic exposition of the dialectic of explanation and understanding, as phases of a unique process, I propose to describe this dialectic first as a move from understanding to explaining and then as a move from explanation to comprehension. The fitst time, understanding will be a naive grasping of the meaning of the text as a whole. The second time, comprehension will be a sophisticated mode of understanding, supported by explanatory procedures. In the beginning, understanding is a guess. At the end, it satisfies the concept of appropriation as the rejoinder to the kind of distanciation linked to the full objectification of the text. Explanation, then, will appear as the mediation between two stages of understanding. If isolated from this concrete process, it is a mere abstraction, an artifact of methodology.

FROM GUESS TO VALIDATION

Why must the first act of understanding take the form of a guess? And what has to be guessed in a text?

The necessity of guessing the meaning of a text may be related to the kind of semantic autonomy that I have ascribed to textual meaning. With writing, the verbal meaning of the text no longer coincides with the mental meaning or intention of the text. This intention is both fulfilled and abolished by the text, which is no longer the voice of someone present. The text is mute. An asymmetric relation obtains between text and reader, in which only one of the partners speaks for the two. The text is like a musical score and the reader like the orchestra conductor who obeys the instructions of the notation. Consequently, to understand is not merely to repeat the speech event in a similar event, it is to generate a new event beginning from the text in which the initial event has been objectified.

In other words, we have to guess the meaning of the text because the author's intention is beyond our reach. Here perhaps my opposition to Romanticist hermeneutics is most forceful. We all know the maxim — which indeed antedates the Romantics, since Kant knows and cites it[1] — to understand an author better than he understood himself. Now even if this maxim may receive different interpretations, even if it may be retained with proper qualifications (as I shall attempt to show below), it led hermeneutics astray inasmuch as it expressed the ideal of "congeniality" or a communion from "genius" to "genius" in interpretation. The Romanticist forms of hermeneutics overlooked the specific situation created by the disjunction of the verbal meaning of the text from the mental intention of the author. The fact is that the author can no longer "rescue" his work, to recall Plato's image. His intention is often unknown to us, sometimes redundant, sometimes useless, and sometimes even harmful as regards the interpretation of the verbal meaning of his work. In even the better cases it has to be taken into account in light of the text itself.

In conclusion, then, there is a problem of interpretation not so much because of the incommunicability of the psychic experience of the author, but because of the very nature of the verbal intention of the text. The surpassing of the intention by the meaning signifies precisely that understanding takes place in a nonpsychological and properly semantical space, which the text has carved out by severing itself from the mental intention of its author.

The dialectic of *erklären* and *verstehen* begins here. If the objective meaning is something other than the subjective intention of the author, it may be construed in various ways. Misunderstanding is possible an even unavoidable. The problem of the correct understanding can no longer be solved by a simple return to the alleged situation of the author. The concept of guess has no other origin. To construe the meaning as the verbal meaning of the text is to make a guess.

But, as well shall see below, if there are no rules for making good guesses, there are methods for validating those guesses we do make.[2]

---

[1] *Critique of Pure Reason*, trans. N.K. SMITH (New York: St. Martin's Press, 1965), A314, B370, p. 310.

[2] E.D. HIRSCH says very convincingly, "The act of understanding is at first a genial (or a mistaken) guess and there are no methods for making guesses, no rules for generating insights. The methodological activity of interpretation commences when we begin to test and criticize our guesses." *Validity in Interpretation* (New Haven: Yale University Press, 1967), p. 203.

In this new dialectic both terms are required. Guessing corresponds to what Schleiermacher called the "divinatory," validation to what he called the "grammatical." Both are necessary to the process of reading a text.

The transition from guessing to explaining is secured by an investigation of the specific object of guessing. We have answered our first question, why do we have to guess in order to understand? We still have to say what is to be guessed by understanding.

First, to construe the verbal meaning of a text is to construe it as a whole. Here we rely more on the analysis of discourse as work than on the analysis of discourse as written. A work of discourse is more than a linear sequence of sentences. It is a cumulative, holistic process.

Since this specific structure of the work cannot be derived from that of the single sentences, the text as such has a kind of plurivocity, which is other than the polysemy of individual words, and other than the ambiguity of individual sentences. This textual plurivocity is typical of complex works of discourse and opens them to a plurality of constructions. The relation between whole and parts — as in a work of art or an animal — requires a specific kind of "judgment" for which Kant has given the theory in the *Critique of Judgment*. Concretely, the whole appears as a hierarchy of topics, of primary and subordinate topics that are not, so to speak, at the same altitude, so as to give the text a stereoscopic structure. The reconstruction of the text's architecture, therefore, takes the form of a circular process, in the sense that the presupposition of a certain kind of whole is implied in the recognition of the parts. And reciprocally, it is in construing the details that we construe the whole. There is no necessity, no evidence, concerning what is important and what is unimportant. The judgment of importance is itself a guess.

Second, to construe a text is to construe it as an individual. If a work is produced according to generic (and genetic) rules, it is also produced as a singular being. Only *technê* generates individuals, says Aristotle, whereas *epistêmê* grasps species. Kant, from another point of view, confirms this statement: the judgment of taste is only about individuals. Concretely, the work of discourse, as this unique work, can only be reached by a process of narrowing down the scope of generic concepts, which include the literary genre, the class of texts to which this text belongs, and the types of codes and structures that intersect in this text. This localization and individualization of the unique text is also a guess.

The text as a whole, as a singular whole may be compared to an object, which may be viewed from several sides, but never from all sides at once. Therefore the reconstruction of the whole has a perspectival aspect similar to that of a perceived object. It is always possible to relate the same sentence in different ways to this or that other sentence considered as the cornerstone of the text. A specific kind of onesidedness is implied in the act of reading. This onesidedness grounds the guess character of interpretation.

Third, the literary texts involve potential horizons of meaning, which may be actualized in different ways. This trait is more directly related to the role of secondary metaphoric and symbolic meanings than to the theory of writing. A few years ago I used to link the task of hermeneutics primarily to the deciphering of the several layers of meaning in metaphoric and symbolic language. I think today, however, that metaphoric and symbolic language is not paradigmatic for a general theory of hermeneutics. This theory must cover the whole problem of discourse, including writing and literary composition. But, even here, the theory of metaphor and of symbolic expressions may be said to provide a decisive extension to the field of meaningful expressions, by adding the problematic of multiple meaning to that of meaning on general. Literature is affected by this extension to the degree that it can be defined in semantic terms by the relation between primary and secondary meanings in it. The secondary meanings, as in the case of the horizon, which surrounds perceived objects, open the work to several readings. It may even be said that these readings are ruled by the prescriptions of meaning belonging to the margins of potential meaning surrounding the semantic nucleus of the work. But these prescriptions too have to be guessed before they can rule the work of interpretation.

As concerns the procedures for validation by which we test our guesses, I agree with E.D. Hirsch that they are closer to a logic of probability than to a logic of empirical verification. To show that an interpretation is more probable in the light of what we know is something other than showing that a conclusion is true. So in the relevant sense, validation is not verification. It is an argumentative discipline comparable to the juridical procedures used in legal interpretation, a logic of uncertainty and of qualitative probability. It follows from this understanding of validation that we may give an acceptable sense to the opposition between the *Naturwissenschaften* and the *Geisteswissenschaften* without conceeding anything to the alleged Romanticist dogma of the ineffability of the individual. The method of converging indices, which characterizes the logic of subjective probability, provides a firm basis for a science of the individual, which may rightly be called a science. And since a text is a quasi-individual, the validation of an interpretation applied to it may be said to give a scientific knowledge of the text.

Such is the balance between the genius of guessing and the scientific character of validation, which constitutes a modern presentation of the dialectic between *verstehen* and *erlären*.

At the same time, we are also enabled to give an acceptable meaning to the famous concept of the hermeneutical circle. Guess and validation are in a sense circularly related as subjective and objective approaches to the text. But this circle is not a vicious one. That would be the case if we were unable to escape the kind of "self-confirmability" which, according to Hirsch,[3] threatens the relation between guess and validation.

---

[3] *Ibid.*, pp. 164-207.

But to the procedures of validation there also belong procedures of invali-
dation similar to the criteria of falsifiability proposed by Karl Popper in
his *Logic of Discovery*.[4] Here the role of falsification is played by the
conflict between competing interpretations. An interpretation must not
only be probable, but more probable than another interpretation. There
are criteria of relative superiority for resolving this conflict, which can
easily be derived from the logic of subjective probability.

To conclude this section, if it is true that there is always more than
one way of construing a text, it is not true that all interpretations are
equal. The text presents a limited field of possible constructions. The
logic of validation allows us to move between the two limits of dogmatism
and scepticism. It is always possible to argue for or against an interpretation, to confront interpretations, to arbitrate between them and to seek
agreement, even if this agreement remains beyond our immediate reach.[5]

FROM EXPLANATION TO COMPREHENSION

The preceding description of the dialectic between understanding
as guessing and explanation as validation was roughly the counterpart of
the dialectic between event and meaning. The following presentation of
the same dialectic, but in the reverse order, may be related to another
polarity in the structure of discourse, that of sense and reference. This
new dialectic can be considered from one point of view as an extension
of the first one. The reference expresses the full exteriorization of discourse to the extent that the meaning is not only the ideal object intended
by the utterer, but the actual reality aimed at by the utterance. But,
from another point of view, the polarity of sense and reference is so specific that it deserves a distinct treatment, which reveals its fate in writing
and, above all, in some literary uses of discourse. The same points will
hold for the counterparts of the theory of the text in the theory of reading.

We have seen that the referential function of written texts is deeply
affected by the lack of a situation common to both writer and reader. It
exceeds the mere ostensive designation of the horizon of reality surrounding the dialogical situation. Of course, written sentences keep using
ostensive devices, but these ostensive terms can no longer hold for ways
of showing what is referred to. This alteration of the ostensive designation

---

[4]   Karl POPPER, *The Logic of Scientific Discovery* (New York: Harper & Row, 1968).
[5]   In this part of my essay I have largely drawn on materials borrowed from E.D.
Hirsch. I am sufficiently indebted to his point of view to say where I disagree with him.
In spite of his insistence on the mute character of the text, he maintains that the aim of
the interpretation is to recognize what the author meant. "All valid interpretation, of every
sort, is founded on the re-cognition of what an author meant." (p. 126) In fact, however,
the intention of the author is lost as a psychical event. Moreover, the intention of writing
has no other expression than the verbal meaning of the text itself. Hence all information
concerning the biography and the psychology of the author constitutes only a part of the
total information which the logic of validation has to take into account. This information,
as distinct from the text interpretation, is in no way normative as regards the task of interpretation.

has positive and negative implications. On the one hand, it implies an extension of the referred to reality. Language has a world now and not just a situation. But, to the extent that this world, for most of its parts, has not been shown, but merely designated, a complete abstraction of the surrounding reality becomes possible. This is what happens with some works of discourse, in fact with most literary works, in which the referential intention is suspended, or at least those in which the reference to the familiar objects of ordinary discourse is suspended, to say nothing for the time being of another kind of reference to some of the more deeply rooted aspects or dimensions of our being in the world.

The new dialectic between explanation and comprehension is the counterpart of these adventures of the referential function of the text in the theory of reading. The abstraction from the surrounding world made possible by writing and actualized by literature gives rise to two opposed attitudes. As readers, we may either remain in a kind of state of suspense as regards any kind of referred to reality, or we may imaginatively actualize the potential non-ostensive references of the text in a new situation, that of the reader. In the first case, we treat the text as a worldless entity. In the second, we create a new ostensive reference thanks to the kind of "execution" that the act of reading implies. These two possibilities are equally entailed by the act of reading conceived of as their dialectical interplay.

The first way of reading is exemplified today by the various structural schools of literary criticism. Their approach is not only possible, but legitimate. It proceeds from the acknowledgement of what I have called the suspension or suppression of the ostensive reference. The text intercepts the "worldly" dimension of the discource — the relation to a world which could be shown — in the same way as it disrupts the connection of the discourse to the subjective intention of the author. To read, in this way, means to prolong the suspension of the ostensive reference and to transfer oneself into the "place" where the text stands, within the "enclosure" of this worldless place. According to this choice, the text no longer has an exterior, it only has an interior. To repeat, the very constitution of the text as a text and of the system of texts as literature justifies this conversion of the literary object into a closed system of signs, analogous to the kind of closed system that phonology discovered underlying all discourse, and which Saussure called *langue*. Literature, according to this working hypothesis, becomes an analogon of *langue*.

On the basis of this abstraction, a new kind of explanatory attitude may be extended towards the literary object. This new attitude is not borrowed from an area of knowledge alien to language, but it comes from the same field, the semiological field. It is henceforth possible to treat texts according to the explanatory rules that linguistics successfully applied to the elementary systems of signs which underlie the use of language. We have learned from the Geneva school, the Prague school, and the Danish school of linguistics that it is always possible to abstract systems from processes and to relate these systems, whether they be phonological,

lexical, or syntactical, to units which are already defined through opposition to other units of the same system. This interplay of distinctive
entities within finite sets of such units defines the notion of structure in
modern linguistics.

It is this structural model that is now applied to texts, i.e., to
sequences of signs longer than the sentence, which is the last kind of
unit that linguistics takes into account.

This extension of the structural model to texts is a daring endeavor.
Is not a text more on the side of *parole* — of speech — than on the side
of *langue*? Is it not a succession of utterances, and therefore, in the final
analysis, a succession of sentences? Did we not show elsewhere the
opposition between spoken and written language, as contained in the
concept of discourse which we opposed to *langue*? Such questions indicate at least that the extension of the structural model to texts does not
exhaust the field of possible attitudes in regard to text. We must therefore
limit this extension of the linguistic model to being just one of the possible
approaches to the notion of interpreting texts. Let us, however, first
consider an example of such an approach in some detail before moving
on to consider a second possible conception of interpretation.

In his essay "The Structural Study of Myth," Claude Lévi-Strauss
formulates the working hypothesis of structural analysis in regard to one
category of texts, that of myths.[6] He says, "Myth, like the rest of language, is made up of constituent units. These constituent units presuppose
the constituent units present in language when analyzed on other levels —
namely phonemes, morphemes, and sememes — but they, nevertheless,
differ from the latter in the same way as the latter differ among themselves; they belong to a higher and more complex order. For this reason,
we shall call them *gross constituent units*."[7]

Using this hypothesis, the large units, which are at least the same
size as the sentence and which, when put together, form the narrative
proper to the myth, will be able to be treated according to the same rules
that apply to the smallest units known to linguistics. It is to insist on this
likeness that Lévi-Strauss calls them mythemes, just as we speak of
phonemes, morphemes, and sememes. But in order to remain within the
limits of the analogy between mythemes, and the lower level units, the
analysis of texts will have to perform the same sort of abstraction as that
practiced by the phonologist. For the latter, the phoneme is not a concrete
sound, in an absolute sense, with its acoustic quality. It is not a substance,
to speak like Saussure, but a form, that is to say, an interplay of relations. Similarly, a mytheme is not one of the sentences of a myth, but
an oppositive value attached to several individual sentences, which form
"a bundle of relations." It "is only as bundles that these relations can be
put to use and combined so as to produce a meaning."[8] What is here called

---

[6] In *Structural Anthropology*, trans. Claire JACOBSON and BROOKE Grundfest
SCHOEPF (Garden City, New York: Anchor Books, 1967) pp. 208-28.

[7] *Ibid.*, pp. 206-7.

[8] *Ibid.*, p. 207.

a meaning is not at all what the myth means, in the sense of its philosophical or existential content or intuition, but rather the arrangement or disposition of the mythemes themselves; in short, the structure of the myth.

I would like to briefly recall here the analysis that Lévi-Strauss offers
of the Oedipus myth following this method. He first separates the sentences of the myth into four columns. In the first column he places all
those sentences which speak of an over-esteemed kinship relation: for
example, Oedipus weds Jocasta, his mother; Antigone buries Polyneices,
her brother, in spite of the order not to do so. In the second column are
the same relations, but inverted as an under-esteemed kinship relation:
Oedipus kills his father, Laios; Eteocles kills his brother, Polyneices. The
third column is concerned with monsters and their destruction. The fourth
groups together all the proper names whose meanings suggest a difficulty
in walking upright: lame, clumsy, swollen foot.

Comparison of the four columns reveals a correlation. Between
numbers one and two, we have kinship relationships in turn over-esteemed
and under-esteemed. Between three and four, there is an affirmation and
then a negation of man's autochthony. "It follows that column four is
to column three as column one is to column two... By a correlation of
this type, the overrating of blood relations is to the underrating of blood
relations as the attempt to escape autochthony is to the impossibility to
succeed in it." [9]

The myth thus appears as a sort of logical instrument which draws
together contradictions in order to overcome them. "The inability to connect two kinds of relationships is overcome (or rather replaced) by the
assertion that contradictory relationships are identical inasmuch as they
are both self-contradictory in a similar way." [10]

We can indeed say that we have explained the myth, but not that
we have interpreted it. We have, by means of structural analysis, brought
out the logic of the operations that relate the four bundles of relationships
among themselves. This logic constitutes "the structural law of the myth"
under consideration. [11] It will not go unnoticed that this law is preeminently an object of reading and not at all of speaking, in the sense of a reciting
where the power of myth would be re-enacted in a particular situation.
Here the text is only a text, and reading inhabits it only as a text, thanks
to the suspension of its meaning for us and the postponement of all actual-
ization through contemporary discourse.

I have just icted an example from the field of myths. I could cite
another from a neighboring field, that of folklore narratives. This field has
been explored by the Russian formalists of the school of Propp and by
the French specialists of the structural analysis of narratives, Roland
Barthes and A.J. Greimas. The postulates used by Lévi-Strauss are also
used by these authors. The units above the sentence have the same

---

[9]   *Ibid.*, p. 212.
[10] *Loc. cit.*
[11] *Ibid.*, p. 214.

composition as those below it. The meaning of an element is its ability to enter into relation with other elements and with the whole work. These postulates define the closure of the narrative. The task of structural analysis therefore consists in performing a segmentation (the horizontal aspect) and then establishing various levels of integration of parts in the whole (the hierarchical aspect). But the units of action, which are segmented and organized in this way, have nothing to do with psychological traits susceptible of being lived or with behavioral segments susceptible of falling under a behaviorist psychology. The extremities of these sequences ar only switching points in the narrative, such that if one element is changed, all the rest is different, too. We here recognize a transposition of the commutative method from the phonological level to the level of the narrative units. The logic of action then consists in linking together action kernels, which together constitute the narrative's structural continuity. The application of this technique results in a "dechronologizing" of the narrative, so as to make apparent the narrative logic underlying the narrative time. Ultimately, the narrative is reduced to a combination of a few dramatic units such as promising, betraying, hindering, aiding, etc., which would thus be the paradigms of action. A sequence is a succession of action kernels, each one closing off an alternative opened up by the preceding one. The elementary units, in their turn, fit in with larger units. For example, the encounter embraces such elementary actions as approaching, summoning, greeting, etc. To explain a narrative is to get hold of this symphonic structure of segmental actions.

To the chain of actions correspond similar relations between the "actors" in the narrative. By this one does not mean psychological subjects, but formalized roles correlative to the formalized actions. The actors are defined only by the predicates of action, by the semantic axes of the sentence and the narrative: the one who does the acts, to whom the acts are done, with whom the acts are done, etc. It is the one who promises, who receives the promise, the giver, the receiver, etc. Structural analysis thus brings out a hierarchy of actors correlative to the hierarchy of actions.

The next step is to assemble together the parts of the narrative to form a whole and put it back into narrative communication. It is then a discourse addressed by the narrator to a receiver. But, for structural analysis, the two interlocutors must be looked for nowhere else than in the text. The narrator is designated by the narrative signs, which themselves belong to the very constitution of the narrative. There is nothing beyong the three levels of actions, actors, and narration that falls within the semiological approach. Beyond the last level there is left only the world of the users of the narrative, which itself falls under other semiological disciplines that deal with social, economic, or ideological systems.

This transposition of a linguistic model to the theory of narrative perfectly corroborates my initial remark regarding the contemporary understanding of explanation. Today the concept of explanation is no longer borrowed from the natural sciences and transferred into a different field, that of written documents. It proceeds from the common sphere of language thanks to the analogical transference from the small units of language (phonemes and lexemes) to the large units beyond the sentence, including narrative, folklore, and myth.

This is what the structural schools mean by explanation in the rigorous sense of the term.

I now want to show in what way explanation (*erklären*) requires understanding *(verstehen)* and how understanding brings forth in a new way the inner dialectic, which constitutes interpretation as a whole.

As a matter of fact, nobody stops with a conception of myths and narratives as formal as this algebra of constitutive units. This can be shown in a number of ways. First, even in the most formalized presentation of myths by Lévi-Strauss, the units, which he calls mythemes, are still expressed as sentences, which bear meaning and reference. Can anyone say that their meaning as such is neutralized when they enter into the bundle of relations, which alone is taken into account by the logic of the myth? Even this bundle of relations must be written in the form of a sentence. In the case of the Oedipus myth, the alternation between over-evaluated and under-evaluated kinship relationships means something that has deep existential bearings. Finally, the kind of language game that the whole system of oppositions and combinations embodies would lack any kind of significance if the oppositions themselves, which Lévi-Strauss tends to mediate in his presentation of the myth, were not meaningful oppositions concerning birth and death, blindness and lucidity, sexuality and truth. Without these existential conflicts there would be no contradictions to overcome, no logical function of the myth as an attempt to solve these contradictions.[12]

Structural analysis does not exclude, but presupposes, the opposite hypothesis concerning myth, i.e., that has meaning as a narrative of origins. Structural analysis merely represses this function. But it cannot suppress it. The myth would not even function as a logical operator if the propositions that it combines did not point towards boundary situations. Structural analysis, far from getting rid of this radical questioning, restores it at a higher level of radicality.

If this is true, could we not then say that the function of structural analysis is to lead us from a surface semantics, that of the narrated myth, to a depth semantics, that of the boundary situations, which constitute the ultimate "referent" of the myth?

---

[12] Lévi-Strauss seems to admit this, in spite of himself, when he writes, "If we keep in mind that mythical thought always progressess from the awareness of oppositions toward their resolution, the reason for these choices becomes clearer." (*Ibid.*, p. 221). And Again, "the myth provides a kind of logical tool." (*Ibid.*, p. 212.) In the background of the myth there is a question which is a highly meaningful one: "Is one born from one or from two?" Even formalized in this way, "Is the same born from the same or from the other?", the question expresses anxiety and agony regarding our origin.

I believe that if this were not the case, structural analysis would be reduced to a sterile game, a divisive algebra, and even the myth itself would be bereaved of the function Lévi-Strauss himself assigns it, that of making men aware of certain oppositions and of tending towards their progressive mediation. To eliminate this reference to the aporias of existence around which mythic thought gravitates would be to reduce the theory of myth to the necrology of the meaningless discourses of mankind.

If, on the contrary, we consider structural analysis as one stage — albeit a necessary one — between a naive interpretation and a critical one, between a surface interpretation and a depth interpretation, then it would be possible to locate explanation and understanding at two different stages of a unique hermeneutical arc.

Taking the notion of depth semantics as our guideline, we can now return to our initial problem of the reference of the text. We can now give a name to this non-ostensive reference. It is the kind of world opened up by the depth semantics of the text, a discovery, which has immense consequences regarding what is usually called the sense of the text.

The sense of a text is not behind the text, but in front of it. It is not something hidden, but something disclosed. What has to be understood is not the initial situation of discourse, but what points towards a possible world, thanks to the non-ostensive reference of the text. Understanding has less than ever to do with the author and his situation. It seeks to grasp the world-propositions opened up by the reference of the text. To understand a text is to follow its movement from sense to reference: from what it says, to what it talks about. In this process the mediating role played by structural analysis constitutes both the justification of the objective approach and the rectification of the subjective approach to the text. We are definitely enjoined from identifying understanding with some kind of intuitive grasping of the intention underlying the text. What we have said about the depth semantics that structural analysis yields rather invites us to think of the sense of the text as an injunction coming from the text, as a new way of looking at things, as an injunction to think in a certain manner.

This is the reference borne by the depth semantics. The text speaks of a possible world and of a possible way of orientating oneself within it. The dimensions of this world are properly opened up by and disclosed by the text. Discourse is the equivalent for written language of ostensive reference for spoken language. It goes beyond the mere function of pointing out and showing what already exists and, in this sense, transcends the function of the ostensive reference linked to spoken language. Here showing is at the same time creating a new mode of being.

Paul RICOEUR,
Universities of
Paris and Chicago.

The New Hermeneutic and the
Interpretation of Poetry

This is not the occasion for a history of hermeneutics in its ancient or modern phases and of the different disciplines affected by it.[1] I shall, though, offer some historical pointers as I examine what I judge as three important contributions of the Hew Hermeneutic, as I will call the movement that springs especially from Martin Heidegger and Hans-Georg Gadamer. This development has had its theological-biblical representatives, in Rudolf Bultmann and Gerhardt Ebeling for examples, and its literary-theoretical representatives who, besides Heidegger and Gadamer themselves, include the recent work of Paul Ricoeur and George Steiner, as well as that of Richard Palmer, and myself. The historical notes will help to situate and to understand what is at issue in the New Hermeneutic, for historical thinking belongs in an essential, not merely decorative or illustrative fashion, to the hermeneutic approach. Even in talking 'about' hermeneutics, one should at the same time be 'doing' it. Beyond the provision that I must confine myself here to historical notes, I must also make clear that I will not so much render an exposition of concepts readily at hand but attempt in a modest way, to forge them so that what is attractive and disconcerting about them for our conception of 'literature' stands out. So that the historical map in which the New Hermeneutic finds its place, and takes place, is not a pacific one but a dialectically clamorous one of question and answer, claim and counter-claim, argument and counter-argument. All map making involves simplification, this one too, but the purpose of a map is to assist in recognition as one passes through a land.

The expression 'hermeneutic' I use in the contemporary sense found in Heidegger, Gadamer, and Ricoeur, to designate the theory of textual interpretation and of the textuality of the text.[2] In earlier periods when this

---

[1] For such a history, see GADAMER, *Truth and Method* (Seabury trans., New York, 1975; German 2nd ed. 1965) *passim;* RICOEUR, "The Task of Hermeneutics", in MURRAY, ed., *Heidegger and Modern Philosophy* (New Haven, 1978); PALMER, *Hermeneutics: Interpretation Theory* (Evanston, 1969); MURRAY, *Modern Critical Theory* (The Hague, 1975); and SZONDI, *Einführung in die literarische Hermeneutik* (Frankfurt am Main, 1975), and the voluminous references cited in these works.

[2] In Heidegger an ambiguity arises about the status of text due to his more frequent use of speech and speaking, an ambiguity that for now I shall ignore. In part I think that what Heidegger says about *sprechen* and *Sprache* can be assimilated to a hermeneutics of the text; in part, though, I agree with those who charge Heidegger with a 'suppression' of the textuality of the text. On the other hand, the liberators of the suppression can be charged with a reverse suppression of speech.

term designated the art or science of interpretation, the texts to be interpreted were Biblical or classical texts, and one of the major controversies
arose from this condition, namely the argument over whether hermeneutics
is always and only peculiar to some type of texts (e.g. to Scripture) or
whether there can not exist a general hermeneutics with universal pretentions. A major trend in the history of hermeneutics has been a movement
from particular to general hermeneutics, and this has led of necessity to an
involvement in philosophical matters and to projects, like those of Dilthey and Heidegger, to establish hermeneutic foundations. The present
paper raises the question of how, in light of these foundational attempts,
we shall conceive the interpretation of poetry.

A second major controversy concerns what is the proper *aim* of hermeneutics. Now for Schleiermacher in the early 19th century and for Dilthey in the late 19th century, and in our own time, for Collingwood, the
aim of hermeneutics was to transport oneself empathetically via written
traces into the mind of an alien other (cf. *Nacherleben*, re-enactment).
Success in this case amounts to achieving union with the other, a psychological proximity or identity between reader and author,[3] and failure
means its converse. In the hermeneutic process thus viewed, the circular
movement of understanding as a back and forth would finally *disappear*
when understanding is attained. There are, we have come to appreciate,
a whole complex of suppositions built into this Romantic historicism, ones
which are endemic to modern 'subjectivism', epistemological theory, and
metaphysics. These are the 'problem of other minds' (here applied toward
predecessors rather than toward contemporaries), and the 'ideal' of knowledge as the attainment of an indentity and abolition of distance and difference. The New Hermeneutic stands opposed to this kind of hermeneutics, and Heidegger gave the main critical and the main positive guidance in the new direction.

Heidegger's achievement was to undercut this problematic of the
stranded Cartesian self and the metaphysics of identity, with his existential
conception of worldly being-with and with the structure of historical
temporality and tradition, which Gadamer has so richly elaborated as a
necessary framework for experience in the realm of the humanities or
Geisteswissenschaften[4] and which he has focussed in a most interesting
way by his rehabilitation of the concept of 'prejudice'. Heidegger gave this
new twist to the task of hermeneutics when he based hermeneutics
not on a 'method' but on a permanent structure of human existence. By
virtue of our language, our traditions and common life, which are prior
to the egological constructions of a subjectivity, we already exist factical-
ly in relations to predecessors and successors. This factical possibility is
ultimately rooted in the way our existence is temporally spread-out, and
the way this temporal extendedness opens up a world to us. This is the

---

[3]   On my view E.D. HIRSCH's work, *Validity in Interpretation* (New Haven, 1967),
revives romantic historicism.
[4]   See *Truth and Method*, pp. 253-274, and Gadamer's constant contrasting of hermeneutic experience with the 'method' of the natural sciences.

'fateful destiny' of men. This meant that time is no impossible chasm to be crossed over but itself a process of disclosure and closure.[5] And secondly, Heidegger, more especially in his later writings, showed that instead of hermeneutic aiming at recovering a psychological individuality (a 'unique' speaker), we need one that focuses primarily on what is said, on the matter of speaking itself.

Accordingly, the New Hermeneutic orients itself toward the saying of what gets said in the text, rather than toward unique personalities behind them, and instead of a conquest of strangeness and unfamiliarity, a task predicated upon the identity model, the New Hermeneutic appeals to a dialectic model of identity and difference encompassing identity-in-difference and difference-in-identity, to cast it in the Hegelian idiom.[6] Or, putting it in the Heideggerian way, we could speak of sameness, not to be confused with identity or equivalence, and of the difference as opening to togetherness rather than as mere oppositeness. Hence the true hermeneutic model must *preserve* the tension between strangeness and familiarity. This is the way to understand that extraordinary resonance that Heidegger discovers in the line of Hölderlin, "Seit ein Gespräch wir sind und hören voneinander" *(Friedensfeier)/*:Since we have been a conversation and hear from one another", and of Gadamer's elaboration of the structure and play of conversation as a fresh way of thinking about language. By basing hermeneutics in this way upon a structure of human being and the state of the human condition, as *Vor-struktur* or precondition of any possible understanding, hermeneutics assumed an ontoligical significance. I may remark in connection with this hermeneutic model, that Derrida's characterization of hermeneutics as "pontification", a bridge-making by pontification which ought to surmount and conquer the strange into the familiar, can at best apply only to the earlier brand of hermeneutics. In other words, Derrida's criticism, here as in other stages along the road to deconstruction, is of Heideggerian extraction.[7]

In the course of hermeneutic reflection, one may discern an impulse from classical Greek sources, since a hermeneutics under the sign of the

---

[5]   "Hence temporal distance is not something that must be overcome. This was... the naive assumption of historicism, namely that we must set ourselves within the spirit of the age, or think with its ideas and its thoughts, not with our own, and thus advance toward historical objectivity" *(Truth and Method*, p. 264).

[6]   By the 'identity model' here and throughout this paper I mean a specific conception of Being, knowledge and language, which goes back to Aristotle and largely dominates Western philosophy. In its ontological version, it conceives the real as that which is permanently self-identical; in its epistemological version, it defines knowledge as the state wherein the mind by grasping its form becomes identical with the thing; and in its linguistic version, it conceives true meaning as univocal, proper, and transparent, as conforming to the A = A or law of identity. In this sphere thought can be *at home*, while fending off all that is improper, obscure, equivocal, and alienating. For Aristotle, though philosophy begins in wonder, it ends in the conquest of strangeness, since the strange is merely the yet-to-be-known. For the New Hermeneutic which rejects this model, thinking is the cultivation rather than the abolition of astonishment, and thus must call on a different understanding of Being, knowledge and language.

[7]   See DERRIDA's works, *passim*.

messenger-god Hermes, must signify the bringing forth of what is to be
said, announced, or 'messaged' in language,[8] as that which is most essential about language. This is the accent heard in Heidegger, Gadamer,
and in his current work, Ricoeur, and with which I would associate myself.
The accent corresponds to a certain independence and impersonality of the
linguistic text. But this impersonality is not to be explained, as a recent
author has done, as a detachability from its utterance origin that is determined by the 'uses' made of texts by societies,[9] but instead from the fact
that the texts continue to speak, across a variety of historical situations,
to have something to say, that we when we hear it, we find ourselves
in need of its saying and respond by interpreting, performing, and preserving the text.[10] In its widest sense, "hermeneutics" has become a kind
of portmanteau category for Continental philosophy of language. This
Continental philosophy of language, however, must be sharply distinguished from Continental would-be 'science' of language and from literary
theory that emulates structuralist semiotic linguistics.

We have suggested the sense in which the New Hermeneutic offers
an alternative path to that of Romantic historicism, but it also offers a way
out of a second impasse of modern literary interpretation, one that is the
very anti-pode of historicism, namely the impasse of Enlightenment formalism, whose heirs are the modern structuralists. By 'formalism' I do not
mean merely a viewpoint that resolves to take 'form' with the utmost
seriousness, because as could be shown such formalism does not take form
seriously enough or, just as relevant, playfully enough.[11] Formalism in
general designates a set of ideas about 'form', about its nature, primacy,
and independence, and even about the irrelevance of content, matter, or
substance. In this sense one can distinguish in literary criticism quite different degrees of formalism, from the informal formalism that characterized
the theory and practice of American New Criticism, ca. 1940-1960,[12] to the
more formal formalism that derives from Russian Formalism (ca. 1915-
1930) and from French Structuralism (from Saussure ca. 1915 to Barthes
and Todorov), which is now enjoying an ascendant moment in Anglo-
American literary theory.[13] For formalism of the latter variety is an exacting kind of aestheticism, which conceives the object of its science as

---

[8]   HEIDEGGER, "A Dialogue on Language", *On the Way to Language* (New York,
1971; German, 1959), p. 29f.

[9]   John ELLIS, *The Theory of Literary Criticism* (Berkeley, 1974), pp. 44-47.

[10]   Herein lies the hermeneutic question of 'application'.

[11]   By claiming that formalists don't take form *playfully* enough, I mean they look
at the form as at any object, withdrawn from letting themselves be put in play and thus
experience the play of language. For the ideal of science lies outside play, in the seriousness
of the *Gestell* (Framework), and it doesn't take form *seriously* enough because it wants it
only to the extent that it can conform to its methodological demands. (On play, see Heidegger
and Gadamer). Of later formalists only Derrida in his Grammatology attempts both with
the result that the framework crumbles, putting him outside of serious semiotics.

[12]   See the chapter "The Old and New Criticism", in my *Modern Critical Theory*.

[13]   See the still excellent presentation of this moment in Edward SAID's *Beginnings:
Intention and Method* (Baltimore, 1975). I raise these questions in a review of Todorov's
The Poetics of Prose in *Philosophy and Literature*, (1978).

outside of history, with neither capacity or need for referentiality and truth, and as instead a search for the technical devices that underlie the aesthetic qualities and allow us to calculate their possible effects, and to supply a method of rigorous 'reading', as distinguished from mere interpretation and from commentary.

The Russian formalists sought a science of poetics that would yield "objective description of the peculiarly literary nature and use of certain 'phonemic' *devices* in the literary work, and not with that work's phonetic' content, its 'message', its 'sources', its 'history'...".[14] For it is the "various devices or techniques *(priem)* which act as agencies of 'literariness'.[15] And while there has been much subsequent work since on specific devices and their taxonomies, the following statement about the early formalist view is one that Todorov and Jakobson can readily endorse today. "Thus the sum total of 'devices' employed in the poem generate and so constitute its range of 'meaning'. In the end, the poem *is* its devices; it *is* its form".[16]

I cannot here consider in detail these formalist claims about literature, their background and critique, but in the discussion to follow their contrast with hermeneutic assumptions and working ideas should be evident.

I referred to a hermeneutic under the sign of Hermes as its Greek connection or root. But a mention of 'enlightenment' formalism should remind us that enlightenment, too, is of Greek origin, and Todorov rightly emphasizes that he resumes a task that was begun by the Sophists, but later mostly abandoned. What is *new* about the New Hermeneutic is to a surprising extent that it resumes a task left off when that task fragmented to pieces in classical poetics. This refers of course to the coinvolved developments of rhetoric, poetics, and dialectics, which expressed the pressures and adjacencies of classical politics, classical poetics, and classical philosophy. A glance in this direction is found in Heidegger's allusion to Mallarmé's 1894 quip that after the great Homeric deviation all poetry had lost its way.[17] The considerable attention which modern hermeneutic thinkers have lavished on Greek philosophical texts confirms this fact,[18] at the same time that they oppose every kind of neo-classicism and humanism based upon a normative idea of the classic.

---

[14]   Terence HAWKES, *Structuralism and Semiotics* (Berkeley, 1977), p. 61.

[15]   *Ibid*, p. 63.

[16]   *Ibid*, pp. 64-65; see TODOROV, *The Poetics of Prose* (Ithaca, N.Y., 1977), p. 236.

[17]   "Naming signifies in Greek already for somewhile declaration *(Aussagen)* ; and declaring means to make something known *as* something. This understanding of language holds predetermined the realm in which Homeric poetry moves (on this consider the far-reaching word of Mallarmé, quoted in Henri MONDOR, *Vie de Mallarmé*, p. 683: "Poetry has, since the great Homeric diviation, entirely lost its track" (HEIDEGGER, *Vier Seminare* (Frankfurt a. Main, 1977), p. 74).

[18]   Say, for illustration, their writings on Aristotle, those of Heidegger on the *Physics* and *Metaphysics*, of Gadamer on the *Ethics*, and of Ricoeur on the *Poetics*.

II. — THE LANGUAGE OF POETRY

So much by way of general orientation about the task of the New Hermeneutic. Next I take up the question of what specifically demarcates poetic language *as* poetic. The answer can be approached by considering the principle dimensions of the poetic text — the *what*, the *way*, and the *import* of poetic saying — and above all the unity that binds them together. (All this, naturally, supposes *that* poetry exists, and that we are already approaching it within the circle of understanding). Once this is ascertained in a tentative way, I shall explore the notions of the truth of poetry and the historicity of poetry.

1.   The What. Poetic speaking — the speaking that takes place in a text — is a speaking that names and calls forth that which it addresses into the presence of its being. The naming act or event is accomplished through the distinctive working of the poetic work which brings about the establishment of a world.[19] This means that poetic speaking is not primarily either self-expression or communication between senders and receivers, and that poetic naming is not the passing out of titles or affixing of labels to things already familiar and at hand. The essence of *inaugural* naming as Heidegger specifies it, is a calling of what is named from out of a distance into presence, out of remoteness into nearness. Yet the bringing near of a thing named does not mean transporting an object from far away into a lecture hall, a gallery, or living room. The museal collecting of things from all different places and times does move things, but it does not obviously bring us closer to these things or these things closer to us not if closeness means in the vicinity of the thing's truth and presence. The naming act, on this view, does not transfer the thing from one spot to another, or multiply the objects in the workd, but rather in calling things calls them that they may come to presence, appear in a way that bears upon men and exert a claim on us. It is through poetic naming that things begin to arrive and reach the concreteness of their being as things.

2.   The Way. The ways of poetic utterance are infinitely creative, and while many insightful and careful things may be said regarding it, I don't think a grammar or a rhetoric of poetry can capture the essence of it. This poetic infinitude is not the same as ordinary infinitude in the sense distinguished by Chomsky as the 'competence' for producing everyday non-parroted sentences, although the poetic infinitude presupposes this competence as well. Yet it should be pointed out that banal, stereo-typical, parrot-like speaking, with little to say, does not at all contradict creative competence in the transformational sense, and makes it trivial by comparison with the creative infinitude of poetic work. The poetic wealth of language is alien to everyday linguistic commerce, in its richness, density,

---

[19]   Elsewhere I take up the structure of this world, in terms of the concepts of ground, horizon, and measure. See my *Hermeneutics of the World in Stevens, Rilke, Faulkner and Broch*.

thickness, in its exuberant heterogeneity, in its rarity and archaism, in its novel coinages, and in its free relation to the whole field of common speech, and to the history of common and literary language. This infinitude operates in all levels of poetic language, from the lexical, syntactic, and phonetic, to the semantic, sentential, and textual dimensions of poetic composition.

3. The Import. Poetic utterance, by its nature, is self-exhibiting, which means that it stands out from everyday and technical kinds of speech and texts, inviting a special attention and experience. This is because of the *elementality* of what it says and the *irrandiance* of how it says, which unite to form the import or poetic force of poetry. In this regard, poetic utterance is self-revealing just as ordinary speech, in ordinary contexts, is largely self-concealing because it is used up in its use and functions. This does not mean, however, and Heidegger has unfortunately not made this so clear, that the poetic manifests a merely anti-thetic relation to the everyday, for it is only *through* the poetic that the everyday can be revealed in its everydayness, and that through it we can discover the sense in which something poetic lies at the base of the everyday world. *An Ordinary Evening in New Haven* is anything but ordinary. Here too once recognises the hermeneutic polarity of familiarity and strangeness.

A version of the thesis about 'self-exhibiting' is recognized in formalist poetics, in its profound insight into the 'fore-grounding' (Russian *aktualisace*) and 'making strange' *(astranenie)* of poetry language. This notion appears strictly analogous to Heidegger's general notion that the work of art, in erecting a world, lets the earth *be* an earth, the stone in the case of the stone sculpture, the word in the case of the poem. Unfortunately in formalism this great insight got wedded to a perverse deduction from it which deprived poetry of its truth-bearing powers. This deduction was legitimated by the assumption that all referentiality must be 'informational' and by the desire to preserve the autonomy of poetry against propagandistic political use and by acquiescence in the positivist idea of science. When Jakobson converts poetry into a model of the pure sign for its own sake, from which it gains its model-theoretic importance for linguistics, he achieves this at great hermeneutic expense. For semiotic linguistics having converted the three term relation of sign in terms of signifier, signified, and thing (or proposition, sense and reference), to a two term relation of signifier and signified, is on its way to embracing a strictly one term term, which as Derrida conclusively shows, finally liquidates the sign. The conception of language as sign that signifies and cypher that encodes belongs to metaphysics, and as such, according to Heidegger, must be surpassed by a hermeneutic thinking of language as signal that indicates and gesture that makes manifest what-is. [20]

Much of the wealth of poetic speech (its polysemy, figuration, violation, originality) is familiar to us, though of course as Hegel stressed its

---

[20] Jacques DERRIDA, "Structure, Sign and Play", *The Structuralist Controversy* (Baltimore, 1970) p. 250 and *Of Grammatology* (Baltimore, 1976) pp. 44-57, *passim*, and HEIDEGGER, *On the Way to Language*, pp. 115, 121, 123.

being familiar does not assure its being understood. Less often noted, yet
of considerable importance, is the significance of what might be termed
the 'replay' of ordinary language in poetry. A therapeutic side-effect of
attending to such replays is how it shows us that many traditional ways
of defining poetry (e.g. poetry as metaphor) will not do, because it is not
just metaphor but rather a kind of metaphor and order of metaphor that
alone makes a poetic difference, what Ricoeur calls 'living metaphor'
(*métaphore vive*).[21] By contrast a theory of rhetoric must be principally
concerned with the standard types of textual figures, with their conventions and classifications. Valuable in its own right as such work is, it
cannot alone determine the nature of the poetic, and the collapse of the
distinction between poetics and rhetoric is a confusion. Moreover, Heidegger's critique of the concept of metaphor in so far as that concept is
dependent upon metaphysics, suggests further its dubious use for a hermeneutic poetics.[22]

The less frequently discussed examples of authentically poetic language I have in mind are of two sorts: (i) those citings of ordinary
speech episodes, perhaps even especially those most repeated, shop-worn,
and banal of expressions, in works of poetry, including novels and dramas.
And (ii) the way that poetic speech has of foregrounding speech-acts as
speech acts, and generally modes of speech as those modes. Both of these
cases we designate the 'poetic-hermeneutic As'.[23] The first sort T.S. Eliot
shows to us in *The Waste Land*, in such lines as:

> 'You gave me hyacinths first a year ago;
> 'They called me the hyacinth girl'.
>
> (from I. The Burial of the Dead)
>
> 'My nerves are bad to-night. Yes, bad. Stay with me.
> 'Speak to me. Why do you never speak. Speak'.
>
> (from II. A Game of Chess)

or in the unforgettable exeunt from the pub, which closes down the second
movement, "A Game of Chess".

---

[21]   Paul Ricoeur, *The Rule of Metaphor*, trans. R. CZERNY (London and Toronto,
1977), French, 1975.

[22]   On this issue, see Ronald BRUZINA, "The Metaphor and Philosophy", in *Heidegger and Modern Philosophy*, ed. M. MURRAY, and compare Ricoeur, *op. cit.*, pp. 309f
and DERRIDA, "White Mythology", *New Literary History*, VI (Autumn, 1974), 5-74 (French,
1971).

[23]   This term borrows partly from what Heidegger says about the hermeneutical vs.
the apophantical 'As' in *Being and Time:* "[the apophantical 'As'] no longer reaches out
into a totality of involvements. As regards its possibilities for articulating reference-relations,
it has been cut off from that significance which as such, constitutes the surrounding world.
The 'as' gets pushed back into the uniform plane of that which is merely present-at-hand.
It dwindles to the structure of just letting one see in a definite way... Thus assertion cannot disown its ontological origin from an interpretation that understands. The primordial
'As' of an interpretation (*ermeneia*) which understands circumspectively we call the 'existen-
tial-hermeneutic As' in distinction from the 'apophantical As' of the assertion" (p. 158),
and from a little noticed passage in "The Origin of the Work of Art": "Such [poetic] saying
is a projecting of the clearing, in which announcement is made of what it is that beings
come into the Open *as*" (*Poetry, Language, Thought*, (New York, 1971), p. 73).

Well, if Albert won't leave you alone, there it is, I said,
What did you get married for if you don't want children?
HURRY UP PLEASE ITS TIME
Well, that Sunday Albert was home, they had a hot gammon,
And they asked me to dinner, to get the beauty of its hot —
HURRY UP PLEASE ITS TIME
HURRY UP PLEASE ITS TIME
Goonight Bill. Goonight Lou. Goonight May. Goonight.
Ta ta. Goonight. Goonight.
Good night, ladies, good night, sweet ladies, good night, good night.

Thence forward the witticism became possible, especially perhaps for non-British readers, that the barmen of England could recite T.S. Eliot.

A second species of the poetic-hermeneutic As are found in the so-called 'speech-acts' that occur in ordinary discourse (though in a hermeneutically embedded and hidden way) and seemingly also occur in literary works of art. Simply, for our purpose, we could say a speech-act is any act of speaking whose utterance also co-constitutes a deed, as in the case of promising, prophecying, making a vow, insulting someone, or making a threat.[24] I said that such speech-acts 'seemingly' occur in literary works because of the difficulty in specifying just what that different way of occuring is. Commonly it is alleged that the ones in ordinary discourse are 'real', whereas the others are 'fictional'; which is the view of Austin and Searle, that the literary speech-acts are play-acting, and parasitic upon the serious, sincere, and original ones.[25]

Many writers have thought that the apparent speech acts in literary works of art are 'imitations' of speech acts, so that the promises, warnings, commands, oaths that occure in literature are in reality imitation-promises, imitation-commands, and so forth.[26] This basically Aristotelian doctrine has affinities with Ingarden's notion of a quasi-judgment, with Richards' notion of a pseudo-statement, and with Gass's more recent Wittgensteinian view that poetry, unlike ordinary speech, never *says* anything.[27] In contrast to these notions I want to explore the thesis that literary speech acts are not so much imitations of speech-acts but instead,

---

[24] The crucial texts for this notion are J.L. AUSTIN's *How to Do Things with Words* (2nd ed., Oxford, 1975), and John SEARLE, *Speech Acts: An Essay on the Philosophy of Language* (Cambridge, 1969). Elsewhere I have tried to show that Heidegger anticipates the theory of speech-acts, against similar opponents, in *Being and Time*. I am also of the view, now fairly widespread, that *all* acts of speaking are speech-acts.

[25] Literature is parasitic and non-serious because (a) literature suspends the rules that govern linguistic practice; and (b) literature breaks the word-world relationships. A quite different view of the same matter would claim that the interruption and suspension of the rules makes possible a revelation of the word-world relation, and that this relation, when ordinarily operative, is concealed from awareness. Yet ultimately this revelation can't be explained by a rule model, or rule-convention model because there is no rule for rule-breaking, and rule revealing lies beyond rule, and deals in the order of originating and founding.

[26] M. Beardsley, R. Ohman, B.H. Smith.

[27] On Ingarden and Richards, see my *Modern Critical Theory*, pp. 38, 49-50, and for William GASS, see "Carrots, Noses, Snow, Roses, Roses", *Journal of Philosophy*, LXXIII, 19 (November, 1976), pp. 736-37, and *The World within the Word*, (New York, 1978).

are self-fore-grounding, self-revelatory speech-acts that reveal the *meaning* of speech acts. This claim is part of the larger thesis that one of the accomplishemnts of poetic truth is to reveal the ordinariness of the ordinary which, like An Ordinary Evening in New Haven, or even in Ottawa, is anything but ordinary.

I shall briefly mention two examples, which unfortunately space does not permit me to develop, one from Faulkner and one from Vergil. The first I have developed in a recent paper, the second I will return to later in this paper. First, consider the promise that Anse Bundren makes, in Faulkner's *As I Lay Dying*, to his wife Addie that she will be buried in Jefferson. "And when Darl was born I asked Anse to promise to take me to Jefferson. I died, because I knew that father had been right..." (Vintage ed. p. 165) and Anse, later in time, remarks to Tull: "I give my promise... She's counting on it" (p. 133). In the novel this promise becomes the vehicle of a revenge against life that propels the family members through fire and flood, saving and transfiguring some (Cash and Jewel), driving some to equivocal madness (Darl), and showing up the inner deadness of others (Anse). [28]

In Vergil's *Aeneid* there appear a number of so-called 'directional prophecies', such as those made to Aeneas by Hector (II.289f), Creusa, Hellenus (III.374f), Apollo, and Celaeno (III.250f), which refer to some imminent stage in his wandering quest. While all may be supportive of the divine ordinance that Aeneas will one day found a new city, which is the overarching storyline that connects the Aeneas legend with the historical present of the Augustan age, these prophecies are "nevertheless", a recent study puts it, "a very misleading and incomplete guide, partly because they do not reveal all — as Hellenus makes clear (III, 379-80), and Anchises' unexpected death illustrates (III, 708ff) — but largely because they give no indication of the relative weight of individual events, so that the same occurrence may have one appearance when predicted and another when seen in the present. All that is predicted happens, or will happen just after the poem's end, but, in entirely suppressing the cost, the struggle Aeneas will face, the prophecy is so oversimplified as to become the vehicle of a terrible irony not fully revealed until the poem ends". [29]

I have proposed that the literary speech act reveals the meaning of the speech act, citing as cases the meaning of the promise and prophecy in Faulkner and Vergil. The work does this by showing that to the performative utterance there always belong a world, and within that unfolding world the speaking is seen to have its place, a certain weight, and significance. As the act of its speaking is revealed, so too is the worldiness of the utterance, in terms of peculiar intersection of customs, conventions, and privacies. While in ordinary situations we are aware of the contex-

---

[28] An extended interpretation of this work was presented in my paper "Clearing, Clearing Up, and Clearing Away: Heidegger and Faulkner", delivered at the Association for Philosophy and Literature, May, 1978.

[29] Sara MACK, *Patters of Time in Vergil*, (Hamden, Conn. 1978), pp. 56-57.

tuality of our discourse, this may not surface into our awareness without effecting a breakdown. For essential to everyday speech acts is that they are somehow concealed from those who perform them, concealed by their very publicity, familiarity, and repetitive averageness. The ordinary speaker of a language is absorbed by his speaking anonymously, in his communicating and purpose intents, especially when he is sincere and serious in a Searle-like way. Poetry can reveal the depths, and the shallows, that underlie and contextualize ordinary utterances or personal thoughts. This means that the dependence of utterance upon language, and the priority of language over speaking, are relations always explored in the poetic work.

But it is not just this general dependence of speech act upon language, but the specific hermeneutic-poetic As that manifests the kinds of speech acts and kinds of sentences. Thus we could say that the literary work gives us the ontological meaning of the command, declaration, interrogation, exclamation, exhortation, or acquiesence as the different ways of sentencing. I say ontological to distinguish it from a factual, informational sort of knowledge. To be sure the giving of these meanings, for they are a gift, by the text does not occur in the degreeless and contextless way that are imagined for 'ideal' meanings, "washed in the remotest cleanliness of a heaven", as Stevens says. Essence or meaning here is not essence in the manner of the steno-signs of mathematics or in the name of a universal formal relevance. Poetic work yields the essence which matters to us, in a way that exerts specific claims upon us, puts us into a new situation as a self, and provides a site or locale wherein things are revealed.

The poetic-hermeneutic As is the achievement of the literary work of art, for it discloses the truth and meaning of our acts of speaking and thus of our lives transacted in them. The literary work is autotelic only in the sense that it does not refer to some object or process in the world that is already understood, mastered, and evidently 'there'. But the peculiar fencing off and self-fore-grounding that characterizes literary language does not prevent it from "saying". What it says, however, is not a function of ordinary communication between a sender and a recipient of messages. *What it says is the ontological meaning of speaking.* Meaning in poetry is always revealed within the concreteness of a world. Ultimately we could say that what the work reveals to us is *the meaning of the world* and what comprises a livable world; that is, of what it is to have , possess, or seek a world. The work shows what it is to be enthralled, thrown, and delivered over to a world, which may include the features of rootlessness, fragmentariness, darkness, and aimlessness. [30]

---

[30]   In the previously mentioned manuscript, *Hermeneutics of the World,* I further define world in terms of its ground, horizon, and measure, and the literary work may be said to nominate and establish world. These terms form a fundamental semantics of poetry.

III. — THE TRUTH OF POETRY

Our discussion has already broached the trugh of the work of art, but we must now consider this topic more expressly as we turn to the second contribution of contemporary hermeneutics.[31] For the New Hermeneutic has both recovered and developed the problem of trugh in a way that is prohibited for both formalism and historicism. Throughout most of the Western tradition, and in a decisive way since the founding of modern aestheticism in the late 18th century, it has been usual for philosophers to divorce poetry and truth, and to treat the notion of truth in and of literature as a category mistake that betrays a confusion of aesthetics with logic and science. (In the older, pre-18th century tradition this relation persisted in a minor way in the oft-heard charge against poetry as lie and deceit, which Nietzsche revived and reversed in his remark that 'we have art in order not to die of the truth').[32] Such a view pervades 20th century discussions, of cricitics as much as philosophers, and I will indicate briefly how it gets expressed in formalist and historicist aesthetics.

Summarizing the thesis of Prague school formalism (Trubetskoy and Jakobson), a recent expositor writes: "(T)he *cognitive* or *referential* function of language operates when it is used for the transmission of information; the *expressive* or *emotive* function is seen... to indicate the mood or attitude...".[33] The latter function is the truly aesthetic or poetic one, and Jakobson's later refinement of this claim in terms of the six functions of language, makes of the poetic-aesthetic function the one that attends to the world of the message (where message means verbal form, not content) for "its own sake". "Verbal art... is not referential in mode... Its mode is auto-referential; it is its own subject", so that the poetic work is "an intrinsic, self-generating, self-regulating and ultimately self-regarding whole". In the view of Barthes "literature's essential nature" is that "in which signifiers are prised utterly free of signifieds, aiming... for a *coherence* and *validity* of response, not objectivity and truth".[33] Todorov proposes *vraisemblance* or verisimilitude rather than truth, for literary truth is a truth of coherence of text with text.[34] Eco asserts a thesis, not just for literature, but for semiotic linguistics generally when he declares that

---

[31] Beside the texts of Heidegger and Bultmann, see GADAMER, "The Retrieval of the Question of Artistic Truth", *Truth and Method*, pp. 73-90, and my *Modern Critical Theory*, pp. 77-81, 176-185. For a contrast with an 'analytic' approach, see Peter McCormack's contribution, "Problems with Literary Truth".

[32] This minority tradition is incomparably more profound than the majority tradition. I should qualify my previous statement about the major tradition by noting that in the epoch of German Idealism, in Schelling, Hegel and Schopenhauer, there occurred a transformation of aestheticism. Still Hegel is *ultimately* ruled by the same traditional conception (see Karsten HARRIES, "Hegel and the Future of Art", *Review of Metaphysics*, 1976); while Schopenhauer partly sides with Hegel and partly with Nietzsche.

[33] Terence HAWKES, *Structuralism and Semiotics*, (Berkeley, 1977), pp. 75, 86 and 156 respectively.

[34] Tzvetan TODOROV, *The Poetics of Prose*, pp. 82-87. For further criticism of semiotic theories, see RICOEUR, *The Rule of Metaphor, passim*.

/peanut butter/ is no different from peanut butter,[35] which one cannot resist extolling as a truly unique way of eating one's words!

Historicism is equally, though differently incapable of understanding the meaning of poetic truth. For historicism concludes, on the basis of a genuine insight into the historical situatedness of every possible speaking, that truth as eternal, necessary, and universal proposition, is shipwrecked. From a perspective determined by skeptical disillusion, it sees no way of re-thinking the nature of truth. Formalism and historicism are thus alike in their abandonment and repudiation of truth, historicism especially as it strives for a knowledge of other minds at other times and places. That historicism could see the epochal and time-boundedness of work only as a form of hermetic cloture, not as a concrete openness, lead as well in its skeptical formulations to the view that the concrete, specific historicity of a given time is ineffable. (Here, again, the identity model dominates).

In the context of this debate, the hermeneutic procedure must be to show a way out that allows us to regain the rightful and appropriate place of referentiality and truth. And yet what we are after will not be just another of the frequently proposed reactionary formulations that offer a poetry of "subjective truth" in contrast to the "objective truth" of science.[36]

In the philosophical tradition, truth has been generally conceived of as a correctness relation between a proposition and an object or state of affairs, or alternately between a mind and its object. This mental and propositional sense of truth is a proper and even indispensable sense of truth. This notion only requires a critique of its concealed implication to be the only proper and fundamental meaning of truth. Heidegger has demonstrated that this implicit claim is untenable and that there must be another prior sense of truth, truth as revelation rather than truth as correspondence, which is proper to poetry and creative language.[37] While this

---

[35] Umberto Eco, *A Theory of Semiotics* (Bloomington, Ind. 1977), p. 7. Compare here Jonathan Culler, in his *Saussure* (London, 1976): "To the semiologist the truth or falsity of the prepositions of a discipline [e.g. astrology or astronomy] will be irrelevant" (p. 102).

[36] Most recently by Robin Skelton, *Poetic Truth* (London and New York, 1978).

[37] Heidegger derives this sense of truth from the Greek *alētheia* (unconcealment) which Bultmann connects with the Biblical *apocalypsis* (uncovering). The claim is that the proposition is not the first or real given of language — that it is a derivative specialized function that presupposes the background of language in speech and word-event. Poetic truth happens only with poetic language.

In some of his last writings Heidegger states that his translation of *alētheia* by "truth" was misleading, though not what was thought through this word, which thereafter he will render by opening or lighting *(Lichtung)*. He also comments that his thesis on a shift in Greek experience from truth as revelation to truth as correctness is no longer tenable, not again because he was after the wrong thing, but because he came to see that even in early Greek thought, poets, thinkers, and ordinary speakers alike, the opening remains unthought (see "The End of Philosophy and the Task of Thinking", *Basic Writings* (New York, 1977), pp. 389-390).

While this 'retraction' may be historically justifiable, he is unwise to withdraw the translation, first because it then loses the notable critical tie with correctness, that is with

truth is pre-propositional, it must be stressed that it is *not pre-linguistic*, for this truth comes about only as a happening of poetic language, that outlines the world in a primordial way and makes manifest what is. This calls for verbs like 'reveal', 'wrest from hiddenness', 'inaugurate', and 'nominate', to describe the semantic action of the poetic working of the work. This articulates further what was involved earlier in our discussion of poetic naming.

I can elucidate this in other terms by saying that the poem establishes a semantic site. By *semantic* site I mean the interplay of the basic meanings of things and of Being, which become discriminatable through the poem and the world of the work. Great poetry, we could say, seeks to institute a world in which the differences and togetherness of the regions of Being are set forth. Heidegger elaborates this in a more substantive way by suggesting that poetry gathers together into proximity and distance the Fourfold *(Geviert)*. The four regions of Being correspond to the Earth and its mortal dwellers and builders, and the Heavens and its divine presiders who are present or absconded from view, with each member of the World-Square ramifying the other. To fully explicate the promise in Faulkner or the prophecy in Vergil for example would be to examine those acts of speaking within the resounding movement of the World-Square of the work. It is of the nature of great poetry, we could say, to establish the ancient and ever-present parameters of the world process, and in this regard poetry constitutes the heart of language. [38]

For us suggestions such as these may sound extravagant and bizzare. Yet an argument can be made that the World-Square, of which Heidegger speaks in his Hölderlin-struck way, is not so much the newest fashion of Continental ontology as the oldest, only humanly universal frame of reference, found everywhere among human societies. [39]

I spoke additionally about the *site* of the semantic action of poetry. The semantic site or topos is a place, but a temporized place, even better an *ex*temporized place. The advantage of this way of thinking the matter is to break away from the subjectivism that burdens and warps all

---

a notion that it must be opposed to. Second, letting go of this connectedness has the effect of allowing highly exclusive claims of correctness to go unchallenged. And thirdly, whether the event Heidegger once thought he had located in Greek, thought (i.e. the shift from unconcealment to correctness) happened or not, the fact remains that even in the usage of Plato and Artistotle there were recognised senses of truth other than correctness, which continues to be named by the many-sensed *alētheia*. In discussion, Charles Segal called my attention to the work of Marcel Detienne, as supportive of Heidegger's previous interpretation of early Greek usage. See "La notion mythique d'*Alētheia*", *Revue des Études grecques*, LXXIII (1960), 27-35, and *Les maîtres de Vérité dans la Grece archaïque* (Paris, 1967).

[38] See "The Nature of Language", *On the Way to Language*, pp. 105-8; "The Thing" in *Poetry, Language, Thought*, and "Hölderlin and the Essence of Poetry", in *Existence and Being* (ed. W. Broch, Chicago, 1967).

[39] See Charles KAHN, *Anaximander and the Origins of Greek Cosmology* (New York, 1960), pp. 134f and the cited works of Meillet. How the World-Square compares and relates to the age of modern technology lies outside the scope of this paper, but not outside Heidegger's thought.

purely intentionalist and expressivistic theories of art. In these sites of creative language, Being calls to man and man, as poet and interpreter, responds to Being.

Because the poetic work establishes a semantic site, which is an occurence of truth, we may speak of the poem as a alethic word-event (from *alétheia*.) The poem is such a happening of truth in a double way. First it casts the participant and communicant in the event into a new situation as a self. The "inaugural naming of the gods and the essence of things" emplaces the self in a new world. Secondly, it affords knowledge of an original though originated, non-derivative order of truth about selves, about things, and about Being itself. Heidegger phrases this another way by saying that the poetic work clears a clearing in which Being is disclosed, irradiated. The clearing, or semantic site, suggests a domain separated off from, but in the midst of beings. As verbal, it suggests a process and even of bringing the dim and concealed into the light. What clears the clearing is different in ontological kind from any other thing found in the surrounding world, for the artwork is "like nothing else in Tennessee". It also suggests a meaning of creativity, for the clearing is created by the unusual being of the artwork, where neither work nor Open existed before. With the side of a creative truth is wed the truth of letting things be, setting them free into the fullness of their natures and into the configuration of their relations.

IV. — THE HISTORICITY OF POETRY

Our discussion of the truth of poetry in the verbal terms of unconcealing, setting-to-work, establishing, and event has spoken in ways that demand that we recognize the historicity of poetry. Historicism, reacting to its distrust in the stereotype of the 'timeless' work of art, takes historicity seriously enough, but its formulations were encumbered with epistemological dogmas and inadequate structural detail, until Heidegger showed how this task might be ventured anew in his *Being and Time*. From the opposing vantage, formalism either ignores this historicity or assings it diachronic status, abstracting from existing individuals and community into a synchronism that is a model of a timeless psychological process. [40]

By the historicity of the poem in the hermeneutic sense I refer to its action of a temporal opening-up of future, present, and past tenses, in the distinctive fashion of the given work. This 'extemporizing' describes the working of the work. All poetry accomplishes such an extemporizing of

---

[40] On this model see Noam CHOMSKY, *Reflections on Language* (New York, 1976) pp. 58; 119-120, 232, n.4, and Jonathan CULLER's book, *Saussure* (London, 1975): "The fact that the sign is arbitrary or wholly contingent makes it subject to history but also means that signs require an anhistorical analysis". According to this view, the radical priority of synchronics over diachronics ensures "the irrelevance of historical or diachronic facts to the analysis of *la langue*", pp. 36-37.

temporality in some degree and manner. Great poetry, we could say, does this to an epochal extent by telling men the time in which they live, which is what Homer or Vergil, Milton or Wordsworth, Hölderlin or Whitman do, and what strong poets have always done. The opening-up of the poem establishes a particular relation between the individual's immediate present and a more encompassing life-time bounded by his death and birth, and between this individual, existential level and the more expansive sphere of historical relation to other lives and other beings. [41] In this sense we may distinguish a poetry of the immediate present, a poetry of individual mortality and natality, and a poetry of destiny or of the historical community. No poetry will merely exemplify one of these kinds, for the actuality of poetry is more complex. The attempted poetry of immediacy is unavoidably affected by the inescapable background of the life-whole and by other lives and beings, which casts a shadow over it. This shows up in all poetry from the *carpe diem* of Horace (*Odes*, Bk.1, 11, 7) to Marvel's "To His Coy Mistress", to this episode from William Carlos Williams' *Patterson*, a work that the author described as "a reply to Greek and Latin with the bare hands".

> We sit and talk,
> quietly, with long lapses of silence
> and am aware of the stream
> that has no language, coursing
> beneath the quiet heaven of
> your eyes
>
> which has no speech; to
> go to bed with you, to pass beyond
> the moment of meeting, while the
> currents flat still in mid-air, to
> fall —
>
> With you from the brink, before
> the crash —
>
> to seize the moment.
>
> We sit and talk, sensing a little
> the rushing impact of the giants'
> violent torrent rolling over us,
> a few moments.

But the shadow falls with unsurpassed pathos when Goethe's Faust declaims to Mephistopholes:

> Werd' ich zum Augenblicke sagen:
> 'Verweile doch! Du bist so schön!'
> Dann magst du mich in Fesseln schlagen,
> Dan will ich gern zugrunde gehn!
>
> Dann mag die Totenglocke schallen,
> Dann bist du deines Dienstes frei,
> Die Uhr mag stehn, der Zeiger fallen,
> Es sei die Zeit für mich vorbei!

---

[41] For the distinctions between the immediate, existential and historical levels, which correspond in the ages of man to childhood, youth and age, see John DONNE, *The Way of All the Earth* (New York, 1972).

If I say to the fleeting moment:
O stay on, Thou are so beautiful!
Then you may throw me in fetters,
Then will I gladly go under!
Then may the death-knell peal,
Then are you freed from your service,
The clock may stop, the hands drop off,
And time for me be done with![42]

Lastly, we might return to Vergil's *Aeneid* which provides one of the supreme Western cases of the experience of the transition from the existential level to the historical level, and in particular to that memorable *ecphrasis* by which Vergil portrays Aeneas experience at the Carthage Temple:

Namque sub ingenti lustrat dum singula templo,
reginam opperiens, dum quae fortuna sit urbi,
artificumque manus inter se operumque laborem
miratur, videt Iliacas ex ordine pugnas
bellaque iam fama totum volgata per orbem
Atridas, Priamumque et saevum ambobus Achillem.
constitit et lacrimans 'quis iam locus' inquit 'Achate
quae regio in terris nostri non plena laboris?'
En Priamus, sunt hic etiam sua praemia laudi,
sunt lacrimae rerum et mentem mortalia tangunt.
solve metus; feret haec aliquam tibi fama salutem'.
sic ait, atque animum pictura pascit inani
multa gemens, largoque umectat flumine voltum.

For while he awaited the queen beneath the great temple,
He looked at its different details; and while he still wondered
At the town's good fortune, the skill and work of its hands,
He found on the frieze the events of the Trojan war,
Set out all in order, its battle known over the world,
The Atreidae and Priam, Achilles so savage to both.
He stood and wept. "What place, Achates," he said.
"What region of earth is not full of our grief? Look at Priam!
Even here there are due rewards for glory.
Life's events bring tears, mortal fortunes touch the heart.
Do not fear: This fame will bring some salvation to you".
So he spoke, and pastured his spirit on empty pictures,
Groaned aloud, till his face was bathed over with tears.

Bk.I, 453-465[43]

Aeneas continues to survey the figures and battles until he comes upon and recognises his own self in the story (I.488).

The basic theme of the *Aeneid*, according to a leading interpreter, is "The struggle and final victory of order — this subduing of the demonic

---

[42]   This translation I borrow from Arnold Toynbee's one volume abridgment of *A Study of History*.

[43]   The Latin text follows R.D. Williams' edition, *The Aeneid of Virgil* (Glasgow, 1972); see his note on 'ecphrasis', p. 192. The translation is adapted from Lind's *Aeneid*. I don't, though, accept Williams' gloss that the *sunt lacrimae* line merely means that the Carthaginian will be 'sympathetic' to his cause, because though we must include this sense, such a reading misses the dramatic tone and the peculiar word order that opens with the ontological *sunt*, as Peter Colaclides noted to me in discussion.

which... appears and reappers in many variations. The demonic appears in history as civil or foreign war, in the soul as passion, and in nature as death and destruction. Jupiter, Aeneas and Augustus are its conquerors, while Juno, Dido, Turnus and Antony are its conquered representatives. The contrast between Jupiter's powerful composure and Juno's confused passion reappears in the contrast between Aeneas and Dido and between Aeneas and Turnus''.[44] The peculiar heroism of Aeneas, we could say, is his unique *pietas*, his uniting in himself past, present, and future — a Homeric *past* of destruction and defeat, a painful *present* of exilic wandering in search of a new home, tormented by awareness of the damage done to other lives by the civilizing process that can be 'justified' only by its inaugural link with the *future* era of Augustus as an ecumenic *Pax Romana*. The *Aeneid* does indeed celebrate "the great victory of the battle of Actium as symbolizing the end of decades of bloody civil war,"[45] yet what distinguishes the *Aeneid* as poetic work from a mere nationalist self-authentication is precisely how it exhibits the conflicting claims of the moment, the life-time, and the time of communal destiny, without reducing them to a false unity. This is the measure which the poet Vergil imposes on the Augustan age. It is through such a time-design that the prophecies of the *Aeneid*, both the particular directional prophecies and the master prophecy of Jupiter in Book I, get their quality of tragic discord between the envisagement and the fulfillment.

The dark, fearful side of the Roman order can only be overcome by something that is newer than the new order, that can only come when Vergil appears in the context of Dante's *amor* and *lume*, but whose advent Hermann Broch dramatizes in *The Death of Vergil* as the vision that elicited Vergil's decision first to burn his great poem, and then finally to make a gift of it to Augustus. In this perspective Vergil appears as the poet between the no longer of the antique world and the not yet of a world to come, a state beyond the comprehension of the incredulous Augustus. Great poetry, we have said, tells men the time in which they live. Hölderlin enter his poethood, according to Heidegger, when he reveals the meaning of the modern Time of Need, as the age between the No Longer of the gods who have fled and the Not Yet of the gods to come. Walt Whitman seeks to define the past and future Vistas of American life, when he poetizes the technological sublime in the "passage to India". The pattern of the No Longer and the Not Yet may perhaps be generalized to great poetry and may describe the historical horizon as disrupted by the event of the poetic word.

Historicity is a mark of ordinary speech, too, so that it is important to explain the difference between the historicity of ordinary speech-acts and the historicity of poetic speech. Just as for some theorists the difference between poetry and everyday language is that poetry does not *say* anything, so others maintain that a further difference is that poetry is not,

---

[44]   Viktor Pöschl, *The Art of Vergil* (Ann Arbor, 1963), p. 18.
[45]   As Kenneth Quinn remarks, *Vergil's Aeneid* (London, 1968).

strictly, historical at all. Ordinary speech is, of course, tensed speech, yet is bound to the time and place of its utterance, and to its speaker and its addressee in a special way. In being spoken, ordinary speech, fitted to uses and tasks, is used up and exhausted. The relevance of poetic speech, by contrast, is not spent at the moment of the original utterance, so that although it has its own determinate situation, it can also speak to men at other times and places, as well as *about other* times and places. And the interpretation of poetry is not a 'reconstruction' of what the author intended but basically an articulation of what the text says to us, whereas in an ordinary communication the question of what the speaker 'meant' may be of great or at least routine importance. Gadamer rightly argues that the meaning of the text can no more be reduced to the intending of an author, than can the understanding of history be reduced to the stated intentions of the protagonsists.[46] (In fact, the truth of this relation between intention and action, meaning and saying, is explored in every novel and drama). The saying of the text goes beyond its author into a history and to concrete interpreters with their own interests and vantage points. The evidence that supports this view is precisely the affect which the work exerts on others who in response seek to preserve the poem. To the true work of art, as to philosophical texts, there always belongs its present and future preservers, those who transmit, care for, perform, and interpret the work.

This does not mean that the work tell us only what we want to hear, and thus only confirms our sense of things, though of course our pre-understanding must have its orientating 'prejudice'. Poetry which did only that would deserve another name, perhaps the name 'literature' could be kept for it.

Poetry can speak to us of worlds past and perished that live on in their words, and reveal to us the specific historicity of 'those who have been there', a There that is at once temporal and spatial. The audience of the Homeric poems were not the immediate members of the archaic community who form the actors in the poem, and Elizabethan drama tells the ancestral history of its people and retells the Greek and Roman stories. And in so far as it anticipates the arrival of a future, the poem is also projective saying that lays open some future possibilities.

Historicity cannot be understood only in a diachronic way, or only in a synchronic way, for the historicity of the poem is not just one more speech performance in a code and in terms of a set of rhetorical conventions. Such an approach cannot suffice because it does not grasp how the poem in saying something new revises and newly transmits the language. Here Todorov makes the entirely telling concession that "The masterpiece belongs to no genre, except perhaps its own".[47] And Ricoeur makes the related point, quoting Genette, that "rhetoric cares little about the originality or the novelty of figures, 'which are qualities of individual speech,

---

[46] *Truth and Method*, pp. 263, 336, 352 and 356.
[47] *The Poetics of Prose.*

and which, as such, do not concern it'''.[48] There are general rules of linguistic conventions, but no rules for breaking them or for new invention
as Kant, despite his aestheticism, recognized so well in his account of
'genius' and his distinction between productive and reproductive imagination. The advent of the new is essential to the historical happening of
poetic language and to its interplay with literary history and world history,
and to this pitch of poetic work hermeneutics draws attention.

A fuller statement of the relation between poetry and everyday
speech, beyond the hints were presented, lies outside this paper. This is
the territory of interanimation between the "sign of the gods and the voice
of people", as Hölderlin casts it, or in Stevens' more quotidian formula:
"The poem goes from the poet's gibberish to/The gibberish of the vulgate
and back again" (*Notes*, II, ix). One of Hölderlin's prose jottings reads:

> Only that is the truest truth, in which error, because it is set within the whole
> of its system, in its time and place, also comes to truth. It is the light that il-
> lumines itself and also the night. This too is the highest poetry, in which the
> Unpoetic, because it gets said at the right time and place in the whole of the
> artwork, becomes poetic.[49]

I might restate this thought in terms of an earlier point in this paper:
speech acts in poetic works are not imitation speech-acts but self-revealing
acts of speech, such as can occur only in the context of the work of art,
just as speech-acts that occur in the everyday world are self-concealing
in their context. They relate not as original and copy, not even as 'actual'
original versus 'idealized' copy, but rather interact as lighting (poetic
world) and darkening (everyday world), in which the darkness gains its
own illumination, both within the work and outside the work.[50]

The poetic work lights up its own time and its participating audience,
invites us to see how that time is the same and how different from ours,
and puts us into questions as we put it into question. This approach allows
us to think the history of poetic works not according to a mechanical

---

[48]   Cited from *Figures I* (Paris, 1966), p. 220 in *The Rule of Metaphor*, p. 148;
see also Ricoeur on the difference between the standardized topes of the marketplace and
those of genuine poetry (p. 63). Tom Martland has recently put this point about art's history
thus: "activities or objects are art if their massed or accumulated impact extends beyond
experiences into which they originally were meant to provide an 'insight'..." and while the
'on-going culture' provides the 'shareable ground', "we expect art to turn men around by its
thunder and move them into a future, into a present, and into a past" ("Art?", *American
Philosophical Quarterly*, 15, No. 3 (July, 1978), pp. 232 and 234).
[49]   *Werke, Briefe, Dokumente*, Stuttgart ed., sel. Pierre Bertaux (Munich, 1977),
p. 502. My translation.
[50]   The other theme that lies outside my paper, but not outside this symposium, is
the nature of hermeneutic discourse itself which in the name of Hermes mediates between
poetic and ordinary speech, which in interpretively preserving participates in *both* the nature
of a speech act *and* in the nature of a poetic word-event, yet which must find its own language if it is to bring about a 'fusion of horizons'. See GADAMER, *Truth and Method*,
pp. 270f, 340, and especially p. 358: "... no text and no book speaks if it does not speak
the language that reaches the other person. Thus interpretation must find the right language
if it really wants to make the text (itself) speak". For my account of the structure of interpretation and the hermeneutic circle, see *Modern Critical Theory*, Ch. IV.

or even a spiritual law, but on the model of a conversation of mankind about what matters to us.

Michael MURRAY,
Vassar College.

Problems With Literary Truths

INTRODUCTION

In one of the most consequential reflections on the problems of literary aesthetics, *The Apology for Poetry*, Sir Philip Sidney wrote that poets
never lie because they never affirm anything.

> "Nowe for ye Poett hee nothing affirmes and therefore never lyeth," Sidney
> writes in the Norwhich Manuscript; "for as I take it; To lye is to affirme that
> to be true which is false. So as ye other *Artists* and especially the *Historiann*
> affirmeing many things cann in the Clowdy knowledge of mankinde hardely
> escape from many; But the Poett as I saide before never affirmeth... and there-
> fore though hee recount things not true; yett because he telleth them not
> for true, he lyeth not."[1]

Sydney's own affirmation has continued to exercise philosophers and
literary critics even today. For his comment raises more than one issue.[2]
Are there indeed literary truths, or is talk of truth in this domain finally
nothing more than another species of figurative speech? If we may speak
properly of not just truths but of literary truths, then just what analysis
of truths as such can sufficiently warrant this talk? More simply, *what* are
literary truths, *how* are they presented in literary artworks, how do we as
readers *come to know* such truths, and exactly what are literary truths
true of?

I should like to address one of these questions only, the nature of
literary truths. After providing an example of the myriad works which
raise this question, I want to exhibit the varied contexts in which this kind
of question arises. Against this background I propose then to contrast two
quite different contemporary accounts of literary truths, an analytic account and a hermeneutic one, before concluding briefly with an attempt to
show how several common features in this set of philosophical disagree-
ments invite further inquiry. Throughout, my concern will be to suggest

---

[1] Sir Philip SIDNEY. *The Apology for Poetry*, ed. M.R. MHAL (Northridge, California, 1969), pp. 31-32, Sidney's emphases. For further materials see *An Apology for
Poetry*, ed. G. SHEPHARD (London, 1965); *A Defence of Poetry*, ed. J.A. VAN DORSTEN
(Oxford, 1966); and J. BUXTON, *Sir Philip Sidney and the English Renaissance* (London,
2nd ed., 1964).
[2] Some evidence of the difficulties here may be had by consulting recent work in
the application of formal semantics, especially Fregean types of analysis, to literary texts.
See, for example, *Literary Semantics*, ed. T. PAVEL and J. WOOD, *Poetica*, 1979; G.
GABRIEL, *Fiktion und Wahreit: Eine semantische Theorie der Literatur*, Stuttgart, 1975;
K. ASCHENBRENNER, "Implications of Frege's Philosophy of Language for Literature,"
The British Journal of Aesthetics, 8 (1968), 319-334; and H. MELLOR, "Literarische Wahr-
heit," *Ratio* 10(1968), 124-140.

for students of classical and modern interpretation theories the interest and
the importance of continuiing philosophical reflection about the nature of
literary truths. Consequently, my aim will not include an attempt to make
and to defend any larger claims of my own about a single satisfactory
account of this issue. In this way I hope best to serve the larger, more
meditatively toughtful, and not just philosophical interests of our conference as a whole.

I. — QUESTIONS ABOUT TEXTS

Here then, to begin with, is a poem, a dramatic monologue by Post-
humus from Act II of Shakespeare's *Cymbeline*.

> Is there no way for men to be, but women
> Must be half-workers? We are all bastards; all,
> And that most venerable man which I
> Did call my father was I know not where
> When I was stamp'd; some coiner with his tools
> Made me a counterfeit; yet my mother seem'd
> The Dian of that time; so doth my wife
> The nonpareil of this. O! vengeance, vengeance;
> Me of my lawful pleasure she restrain'd
> And pray'd me oft forbearance; did it with
> A pudency so rosy the sweet view on't
> Might well have warm'd old Saturn; that I thought her
> As chaste as unsunn'd snow. O! all the devils!

Now, on reading such texts carefully we sometimes find ourselves
asking different kinds of question. What kind of text is this? How does
this poetic statement differ from other kinds of literary statement? Are
such fictional statements ever true or false? How are we to describe
the content of this text? Are there procedures available for interpreting
this text in an unambiguous way? How are we to evaluate the success
or failure of this work? How can we assess the propriety of a particular
performance of this monologue? What does this text mean? And, most
centrally for our present concerns, just what would allow us rightly to hold
that such a text exhibits literary truths?

These questions are not idle ones as George Steiner's magisterial
analysis of the many difficulties in just this text has amply demonstrated.[3]
We find here lexical problems (the term "pudency"), syntactic difficulties
("and pray'd me oft forebearance"), semantic problems ("chaste as un-
sunn'd snow") rhetorical issues ("O! vengeance, vengeance"), textual
problems (what was the original version of these lines?), performance problems (is the conventional Elisabethan presentation of such monologues
normative in any faithful production of the text?), and on, and on.

Shakespeare's monologue then and — to multiply the genres for what
follows — such texts as the choral ode in Sophocles' *Antigone*, or Dante's
geometrical vision at the end of the *Paradiso*, or the hunt scene in Tolstoy's *War and Peace*, raise a variety of issues which require some sorting.

---

[3] *After Babel* (New York, 1975), Chapter 1.

We do well to notice here initially what Beardsley has referred to in his standard history of aesthetics as three different levels of questions.[4] There are first "particular questions about particular works."[5] Here, for example, someone may well ask whether the choral ode from *Antigone* is the turning point in the play, or whether Sakespeare's Sonnet 116 is a misleading example of the form we know as the Shakespearean sonnet, or whether the hunt scene in *War and Peace* is properly speaking an instance of pastoral. Questions of this first sort are those for the practitioners of criticism. "They do not require theoretical reflection, but demand true information and interpretive skill."[6]

Other questions may be asked of these works at a more general level. Thus, someone may inquire whether all tragedy requires explicit generalization as in Sophocles; or whether the epic can only be understood as a rhymed poem as in Dante or also as allowing realization in prose as in Tolstoy's epic novel; or whether the Shakespearean monologue is but an instance of the lyric and not a genre in its own right. Questions of this second sort insist on systematic knowledge of the arts, the kind of knowledge we have come to expect of a theorist of the arts or, in short, of an aesthetician in the broad sense.

Finally, still other questions may be raised about such texts at even a more general level just in those cases where the texts themselves, say Pope's *Essay on Man*, or Boileau's *Art poetique*, deploy a certain range of critical terms in their own right. Thus, someone may ask whether the critical term "unity" is not used equivocally in Pope's essay, or what are the assumptions about mind made in Sophocles' use of the term "*hamartia*", or whether Dante's understanding of harmony is logically consistent with Aquinas' interpretation of Aristotle's physics. These questions, while clearly involving some attempt at systematic inquiry, are usually understood as more than just aesthetic concerns; in fact, they are taken as philosophical concerns above all. We have then critical, aesthetic, and philosophical questions as instances of at least some but not all of the many kinds of issues which literary texts raise in a preeminent way.

But this division is not yer very clear. We ought then to explicitate briefly the last two of these kinds of questions.

It is not only linguists, rhetoricians, literary critics, textual editors, translators, actors, men and women of letters, and so on who turn to literary texts but philosophers as well. The logic of fictional sentences, for example, in such literary artworks as the poems of Baudelaire is of increasing interest to formal semanticists and philosophers of logic. The kinds of entities whose descriptions one finds in such literary artworks

---

[4] M. BEARDSLEY, *Aesthetics: From Classical Greece to the Present* (New York, 1966).

[5] BEARDSLEY, p. 13.

[6] BEARDSLEY, *loc. cit.*

as, for instance, the "ficciones" of Borges together with the conditions and criteria which govern their identity are of continuing interest to ontologists. The nature of judgements which are expressed in such literary artworks as, for example, the plays of Molière both by fictional characters as well as by authors' *personae* or authors themselves remain a fruitful area for the inquiry of epistemologists. And the peculiar features of particular literary plots — thing of the novels of Dostoyevsky or George Eliot or, more recently, Iris Murdoch — attract the interest of some specialists in moral philosophy and even in the philosophy of religion. Here are then just several of the many examples which could be cited and at much greater length in support of the claims that literary artworks invite the serious attention of philosophers.

The interest of philosophers of art however (or aestheticians — and I will use the latter term hereafter in its narrower sense as a shorter expression for the former) are somewhat more difficult to make precise. For even when we artificially narrow the sense of the word "aesthetics" to include philosophical issues only, it is not immediately evident that there is any further set of questions for the aesthetician to investigate than just those which we have already noted as topics of interest for the logician, the ontologist, the epistemologist, and so on. The independence of aesthetics as a philosopher's discipline, in short, is controversial. For whatever questions would seem to be grist for the mills of aesthetics, the frequent claim is, turn out after some grinding to be the stuff of epistemology or moral philosophy or whatever.

One counter move to this reductive strategy however is particularly prominent in the specialized journals. However much analysis is undertaken, the counter claim here goes, there is at least one set of questions about objects, perceptions, judgements, predicates, values, criteria, and so on which is not reducible to the actual concerns only of other traditional branches of philosophy. And this set of questions concerns aesthetic objects, aesthetic perceptions, aesthetic judgements, aesthetic predicates, aesthetic values, aesthetic criteria and so on.

With this dispute in mind then we may proceed as follows. There is at least one philosophical question which some of these texts cited or others like them may be taken as raising. And this question is a question about aesthetic truth. Do some artworks provide us with what ma properly be called aesthetic truths, or not? More specifically, do some literary artworks present us with a set of truths about, say, persons which may properly be called aesthetic truths in general and, in instances like those which I have referred to, literary truths in particular? This is the issue which we now need to bring into sharper focus with the help of a contrast.

II. — LITERARY TRUTHS — AN ANALYTIC PERSPECTIVE

I begin then with a rough characterization of some analytic views about truths in literature. Although I shall not rely exclusively on their works alone, I shall be referring most often to the views of Weitz, Mandel-baum, Beardsley, Hospers, and more recently, Purtill, whose work in this area continues to be representative.[7] The view I present however is a construction and not attributable to any one thinker alone.

Many but not all analytic philosophers who are interested in the literary work of art often begin with a familiar observation. Literary works of art consist of different kinds of sentences about different kinds of things. Moreover, some of these sentences — we might call them here "literary statements" — often purport to be communicating truths about many important matters.

Scrutinizing any classic work of fiction, say *War and Peace*, is usually sufficient to see that this observation is correct. Literary works of art like *War and Peace* do consist of many different kinds of sentences. There are, to keep our list short, statements, dream accounts, questions, exclamations, commands, curses, prayers, and so on. Moreover each of these items appears in more than one guise. For we have foreign language expressions, ideolects, slang, broken utterances, incomplete sayings, and so on. The variety is very great both of kinds of sentences and of the variants these sentences assume. Examination of literary works and linguistic analysis of such works provides a welter of further data for those who would wish to itemize further.

If the kinds of sentences in literary works then are numerous, the matters these sentences deal with are even more extensive. Even when we confine ourselves to literary statements alone, we find all kinds of topics in evidence. Literary statements for example often propound putative truths about those features of the world which the natural sciences are accustomed to describe. We can read claims being made about the nature of society, culture, and human institutions in a vein we have come to expect most often in the social sciences. Truths are offered about historical events and human actions in a way historians most often use to formulate such matters. Literary statements are made too about the nature of mind, about human ideals, about even such important but surely obscure matters as individual destiny.

Now with these vague but non-controversial observations in hand analytic philosophers proceed to sharpen their concerns by operating several exclusions. The point of interest is not, initially at any rate, understood as a set of questions about the *values* we catch sight of when dealing sympathetically with literary works of art. The accent falls rather on truths.

---

[7] See for several but not all examples, M. WEITZ, "Truth in Literature," *Revue Internationale de Philosophie*, 9(1935), 116-129; M. MANDELBAUM, "Family Resemblances and Generalizations Concerning the Arts," *American Philosophical Quarterly*, 2(1965), reprinted G. DICKIE and R. SELAFANI, eds. *Aesthetics* (New York, 1977), pp. 500-515; M. BEARDSLEY, *Aesthetics: Problems in the Philosophy of Criticism* (New York, 1958); J. HOSPERS, *Meaning and Truth in the Arts* (Chapel Hill, 1946) and "Implied Truths in Literature," *The Journal of Aesthetics and Art Criticism*, 19(1960/61), 37-46; and R. PURTILL, "Truth in Fiction," unpublished manuscript, 1977.

Moreover, the concern is not with *truths of any great* stature in the way for example that didactic theories of art, so important to Plato in several periods of his thought, focusses narrowly on the presence or absence in literary art works of "great truths." Nor finally is the analytic philosopher usually concerned with *symbolized truths* in the peculiar sense of what so many readers find themselves responsive to, say in Kafka's work — putative truths about the world which they are not able to formulate in non-figurative terms. On course there are important questions, and indeed philosophical ones, which concern values, great truths, and symbolic truths. And some might even hold that at least paradigmatic cases of successful literary art works provide priviliged access to such matters. But for the most part analytic philosophers are almost always concerned with what they like to refer to as the everyday garden variety of common-sense truths, not then the pâté de grives and the canard à l'orange but the peas and carrots on the philosophical menu. The accent then falls squarely on the question whether some literary statements in literary art works can be said to deal with truths at all, and if so then just how?

If a start is made with observation about sentences and a preliminary formulation of the matter at hand is something like what I've just described, then what is the usual answer to the question? Before looking at the response three distinctions of unequal importance should be noticed.

We need to distinguish first between sentences within the literary work and sentences about such a work. The distinction is of course commonplace. Yet it is one we need to make explicit if we wish to avoid slipping from talk about truths which sentences within literary works refer to and truths which sentences within literary-critical works refer to. This second variety can be extensive in its own right once we begin to reflect on critical practice. But the set of expectations we bring to works of literary criticism are very different indeed from those we bring to literary works of art. Sometimes, it is true, these expectations overlap as in those cases where many works of literary criticism would seem to have aesthetic pretentions of their own quite apart from the artworks they purport to be reflections on. Yet in general and however difficult any anatomy of these sets of expectations might prove, the fact of such difference is plain enough.

A second distinction some analytic philosophers continue to find useful is a more slippery one, that between propositions and predications.

Despite almost one hundred years work in modern philosophy of logic, propositions remain elusive entities which appear to many philosophers at best only half real. Propositions, some would argue, are not themselves linquistic entities although, if they are to be found at all, they are to be found only in the company of sentences. "Predication" on the other hand is a technical term in the context of this discussion. The relevant sense here is almost exclusively confined to the kinds of issues philosophers struggle with when they raise questions about saying and showing. This sense has been construed as "each distinguishable respect in which a discourse or part of a discourse may be said to be true or false."[8] Thus a statement that says one thing and suggests another is taken here to be making two predications. An example might go like this. "Peter is not the worst player in the tennis tournament," which says that at least one player is worse than Peter and suggests further that Peter is at any rate a pretty bad bet. Now, the truths in literature which philosophers are concerned with are not those which assume a propositional form but those which are expressed in the predications which occur in many of the sentences comprising the literary work.

A third and final distinction we need to notice turns on a contrast between the kinds of interest analytic philosophers have with the sentences in a literary work and the interest which the literary critic has.

The literary critic, we might say with Monroe Beardsley, is largely concerned with three tasks. The first is that of explication, the attempt that is"... to determine the contextual meaning of a group of words... given the standard meanings of the words plus information about their ranges of connotation." The second is that of elucidation in the sense of determining"... parts of the world of the work, such as character and motives, that are not explicitly reported in it, given the events and states of affairs that are reported plus relevant empirical generalizations..." And the third is interpretation in the sense of determining not the thesis of a work, that is, "its doctrine or ideological content," but the themes of the work, that is, "something named by an abstract noun or phrase" such as, say, the tragic character of poverty.[9]

Philosophers, by contrast, usually are concerned only with what can be properly termed true or false in the literary work. This may well turn out to be the thesis which the critic has been able to isolate with the help of his different training, skills, and sensibility. The philosopher however will go on to ask his characteristic questions about such theses, questions for example about the world, or just how such truths are presented whether by statement or assertion or whatever, or just what kind of truth or falsity such statements can be properly said to have.

Now each of these distinctions raises questions in its own right. But these questions need not occupy us here. Rather we have to notice, now that the starting point, the issue, and the relevant distinctions are in mind, just what answer the philosophers are wont to provide to their own question.

One way to get clearer about the answer is first to cast the initial question in a more general form to see just what positions have been taken in its regard. The problem is just how do fictional statements differ from non-fictional ones, or how does fiction differ from non-fiction. And this has generated at least five kinds of responses which are worthwhile summarizing here quite briefly.[10]

---

[8]   BEARDSLEY, p. 404.
[9]   BEARDSLEY, pp. 401-403.
[10] See BARDSLEY, pp. 419-420.

(1)   The first view holds that fiction is not true while non-fiction is true. Yet there is a difficulty here with saying just how we are using the vague word "true". However and more seriously, the main problem with this view is that many fictional works contain true statements (say, *War and Peace*), whereas many non-fictional works contain false statements (say, *Principia Mathematica*).

(2)   A second view holds that fictional works consist of sentences which are neither true nor false, whereas non-fictional works consist of sentences which are either true or false. But the same kind of consideration that proved fatal to the first view proves fatal to the second as well. For some non-fictional works contain sentences which are neither true nor false (commands, say, in programmed logic texts), and some fictional works contain sentences which are either true or false (census figures for small Pennsylvania towns in the 1920's in John O'Hara novels).

(3)   A third view holds that all declarative sentences in fictional works are disguised imperatives of the form "suppose that..." or "let us pretend that..." whereas no such disguised imperatives are on the loose in non-fictional works. When we reflect on the variety of uses to which declarative sentences are put, however, this view appears overly ingenious.

(4)   A fourth view locates the differences between fictional and non-fictional works in readers' attitudes rather than in the sentences of the work. The attitude of a reader who takes up *War and Peace* to determine Tolstoy's philosophy of history is different than the attitude of a reader who takes up *War and Peace* to enjoy a novel. But this view, like the preceding one, also seems overly ingenious. As Beardsly puts it, "you do not have to ignore the truth-value of a discourse for it to be literature, and ignoring the truth-value of the *Principia* does not make it fiction." [11]

(5)   A fifth view turns on a distinction between uttering a sentence and asserting one. A journalist may, for example, utter a sentence in reporting Mr. Trudeau's views about the Canadian Constitution. But he is both uttering and asserting such a sentence when he utters the sentence in such a way as to communicate to his listeners that he believes the sentence is true. Fictional works then are construed to include truths of utterance only, whereas non-fictional ones include truth of utterance and truth of assertions. It is not difficult however, as the journals show, to raise important doubts as to the well-foundedness of such a distinction without even multiplying those doubts by considering the legitimacy of its application to literary works.

With these five general views as background I turn to the usual response given to a narrower question. The question here is not how do fictional works differ from non-fictional ones, but how do putative truths found in literary texts differ from truths found in non-literary ones. And the most commonly held response to this question goes as follows.

---

[11]   BEARDSLEY, p. 420.

Truths in literary works differ from truths in non-literary works in the way that suggested truths, the truths of predications, differ from asserted truths, the truths of propositions.

But just how *are* truths suggested in literary works?

Literary works do not suggest truths either in the sense that these truths are intended by the author or in the sense that these truths are graspable by the audience. Thus neither writers' intentions nor readers' responses do sufficient justice to the work itself.

"We want to be able to say," John Hospers writes, "that something is implied [suggested] even though the author may not intend it and be quite unaware of it, and even though the audience [reader] may be so imperceptive as not to grasp it."[12]

But just *what kind* of truths are implied in this large sense of implication as suggestion?

"Works of literature," Hospers continues, "are able... to suggest *hypotheses* about human behaviour, human motivation, human action, and sometimes about the social structure... These works may suggest or intimate (say without saying) numerous propositions [predications in our terminology]... about the world, about the subject matter of the work itself. And since some of these suggested propositions are doubtless true, we have here surely an important sense of truth in literature..."[13]

So much then for an analytic perspective on literary truths.

III. — LITERARY TRUTHS — A HERMENEUTIC PERSPECTIVE

I want now to look at an alternative approach to the problem of literary artworks and putative truths. This approach I will characterize simply as a hermeneutic one. Again, without restricting the presentation to their work alone, I will here be mainly concerned with the work of H.G. Gadamer and in part with the connections between his hermeneutic philosophy and the earlier reflections of Dilthey, Husserl, Ingarden and Heidegger.[14] So marxist thinkers, formal logicians, thomists, and so on are not included. It is important to recall that neither here nor earlier is there any attempt to represent any one particular position as such. Rather the concern is with sketching the main features of a general position most of whose elements a certain group of thinkers would characteristically find to be important in the light of their own individual views. I shall follow the same division here as I have used earlier, beginning that is with a starting

---

[12] HOSPERS, reprinted in J. MARGOLIS, ed., *Philosophy Looks at the Arts* (New York, 1962), p. 203.

[13] HOSPERS, p. 213.

[14] The major text here is GADAMER's *Wahrheit und Methode*, translated anonymously New York, 1975.

point and an issue, then sketching more fully the context and the formulation of the point at issue.

Non-analytic thinkers concerned with questions about truths and literary artworks have a different point of departure than their analytic colleagues. Instead, that is, of remarking the curious fact that many statements appearing in literary works of art are both similar and yet importantly different from those which occur in non-literary texts, hermeneutic thinkers are struck for example by the way temporality and history are represented in such texts, by the play of language and silence in literary texts, and especially by a peculiar expectation of literary artworks as of all art. This expectation might be put as follows. Hermeneutic philosophers are less concerned to analyze the truth conditions of different kinds of sentences whether literary or non-literary than they are intrigued by the possibility that artworks may provide access to truths that are otherwise unavailable elsewhere. The starting point here then, if we confine ourselves to questions about literature and truths, is not an observation but, roughly speaking, an assumption.

We need to try to get clearer however about what the issue may be here. Hermeneutic philosophers are not characteristically concerned with whether or not a certain class of sentences can be said to be true or false on some analyzed sense of those cardinal terms. Rather a general assumption has already been made before the literary artwork is approached. And this assumption is a general one in the sense that it accompanies hermeneutic reflection not just on literary artworks but on artworks of every kind. The assumption, as I understand it, comes to something like this: artworks present truths about many things. Literary artworks present truths especially about persons (characters) and about their actions (plots).

The point then is that whether artworks present truths at all is not at issue for the hermeneutic thinker. Rather what summons his reflection is, granted that artworks present truths, just what are these truths about and just how do artworks present such truths. Most interesting is what I referred to above as an assumption. For work on these questions is characteristically in the service of a larger interest, the question whether some artworks present some truths about persons and actions which are not available anywhere else, a class of truths available that is only in our interaction with some artworks. Moreover literary artworks with their peculiar linguistic medium are taken to be in some as yet unclarified sense privileged sites for the manifestation of such occult truths. The issue here then does not turn on the similarity between literary and non-literary texts (both comprise sentences), but on the dissimilarity between a peculiar class of truths accessible in literary artworks preeminently and the inaccessibility of such a class of truths elsewhere.

If these, or something much like them, are the starting point and the main issue of a hermeneutic reflection on literary artworks, what then is the further context we need just now to make an initial formulation of the question here a bit more understandable? I think we need especially to appreciate the polemical character of hermeneutic thinking about the nature of aesthetics.

Hermeneutic reflection, in proposing for investigation what seems to be an intriguing property of literary artworks which is not found to the same degree in other artworks or indeed outside the realm of art, is self-consciously trying to contest certain consequences of an established scientific world view. Consequently the issue which this view is calling to our attention is to be understood inside a critical understanding of the history of modern aesthetics. Aesthetics, this larger claim goes, has been understood up to the present as a progressive and helpful subordination of a philosophical discipline to one only of a member of possible interpretations of science. Aesthetics thus has come to function as an investigation of particular kinds of objects with the help of a methodology extrapolated from the models of modern mathematics and physics. More specifically, whatever kinds of truths are taken to be aesthetic truths are as such almost all construed further in terms of concepts derived from our contemporary understanding of the nature of science as an intelligible discipline and our understanding of the truths which science is concerned to formulate.

So, in locating the issue in terms of some hypothetical feature of artworks alone, the hermeneutic view is indirectly contesting the model we habitually work with in delimiting certain questions as problems in aesthetic say rather than as problems in ontology. And this view is also contesting indirectly the model we habitually bring to bear on questions pertaining to the nature of truths. In short, part of the background here includes a polemic against a construal of the separate domains of philosophy after the model of the mathematical understanding of modern science and a construal of truths in artworks on the model of the truth functional analysis of scientific truths. Questioning the understanding of truths in literature which analytic philosophy presents, then, involves questioning the understanding of truths in literature which analytic philosophy presents, then, involves questioning the understanding of modern aesthetics as a philosophical discipline.

But, even supposing that such a polemic were largely if not in all its details justified, just what alternatives does the hermeneutic view propose?

It is important to see that *some* alternative is proposed and hence the need for a positive account of both aesthetics and literary truths is acknowledged. The problem then is not with the denial that more than a negative account is required, but with the particular positive account brought forward. For this alternative is a murky one. Beyond holding out the hope for literary artworks presenting different kinds of truths than the naturel sciences do, this position draws attention to the kinds of indirect knowledge that have traditionally been associated with humanistic traditions. Gadamer, for example, wants to hold that the humanities have preserved until recent times a different, looser, more opne-ended, one might even want to say more contextual understanding of truth than the natural sciences have. This understanding, so the story goes, is still operative in the early Dilthey until the struggles with psychologism finally move Dilthey beyond the perduring insights of his neglected masterpiece, the biography of Schleiermacher. With important qualifications, a similar understanding is to be found also in parts of Collingwood's work, for example in his treatment of the logic of question and answer which Gadamer refers to explicitly. Still, we must persist in asking just what the positive element in this different understanding of truth looks like.

One important element in this account is the contention that, whatever characterization we settle on for those non-objective, non-verifiable, non-scientific truths in literature, we must situate those truths neither in the sentences in the work nor in those about the work. Rather these truths are to be identified within the *understanding* of the texts. And such an understanding may assume, as the case of dramatic production clearly indicates, more than a sentential form only.

But doesn't this further contention bring back into play all the versions of intentionalism, whether centered on authors or performers or audiences, which both analytic and hermeneutic philosophers have been so ingenious in disqualifying? This is not clear. In fact, it would be necessary to look much more closely at just what intentionalism is before trying to judge this matter intelligently. What should be noted for now however is the characteristic way in wich the hermeneutic thinker responds to such a query. "... the experience of the work of art always fundamentally supposes every subjective horizon of interpretations," Gadamer writes. Moreover, his own work in large part aims to "...show that understanding is never truly subjective behaviour toward a given 'object,' but towards its effective history — the history of its influence; in other words understanding belongs to the being of that which is understood."[15]

Most of this may be the case. The persistent problem is finding persuasive reasons, and reasons of a sort that analytic philosophers would accept, for justifying holding such a view. We have, at least in the remarks above, no such arguments but assertions only. They may be true, and then again they may not be. What we require from the hermeneutic philosopher, however, and precisely here, is less assertion and more argument. But this final point requires more elaboration.

Notice then both how important the point at issue here is and how the hermeneutic thinker retorts. The point at issue of course is just how we are to know what stands for or against the kind of suggestive but hardly rigorous reflections put forward so far. How are we to evaluate such reflections? And if we do not settle on a solution to this puzzle, then exactly why need we try to look further into the nature of truths in literature than our analytic colleagues are already doing? At least we know what can count as an answer to the questions *they* are asking. At

---

[15]   GADAMER, pp. xix and xxi.

least we know what form such answers should take even if these answers are not yet all in hand.

The hermeneutic thinker characteristically replies to this cardinal objection in some such terms as these. To meet the conditions analytic philosophers impose on putative aesthetic theories about truths and literature would be inconsistent with the critique of a one-sided view of scientific truth. To put hermeneutic reflections then into such an acceptable form would be to practice just that kind of powerful but overly-narrow kind of thinking which these reflections have been assigned to question. Perhaps not all the issues we have to raise about truths in literature can be poured into the mold of problems seeking solutions. Some of these issues we may not even yet be able to get into proper question form. So much then for the starting point, the focus, the contexts, and the point at issue of a second set of needs about literary truths.

And so the dispute about what is to count as a proper theory of truths in literature continues. But we need not pursue it further here. More important are several further features of the hermeneutic approach, features which indicate like the elements noted so far, a resistence to any easy method of critical evaluation.

IV. — INVITATIONS TO FURTHER INQUIRY

In this fourth and final section of my paper I want now to pursue somewhat further at least one basic opposition between the two perspectives which I have been at some pains so far to sketch.

If the characteristic form for the questions analytic philosophers bring to literary texts is something like "just how do truths in literature differ from truths elsewhere?" what if any question characterizes the other approach? With the polemical context still in mind I think we can put this questions something like this: "Just what if any truths make themselves manifest in the understanding of literary works of art and not elsewhere?"

Here again we require some background.

Putting our question this way and not another stresses the idea, now more familiar since careful critical reflection on Roman Ingarden's work has started, that the literary work of art is in some important sense a process-like phenomenon. An aesthetic object, this story goes, is constituted in the interaction between the stratified structure of the literary work of art and the active understanding of its readers. The claim then is that the work of art is a kind of event, in fact an ontological event in the sense that such an event brings about the appearance of one species of objects, the aesthetic object, makes this appearance manifest to the sympathetic understanding of a reader, and makes available in this phenomenon access to truths about persons and actions.[16] It is capital here to recognize

---

[16]   See GADAMER, p. 134.

the primacy of the artwork over the imagination. For if there is a way out of the impasses of psychologism which continue to threaten hermeneutic theories of aesthetic truths, as I think there is, then such an issue cannot be found in the direction of subjectivity alone, no matter how deeply we pursue the archeology of knowledge. Husserl's greatest attempt at doing phenomenology and not just writing one more theory of phenomenology, his endless studies on temporality, have demonstrated this point. And Husserl himself, as the tortured drafts of his intersubjectivity materials show unequivocally, came to understand the point of his interminable beginnings, a lesson which Heidegger learned early on. That is why, while insisting on the understanding of the literary work of art as that area in which there comes to presence whatever truths literature yields, Gadamer writes: "Literature as an art-form can be understood only from the ontology of the work of art, and not from the aesthetic experience that occurs in the course of that reading."[17]

But what more precisely is it that such understanding is active upon? And what is it in the literary work of art that makes such presences possible?

Both the hermeneutic and the analytic philosopher here appeals to the peculiar role language plays in literature. For the hermeneutic philosopher however, language is no longer viewed as simply a means of communication and therefore an entity to be understood in terms of either sophisticated mathematical theories like Shannon's or imaginative structuralist theories like Jakobson's or metaphorical self-referential theories like Derrida's. Nor is literary language to be construed simply as a means of expression and therefore to be subjected to all the puzzles of expression theories of art. Rather language in the literary work is listened to with something like the ear we see at work in Heidegger's meditations o Trakl's color symbolisms or George's formalisms or most notably Hölderlin's lyric memorializings. That is, language on the hermeneutic view is habitually understood not in the sense of a formal system but in the obscure and almost mystical sense of a speaking event, a verbal happening. The text speaks or, as Heidegger never tires of saying in *On The Way To Language* in one of his most carefully deployed tautologies, "Language speaks," "the essence of language is the language of essence," "Das Wesen der Sprache ist die Sprache des Wesens."

This is part of what lies behind some of the cryptic statements in Gadamer's work about cultivation, common sense, taste, and tact as modes of indirect knowledge, about inexplicitness and inexpressibility.[18] "...all encounter with the language of art," he writes, "is an encounter with a still unfinished process and is itself part of this process." The controlling idea is that the peculiar kind of speaking that goes on the literary work of art is a domain, a site, a *topos* where we are summoned, as Heidegger likes to say, by the unarticulated possibilities of a world breaking

---

[17]   GADAMER, p. 143.
[18]   GADAMER, pp. 34-36.

through the language of the text to our understanding. *This* kind of language, the claim here goes, *may* make available to us truths that are otherwise unaccessible.

Again, I think we need to say plainly that this kind of talk is for many of us unsettling. I have tried to examine these Heideggerean matters sympathetically yet critically elsewhere so I will not delay here.[19] What should be noted however is the primacy, in such unusual talk about language as speaking, of an experience with language rather than of a concept of language. If we are ever to come to critical terms with the central oppositions between analytical and hermeneutic approaches to truths in literature, as I think we must, we need to recognize this central opposition between a concept of language and an experience of language. The former is a difficult enough affair; but the latter refers us exasperatingly to time, to history, to, for one example only, the mysteriously priviledged speaking of language that characterized the ritual of Greek tragic drama at Athens.

One final point now should be made. Wit this focus on the process character of the literary work of art as an event and the speaking of language that comes about in the understanding of such a work, clearly the accent in the hermeneutic view falls on some as yet unexplicitated account of experience. Dilthey of course, worked long and hard at developing a more comprehensive account of experience than the empirical account he continued to be bothered with even after his reading of Kant. And Husserl too in a quite different vein looked towards reconstructing a view of experience that would be up to the measure of what he called the life world. Regardless of the different problems each of these attempts foundered on, a common and enduring feature of both was the stress on time and history. The objectivities of science were to be set aside, or got around, or even transcended in the vital interest of situating things and events anew at the center of a history of understanding. So the hermeneutic approach characteristically stresses origins while skirting biographical fallacies, and stresses traditions while side-stepping historicisms. "If it is acknowledged," Gadamer writes, "that the work of art is not a timeless object of aesthetic experience, but belongs to the world that endorses it with significance, it would follow that the true significance of the work of art can be understood only in terms of its origin and genesis in that world."[20]

But does this text give us access to truths which are otherwise unaccessible? To the contrary. It would seem without forcing all truths into the form of sentences, we still can notice that the truths which the hermeneutic approach directs us to seem more like old chestnuts than novel revelations. What could be more familiar than the cycle of seasons, the cycles of childbearing, the cycles of birth and death, the cycles even of our knowledge and our ignorance?

---

[19] See my book, *Heidegger and the Language of the World: An Argumentative Reading of the Later Heidegger's Reflections on Language*, Ottawa, 1976.
[20] GADAMER, p. 148.

I think we have to recall than here the early contrast between a concept of truth and an experience of truth. Granted that we are not a all clear about just how the term experience is to be reconstructed, we do understand nonetheless that truths in the second sense are more happenings than mental constructs. So in asking just what truths this text gives us access to, we need to reflect on the possibility that such a text does not so much afford us insight into novel concepts but, the claim is, occasionally brings about some kind of event of understanding.

Our initial problems then return, but now in a different form. For we are pressed to ask just how are we to know when such events come about, just how are we to characterize such events, and, most importantly, just what such events, if there be any, have to do with if not concepts then, to use the recommended phrase, experiences of truth?

Neither the analytical nor the hermeneutic thinker provides an unambiguous response to such difficulties. Each merely raises again the doubt that this kind of difficulty about the nature of literary truths, namely the tortured relations between their contents and their understanding, allows no consistent solution without a reexamination of the paradigms themselves within which we do philosophy.

CONCLUSION

The poet Sidney's affirmation that the poet never lies because "hee nothing affirmes", raises, I have tried to show, a number of confusing issues about the nature of aesthetic truths in general and literary truths in particular. In this paper I have been concerned to illustrate and then to clarify by contrast at least some of the central elements these issues involve. More specifically, I have suggested that the fact of representative contemporary philosophical disagreement about the nature of these details invites renewed inquiry. Before that investigation can be pursued in a thematic fashion however, it is necessary to win some critical distance on such contemporary formulations of the problem of literary truths as we have noted here by examining the historical contexts and interpretations which thoroughly condition these formulations even if they do not determine them. But that is another story, a philosophical story, a kind of fiction perhaps but precisely as a fiction a story which may, at least on some interpretation, be allowed as making certain claims to truth.

Peter McCORMICK,
University of Ottawa.

Must We Say What We Mean?

The Grammatological Critique of Hermeneutics

Are there texts that it is impossible to understand and interpret? Is there a minimal set of conditions which must be satisfied before an interpreter can claim to have understood a text? Those familiar with the problems of interpreting the writings of antiquity will know that these are old questions, perhaps as old as the writings themselves. The Anaximander fragment, for instance, is a notirious example of the difficulties of interpretation, and it has had widely variant readings, such as Nietzsche's, or Heidegger's (who generated his reading by criticizing Nietzsche's blindness to the proximity of Nietzsche's own metaphysics to Anaximander's). The Anaximander fragment is thus now part of an intricate web of readings, or of what has recently been called intertextuality. Presumably we are so enmeshed in this web that it is impossible to read the text independently of its intertextual toils. Our entrapment in this famous hermeneutic circle is so complete that we should perhaps not even desire to escape.

Recently, however, the questions of the limits of interpretation has been raised in a provocative way be the French post-structuralist, Jacques Derrida. Both *Of Grammatology* (Baltimore, 1976) and *Spurs: Nietzsche's Styles* (Venice, 1976) represent a thorough-going challenge to hermeneutical philosophy. In *Spurs* Derrida makes his point with a curious example — one that is closely related to Heidegger's reinterpretation of both Anaximander and Nietzsche through a rereading of the Anaximander passage. Derrida's example is a piece of scrap paper from Nietzsche's *Nachlass* on which is written, in quotation marks, "I have forgotten my umbrella." Derrida suggests, probably correctly, that no amount of traditional philological interpretation will enable us to decide the meaning of this "text". It thereby becomes for him a paradigm case, one that can be elaborated infinitely through his own method of deconstruction even though the text itself is beyond the limits of "interpretation," traditionally understood. This particular text is a paradigm precisely because it has, in Derrida's words, "no decidable meaning."

This undecidability is both the bane of hermeneutical philosophy and the hallmark of grammatological philosophy. Grammatology is thus conceived as the antidote to the traditional metaphysical assumptions about the nature of language, meaning, and truth. These assumptions are not simply matters about which only philosophers should worry since they bias the practical procedures of all the interpretive disciplines.

Whether the grammatological attack on hermeneutics really has such a sweeping critical scope as Derrida implies must, however, be questioned. Hermeneutical philosophy itself has a history, and criticism of older versions do not necessarily apply to newer ones. To avoid misunderstanding, then, a brief explanation of "hermeneutics" as it is currently conceived is in order.

I. — HERMENEUTICS AND GRAMMATOLOGY

Hermeneutics is essentially the philosophical concern with the theory of understanding and interpretation. For philosophers the primary interest in hermeneutics depends on whether it can generate a successful critique of traditional epistemology. Since Kant epistemology has been conceived as a foundationalist enterprise — one that attempts to separate knowledge from other forms of belief, with the intention of ascertaining what is objectively certain. Hermeneutics, in contrast, rejects the idea that the primary task of philosophy is to supply foundations and guarantee certainty. It sees knowledge as pragmatically relative to contexts of understanding. The paradigm of the phenomenon of understanding is the interpretation of texts, and hermeneutical theory maintains that while there is no physicalistic "fact of the matter" to be properly or improperly *represented* by interpretations, nevertheless there *are* determinate constraints on what gets taken as proper or improper interpretation.

Perhaps only because the theory of knowledge (epistemology) and the theory of understanding (hermeneutics) have traditionally been preoccupied with different paradigms, they have evolved into competing views about what philosophical theories must do. An extremely condensed account of the contrast between them can be given by characterizing them in terms of four presuppositions on which they differ. The traditional notion of knowledge presupposes (1) a privileged standpoint as the guarantee of certainty; (2) perception as the paradigm case; (3) the atemporal truth of instances of knowledge claims; and (4) the impotence of reflection to disrupt self-evident tenets. In contrast, hermeneutics maintains that understanding is always interpretive, and thus, (1) that there is no uniquely privileged standpoint for understanding; (2) that reading rather than seeing is the paradigm case for the phenomenon of understanding; (3) that understanding changes, and thus interpretations require continual re-examination; and (4) that any interpretive understanding is laden with self-understanding, however implicit, so that changes in the latter eventuate in changes in the former.

To the confirmed epistemologist hermeneutical philosophy will sound like yet another version of relativism or idealism. To this the hermeneutical theorist should reply not by defending relativism against objectivism, intertextuality against historical realism, coherence against correspondence, but rather by pointing out that even seeing these as the only *philosophical* alternatives involves a peculiarly Kantian or epistemological "theory of theories" — one that unwarrantedly believes that various fields of inquiry are in a state of crisis if *philosophy* has not proved that mind can mirror nature, or that the reader can be sure of capturing a particular poem and not some other poem in the one right interpretation. In fact, "realism" and "nominalism" are more relevant to a debate *within* hermeneutics than they are as philosophical labels to be attached to either hermeneutics or epistemology when these are viewed from *outside* each other. A heavy infusion of Peirce into recent hermeneutical literature seems to have reintroduced that traditional philosophical quandary into debates about the propriety of interpretations and the limits on readings. Derrida's apparent nominalism can be viewed as an attempt to take post-Heideggerian philosophy in a different direction from that taken by hermeneutic philosophers like Hans-Georg Gadamer. Both camps are allied in their opposition to traditional epistemology, but more interesting are their radical internal differences.

Both grammatology and hermeneutics are theories of understanding as reading, and thus they emphasize reception and intertextuality (not psychological response). The semiotic notion of intertextuality involves, however, a different theory of language from that found in Gadamer's notion of linguisticality. Whereas Gadamer thinks of texts as being engaged in dialogues with one another — thus relying on the Platonic notion of dialogue as a concern with the truth of the matter — the post-structuralists' notion of discourse prescinds from terms like "meaning," "reference," "significance," and "intention." The semiotic notions of text and intertext represent a fundamental challenge to the traditional aesthetic conceptions of the nature of the work of art, conceptions which the semioticians think are still retained by contemporary hermeneutic theorists who follow Heidegger. Hermeneutics, like Heidegger, is accused of presupposing, contrary to its intentions, a philosophy of presence, that is, an implicit ontological (or "onto-theo-logical") commitment of the sort that Heidegger wanted to overcome. This commitment manifests itself in the fact that when hermeneutics insists that the tradition *(Wirkungsgeschichte)* inevitably influences the understanding and interpretation of artworks, it does not question sufficiently the traditional metaphysical assumptions built into the very concepts of artwork and tradition.

The grammatologist replaces the notion of the *work* of art, "l'œuvre," or "the book," with the more neutral notion of the *text*, and it substitutes the concept of intertextuality from that of the tradition. "Text" and "intertext" are thus technical terms in the vocabulary of the post-structuralist research program, and their usefulness can be appreciated, it would seem, only after giving up the traditional metaphysical vocabulary still retained by hermeneutics.

According to the grammatological critique of hermeneutics, the concept of the *work* of art entails that any written work which is properly literary must be characterized by five features: (1) unity, (2) autonomy, (3) intentionality, (4) self-referentiality, and (5) a self-conscious literariness. This last feature summarizes the previous four in that it depends on a sharp distinction between the literary and the literal, between artistic and ordinary language. This distinction is itself possible only if the interpretation of a work can show it to have an internal unity and an autonomous uniqueness. This conception of the artwork gives interpretation its taks of investigating both the intrinsic structure of the work and the extrinsic sources and setting of the work's production. Precisely because what is under investigation is a work, and a work is assumed to be a production by somebody, the intentionality that pervades the work can be a guide to the interpretation. But since the work is a work of *art*, the interpretation need not be limited by the reference of the work to the world in which it is produced if the work itself can be said do produce its own world.

Given these features, the grammatologist's technical term "text" does not simply substitute for the hermeneutical term "work" since the grammatologist's or semiotician's research program is not committed to these traditional assumptions. Instead of "interpretation" the grammatologist's investigation is characterized as "deconstruction" or "dissemination." It does not search for the hidden intentional unity of the text, but it decodes the lack of such unity by searching out the tensions, oppositions, and even the incoherence that propagates further writing. Literary language is no longer privileged over against ordinary langauge since both are characterized by the same possibilities. Thus, self-referentiality is not a special feature of literary language alone, and there is also nothing like a "hidden meaning" which the hermeneutic interpretation must uncover. The text is not autonomous, but is the interplay of an infinity of other texts.

For the grammatologist, who starts from the linguistic, Saussurean notion of the "arbitrariness of the sign," the text is only a chain or a fabric of signs. Derrida's "fabric of signs" metaphor works like the more familiar "web of beliefs" metaphor in that there is no independent access to the fact of the matter, to the thing represented, to the transcendental signified, to Being, or to whatever other transcendental ineffable one wants to substitute. Signs refer only to other signs, and Derrida thus cites Peirce's claim that "we think only in signs." This arbitrariness of the sign leads both Saussure and Derrida to stress what Derrida calls the "immotivation and discontinuity" of the structure of the sign (*Of Grammatology*, p. 326). These features are carried over into the conception of the text, which is not a "work" — that is, a unity generated by a producer's intention. The text, like all language, is discontinuous within itself. It is itself enmeshed in a fabric of texts, in a system of systems, which is now called intertextuality.

Working in a research program in which tradition is a central concept requires the interpreter to be aware of the influences on the genesis of the work, and perhaps of the work's own influence on other works (that is, the history of its reception). Understanding a work can thus be helped by understanding both its sources and its own importance as a source. In the alternative research program "intertextuality" replaces such traditional "source study," although it is not to be taken as being identical in practice to source study and is not merly a more fashionable way of describing the tradition. For the grammatologist "tradition" is linked conceptually with a theory of history and historical development containing vestiges of teleological, holistic metaphysics.

As the totality of works, tradition presupposes the notions of (1) continuity, (2) commensurability, (3) charity, (4) commonality, and (5) progress (toward consensus). That none of these associations accompany the concept of intertextuality can be seen by taking each feature in turn.

CONTINUITY

Although historians and philologists recognize historical changes resulting in differences over time, they ordinarily assume that history is continuous. "Tradition" may not be as sweeping a term as "history" since history includes many traditions, but it is nevertheless true that tradition is of a piece. Recently, however, historians have become more skeptical of such holistic assumptions, and many have come to suspect that the unity linking historical events into a causal chain is really more a function of the historian's narrative than of the observable, empirical events. This skepticism is not new, of course, since it goes back to the historian, David Hume, but post-structuralist theorists like Michel Foucault have added new rhetorical twists. Against the usual assumption by historians of ideas that history is continuous, Foucault spells out in *The Archaeology of Knowledge* (New York, 1976) a methodology based on the thesis that history is discontinuous.

Hermeneutic theorists like Gadamer argue that the interpreter's own tradition necessarily conditions his or her understanding of the past. The hermeneutic theorist could not insist on the inevitability of such conditioning, and of the hermeneutic circle, unless the process leading from past to present were continuous. Since the post-structuralist methods of historiography are designed to avoid the very idea of continuous development, there would appear to be a basic disagreement between hermeneutics and post-structuralism.

While there may in fact be differences between those who use the methods of the analists and those who do not, these differences do not in fact result from a real philosophical issue of the sort Foucault raises. His point is best taken as saying that "continuity" and "discontinuity" are not features of the empirical events but rather as regulative ideals for the historiographical writing itself. Some historians will think, of course, that if another historian such as Foucault identifies a discontinuity, a break or rupture, in the historical process being described, then the research has not been completed, as the historian ascribing to the ideal of discontinuity would think. Rather, the research has just begun, according to the historian of continuity, since now one must explain that discontinuity, showing how it came about and how it could have been produced out of what preceded it.

This is, however, only a practical question and not a theoretical one. There is always more to be explained, and all historians must limit the scope of their accounts (whether temporally in terms of dates or methodologically in terms of what is to be described). Foucault overstates his case against the traditional historian by implying that the claims that history is continuous and that it is not continuous are contradictories. Presumably no one could say that history as a whole (or even a subdivision of history, like *the* history of thought) is continuous, and this observation should make it clear that the predicates "is continuous" and "is discontinuous" apply not so much to the events themselves as to the historian's "story." Since there is no standpoint from which these predicates could be applied to all of history, they should be taken as reflections on the success or the limits of particular narratives. "Some histories are continuous" and "some histories are discontinuous" would then not be misunderstood as logical contradictories. They are at best logical subcontraries, which means that although both cannot be false, *both* might very well be true.[1]

COMMENSURABILITY

This long discussion of the notion of continuous development should help to deflate some of the rhetoric involved in worries about terms like "discontinuity," "rupture," or "paradigm shift" and to elucidate the other components of the traditional notion of tradition. Tied to the assumption that a tradition is essentially continuous is the belief that it consists of entities that can be circumscribed in a commensurate discourse, no matter how diverse these entities are from one another. One might think, for instance, that the very idea of a history of art or of literature is paradoxical since a work of art or literature is supposed to be a unique, autonomous whole and therefore to have no internal links with preceding or subsequent works or with external reality.[2] Individual works, or perhaps individual groupings of works (whether by author or by period), are thus incommensurate with one another.

Such hermeneutical incommensurability would indeed seem to make adequate understanding an impossible ideal. As a further consequence, would interpretation also become "undecidable"? To make this grammatological inference would be to conflate "adequate understanding" with "assimilation." The hermeneutic theorist can block this move by insisting that we can understand another culture or cultural artifact adequately even if we do not share that culture's beliefs. Much the same point has been made about understanding primitive societies or other religions. Similarly, we can understand and be moved by literary works against the background of our understanding of other ones that may be temporally and generically quite different. While the strategies for construing a history of literature

---

[1]   See Hans Michael BAUMGARTNER, *Kontinuität und Geschichte: Zur Kritik und Metakritik der historischen Vernunft* (Frankfurt, 1972), pp. 301-312.
[2]   For further discussion of the paradox of literary history, see Chapter Five of the author's *The Critical Circle: Literature, History, and Philosophical Hermeneutics* (Berkeley, Los Angeles, and London, 1978).

or of art may be complex and debatable, the discontinuity of history and the concomitant incommensurability of various discourses do not constitute a *practical* obstacle to our understanding of other times and discourses.

CHARITY

Derrida's and Foucault's arguments sometimes indicate, however, a way in which the incommensurability of discourses may constitute a *theoretical* obstacle for the hermeneutical theory of understanding. Their position is often expressed in terms of a theory of language which has as a consequence the rejection of what philosophers of language call the principle of charity. This principle is a constraint on translation such that if a purported translation did not preserve the maximal number of truths, or the least number of falsehoods, in English (that is, as determined from *our* point of view), then it would not be a proper translation. It would have to be discounted a priori as an implausible attempt that simply failed to understand the other language.

However essential this principle may be as a constraint on translation, it would not be a desirable regulative principle in a theory of understanding and interpretation. As such, charity would be like the old hermeneutical view that we could not be said to have understood a work of the past (the Bible, for example) until we had interpreted everything that seemed strange about in into familiar terms. Derrida often criticizes hermeneutics in general for wanting to make the strange familiar, and his program of deconstruction is designed, it would seem, to preserve the strangeness of the text, and even to make familiar texts become strange. Yet a modern hermeneutics could readily accept this method of reading as a strategy that is useful in preventing us from reading our own expectations into everything. This strategy would make us more aware of our expectations so that we do not become overly enclosed in the circle of our own subjective understanding. Deconstruction may thus be a necessary moment of the hermeneutic circle, which is a ceaseless, open-ended activity. The deconstructive movement away from what is familiar should not, however, obscure the equally necessary movement back toward a hermeneutic self-recognition in the text. There must be *some* shared belief if there is to be any understanding at all. The hermeneutic theorist can say this and still balk at accepting the principle of charity as a necessary condition of understanding. Since charity is the assumption that *most* of the beliefs must be shared, it is a much stronger claim than is required by a plausible theory of understanding.[3]

---

[3] The principle of charity could also be accused of repeating a concealed ideology, namely, that implicit in the idea of the social melting-pot, where it is assumed, of course, that "they" will become like "us" rather than "we" like "them." Ian Hacking makes a similar point in *Why Does Language Matter to Philosophy?* (Cambridge, 1975), p. 149. For further discussion see D. C. Hoy, "Forgetting the Text: Derrida's Critique of Heidegger," *Boundary 2*, Fall 1979; and "Hermeneutic Circularity, Indeterminacy, and Incommensurability," *New Literary History*, X:1 (Autumn 1978), pp. 161-173.

COMMONALITY

When charity is taken as a psychological rather than a semantic principle, it raises a difficulty that is familiar from the history of hermeneutics. Charity presupposes the essential commonlaity between the author and the reader such that whether the hermeneutical theory emphasizes genesis or response, it is describing psychological processes in individual minds. While the hermeneutic philosophies of Schleiermacher and Dilthey go beyond the Enlightenment assumption that peole are everywhere and always the same, their theories rely on notions like empathy to bridge the hermeneutical gap between the author and the interpreter.

This psychologism is attacked by critics of hermeneutics like Derrida and Foucault, who prefer to think of the object of their investigations as "discourses" and "texts" rather than "minds." This is not, however, a fundamental criticism of hermeneutic theory as such, but only of an outdated version of it. In varying degrees, contemporary theorists like Gadamer and Habermas have taken philosophical criticisms of psychologism into account and formulated their hermeneutical theories in such a way that there is no real conflict with the post-structuralists' linguistic methods.

PROGRESS AND CONSENSUS

More to the point than the charge of psychologism is the criticism of hermeneutics for being encumbered with the vestiges of an undesirable teleology. Thinking of history as a developmental process in which all epochs are linked by common characteristics in such a way that improvement is possible leads naturally to a belief in progress. This notion of progress can be a weak one, as in Habermas's Peircean theory of the ideal speech situation. The original intuitions of hermeneutics were indeed that if everybody were able to think and discuss an issue in an unconstrained way, such discussion would inevitably resutl in agreement, and thus in convergence on the truth, the *consensus omnium*, the universally commensurating discourse about all possible discourses.

This view of Habermas's, however, has been contested by other hermeneutic theorists, including Gadamer, who posits instead an indefinitely open-ended development. Progress thereby becomes a more specific notion. Whether progress has been made could not be decided in global terms, but only in regard to specific social institutions, whose existence in and of themselves is not a priori necessary. Since there would be no transhistorical standpoint from which history or civilization could be said to have progressed, this piecemeal but plausible outlook would not be guilty of presupposing an implicitly teleological metaphysics like that found in most developmental theories of history.[4]

---

[4] For further discussion see D. C. HOY, "Taking History Seriously: Foucault, Gadamer, Habermas," *Union Seminary Quarterly Review*, XXXIV:2 (Winter 1979), pp. 85-95.

II. — INTERTEXTUALITY AND INTENTIONALITY

Whether there is a real opposition between hermeneutics and grammatology, and whether the standard conceptions of the literary work and the literary tradition are indeed undermined by the interpretive undecidability implied by the concepts of text and intertextuality, has not been sufficiently argued by the post-structuralists. Much depends on how such notions as intertextuality are taken. Is there, for instance, a real theoretical and practical difference between a methodology relying on the notion of intentionality and one relying on intertextuality? If there is, then the grammatological critique of hermeneutics may entail a genuine alternative. If there is not, then whether particular grammatological criticisms of traditional ways of doing research in the humanities are valid is still an important matter, but one that is better decided in terms of particular disciplines and interpretations.

Focusing specifically on the field of literary criticism, then, it should be emphasized tha unlike the term "undecidability," which is part of Derrida's metaphilosophical polemics, the terms "intertextuality" names a specific concept in a research program of practical criticism. It is used particularly by semiotic theorists like Julia Kristeva, Roland Barthes, and Michael Riffaterre. Kristeva defines the concept succinctly in *Semiotiké* (Paris, 1969): "le texte poétique est produit dans le mouvement complexe d'une affirmation et d'une négation simultanées d'un autre texte" (p. 257). She also claims at the same place that it is a "fundamental law" that "les textes poétiques de la modernité... se font en absorbant et en détruisant en même temps les autres texts de l'espace intertextuel." Her view is thus comparable to Harold Bloom's theory of poetic influence as a patricidal series of misreadings. Kristeva's and Bloom's approaches are of a different order in practice, however, and Jonathan Culler has argued convincingly that Bloom's conception of intertextuality is too general and "Romantic," lacking the practical specificity of the semiotic notion.[5] Intertextuality has even been applied outside of literature, and the historians Hayden White and Michel Foucault clearly rely on related strategies.

Derrida's relation to these practical pursuits is rather complex. As a historian of philosophy he could be said to be putting the notion of intertextuality to use in that specific area. As a philosopher in his own right he is mapping out the grammatological theory without which the notion of intertextuality would lose its force. In fact, there is a disturbing tendency for both literary critics and historians to say that since *philosophy* has now *proved* that nothing exists but texts, or that we think only in signs, or that "die Sprache spricht," this now makes the methodology of intertextuality applicable to all scientific inquiry, and even perhaps all there is to any science.

---

[5] Jonathan CULLER, "Presupposition and Intertextuality," *MLN* 91 (1976), pp. 1380-1396. My thanks to both Jonathan Culler and Cynthia Chase for a helpful discussion of this paper.

This reasoning would indeed by guilty of hasty ontologizing, and it would lead too quickly toward an unabashed nominalism. It goes against the grain of Derrida's own metaphilosophical view that philosophy cannot "prove" anything, and certainly not anything ontological. There are thus two ways to take the philosophical import of the notion of intertextuality. The wrong way is to think Derrida's famous claim that "il n'y a pas de hors-texte" (*Of Grammatology*, p. 158) is a new version of idealism (perhaps in the vein of Cassirer's or Whorf's *Sprachidealismus*). Grammatology would then be an ontological overdramatization of what literary critics call formalism. A better way to take intertextuality is as the basic concept of a research program which is only exercising an option to choose its vocabulary and to restrict itself to specific kinds of analysis. This program thus abandons any ontological claims since it is rather an attempt to de-ontologize its object of study be avoiding laden terms like "intention," "author," "meaning," "meaningfulness," "value," and "reality" as well as the distinction between metaphorical and literal, or serious and non-serious discourse.

A research program is certainly entitled to select its own vocabulary, but the next question is whether it will have practical results that are not parasitic on the alternative vocabulary. Citing Bakhtine, Kristeva in *Semio-tiké* notes that the importance of intertextuality is that it replaces inter-subjectivity (p. 146). Because intertextual criticism does not want itself confused with traditional source study, it will go to any lenghts to avoid the concept of intention. It even makes the poet's knowledge of other not texts irrelevant. Harold Bloom goes so far as to say that the epheb need to have read the precursor poem that his own poem "misreads" (*The Anxiety of Influence*, New York, 1973; p. 70). Presumably Bloom is saying more than he really means, however, for he is probably imagining that the ephebe knows some of the precursor's poetry, but may not happen to know a specific "central" poem — central to both the precursor and the ephebe precisely because its centrality may be perceivable only after the ephebe's own poems have caused a swerve in the history of poetry. The poem, while not known, could plausibly be said to have been inferable, and Bloom's claim is not as paradoxical as it sounds.

The irrelevance of what the poet knew or intended is also apparent among the Franch critics. Like Kristeva, Roland Barthes also dissolves the concept of subjectivity into that of the text:

> *je* n'est pas un sujet innocent, antérieur au texte... Ce « moi » qui s'appro-
> che du texte est déjà lui-même une pluralité d'autres textes, de codes infinis,
> ou plus exactement: perdus (dont l'origine se perd). [6]

Barthes's claim makes clear that the intertext implied within a text need not be another literary text (contrary to Bloom). That it often is, however, seen by Barthes himself in *The Pleasure of the Text* (New York, 1975):

> I recognize that Proust's work, for myself at least, is *the* reference work, the
> general *mathesis*, the *mandala* of the entire literary cosmogony — as Mme de

---

[6]   Roland BARTHES, *S/Z* (Paris, 1970), p. 16; cited by CULLER, p. 1382.

Sévigné's letters were for the narrator's grandmother, tales of chivalry for Don Quixote, etc.; this does not mean that I am in any way a Proust "specialist": Proust is what comes to me, not what I summon up; not an "authority," simply a *circular memory*. Which is what the inter-text is: the impossibility of living outside the infinite text — whether this text be Proust or the daily newspaper or the television screen: the book creates the meaning, the meaning creates life [p. 36].

These two passages from Barthes reveal how difficult it is to break completely with the concept of subjectivity. Whereas the first passage says the "I" is not anterior to the text but is already a plurality of other texts, this does not seem to be *all* that is true about the "I" in the second passage. Although it is impossible to live outside the infinite text, can the "I" be just the infinite text? If the "I" is an infinity of texts, then it lacks the identity necessary to being an "I." If the identity is provided by a primary intertext, as Proust's is for Barthes, then who or what does the reading, the expanding of the text's infinite relations?

The semiotic notion of the text as an infinity of connections with other texts, as a universe that is both microcosm and macrocosm, is troubling. Kristeva also says that "tout texte est d'emblée sous la jurisdiction des autres discours qui lui imposent un univers."[7] This metaphorical insistence on the network of texts as an infinite universe is obviously more theoretical than practical. It follows from Saussure's thesis of the arbitrariness of the sign, but it is applied rather differently at the level of practical criticism. As Culler aptly points out, "it is difficult to make that universe as such the object of attention" (p. 1384). He notices that Kristeva herself pays attention to which editions an author could have known when that would make an interpretive difference. The intertextual domain thus in practice becomes narrowed down to specific texts, and perhaps even to one text.

Exactly what principle governs this narrower selection of the relevant intertext is not clear from the theory itself. The advantage of the alternative research program making use of intention is that it can state precisely what its principle of selection is and how it will handle hard cases. For instance, in one of the better formulations of intentionalist interpretation, namely, Stanley Cavell's *Must We Mean What We Say?* (New York, 1969), the critic can decide when he or she is properly attributing an implied reference in the text (or film) and when that allusion is merely being read into the text arbitrarily. "It makes sense," Cavell argues, "to say Fellini intended (that is to say, Fellini can have intended) the reference to Philomel if he knew the story and now sees its relevance to his own, whether or not the story and its relevance occurred to him at the time" (p. 233). Cavell thus maintains that although there can be inadvertent intentions such as this case illustrates, knowing is still a necessary (but not a sufficient) condition for intending.

Some principle such as this would also be required by the intertextual critics when they move from the infinite universe of intertextual reference

---

[7]   Cited by CULLER, p. 1384.

down to the selection of specific texts and codes. If their choice of inter-
pretant is not just arbitrary, there must be constraints on it. Without a
specific principle stated in a nonintentionalist vocabulary the intertextual
research program risks being in practice merely parasitic on the traditional
philological program.

Whether one should want to be entirely free from criticism based on
the vocabulary of intersubjectivity depends upon how restrictive that vocabulary actually is. Derrida himself has been interpreted as denying the role
of intention altogether, but in fact his view about intention is more subtle,
as is evident in his exchange with the American philosopher of language,
John Searle.[8] In the course of criticizing both hermeneutics and speech
act theory, which make comparable mistakes, Derrida says he does not
wish to get rid of the concept of intention but only to give it a different
place, a less priviledeg one.[9] Intention will no longer be constitutive of the
meaning of the work. The lack of any sufficient condition for the reading
of a written text will allow Derrida to replace ''interpretation'' with ''deconstruction'' or ''dissemination,'' an infinite play of possibilities built into
the play of the text. ''Play'' is itself a technical term for the absence of
a transcendental signified — the goal of traditional interpretive searches for
''the meaning'' of the work.

To condense the debate between Searle and Derrida one can invert
Cavell's titular question and ask, must we say what we mean? On
Searle's theory it turns out that in a certain sense we *must* say what we
mean, since what a sentence says is a function of the speaker's or the
author's intentions. For Searle sentences just are ''fungible intentions,''
and ''to the extent that the author says what he means the text is the
expression of his intentions'' (p. 202). In contrast, Derrida's view seems to
be that we *cannot* say what we mean, and often he purposefully does not
say what he means, or does so only ironically. He rejects the idea that the
intention necessarily determines the meaning of the text on the grounds
that intention is in fact more problematically disjointed or divided within
itself than intentionalist theorists realize. Derrida maintains that intention
is never fully present to itself, and is not transparent, even to the inten-
der. The nonserious, the *oratio obliqua*, will thus never be excluded from
even the most ordinary language, contrary to what Austin and Searle seem
to think.

More interesting than the differences between Searle and Derrida are
the differences between Derrida and Cavell. Whereas Searle and Derrida
have nonequivalent concepts of intention, Derrida and Cavell appear to
agree, especially since Cavell can allow for inadvertent intentions. Yet

---

[8] For the Searle-Derrida exchange see J. DERRIDA, ''Signature Evenement Contexte,'' in *Marges de la philosophie* (Paris, 1972); English translation in *Glyph I* (Baltimore,
1977), pp. 172-197, which is then followed by J. SEARLE, ''Reiterating the Differences:
A Reply to Derrida'' (pp. 198-208). Derrida's rejoinder, ''Limited Inc: a b c...'' appears
in *Glyph*, 2 (Baltimore, 1977), pp. 162-254.

[9] DERRIDA, ''Signature Event Context,'' p. 192. One must keep in mind that in
French the verb for ''to mean'' is *vouloir-dire*.

while Cavell emphasizes the importance of the appeal to intention, Derrida diminishes it. To understand why this is so, one must first understand that there is considerable agreement between Derrida and Cavell about the nature of philosophical theories. This agreement may also explain the obvious metaphilosophical disagreement between Derrida and Searle.

Cavell's question is, must we mean what we say? His answer is, it depends. In the essay, "A Matter of Meaning It," he says, contra Beardsley, that the appeal to the intention of an utterance is sometimes appropriate and sometimes inappropriate as an explanation. The appeal to the intention is for Cavell much like the attempt to explain any remark o action in order to determine responsibility. Intention is useful in figuring out "the point of the work," or "why it is as it is." But Cavell also thinks the attempt to explain the work by determining its intention forces one further *into* the work. So there is a significant difference between his intentionalism and the view Beardsley is attacking. To avoid confusion Cavell should perhaps have been willing to speak of the text's rather than the author's intentions. That he did not do so is explained by the fact that his view is not a different theory of intention so much as a different view of philosophy from Beardsley's. Seeing the critic making implicit or explicit intentional claims when faced with the question "Why this?" Cavell thinks the philosopher has two choices: either to repudiate this description of the activity of criticism "on the ground that they [the intentional cliams] *cannot* be true (because of his philosophical theory — in this case of what poems are and what intentions are and what criticism is)," or to "accept them as data for his philosophical investigation, learning from them what it is philosophizing must account for" (p. 227). On the one hand, then, philosophers like Beardsely and Searle who think of philosophy as a prescriptive, foundationalist enterprise reject certain descriptions of liberary criticism because their theories tell them that things cannot be that way. On the other hand, philosophers like Cavell and Derrida who think of philosophy as nonprescriptive, anti-foundationalist writing look at what is being done, note how philosophy makes false problems out of its own ruminations, and develop their own view more as a critical undercutting of the philosophical theory that does not question itself than as an ideal guide for the practical discipline in question. In the latter theory intention is not a constitutive entity but a procedural strategy of reading. As such it can be emphasized or ignored to the extent that the reading requires.

Of course, Cavell and Derrida do have their differences, but probably only because the critics Derrida is reading now are quite different from those Cavell was reading in 1957 or even in 1965 (the dates of the two essays by Cavell under discussion). Derrida is not faced with critics who worry about the question "Why this?" whereas "Why?" is the paradigm question for the philosophical literature on the theory of action (such as Anscombe's 1957 work, *Intention*). To Cavell's claim that we need to appeal to intention to explain the *point* of the work, Derrida could replay his theme that there is no way the critic can "faire le point" ("mark the point," or better, "take bearings") since there is no punctual position, no unilinear text signed by a "single" (singly intentioned, or "single-minded") author. Even Cavell's procedural notion of intention as that which forces the reader to go further into the text might be met with skepticism. Go further into the text, says Geoffrey Hartman in his *Georgia Review* essay on Derrida's *Glas*, and you only encounter the essential un-intelligibility of the literary work. [10] The metaphysics of presence is insidious, Derrida could say, and still contaminates Cavell's thought insofar as he believes intention to be equivalent to what the peom means and appeals to it as the basis for explaining the "unity of the work" and "trust in someone as an artist" (Cavell, p. 237).

Derrida's distrust of these traditional aesthetic categories leads him to make his own claims sound more controversial than they probably are. Something like *Sprachidealismus* may seem to be implied by such statements as "there is nothing outside of the text" and "the thing itself is a sign" (*Grammatology*, p. 49). "Reality" itself becomes merely a textual entity, a construct in the text of philosophy, since there is no "natural attachment" to a real referent (p. 46), no "flesh and bone" referents even for proper names (p. 159). These claims are to be true not only of literary writing, as we would normally assume, but of all kinds of writing, not just the doubling commentary of the literary interpreter, but also the writing of "the philosopher, the chronicler, the theoretician in general, and at the limit everyone writing" (p. 160).

Of course, nobody really thinks he or she is merely a fictional entity, so Derrida's point must be overstated. His claim that there is no signified outside the text, no real referents, is a rather dramatic way of saying there is no such thing as *the* signified, no transcendental signified entirely independent of the signifier-signified relation. Take Derrida's own suggested cases, the historian and the philosopher. Unlike the novelist they both seem to write with a commitment to the actual existence of real events or definite truths. They write so that their signifiers *will* disappear into the signified. In conversation one historian tried to defend the idea of inter-textuality by denying that there were real events in the past. The fall of the Bastille and the shooting of John Kennedy were for him to be *only* textual constructs. When asked contentiously whether being shot himself would be only a textual event, the historian's amusing reply was to insist that the "event" could only be said to have occurred when people started talking about it. What, however, would the *first* person who said anything be talking about? And what would the wounded man himself have experienced?

Clearly the more adequate response is not to deny that there are real events, but to insist that any event is only ever captured in a description, that is, in a context that is itself not an event but a discursive variable. Derrida himself in his reply to Searle insists that he does not deny the necessity of having some context or other, but only the idea that any given

---

[10] Geoffrey HARTMAN, "Monsieur Texte II: Epiphony in Echoland," *The Georgia Review* XXX:1 (Spring 1976), p. 182.

context is more necessary or privileged than any other. Derrida's point thus appears to be the quite plausible one that all we have access to in interpreting texts is the system of inferences formulatable from that text and others, or at least from other text-like constructs such as Barthes's television screen. The assertion that there are real events is trivial and uninformative if it is also true that events are only ever comprehended under a discription. Derrida need not deny that there are real events, or that there is a "flesh and bone" genesis of the text, and indeed he does not.[11] When he says, for instance, that "what opens meaning and language is writing as the disappearance of natural presence" (*Grammatology*, p. 159), he is not asserting the nonexistence of natural presence. He is only implying that anything said after that is not a matter of fact but of interpretation. In the history of philosophy we are used to the idea of natural presence disappearing right at the beginning — as it does, for instance, with sense-certainty in Hegel's *Phenomenology of Spirit*.

Derrida's theory of reading is thus not so radical that it rejects the classical exigencies of traditional criticism. These still do obtain, and reading "must be intrinsic and remain within the text" (p. 159). Given this admission, however, it is then quite legitimate for Derrida to insist that reading not restrict itself to repeating or doubling "the conscious, voluntary, intentional relationship that the writer institutes in his exchanges with the history to which he belongs" (p. 158). Reading must open the text by supplementing it. This supplement is not a capricious addition by the reader, though, for it must already be contained in the text, which is never fully present to itself, even form the beginning.

Derrida's philosophy is not as complete a break with the history of philosophy as many would like to believe. On the contrary, he is best understood as the latest development of a tradition going back to Kant and Hegel, a tradition which includes contemporary hermeneutics as well. Of course, to see Derrida as part of a tradition is itself a hermeneutical move — one that may manifest a desire to control his texts by making what is strange in them appear quite familiar. To conclude this would be to underestimate the complexity of the hermeneutic process, however, since the act of finding a tradition for his work — or alternatively expressed, finding the particular intertextual matrix in which his texts are determinate intersections — is only the start of the uncertain task of interpreting them. This difficulty is compounded by a writer who does not wish "to say what he means" and does not think that "saying what one means" is even desirable as a regulative ideal. Such compounding, however, does not make interpretation impossible. There may well be texts impossible to

---

[11] Derrida's position is in spirit not that remote from Nelson Goodman's nominalism. In like manner one could say that in *Ways of Worldmaking* Goodman goes too far when he speaks of there being not one but many worlds. It would seem perfectly adequate to speak of a plurality of world-versions. His point, though, is that if there is no other access to a world than through a particular version, the term "the world" has no use except one internal to a version.

interpret in practice, but there is no reason to think that anything readily identifiable as a text is uninterpretable in principle.

David Couzens HOY,
Barnard College,
Columbia University.

II. — Philological Interpretation:
Theory and Practice
Interprétation philologique:
théorie et pratique

The Interpretation of the Greek Lyric Poets in Our Time

Synchronism and Diachronism in the Study of an Oral Culture*

Any attempt to interpret the archaic Greek lyric poets today, any question of how and to what extent it is possible to present them to our contemporaries without academic abstraction, necessarily comes up against that great basic problem — the problem of the survival of the classical world in our culture. What meaning can archaic Hellenism have in a modern technological civilisation which rejects history and imposes itself as a civilisation which is at once new, integrated and alienated (or so the sociologists define it) because it has irrevocably deprived the world of its own historical dimensions? The result of this irreversible situation is known to us all: a major crisis of all values, whether ethical, political or expressive. If we cast a glance at contemporary culture and the latest movements of the European neo-avant-garde, we see that the state of crisis may well have attained its limits. For an immediate theoretical understanding of modern poetry we need only refer to the categories formulated by a German writer, Hans Magnus Enzensberger: assembly and ambiguity, dissonance and absurdity, alienation and mathematisation, irregular rythm and experimentation with new syntactic connections,[1] in a word, laboratory poetry, poetry of the absurd which is the absurdity of a common existential state — but, in the best of cases, also a poetry of challenge, of provocation and, implicitly, of the rejection of an alienating and ahistorical reality.

---

* This essay is the updated English (translated by Alastair Hamilton) text of a paper in Italian read in Bonn on 4 September 1969 at the 5th International Congress of Classical Studies (FIEC), and published in *Quadrini Urbinati di cultura classica,* N° 8 (1969), pp. 7-21.

[1] *Einzelheiten*, Frankfurt am Main 1962, p. 260.

Now, in such an unpredictable cultural context, in which the alienation from any value judgement ("Wertverfremdung") in the name of a supposed scientific objectivity seems to be the common operative norm, it is
hard to conceive the existence on a cultural level of an art form like
archaic Greek lyric poetry which, in its multiplicity of human dimensions,
its vision of the world and its direct relationship with the public, is very
remote to us. To present it by way of an interpretation based on old humanist aesthetics or the neo-humanist ethics of Jaeger would seem nothing
if not anachronistic. Nobody, nowadays, would be prepared to revive the
traditional humanist interpretation of Greek poetry as an eternal natural
history of taste and art, or the neo-humanist idea that Greek culture from
Homer to Plato represents a relevant norm of political behaviour which
safeguards the dignity of man in all he does. Less still would anyone be
prepared to submit to the vain illusion that those static marble models of
quality and value, those models of an exemplary Hellenism, can really
become effective in a cultural and political sphere. The immediate post-war
years witnessed the rapid decline of ethical neo-humanism everywhere.
This was caused in part by the new European political reality which arose
from the ashes of those values which neo-humanism itself had championed,
but above all by the ideological anxiety of the recent generations and the
swift advance of science and technology. In what sense could Hellenism
— and, more specifically in the context of this paper, archaic Hellenism
— be considered relevant, if the steady attempt to return to it as a culture
both hegemonic and endowed with the privilege of representing ideal
models of life and thought had failed irremediably? The more attentive and
committed critics were quick to spot the profound crisis of traditional humanism and the rise of fresh cultural problems presented by the new
human sciences and by a deeply innovative linguistic science.

The research of Bruno Snell, Hermann Fränkel, George Thompson,
Eric Dodds and Moses Finley (to mention only the more representative
scholars) and, more recently, of Jean Pierre Vernant and Eric Havelock,[2]
offers a very wide range of methodological instances and implications determined by the awareness of a new general situation. We see a critical
operation at work which, despite the diversity of interests and aims, has as
a common requisite the effort to obtain a concrete understanding of the
mentality of archaic Greek man, his linguistic structures, his mental and
psychological categories, the substance and form of the subjects of his
thought and his art, the living aspect, in short, of Greek man at the moment
in which he becomes aware of himself and of his position before others. We
have a critical line in which the question, the categories and the instruments
of the modern human sciences converge: from semantic lexicology to social
psychology and psychology of history, from sociology to anthropology.
We thus look out onto a polycentric perspective which dissolves that false
metaphysical view which the idealist critics had of Greek man as a reality
separate from nature, and gives us, rather, as the object of research, the

---

[2] *Preface to Plato*, Cambridge Mass. 1963; *The Greek Concept of Justice From Its
Shadow in Homer to Its Substance in Plato*, Cambridge, Mass. — London 1978.

concrete problem of man on the various planes of his individual and social life. In this movement towards the concrete, in this conception of reality which rejects the study of the phenomena of consciousness outside real situations, in this line of thought which is the thought itself of contemporary philosophy, we must seek the authentic meaning of archaic Greek lyric poetry and present it as a living example of the act of poetic *creation* at the beginning of our history.

To describe Greek lyric poetry in the act of its *creation*, and consequently in its *creativity*, that is to say as an intervention in the human process in which it participates, requires certain preliminary observations which will allow us to present the phenomenon of its unity and its entirety in a synchronous dimension. A common feature of Greek lyric poetry, and indeed of Greek poetry in general, up to the end of the fifth century, is the type of communication to which it was entrusted: not written but oral communication. It was a poetry which appealed to the ear, as Plato described it in contrast to painting, which appeals to the eye.[3] Our own tendency, whether conscious or unconscious, to approach it as if it were a *literary* phenomenon in the modern sense is contrary to all we know about the origin and spread of the book in ancient Greece. The conclusions to be drawn from the evidence of the fifth and fourth centuries B.C., and from the most authoritative studies on the subject,[4] prove beyond a doubt that it was only at the end of the fifth century that a new technology of the written transmission of works started with the spread of the book. But an oral poetry, precisely because of its direct and immediate relationship with a public which listens, comprises modes of expression and mental attitudes different to the poetry of written communication. It is based on a technology of writing which can be examined psychologically and linguistically in the poetic contexts of other oral cultures — and even, we might add, in the structures of dictation (already observed by contemporary linguistics) of a text written for a broadcast or a public speech. To proceed with short sentences and with paratactical and not

---

[3] *Resp.* X 603 b.

[4] E.G. TURNER, *Athenian Books in the Fifth and Fourth Centuries B.C.* London 1952; E.A. HAVELOCK, *op. cit.*, pp. 36-60 and more recently J. POUILLOUX and N.M. KONTOLEON in *Entret. Hardt* X (1963), pp. 171 ff.; 175 ff. I think it is superfluous to return to the much debated problem of whether orality means the oral composition of the ode, as was assumed of the Homeric epic. As far as lyric poetry is concerned, at all events, the oral aspect should be understood in the sense of oral communication, publication or transmission. A balanced re-examination of the problem in the sense or orality as oral communication also in connection with epic poetry is to be found in A. LESKY, *Festschr. D. Kralik*, Horn 1954, p. 1 ff. = *Gesammelte Schriften*, Bern u. München 1966, p. 63 ff. and in R. MUTH, *Wien. Stud.* 79, 1966, p. 246 ff. For useful and acute observations and a wide documentation on the predominance of the spoken word over the written word in Greek culture see W.B. STANFORD, *The Sound of Greek*, Berkeley and Los Angeles 1967, pp. 1-26. Cf. also A. DIHLE, *Homer-probleme*, Opladen 1970; E.A. HAVELOCK, *Origins of Western Literacy*, Toronto 1976; 'The Preliteracy of the Greeks', *New Literary History* 8, 1977, pp. 369-391; *Communication Arts in the Ancient World* (edited by E.A. HAVELOCK and J.P. HERSHBELL), New York 1978, and J.A. RUSSO, 'Is "Oral" or "Aural" Composition the Cause of Homer's Formulaic Style?', *Oral Literature and the Formula*, Ann Arbor 1976, pp. 31-54.

hypotactical figurations, to avoid allocutions of "mental" origin, to avoid
the use of the first person singular, idiosyncratic because of its "exhibi-
tionistic and indiscreet" nature, to avoid syntactic suspensions, and, more
generally, to use a clear and concrete language in order to express attitudes
of thought which are immediately perceptible to the public and which make
it prepared to listen — these are "essential" rules for any text of oral
communication.[5] In this respect there is no interruption in the continuity
between Homeric poetry and lyric poetry. By and large Snell's remarks on
the concreteness of the Homeric language of the mental process can also
be applied to the language of lyric poetry. The Homeric tendency to represent emotions and states of mind as a "personified exchange"[6] between
the hero and a god, or between the hero and one of his organs (thymos,
kradie), in a sort of soliloquy between the subject and a part of himself,
is still operative in archaic lyric poetry, as we see, for example, in Archilochus apostrophe to his own thymos[7] or in Sappho's conversations
with Aphrodite in reality and in a dream. It is to this mental attitude, or
to what has been described[8] as this "psychology of poetic performance"
which aims at native public the personal and the subjective to render it
immediately perceptible and to involve the public emotionally, that the
series of metaphors, images and similes which animate the language of
lyric poetry lead us. A synchronous analysis of erotic language would illustrate amply the value of the metaphor and the image as instruments
which capture idiosyncratic psychic and emotional states — a broad in-
ventory of sexual, animal, agonistic, nautical, agricultural, ithyphallic and
symposial metaphors, and images of Eros as a wind, a carpenter, a boxer,
a guard, a hunter, a winged child, which describe the multiplicity of the

---

[5]   Cf. Pseudo-Gadda, Il Caffè XVI 1, 1969, pp. 3-19. It is the merit of linguistics
and contemporary criticism, especially that performed in the English language to have
reawakened an interest in oral culture and, more important still, to have identified its linguistic structures, aspects and stylistic procedures. The work of M. McLuhan, The Guten-
berg Galaxy: the Making of Typographic Man, Toronto, 1967, represents an important attempt to analyse aspects of oral culture from Homer to the modern age. For developments
of these tendencies in present-day criticism cf. the studies of R.M. Dorson, "Oral Styles
of American Folk Narrators" and Th.A. Sebeok, "Decoding a Text: Levels and Aspects
in a Cheremis Sonnet", in the volume edited by Sebeok, Style in Language, Cambridge
Mass.[2] 1964 (with an extensive bibliography). On the criteria for distinguishing between a
written system and a spoken system see also the precise and accurate clarifications of
G. Calboli in Rendiconti, fasc. 11-12, 1965, pp. 422-428 (esp. p. 426 ff.) The revival of
oral poetry, from American Folk Songs (cf. N. Frye, "Mito e Logos", Strumenti critici
9, 1969, p. 141 ff.) to the protest songs in Russia (cf. A.M. Ripellino, "Ivan protesta
cantando", L'Espresso 21, 25-5-1969, p. 10 ff.), from the radio to the television and the
cinema, the new vehicles of the spoken word, has made us more sensitive and more attuned
to the constant danger of approaching an oral poetry with the mental patterns and the
coherent logic derived from written culture — more sensitive, perhaps, than the students of
the Homeric world, Parry and Lord, who are rightly regarded as the true promotors of
research into oral poetry in the last thirty years. An interesting critical review of the problems of poetic techniqhe inherent in the oral nature of the archaic epic, with original suggestions, is to be found in R.Di Donato, Ann. Scuola Norm. Sup. di Pisa 1970, fasc. 1.
    [6]   Cf. now J. Russo-B. Simon, Journ. Hist. Ideas 29, 1968, p. 487.
    [7]   Fr. 67a D (118 L.B., 105 Tarditi).
    [8]   E.A. Havelock, op. cit., p. 145-164.

aspects and levels of a love affair. The same applies to the metaphors and similes in the sphere of socio-political ideology — they are mainly animal ones, suitable for characterising moral attitudes and political behaviour: the image of the fox in Solon[9] and Alcaeus[10] is a concrete representation of the vain cunning of the Athenians or the strategic ability of Pittacus in the game of political factions. In *Pythian* II Pindar uses one metaphor after the other — the monkey, the fox, the dog and the wolf — for a paratactical presentation of his political advice to Hieron. Similar, too, is the function of the myth, of that vast phenomenological repertory both divine and heroic which constituted the connective tissue of oral culture and was a social instrument intended to unite past and present, tradition and actuality, poet and public: the mythical episode becomes the exemplification of a norm, of an aphorism or of an aphoristic preamble ("Priamel") or, according to the occasion and the situation of the poem, the exemplary performance of an action either commendable or reprehensible. In their most relevant formulations poetics correspond to the psychology of oral communication — poetics of mimesis which understand the act of poetic creation ($\pi o\iota\varepsilon\tilde{\iota}v$)[11] as reproduction or imitation. The pronouncement of Alcman[12] on the modes of poetry, his claim to have found his words and his song by transforming the cry of partridges into language, can only be understood as the idea of mimesis of an auditory element. Equally consonant with the idea of the element both visual and auditory is the technical poetry of Simonides, with the formulations of his two objectives, poetry as speaking painting[13] and the word as the image of the thing.[14] The tactile sense of the voice "which cleaves ($\alpha\rho\alpha\rho\varepsilon\tilde{\iota}v$) to the ears of men",[15] the curling of the waves represented as a nautical tattoo,[16] the "doorless mouth"[17] of the malicious gossip or the figurative-emotional language of the *Danae*, are among the most significant examples of poetics

---

[9] Fr. 8,5 D.

[10] Fr. 69,6 L.P.

[11] I use the terms "institute" and "poetics" in the sense theorized by Anceshi (*Le istituzioni della poesia*, Milano 1968), i.e. in a sense which is particularly valid and suitable in its theoretical and methodological dimension for a concrete discussion of the phenomenon of Greek lyric poetry: "Le istituzioni... saranno quelle norme, quel complesso organico di norme o quel sistema di norme che riguardano il *fare* [my italics] letterario nelle sue varie forme e... che tendono a porsi come norme intersoggettive, costituendo così *un aspetto sociale* del fenomeno letterario [my italics]" (p. 20): "Quanto alle poetiche, esse... riguardano strettamente il fare, nascono, anzi, dal riflettere sul proprio fare da parte di chi l'arte realmente fa, e all'arte propongono ideali, principi, concetti operativi, acquistando il loro pieno significato nel fatto che esse, in generale, qualunque sia il modo del loro orientamento, tendono a servirsi di tutti gli aspetti della realtà di cui è possibile servirsi al fine che essi si ordinino a rendere l'arte sempre più consapevole di sé, del suo fare, e dei principi di questo fare nella situazione in cui, volta a volta, essa si trova a decidere di se stessa, a stabilire le sue scelte costitutive... La poetica si dà, dunque, *in un orizzonte pragmatico* [my italics]" (p. 21 ff.).

[12] Fr. 39 P.

[13] Plut. *De gloria Ath.* 3, 346 ff.

[14] Fr. 190 b B.

[15] Fr. 595 P.

[16] Fr. 600 P.

[17] Fr. 541, 2 P.

which tend to visualise and describe every element of sensory experience.
Like every other human activity, the art of poetry, too, is conceived as an
ability, a capacity, the mental possession of notions: hence the emphasis
on the idea of *mathesis* corresponding to the poetic idea of imitation. Pindar himself, despite his claims to originality and his refusal to follow the
path trodden by Homer,[18] also works within the pale of this common
technical concept of poetry, as we see from the frequent metaphors
taken from sculpture and architecture relating to his technique and his
poetic objectives.[19]

The paratactical structure on the level of syntax and composition
happens to be an absolute norm of the linguistic codes of this culture of
oral communication, from the poetic code to the cosmological and philosophical ones.[20] There are too many examples to be able to mention
them all here. Whoever is at all familiar with lyric texts, from Archilochus to Pindar, will know that parataxis in the syntactic structure is a
procedure common to the language of lyric poetry. Sappho and Anacreon
are the best examples of such a linguistic norm. We might almost call it
a paratactical mental state which shuns the relationalistc analysis of experience, the logical sequences of cause and effect — a means of formula-
ting emotions and thoughts for aphorisms and peremptory affirmations
arranged in a graduation of visual and auditory effects by way of climax
and anticlimax and in rigid figures of polarity and analogy. As an immediate
example we need only recall the Sapphic ode of erotic emotions,[21] or ca-
tegorical assertions such as "gold cannot be corrupted, Truth is sovereign,
smoke has no effect",[22] which contrast perennial and incorruptible values
with other evanescent and fallacious ones, or, outside the field of lyric
poetry, the antithetical couples War and Love in Empedocles, and being
and non-being, Truth and Opinion in Parmenides.[23]

These figures of thought correspond to analogous figures of structure
in the composition of the poem. The Sapphic ode furnishes a typical example, even from a rhythmic point of view (monostrophic pattern), of paratactical structure — the presence in the same poem and a repetition in
different poems of the game motifs and the same situations, such as love
problems, separations, mythical episodes, floral scenes and divine visions.
In Anacreon's ode on Artemon[24] the characterisation of the enriched
peasant is visualised in a paractical series of acts and ways of life which
contrast in a powerful antithesis the earlier and the later Artemon. Iden-

---

[18]   *Pae.* 7 b, 10 ff.
[19]   A systematic collection of the material is to be found in P. BERNARDINI, *Quad.
Urb.* 4, 1967, p. 80 ff.
[20]   For parataxis in the epic see J. A. NOTOPOULOS, *Trans. Proc. Am. Philol.
Assoc.* 80, 1949, pp. 1-23; in the elegy and in Alcman, B. A. VAN GRONINGEN, *La composition littéraire archaïque grecque*, Amsterdam² 1960, pp. 40 ff.; 124 ff.
[21]   Fr. 31 L.P.
[22]   Simonides, fr. 541, 3-5 P.
[23]   On the linguistic structures of archaic political philosophy see the new analysis
by G.E.R. LLYOD, *Polarity and Analogy*, Cambridge 1966.
[24]   Fr. 82 Gent., 388 P.

tical, too, is the compositional technique of the choral poem in the paratactical structure type of actuality-myth-actuality, where we search in vain for a logical and aesthetic unity: the unity is provided by the occasion of the poem and its function for the purchaser and the public.

Buth the oral type of publication is not only produced by way of recitation, song and dance, before a particular public, but also by the prevalently oral spread of the text in space and time. It necessarily entails — as we see from comparative ethnology — mnemotechnics, a technique of memorization which thus becomes the instrument or the depository of a cultural tradition. A symbol of this technology is *Mnemosyne*, frequently invoked in poetry, who, as a divine person, transmits to the poet the extraordinary power of the art of memory. All this explains the frequency of the concordances and the *loci similes* not only in the language of the lyric poets and of the epic and the hexametrical and elegiac inscriptions, but also in the context of the language of the elegy and the lyric poems themselves — a fruitful common patrimony of formulary and stylistic materials which deserve a systematic analysis dictated by a more modern methodology.[25]

The synchronous dimension does not, of course, exhaust the problem of interpretation. It helps us to understand certain common aspects of a mental and linguistic system, certain forms of organization of culture, but it does not offer perspective parameters which allow us to understand the mutations of meaning within identical linguistic structures in relation to the altering situations. Since lyric poetry was bound to situational contexts different from those of epic poetry, it expressed more realistic subjects, new existential experiences connected with the different socio-political conditions of the archaic polis. It was a type of pragmatic poetry on account of its admonitory, didactic and celebrational function, its choice of themes stimulated by events in military and political life, by the real situations of social life, banquets, religious feasts and athletic competitions, according to the request of a purchaser, a public of "friends" (male or female) of a thiasos of girls, or a political faction of identical social rank. In the diachronous perspective of the situations the phenomenon of lyric poetry stands between tradition and innovation not only in its choice of words,[26] but also in its structures and semanthemes with the emergence of new cultural and political connotations. Solon[27] and Theognis[28] lament the

---

[25] Useful in this respect is the systematic research by R. FÜHRER, *Formproblem-Untersuchungen zu den Reden in der frühgriechischen Lyrik*, München 1967, which shows a substantial continuity between the epic and the lyric in the technique of introductive and conclusive formulas in direct speech. For Archilochus and the epic language see D. PAGE, *Entret. Hardt* X (1963), p. 119 ff. A panorama of structural and verbal concordances between elegiac inscriptions and archaic elegy is contained in B. GENTILI, "Epigramma ed elegia", *Entret. Hardt* XIV (1968), p. 69 ff. and between hexametrical and elegiac inscriptions and epic poetry in Z. DI TILLIO, *Quad. Urb.* 7, 1969 p. 45 ff.

[26] Cf. M TREU, *Von Homer zur Lyrik*, Müchen ²1968 and B. SNELL, *Dichtung und Gesellschaft*, Hamburt 1965.

[27] Fr. 3, 6-11 D.

[28] Vs. 39-50.

political evils of their city, attributing the cause to the foolishness of the leaders in an almost identical linguistic context. The words, however, have a completely different political conditions of Athens and Megara: the leaders (ἡγεμόνες), to whom Solon alludes, are excessively conservative aristocrats; for Theognis, on the other hand, they are the progressive aristocrats. Substantially, then, as we know from ethnolinguistics,[29] the semantic problems of language are the problems inherent in the significance of those cultural phenomena of which words are symbols. Words of value are laden with different denotations, or lose their traditional meaning even in contexts which repeat the linguistic patterns of poetic tradition.[30] The word *arete* in the poetry of Tyrtaeus has situational premises different to the Homeric *arete*; as its presupposition it has the community ethics of seventh-century Sparta; it is a civic "virtue", a property common to city and people.[31] In the realistic thought of Simonides words like *arete, agathos, esthios*, although included in the ideological connotation of an aristocratic ethic, lose their basic semantic value and become utopian because they can no longer be applied to the condition of the man obliged to work within the limits of certain necessities intrinsic to his nature and social situation, "the wish for profit, love and ambitions". The old absolute values are replaced by new relative values. The idea of success based on exceptional capacity and compliance with the divine will is replaced by a new idea of man, not of the man capable of performing the highest feasts of aristocratic virtue, but of the man operating in the respect of a justice "useful to the city". This is the meaning of the ode to Scopas[32] and of the papyrus fragment from Oxyrhynchus 2432.[33] There is, as we see, a desecration of aristocratic values, well documented, moreover, by the testimony of Aristotle[34] who attributed to Simonides the shrewd aphorism that the nobles by birth (εὐγενεῖς) are the rich of ancient times (οἱ ἐκ πάλαι πλούσιοι).

---

[29] Cf. E. NIDA in *Language in Culture and Society. A Reader in Linguistics and Anthropology*, ed. D. Hymes, New York 1964, p. 90 ff.

[30] On the reuse of the formulas and expressions of the epic in the elegy and lyric poetry only partial research has been performed. It is now indispensable that someone should undertake a systematic analysis of the functionality of reuse on a conceptual and stylistic level, an analysis which does not lose sight of, and does not underrate, all the material of the archaic metric inscriptions. The present state of research entitles us to talk of the *polysemanticity* of the epic formula and expression. For Tyrtaeus and Mimnermus see my piece in *Maia* 17, 1965, p. 383 ff. and my comment in *Polinnia, poesia greca arcaica*, Firenze ²1965, pp. 7-18; 34-48; Chr. M. Dawson, *Yale Class. Stud.* 19, 1966, pp. 42-53; C. Prato, *Tirteo*, Roma 1968; B. Snell, *Tyrtaios und die Sprache des Epos*, Göttingen 1969.

[31] Fr. 9, 15 D., 9 Prato.

[32] Fr. 542 P.

[33] Fr. 541 P. This new fragment elucidates and completes the meaning of the ode to Scopas, as I have shown elsewhere (cf. note 44 and *Polinnia*, pp. 306-320). I regard as correct the interpretation of Arthur W.H. Adkins (*Merit and Responsibility. A Study in ˍ ˋeek Values*, Oxford 1960, p. 355-359) who tends to place the enconium to Scopas in the wake of traditional ethics (but he could not have known the new fragment from Oxyrhynchus which was published barely a year before his book appeared); and I regard as partial the interpretation of Hugh Parry (*Trans. Proc. Am. Philol. Assoc.* 96, 1965, pp. 297-320) based exclusively on the synchronous aspects of the language of the ode.

[34] Fr. 92 R.

In the broad panorama of these complex problems which had their premises in the irreversible evolution of Greek society we also find the great theme of being and becoming, of truth and opinion, which affects all late archaic culture from Simonides to Parmenides, by way of a common language, common metaphors and typical words (such as "violate, exert violence"[35], but with different and contrary ideological and artistic consequences. The antithesis of being and appearing, even if not explicitly formulated, was already present in the earliest culture.[36] Its matrix was in the Homeric idea[37] that man has an inconstant and changeable character. But its later developments are explicit. To the volubility of the human mind, to the phenomenal becoming of the man-shadow dreaming that he is and is not[38], Pindar opposes the solid consistency, the perennial certainty of Truth in mythical action and in human action, "the principle of great virtue",[39] the inalienable property of the man who is valiant and of noble birth. To Truth Simonides opposes the power of opinion,[40] to the certainty of today that of the "god tomorrow",[41] so swift is the state of flux of the human condition.[42] These are two contrary world views, the former conservative, the latter dynamic and realistic, which underlie two precise political and cultural positions. The irreconcilability of these two views of reality is conceptualised in Parmenides by way of a procedure which we could call informal logic,[43] truth being identified with being which is the only thing we can know, and opinion with non-being, nothingness. Simonides accompanies the paratactical structures of antithesis and analogy with free movement speculiar to discourse and the language of controversy, polemically introduced to mark an ideological and stylistic break[44] — the same coexistence in the accumulation of semantic denotations in one word, the traditional archaic one and a new denotation which marks a turning point in thought or the fulcrum of a new idea. Thus we have νοεῖν and λόγος in Parmenides, the former taken in its archaic sense (defined by von Fritz[45] as "to perceive", "to plan"), and in the new sense of "to know" (γιγνώσκειν)[46], the latter in its sense of "word, discourse"

---

[35]   βιάομαι or βιάζομαι, to designate the tyranny of falsehood, lies and, in general, all that causes damage or ruin. Cf. *Il*.23, 576; Simon. frr. 541,8; 598 P.; Pind. *Nem*. 8, 34; Parmen. fr. 7,3 D.K.; Emped. fr. 3,5 f. D.K.

[36]   We need only think of the odes by Anacreon on Artemon, the enriched peasant (fr. 82 Gent., 388 P.) for the girl-foal (78 Gent., 417 P.) and for Erotima (fr. 60 Gent., 346, 1 P.), on which see now G. Serrao, *Quad. Urb*. 6, 1968, p. 36 ff.

[37]   *Od*. 18, 130-137.

[38]   *Pyth*. 8, 95 f.

[39]   Fr. 205 Sn.

[40]   Fr. 598 P.

[41]   Fr. 615 P.

[42]   Cf. fr. 521 P.

[43]   Cf. Lloyd, *op. cit.*

[44]   Cf. *Maia* 16, 1964, p. 293 f.

[45]   *Class. Philol.* 38, 1943, p. 79 f.

[46]   Fr. 3 D.K. τὸ γὰρ αὐτὸ νοεῖν ἐστίν τε καὶ εἶναι. There is no point in my considering here the many suggested interpretations of the fragment, on which see now L. TARÁN, *Parmenides*, Princeton 1965, p. 32 ff. I should simply point out that the formulation of Parmenides should be interpreted in the context of fr. 2, where we read about the ways of thought which we can νοεῖν (v.2), the way of being and the way of non-being. But we then read that

and in its new meaning of "reason".[47] Similarly in Simonides the adjective
κακός is taken both in the archaic agonistic sense of "not valiant" and
as meaning "wicked" in a moral sense.[48]

Consequently a new meaning survives alongside the old one, but
operates in different directions with the identical object of attaining a
new awareness of the problems of reality and a new method of thought.
Simonides suggests a radical solution to the problem of the freedom of will
in man's actions: each man can do evil involuntarily, when compelled by
necessity; what is important is that he should not do it voluntarily.[49]
There is, therefore, the wish for a moral choice in the action connected
with respect for a justice useful to the city, in other words, as we know
from a quotation in Plato,[50] for the just norm of giving everyone his due.
Where the useful is concerned Simonides is in line with his contemporary
Xenophanes who contrasted the useless *arete* of the athlete with the *so-
phia* of the poet as the highest virtue because it is fruitful for the community,[51] but Simonides is more radical and progressive in acknowledging
as the only possibility the civic virtue not of an élite of intellectuals, but
of any citizen, and the community of the polis as the formative instrument
of man.[52] Parmenides, on the other hand, from a different, static and conservative ideology, perfectly suited to the political situation of the oligar-
chic Elea,[53] and still in the tradition of the didascalic poetry of Hesiod,
performs the bold experiment of talking to his fellow citizens with the persuasive force not of opinion and myth, of which he decries the fallacious
power, but of the *logos*, of conceptual thought as idea and as method. In
the precarious climate of this crisis of traditional values we find the forms
of the thought and language of the new culture of the Sophists and of
Plato, of the culture of written communication in which the word (according to a maxim of the Viennese critic Karl Kraus) will be the personification
of a thought and not the shell of a sociable opinion. A telling symptom
is the demythization of *Mnemosyne* performed by Simonides:[54] *Mnemosyne* turns into a technical exercise of the memory regarded purely and
simply as a mental phenomenon.

---

we cannot know (γιγνώσκειν v. 7) what is not, since only what is can be known. It is therefore evident that the νοεῖν of fr. 3, identified with being, does not have the same value as
the νοεῖν in fr. 2, which should be understood in the archaic sense of "to perceive" or
"to plan", since the ways of thought of being and of non-being are perceptible, but only
being can be know. Consequently if νοεῖν and εἶναι are the same thing, νοεῖν in this case
would mean "to known" (γιγνώσκειν), because only being can be known; hence the identity
between being and knowing.

[47]   Fr. 7, 5 D.K.
[48]   Fr. 542, 15 and 34 P.
[49]   Fr. 542, 27-29 P.
[50]   *Resp.* I 331 e; cf. Aristotle fr. 85 R.
[51]   Fr. 2, 1 ff. D.K.
[52]   Fr. 53 D. = p. 310 P. πόλις ἄνδρα διδάσκει.
[53]   On the political constitution of Elea in the time of Parmēnides see now E. Le-
pore, *Parola d. passato 21*, 1966, p. 255 ff.
[54]   See G. CHRIST, *Simonidesstudien*, Freiburg 1941, p. 76 f. and above all the intel-
ligent observations of M. DETIENNE, *Les maîtres de vérité dans la Grèce archaïque*, Paris
1967, pp. 110 f; 123.

Essentially speaking, the only object of my analysis is to suggest certain trends of research which might place the problem of interpretation in the broader perspective of that idea to which contemporary anthropology aspires of interpretation as communicability between cultures both different and distant in time. Just to give some of the more significant examples: I do not know how far it is possible to understand certain elements and aspects of love in the partheniads of Alcman and the poetry of Sappho and Ibycus without the help of a comparative analysis with other cultures, even with primitive ones. For many of these elements, like the competitive element in love life, the ritual aspects peculiar to initiation rites and the psychology of veneration for fascination and beauty, are no longer relevant to us. If we observe the phenomena of character and personality, here, too, ethnological comparisons will enable us to understand how, in an age in which the human being was regarded as "an open field of forces", and not as "a compact and closed entity" (to use Fränkel's excellent description),[55] Sappho could express the idea of the self's "awareness" of itself, of the interior awareness of some thing or act probably offensive to its own person.[56] It enables us to understand, outside the old scheme of mythical mentality and rational mentality,[57] that the absence of a word does not necessarily entail the absence of the corresponding notion. The phenomena of character were familiar to the archaic poet; it is only that they were expressed in a language suited to his psychological and intellectual life[58] which entailed, as we have seen, the tendency to make objective and public the idiosyncratic and the personal. In this way we understand how the poetry of Sappho could contain modes of expression

---

[55] *Am. Journal of Philol.* 60, 1939, p. 477.

[56] Fr. 26, 11-12 L.P. [.αν, ἔγω δ'ἐμ' [αὖτα / τοῦτο σύ] νοιδα. The state of the text does not allow us to understand exactly what τοῦτο alludes to. It seems certain, at all events, that it must have been about a personal matter, as we see from vs. 2-4 (ὄ] ττινα [ς γὰρ / εὖ θέω, κῆνοί με μά] λιστα πά [ντων / σίνοντα] ι), in which Sappho refers to people who are ill-treating her, who have an offensive attitude towards her, different from hers towards them, and she suffers from it (cf. vs. 10 τοῦ] το πάθη [ν: the supplement, which is by Diehl, can be regarded as sure, cf. M. TREU, *Sappho*, München 1968, p. 44). There is therefore a state of tension, of polemics between herself and people very close to her, which she fully realises, of which *she is well aware* (for the τοῦτο of vs. 12 cf. vs. 10). Other pertinent observations are to be found in B. SNELL, *Gnomon* 6, 1930, p. 24 = *Gesammelte Schriften*, Göttingen 1966, p. 12; O. SEEL, *Festschr. Dornseiff*, Leipzig 1953, p. 312 f.; A. CANCRINI, *La cultura* 7, 1969, p. 53 f.

[57] This scheme, which has influenced most of the studies on *Hellenism* from Homer to Plato, comes, as we know, from the hypothesis advanced by Lévy-Bruhl in connection with primitive societies (*Les fonctions mentales dans les sociétés inférieures*, Paris 1910) about a "prelogical", "mythical" mentality which knows nothing of the law of contradiction; hence the distinction between mythical mentality and logical mentality as progressive moments in the evolution of thought. Today this hypothesis is no longer valid, as has been recently proved by Lévi-Strauss (*La pensée sauvage*, Paris 1962; *Du miel aux cendres*, Paris 1966, p. 407 ff.), and indeed, it was no longer even valid for the man who formulated it. Many years later Lévy-Bruhl profoundly modified his ideas, regarding his first hypothesis as "unfounded" and unfortunate, cf. *Rev. philos.* 1947, p. 258. It is this same hypothesis that the recent essay by V.N. Jarcho, "Zum Menschenbild der nachhomerischen Dichtung", *Philologus* 112, 1968, p. 147 ff. finds its theoretical support.

[58] For the Homeric age see the perceptive and commendable observations of F. CODINO, *Introduzione a Omero*, Torino 1965, p. 134 f.

of her own self taken at one moment as a field open to free factual and psychic forces,[59] and at another as a state of awareness or of consciousness, this latter attitude being one which was evidently suited to the situation or the somewhat personal and confidential theme and tone of the poem.

In its broader methodological range this different perspective allows us to respond with more appropriate instruments of research to the necessity of respecting, but at the same time fully understanding, the text, not only in all its linguistic connotations, but also in all the extralinguistic reality of the poetic proposition. In order to guard against the danger of arbitrary travesties we should keep in mind the words of T.S. Eliot:[60] "We need an eye which can see the past in its place, with its definite differences from the present, and yet so lively that is shall be as present to us as the present."

Bruno GENTILI,
University of Urbino.

---

[59]   Cf. *Quad. Urb.* 2, 1966, p. 61.
[60]   *The Sacred Wood: Essays on Poetry and Criticism*, 1969, p. 77, on G. Murray's translations of Euripides.

The Interpretation of Images and Symbols

I address you as a classical philologist and as one who is devoted to the tradition of this science. In the 19th century, classical philology showed itself capable of outstanding achievements; it had developed excellent methods of criticism of texts and sources; it had produced thoroughgoing editions and laid down the foundations for a comprehensive study of antiquity. Added to this, it had also interpreted poetry. But here there arose a peculier contradiction. While it applied the greatest stringency to the narrower field of philology, at the same time placing great value on the exactitude of method — the "philological method" was regarded by it as a sacred concept and even today philologists are fond of talking about 'method'[1]. As far as the interpretation of poetry was concerned — that is to say, in describing what went on in a piece of poetry — it was appallingly inexact. It would be easy to illustrate this by citing, for example, Wilamowitz' interpretation of poems by Catullus or some of the poems of Horace treated by Pasquali. Notwithstanding, both Wilamowitz and Pasquali were outstanding scholars. I once came across a French author who compared the intelligence of a highly gifted human being with the striped appearance of the tiger; its coat is shot through with dark stripes and these dark stripes, maintained the author, can be thought of as representing the lack of insight into matters where their intelligence falls short, and the lighter as representing other areas where it has proved itself superbly. As far as the philologist is concerned, the dark stripes make themselves apparent as soon as he begins to analyse poetry or, for that matter, any kind of work of art in speech. He is inclined to regard a piece of poetry as a piece of prose which has a metrical form and which is vaguer and less exact than an objective description.

This very vagueness may have caused many a philologist to be even vaguer in his interpretation than the poem itself. They did not discern that a poem is a universe in which other laws apply and other exactitudes obtain than those which belong to prose. Only he to whom it is possible to display these laws and this exactitude — Herder spoke of the metaphysical exactness of a poem, an excellent expression —, only he to whom it is possible to describe its structure (to use a much over-worked word), can hope adequately to comprehend the imagery, the similes, and the symbols of the poem, which are the heart of poetry. The philologist then comes close to the normal receptive reader who absorbs a work of art because he feels himself attracted to it and because he finds pleasure in it; the reader, that is, who needs culture and literature and in whose need Nietzsche saw

---

[1] In GADAMER's *Truth and Method* however, the word is not used without irony.

a basic motive for the concern with culture and literature. He comes nearer to the reader for whom the poet wrote, since no work of literature was ever written for philologists (W. Bulst, quoted by Jauss, *The History of Literature as Provocation*). The philologist thereby becomes a literary critic.

But is literary criticism a science? Can it come to results which one can consider binding? Can the meaning of poetical imagery, with which we have to concern ourselves here, and which has been a point of controversy in the past and will be in the future, be supported by criteria that can take away the suspicion that it is merely subjective and arbitrary? Would it not be better for the philologist not to bother with such things at all? Indeed, traditional philology for a long time gave little or no attention to the phenomena of poetic symbolism. In the commentaries (to poems) one simply ignored it and nothing shows more clearly that philology confounded poetry with non-poetry than the fact that metaphors, similes, mythological examples and the like, were seen as "decoration"; decoration, so one believed, which could easily be reduced to a prosaic "content". A good example of this is the manner in which mythological allusion was treated: in Augustan poetry, for example, it is simply dismissed as "Alexandrian studiousness", which required an unusually sublime expression. This is not wrong, of course, but the phenomenon is not thereby wholly apprehended. In Horace's Cleopatra Ode, the Egyptian queen is chased from Italy by Octavian's fleet as the hawk routs the doves, or as the swift hunter pursues the hare on the winter fields of Haemonia. For a long time no one noticed at all that the swift hunter was in fact Achilles of the podas okys — Octavian, that is, elevated to the epic sphere of Homer and made equal with the heroes of the *Iliad*. Further, one did not notice the symbolic suggestion contained in the mention of 'haemonia'. The commentaries content themselves with the declaration that Haemonia is Thessaly which, by the way, accounts for the figure of Achilles, since *the* mythical hunter of Thessaly was Achilles. On the Thessalian Pelion he had, as a young hero, hunted down the fastest beasts. In 'Haemoniae', the reader versed in Greek heard — one must not forget that this culture was bilingual — the word 'haema', 'blood', or could at least imagine himself to have heard it. Sound-symbolism also played a role: the two 'ae' in 'Haemoniae' are the sounds of pain whose character is probably in keeping with the final, deadly chase in which Cleopatra was involved. Sophocles uses the names of Haimon and Aias in the same expressive way. That the contemporary reader had an ear for the symbolism of sound can be proved beyond doubt from Quintilian's accounts and from the writings of Greek scholars. This case shows once more that one cannot get along simply with the immanent poetic interpretation of the formalists, but that one must interpret 'historically'. One must take into account the horizon of the contemporary reader in order to acquire a satisfactory understanding. The case of Haemonia belongs to a very subtle category, and before we concern ourselves with such subtle forms, we should perhaps consider simpler forms a little more closely.

There is a type of symbolism for which philological poetic interpretation has at all times had an open ear, often enough an ear that was too widely open. I refer to allegory. An image, a poetically presented passage or a poetical figure, is only allegorical when, in an encoded form, it indicates something else and when its meaning can only be arrived at through this relation. The animals at the beginning of Dante's *Divine Comedy* are allegories for the sins which threaten humankind. Sees as an actual encounter with wild animals, the figure misses its proper meaning. Allegorical poetical interpretation has played an enormously important role since the 'Allegoriae Homericae'. That Circe turns the companions of Odysseus into wolves and swine is an indication that licentiousness can transform men into beasts. This, according to Xenophon (*Mem.* 1.3.7) was what Socrates taught. This meaning finds expression later in Horace, in his second Epistle, and again it is to be found in Dio Chrysostom (8.21) and also in Erasmus' *De Ratione Studii.* [2] Orpheus, Horace informs us, was able to dissuade those men that lived in woods from murder and from their gruesome appetites. This could well be the meaning of the saying that he was able to charm beasts (Ap 391 ff.). In this way, Orpheus becomes the symbol of the culture-bestowing poet and his pedagogical message, the mythological archetype which Horace himself aspires to. Christian writers further elaborated allegorical meanings and myth and poetry became thereby allegorical metaphors for Christian morality and Christian teaching. [3] They are divested of their original meaning and acquire a new meaning which one takes as the true meaning, or at least as one that can be used.

The allegorical interpretation of poetry against which one has serious reservations may be motivated in various ways. In the first place, it serves the purpose of saving poetry, of not allowing the greatness and beauty of poetic tradition which, in spite of all reservations, one admires, to fall into oblivion. One does not want to banish Homer and the tragedies, as Plato had wanted or — as Plato also suggested — to incarcerate living poets; but by allegorical interpretation one divests them of their danger.

In the second place, one knows very well that a figurative representation is more easily remembered and more impressive than an abstract warning or a theoretical analysis; one knows that poetry is more powerful that these, and so, allegorically interpreted it can be useful in promoting and promulgating whatever moral one wishes to promote and promulgate. But this allegorical interpretation amounts to a movement away from poetry to something lying outside it, to an objective which is didactic, propreptical, political and so on. Impressive examples of the changes of ancient mythology into stories expressing Christian sentiments are to be found, incidentally in the *Protreptikos* of Clement of Alexandria. Poetry becomes an illustration of one's own programme, one's own message. In the first place, the programme is there and to this the poetry is made amenable, not without violence. This kind of allegorical interpretation is

---

2   W.J. VERENIUS, *Homer, the Educator of the Greeks,* Mitteilungen der kgl. niederländischen Akademie 1970, 13, Anm. 54

3   With regard to this: Reinhard HERZOG, "Metapher, Exegese, Mythos, Interpretation zur Entstehung eines biblischen Mythos in der Literatur der Spätantike", in: *Terror und Spiel, Probleme der Mythenrezeption* (M. Fuhrmann, München 1971.)

therefore not a path towards poetry, but a path that takes us away from it. For us, however, it is important to get at the poetry, the thing itself.

In addition to these two motives for allegorical interpretation —

(i) the intention to "save" the poetry of the past, to protect it from possible accusation, and

(ii) the desire, with the help of poetry, to give emphasis to the particular message which one wants to delcare, to appoint the poets as crown witnesses in one's own affairs —

there is a third: the intellectual gratification that is to be found in giving the vacillating shape of poetry a firm, rational, comprehensible, unequivocal meaning. It is here that the abstract, scientific approach of the philologist finds satisfaction. He can indulge in his predisposition to turn poetry into prose, and that is the reason why even today the interpretation of images is so popular. Since it has become known that imagery means something and must be interpreted, one goes in for images interpretation, too, and feels happiest in dealing with straightfoward allegorical interpretation. All these interpreters, both ancient and modern, are in no way aware of their motives. They are of the firm belief that they understand a work of literature better than their predecessors and are of the opinion that they bring to light aspects which have been hitherto neglected or overlooked. We all do this all the time; it is not only legitimate but necessary. Poetry lives by giving rise to a sucession of different interpretations. We must concede the same integrity of purpose to the moralising Christian interpreters as we do to modern interpreters who bring to their interpretations of ancient works their knowledge of modern social, religious, political science and newer aspects of psychology, anthropology and philosophy, in short, the ideas and prejudices of their time.

As far as the interpretation of images and symbols is concerned, Freudian psychoanalysis has also played a role and opened up new vistas which have encouraged some to discover sexual symbols at every turn. This had led, for example, to Lesbia's sparrow being interpreted as a male symbol. It is easy to laugh at such aberrations. But, on the other hand, we must by no means exclude the possibility of gaining new insights and being able to interpret poets differently, just as Sigmund Freud himself found, for example, in his explanation of Schilter's Vallenstein what has become known as the Freudian slip. We should be cautious about condemning psychoanalysis altogether as an aid to the interpretation of texts. One significant cause of the blindness of interpreters, which we must not overlook, is prudery. I could cite as examples here Eduard Fraenkel and Friedrich Klingner to prove the point. Here there are many discoveries to be made: in the erotic field "double entente" appear in all cultures, not simply from motives of prudery but as the expression of quite natural feelings of joy at play. One must be aware also of the fact that in erotic matters the direct and rational aproach is neither the best nor the most natural, as indeed research into the behaviour of animals has most clearly confirmed. One of Horace's love poems illustrates this rather well. It is the last love poem of the three volume collection of odes, and is for that very fact the more noticeable. One has always regarded it as a poem that has nothing of particular import to express. In it, Horace is counting the love-songs which he will sing together with the maiden Lyde, with whom he is celebrating the feast of Neptune. The fact that behind these songs, which allude to mythological notions, there is something else hidden, suggested by an allusion at the beginning of the poem:

> Do this well-warded wisdom violence,
> You sense that midday has already shown itself
> As though fleeting day should halt;
> You are too thrifty to bring hither
> The hesitant amphora of the Consul Bibulus
> From where it is kept.

> Inclinare meridiem
>   Sentis et veluti stet volucris dies.
> parcis deripere horreo
>   cessantem Bibuli consulis amphoram.

What is concealed behind this exhortation, and what sort of violence might be done to the girl's well-preserved wisdom are not difficult to conjecture; it is also pretty clear that not only the amphora will yield in its hesitation. Then come the songs. Firstly, Horace wants to praise Neptune and the daughters of the sea with their green hair, the erotic element somewhat in the background. Then, however, Lyde, to whom the poem is addressed, is to sing about Latona and the quick arrows of Diana, the chaste goddess who knows how to defend herself against importunate advances; at the end Venus is sung, the goddess who ruled over Knidos and the shimmering Cyclades, and of Paphos, her sanctuary, which will be visited by a carriage drawn by two swans. The two swans which the goddess guides hint at the happiness of a loving pair, the joy to which the poet aspires, both for himself and for the girl, on this festive occasion. Having said as much, one has almost said too much. It is really enough to have read this mischievous, loving poem, to have appreciated its innuendo, its double ententes as Lydia would have done.

This example well shows what is involved in the interpretation of a poem. It does not consist in demonstrating unequivocally the sense of the poem. Neither does it consist in giving an allegorical equation A = B: "I intend to embark upon a theme which is erotically tinged: Neptune and Nereides: you will at first hold me at arm's lenght: Lyde Diane; and then finally we'll join together in happy love-making: Venus and the swans." No. It is all understandable, and meaningful too, when one merely talks about the songs in which the gods are hymnally praised; the dull reader will hear nothing else, and indeed up to now every interpreter has been dull. But certainly Lyde would not be so dull. We are then here not concerned with crude parallels, but with tender references about whose interpretation we need not go into detail. The reader himself must play the role of Lyde, feeling himself spoken to as one of the lovers to whom the poet is talking. This does not apply only to the poem in question. Every poem opens itself up to us when we, like a lover, are willing to listen for its nuances.

Great poetry does not receive its greatness from the fact that it can be interpreted rationally, unequivocally and be completely expressible in prosaic terms. The ability to perceive the implicit challenge, as also the allusions in the poem, and to follow up the associations, this is a subtler art. Paul Valéry's description is very helpful in this connection:

> The poetic condition, or poetic awakening, seems to me to lie in the development of a special manner of perception (dans une perception naissante) which is such as to apprehend the world as a system of references. Within this, human beings see things, events and actions which, although they ressemble those that populate and make up the world of ordinary cognition, are nevertheless related in a wonderfully appropriate way to the forms and laws of our sensibility as a whole. The things and forms we perceive then somehow acquire another value. They call each other forth; they associate themselves in quite another way than they do under normal circumstances; they are 'musicalized'. (ils se trouvent musicalisés.)

The analogies which Valéry finds for this created poetic condition are music and dream, where the borders set by the real world for things and processes can be crossed without difficulty. A poem makes use of words of which the normal language makes use too, whereas music, unfolding itself quite differently, removes us to another world from the very beginning. It is this that makes it difficult for us to comprehend the peculiarity of poetry. Another illuminating analogy which Valéry introduces is dance. The dancer makes use of the same muscles and limbs as a person who walks, but he does not walk. Poetry is as different from usual speech as dancing is from walking. The critical factor in this is that Valéry speaks of the *émotion poétique*; it is *this* which is first engendered by the poem; it is this which makes it possible for things to enter into a relationship with one another which is wonderful. It is then more a process of feeling than a rational process which takes place in the mind of a reader or listener. If he allows himself to be absorbed by the poem and follows the movements of the poem within himself, if he dances with it, so to speak, then — and only then — can the images and incidents within the poem quite spontaneously call forth those relationships which are beyond that which is merely said. The reader and the interpreter of a poem must learn to sink himself utterly in the poem. He must practice careful listening; he must train himself to acquire *aures religiosae*, ears which possess *religio*, to use Cicero's fine turn of phrase. That is to say, he must learn to understand how to hear secret voices, for here *religio* is used in the Latin sense, i.e. as the capacity of giving attention to secret, divine signs and voices.

The danger, however, is that he misunderstand the implicit challenges within the poem, that he undertake too great an exertion in order to realize a deep underlying meaning, so that coarseness takes over where gentleness is appropriate — where the *sensibility* of the reader is required. That this sensibility is characterized by what the reader brings to the poem, by what he has experienced and how he has lived, is of course self-evident. But rational considerations must also play a part. With regard to a poem which stems from another historical period, one must know what kind of outlook an educated reader of that age would have had respecting images and mythologies. But the most important thing is that one not confuse allegory and symbols. The Soracte Ode of Horace is susceptible to this. It begins wit an image of Roman winter, and the mountain, Soracte, is covered with snow. The trees groan under their burden, the ditches are frozen over. The poet orders his boy, Thaliarch, to heat the fire with wood and bring wine in abundance. The cold of winter shall be countered by the comforst of home. Immediately afterwards the warning — this is the first antithesis —: Leave everything to the gods. As soon as they have brought the wild winds to peace, the cypresses and the old oaks will no longer be shaken, i.e. storms do not last long. That which harasses and troubles one will pass. This then is the second antithesis: inevitable harassment and the consolation that it will pass. And finally: Think not of the morrow; consider each day which destiny grants you as your profit; enjoy your youth as long as old age is still far off. The third antithesis is, then, youth and age. We have a graduated poem before us. Three adverse things are to be fought against: the raw winter by fire and wine, storms which whip their victims by the comfort that they will not last forever, and threatening age by the exhortation to enjoy youth as long as it is possible. Behind the idea of age there is the thought of death, as is suggested by the sentence: each day lived is a day won. But what do the interpreters make of all this? They say that the winter of the first verse means age; and the storms which come to rest so that the storm-whipped trees finally will not be swayed backwards and forwards they interpret in Goethe's sense, that is, "Above all peaks there is peace,", and, by this, death is meant. This, according to one interpretation known to me, is underlined by the fact that the cypresses are the trees of death and that the ash trees are old. All this, however, is illicit allegory, for it destroys the richness of the poem. The only thing remaining is that the poet, because he fears age and death, recommends to us that we enjoy today and our youth. But above all, by applying this allegorical interpretation, we lose sight of the point that a poem by Horace is a process, one that, step by step, leads us to something. If we take 'winter' right at the beginning of the poem to mean age, the storm-thrashed trees which eventually find rest mean death, then this process is destroyed. When he hears the mention of winter, the listener is not to know how the poem will develop, but he will nevertheless be prepared for what is to come. Later, he might come to sense that the winter has to do with the winter of life. In this, however, there is, so to speak, a "musical" connection (you will remember Valéry's "musicalized") between storms and real winter which serves as a comparison between death and old age which, not incidentally, is *described* as *canities*, greyness. *Canities* is placed in opposition to youth, described as *viridis*, a metaphor taken from the plant world. Plant symbolism appears in all three antitheses. The woods which cannot bear their burden, the storm-ridden trees and this *viridis*. With the old ash trees, in addition and for the first time, there appears the conception of age in the poem which then extends to *canities morosa*. The winter of the first stanza is not to be equated with old age, but it prepares one for the mood of *canities*. The trees which cannot carry their weight anymore stand in context with the storm-whipped trees of the second antithesis. One gathers from the whole that Nature and Man are doomed to suffer, that there are harsh and powerful realities — how powerful is the image of the winter of the opening stanza! —, but that there is healing, a means to overcome suffering or to counter it. The images, which belong together, indicate with that "metaphysical exactitude" of which Herder speaks, a context of being in which man finds himself.

Here is yet another example of misinterpretation in one of Horace's poems. The last ode of the first book "Persicos odi..." as Nisbet rightly points out, has suffered from symbolical interpretation. Horace declares that he rejects Persian drink, Persian pomp and wreaths bound with lime fibres; he forbids his slave boy to go looking for a late-blooming rose to add to a simple crown of myrtle; simple myrtle is quite sufficient for pouring and drinking wine beneath a grape bower. Fraenkel interpreted the poem symbolically as a declaration that Horace preferred simplicity in poetry. Nisbet, for his part, rejected this and rightly. However, this did not hinder Kenneth Reckford from reviving the idea and associating it with a remarkable explanation of the word 'philyra' (linden bark). Horace says: "displicent nexae philyra coronae". In the word 'philyra' Reckford sees a reference to 'φιλία' (friendship) and 'lyra" and he is of the opinion that Horace rejects friendship and the lyre, which is really absurd. I have myself tried to clarify the word 'Haemoniae' in the Cleopatra Ode from the point of view of the sound of the word and its meaning, but that does not mean that one must always be counselled by etymology and sound relationships. Nisbet also rejects Pasquali's interpretation of "Persicos odi" where he sees an allusion to love in the myrtle garland of Venus. This though, seems to me to be a correct interpretation, since myrtle is in fact dedicated to Venus. Here there is a relation between Horace and the surroundings where he drinks his wine, which corresponds both to the mind of Horace and to ancient lyrics and mythology. But there is something else in the poem. *Persicos apparatus* does not only mean Persian splendour, but awkward, expensive extravagance as well; his dislike and rejection of garlands which are bound together with lime fibre and his instruction to the boy not to exert himself to find more flowers are symbols for Horace's admonition that we enjoy the present in a simple way and not lose too much time. It is then a variation on the Horatian basic theme of *carpe diem*.

Finally, I would like to point out another kind of allegorical misinterpretation. In the first *Eclogue*, the shepherd Tityrus expresses his thanks to the *puer* in Rome that he is allowed to continue to sing to his Amaryllis, that he, unlike the other shepherd, Meliboeus, has not fallen victim to expulsion as was generally the case in Rome after the battle at Philippi. Tityrus has benn seen as an allegorical representation of Virgil. On the other hand, it has been objected that Tityrus was an old man whereas Virgil, at the time he wrote the *Eclogues*, was not; it could be, then, that it rather concerns Virgil's father. Here there is something quite important to point out.

It is the nature of comparison that two things are compared with each other which, in a certain way, are the same and yet not the same, and this also is true, *mutatis mutandis,* for the interpretation of mythological and poetical figures. Tityrus is Virgil and is not Virgil. He is more than Virgil, something more general, and precisely this feature, that he is an old man, excludes an allegorical interpretation which leaves nothing behind. This is also true of the figure of Aeneas. Aeneas is Augustus, and he is also Aeneas, the exemplary man and forefather of Augustus. He is the precursor of Augustus and prepares the way, and is also his ideal and so, in a certain sense, he is more than Augustus. In Dido, there is the remembrance of Cleopatra, and when, in Carthage, Aeneas forgets his message, one naturally thinks of Caesar and Antony who have been involved with Cleopatra. In a similar way, one must see in the fight between Hercules and Cacus, and the struggle of Aeneas against Turnus, a relationship indicating the battle between Octavian and Antony. In a mythological example something general is made concrete, under which a special, modern case can be subsumed and the contemporary reader will sense the related contexts.

We are then completely justified, also with regard to the strange conclusion of the *Aeneid* which has given rise to so many controversial interpretations, in asking what the essential meaning is, — here again, though we are faced with the danger inherent in an interpretation which strives for an unequivocal solution. After Turnus has been seriously wounded in the leg and lies on the ground and begs Aeneas who has defeated him for mercy, Aeneas hesitates for a moment to kill him. But when he sees the sword belt of Pallas, his friend, whom Turnus had killed, he is enflamed with anger and fury and he thereupon kills Turnus. This has led Putnam, for example, to declare Aeneas a failure and Juno victorious. The circle of madness begins anew. What has happened here? Modern sensibility has found Aeneas' cruelty revolting, and in order to defend the poet against this accusation, one has manipulated the poet's meaning and interpreted the author as condemning Aeneas' cruelty. On the other hand, there are those interpreters who have brought forth the idea that the revenge for Pallas stands for that which Octavian wreaked on the murderers of Caesar, and which was something definitely in line with Roman feeling. That is certainly correct, but one must give due place to ambiguity in the connection. Today one would, at least officially, condemn a man that behaved as Aeneas did. Virgil himself, however, saw both sides, the pain of Aeneas which forced him in the name of a friend to wreak vengeance — in fact since the death of Pallas nothing else had been his objective — and the indignation of Turnus (*indignata*) which conveys his soul awa *sub umbras,* also no without justification. *Clementia* towards the defeated enemy who pleads for mercy, and *fides,* faithfulness to a dead friend and father, stand in a conflict which cannot be resolved. One way or the other, Aeneas has to be guilty. But the idea that there is a duty to take revenge for a friend on his killer is archaic and does not belong to our code of morals. One can perhaps criticize Virgil, but one may not foist our interpretation, our judgement, on him, otherwise we will find ourselves doing basically the same thing as the old allegorical interpreters of Homer did in order to save their poet and appropriate him to their ideas. But apart from that, there seems to me to be a deep truth embodied in this final scene in which Aeneas stands, a figure in an unresolvable confict. Between humanity and policy there is always a tension which cannot be fully overcome. It is not always possible to act prudently without doing somebody wrong.

Viktor POESCHL,
University of Heideberg.

La philologie et la linguistique
dans l'interprétation des textes latins [1]

Peut-être personne ne sera surpris si nous abordons notre sujet en nous demandant ce qu'est la linguistique. Dans son développement accéléré la linguistique moderne, qui est devenue un modèle pour les sciences dites humaines, semble avoir laissé loin en arrière la vénérable philologie classique.

Comme chacun sait, le contact entre la linguistique comparée créée par Bopp au début du XIXe siècle et la philologie traditionnelle, l'héritage de la science des humanistes et des anciens grammairiens, loin d'être facile, fut plutôt tardif et s'établit plus dans le domaine du grec que dans celui du latin. Il y a un peu plus d'un siècle les philologues regardaient encore avec mépris les tentatives d'explication des comparatistes. Les commenteurs de Virgile et de Cicéron, les spécialistes de la question homérique, se rebellaient à l'idée que les langues classiques et celles des peuples barbares de l'Europe et de l'Asie puissent avoir une origine commune. À vrai dire, c'est seulement à partir de Bopp qu'il y eut des linguistes dignes de ce nom. Il est vrai que les philologues, eux aussi, prirent leur nom à partir de F.A. Wolf, mais la distance d'une génération qui sépare Wolf de Bopp signifie beaucoup dans l'Allemagne de cette époque-là. De la même façon que les philologues antérieurs à Wolf avaient été d'habitude théologiens, juristes ou médecins, les linguistes antérieurs à Bopp avaient été, si non philologues, polygraphes ou savants universels, ou bien philosophes. C'est ainsi qu'apparaissent aux origines de la linguistique un Leibniz et un Adelung, mais aussi un Hervás ou même un Friedrich Schlegel.

Quiconque s'est formé, comme moi, à l'intérieur de la linguistique historique pourrait croire que la méthode critique et stricte de la philologie classique devrait être considérée comme une conséquence du développement de la linguistique historique comparée.
Mais il ne faut pas nous laisser aveugler par le prestige de la linguistique comparée, car la rénovation de la critique, aussi bien en philologie qu'en linguistique, n'est qu'un phénomène du progrès général de l'âge

[1] Cet article fut écrit à la demande du Comité d'organisation du Ve Congrès international d'études classiques tenu à Bonn en 1969. Un bref extrait en allemand parut dans la brochure *Die Interpretation in der Altertumswissenschaft* publié par Wolfgang Schmid, Bonn, 1971, 141 p. Le texte espagnol est paru dans la revue portugaise *Euphrosyne*, nouvelle série, vol. V. pp. 403-414. La traduction française que nous publions ici est de Bohdan Plaskacz, professeur à l'Université d'Ottawa; elle a été revue par E. Gareau, professeur à la même université.

moderne. Les deux ont bénéficié du développement du nouvel esprit critique, quoique au départ la philologie ait bénéficié d'un peu d'avance,
supériorité qui est à l'origine de l'affrontement initial entre ces deux disciplines.

Nous ne pouvons pas aborder ici l'histoire des rapports entre la nouvelle linguistique comparée et la philologie toujours traditionnelle[2] : il suf-
fira de rappeler les attaques de G.A. Hermann et de Chr. A. Lobeck
contre Bopp, ou le rôle de Th. Benfey et l'attitude médiatrice de Georg
Curtius entre les deux sciences. Nous pouvons aussi nous en rapporter
à l'œuvre de Adalbert Kuhn, qui contribua avec succès à vaincre la ré-
pugnance et la défiance des disciplines qui étaient solidement établies dans
un terrain bien connu face aux sanskritistes et autres polyglottes en
dehors de tout ordre traditionnel[3].

Les instruments grammaticaux de la nouvelle philologie critique
étaient encore en 1800 peu différents de ceux qui existaient deux ou trois
siècles avant. En 1804 la *Minerve* de Francisco Sánchez, el Brocense
était encore imprimée à Leipzig. Cette œuvre était donc encore actuelle
dans le domaine de la grammaire latine, quoiqu'elle eût été rédigée à
Salamanque vers 1560 sous l'influence de J. C. Escaligero et de P. Ra-
mus[4]. Vers 1800 Gottfried August Hermann, l'un des fondateurs de la
philologie moderne, voulait encore voir les cas latins comme une merveil-
leuse divination de la philosophie, une UERI PRAESAGITIO, comme il
dirait, exacte expression des catégories philosophiques, par laquelle « le
nominatif exprime la modalité de la réalité, le vocatif celle de la possibilité, et les autres cas celle de la nécessité[5]...», de sorte que la langue
latine, était *la* langue, la *forma mentis* universelle de l'homme. On comprend que, dans un monde où régnaient de tels modes de penser, la linguistique historique empirique aît trouvé des difficultés à s'imposer.

Le succès postérieur de la linguistique nous donne maintenant l'impression que ce fut elle qui entraîna la modernisation de la philologie ;
cependant si nous considérons plus attentivement ce point de l'histoire de
la science, nous constatons que tel ne fut pas le cas. Lorsque Mommsen
publia en 1845 son article « Oskische Studien[6] » il était encore très loin
d'utiliser la linguistique comme un instrument nécessaire dans l'interprétation des textes. En abordant ces inscriptions, suite au labour préalable
du déchifrement de l'écriture accompli par l'orientaliste Lipse, Mommsen

---

[2]   Le lecteur trouvera un chapitre très clair et intéressant intitulé *Comparative
Linguistics* dans *A History of Classical Scholarship* (Cambridge, 1908-1921) de J.E. SANDYS,
III p. 205 ss.

[3]   W. SCHULZE, *Kleine Schriften*, Göttingen, 1933, p. 8.

[4]   Je profiterai de cette occasion pour attirer l'attention sur la découverte dans
la Bibliothèque de Salamanque d'une première édition, inconnue auparavant de cette
œuvre : voir la thèse doctorale de J. Liano Pacheco parue en 1971. Voir maintenant *Minerve* (1562) par F. Sanchez de las BROZAS, intr. et éd. par Eduardo del Estal, Salamanque, 1975.

[5]   J. WACKERNAGEL, *Vorlesungen über Syntax*, Bâle, 1928, I, p. 29.

[6]   Zeitschrift für geschichtliche Rechtswissenschaft XIII. Ce n'est pas inclus dans
Gesammelte Schriften, 8 volumes, Berlin, 1905-1913.

déclarait que pour lui « tractare et retractare était une nécessité » et qu'il considérait son travail comme une anticipation : « Nous croirons être récompensés de nos efforts, écrivait-il[7], si, dans un temps pas trop éloigné, la linguistique comparée entreprend cette recherche et reconnaît que l'histoire lui a ouvert la porte. Pour nous la linguistique comparée n'est qu'un moyen, et notre problème n'est pas de déterminer la place que l'osque occupe dans le système des langues, mais bien celle des Osques en Italie ».

Par cet emploi fait en passant de l'expression « système des langues » Mommsen exprimait les limites de la science linguistique telle que la voyaient les philologues et ceux que l'on appelait toujours antiquaires à l'époque.

Mommsen s'opposait en outre à Pott au sujet de l'ombrien qui, comme l'osque, était pour lui une langue non sanskrite et mêlée d'une façon inorganique à des éléments latins[8], et ainsi il osait avant les comparatistes interpréter les monuments linguistiques de l'osque en s'appuyant sur les disciplines traditionnelles qui se trouvaient à cette époque en plein développement : la science hitorique, celle du droit, l'archéologie et la philologie des antiquités.

F. Ritschl est considéré avec raison comme le premier à avoir abordé les textes latins avec les méthodes de la linguistique comparée. Cependant, si nous examinons de plus près son œuvre, nous trouvons que Ritschl se rattache à la pure tradition philologique. L'un de ses disciples[9] nous informe que, lorsqu'il travaillait sur le palimpseste milanais de Plaute, il reçut des incitations linguistiques, sans s'y attendre bien sûr, du poète Manzoni, qui surprit le jeune érudit non seulement par sa familiarité avec Plaute, mais par la clarté de ses idées des rapports entre le latin archaïque et les langues romanes.

Ritschl restait fidèle à la tradition philologique, mais déjà pendant son voyage en Italie il eut une idée approximative de la nouvelle science. À la Bibliothèque Vaticane il put admirer le polyglottisme du fameux Mazzofanti, mais aussi se plaindre qu'une curiosité infatigable et une mémoire si fabuleuse n'apportassent rien à la science. « Quelle contribution cet homme pourrait faire à la grammaire comparée ! » s'exclama Ritschl[10], « mais il n'en a pas la moindre idée ! »

Néanmoins Ritschl n'avait pas opté pour une combinaison de la linguistique et de la philologie. « Tu ne rumineras pas de racines sanskrites ni ne dédaigneras ma manne » — disait l'un des dix commandements pour les philoloques classiques que Ritschl et Lehrs promulguèrent humoristiquement[11].

----

[7]   P. 5 du tirage à part de l'article.
[8]   *Ibid.*, p. 6.
[9]   O. RIBBECK, *F.W. Ritschl, Ein Beitrag zur Geschichte der Philologie*, Leipzig 1879-1881, I, p. 179 s.
[10]   *Ibid.*, I, p. 196.
[11]   *Ibid.*, II, p. 449 s.

Nées du même esprit historico-critique, la philologie et la linguistique progressèrent l'une à côté de l'autre. Il va sans dire que la linguistique historique comparée put être spécialement utile là où il fallait expliquer une évolution préhistorique. Cependant, même dans son fameux commentaire de Lucrèce, un Lachmann considérait purement la tradition interne du latin, sans chercher de correspondances dans d'autres langues indo-
européennes. Les études linguistiques ne furent possibles que lorsque la
paléographie et l'épigraphie mirent à notre disposition des textes authentiques. Les travaux de Ritschl et de son école sur Plaute et plus tard sur
les Glossaires, et ceux de Lachmann sur les manuscrits lucréciens les plus
anciens, mirent à la disposition des linguistes les premiers textes dignes de
crédit. Ainsi, grâce seulement à des travaux épigraphiques, Ritschl put parler en 1861-1862 de dialectes latins et analyser par exemple le latin de
Préneste. À ce sujet il ne faut pas oublier que seule l'invention de la pho-
tographie et son application à des manuscrits et à des inscriptions rendit
possible un travail critique sous un aspect linguistique.

La sécurité à laquelle on était parvenu en linguistique historique
moyennant ce travail critique a fait croire aux gens de ma génération,
à une collaboration indubitable et féconde entre la philologie et la linguistique. Cependant, il est évident à la lumière de l'histoire de la science,
que les rapports entre ces deux disciplines furent souvent dans le passé
imprégnés d'une défiance réciproque, une défiance très semblable à celle
qui existe encore entre la philologie traditionnelle et les courants récents
de la linguistique. D'autre part, il y avait assez de gens pressés qui d'une
façon prématurée et dépourvue de sens critique appliquaient les méthodes de la grammaire historique comparée aux langues classiques. Ainsi W.
Corssen, l'un des premiers hommes à travailler d'une manière critique en
linguistique historique du latin, écrivait que «à côté de bons et abondants
fruits, bien des mauvaises herbes ont poussé aussi dans ce champ[12].»
Corssen devait se plaindre des comparatistes présomptueux qui auraient
voulu réduire tous les suffixes latins à un couple de suffixes sanskrits
lorsqu'ils eurent découvert par exemple «le suffixe sanskrit vaut en
plusieurs formations latines, comme uer-utum, sang-uen, it-in-eris, sobr-in-
us» et dans une série de formations très diverses, ce qui est simplement
absurde[13] La grammaire comparée n'avait pas gagné en un jour cette as-
surance qui nous soulevait d'admiration dans nos jours estudiantins.

Cette brève revue des anciens rapports entre la philologie et la
linguistique nous permet de conclure que l'interprétation linguistique de
vieux textes demande de l'expérience et des aptitudes critiques dans les
deux disciplines.

À première vue il semble même que la linguistique a contribué peu ou
rien au progrès de la philologie. Mais en vérité, les deux sciences ne s'é-
taient pas bornées à se développer avec une exigence critique de plus en
plus grande l'une à côté de l'autre. Les méthodes de la linguistique avec

---

[12] *Krit. Beiträge zur lateinischen Formenlehre*, Leipzig, p. V.
[13] *Ibid.*, p. VI s.

lesquelles on étudia les documents non littéraires aussi bien que les textes eux-mêmes contribuèrent en effet à doter la philologie classique de la forme scientifique que le positivisme exigeait dans la seconde moitié du XIXᵉ siècle.

Les philologues sentaient que la science linguistique pouvaient leur offrir une vision plus profonde des textes. Quand la linguistique historique se fut imposée — et il y a un demi-siècle elle pouvait parfois regarder de haut la philologie traditionnelle — le grand latiniste J. B. Hofmann pouvait écrire: « Si l'on est placé devant l'alternative de « Comparaison ou de philologie? » en général on preférera la méthode linguistique à la méthode purement philologique, d'autant plus que les langues indo-européennes récemment découvertes... constituent la preuve d'un développement achevé il y a longtemps dans la préhistoire, ou déjà en germe[14]. »

La question à laquelle J. B. Hofmann touche ici en passant signifie la découverte d'une nouvelle dimension dans l'interprétation des vieux textes. Dans les documents de n'importe quelle langue nous trouvons « la preuve d'un développement achevé il y a longtemps dans la préhistoire », mais aussi bien l'anticipation de phénomènes linguistiques capables plus tard de subsister pendant des siècles. Dans le texte latin que les anciens commentateurs avaient devant eux il y a deux mille ans, la linguistique historique découvre en quelque sorte une étape intermédiaire entre l'indo-européen et les langues romanes. De la même façon que les auteurs archaïques et les inscriptions les plus anciennes peuvent jeter de la lumière sur le lointain passé indo-européen, les œuvres de la période classique et post-classique peuvent être considérées comme un prélude à la période romane postérieure et moderne.

Les problèmes linguistiques du latin post-classique furent posés de toute façon plus tard que ceux du latin archaïque. La philologie romane ayant été créée sur la base des langues littéraires, des décennies durent passer avant que l'esprit cherchât d'autres objets. Quand les méthodes des néogrammairiens furent pleinement développées, il devint plus facile pour les spécialistes de reconstruire une « forme primitive », laquelle, une fois déduite, était pourvue d'un astérisque, que d'en chercher un témoignage effectif dans le désert des auteurs latins tardifs encore mal édités et corrigés là où on voyait auparavent une faute honteuse. Limitons-nous à un seul exemple: pour l'infinitif de *SUM* on avait déduit correctement une forme ESSERE de l'italien ESSERE, vieux français ESTRE, etc. Et cette forme continue à être donnée avec astérisque, ainsi par exemple dans Meyer-Lübke ou dans Kieckers[15], bien qu'elle soit attestée au moins dans une inscription de Rome du haut Moyen Âge[16].

---

[14] Ainsi encore dans la nouvelle édition de 1965 de la grammaire de Stolz-Schmatz, II, p. 333.

[15] *Hist. Gramm. des Lat. Formenlehre*, p. 318.

[16] E. DIEHL, *Inscriptiones Christiane*, 3865. La date de cette inscription n'est pas antérieure au VIIᵉ siècle.

Seul un linguiste qui fut toujours un critique des jeunes grammairiens, Hugo Schuchardt, se rebella avec un sens aigu de la réalité linguistique contre l'idée d'une régularité schématique du latin vulgaire. Dans sa thèse doctorale de 1864, parue peu après amplifiée en trois volumes sous le titre de *Der Vokalismus des Vulgärlateins,* il devança la correction de la théorie de l'uniformité du latin vulgaire reconstruit par les néogrammairiens. Il appuya sa démonstration sur un ensemble de matériaux qui par sa richesse excite l'admiration, surtout lorsqu'on pense qu'à cette époque n'étaient disponibles ni le CIL, ni l'édition de Goetz des Glossaria Latina, ni les éditions critiques de presque aucun auteur latin tardif. Schuchardt entreprit alors avec audace de chercher des indices d'évolution romane dans les sources de l'antiquité et de la transition au Moyen Âge. Malheureusement cet ouvrage, de parution précoce, resta presque isolé.

En rapport avec le latin tardif nous devons rappeler ici un théologien: Hermann Rönsch, précurseur de l'étude linguistique moderne du latin chrétien. Dans son livre *Itala und Vulgata* (1868) et dans ses *Semasiologische Beiträge zum lateinischen Wörterbuch* (1887-1889) il signala de nouveaux sentiers. Avec un sens aigu de la vie des mots il poursuivait l'histoire de vocables latins jusqu'aux langues modernes, dont les éléments latins tardifs, aussi bien que les éléments scolastiques médiévaux sont d'habitude inconnus.

L'intérêt pour la langue latine tardive ne s'éveilla que peu à peu. La linguistique historique préféra toujours s'occuper de la préhistoire et des origines des langues, plutôt que de leur développement ultérieur. En outre, le vulgarisme des textes tardifs de la latinité était beaucoup moins attrayant que les particularités de la langue d'un Plaute ou d'un Lucrèce. Avant que les philologues ne se fussent consacrés aux difficiles problèmes d'édition des textes latins tardifs, les jeunes grammairiens avec leur latin vulgaire schématique avaient pourvu les romanistes d'une explication simplifiée de la formation des langues romanes. Comme nous l'avons déjà indiqué, malgré le livre de Schuchardt, jusqu'au moment où on commença à tirer des leçons des atlas linguistiques, le latin vulgaire continua à être expliqué par la voie «linguistique», c'est-à-dire par une reconstruction comparative. Beaucoup plus tard, on entreprit la tâche infinie de chercher les faits attestés dans les textes d'auteurs, dans les inscriptions et autres documents.

Un texte comme la *Peregrinatio ad loca sancta* fut découvert et publié en 1887. Si nous nous imaginons ce que les érudits du XVIIe ou XVIIIe siècle auraient fait avec le texte de cette œuvre lors de son édition, et si le manuscrit original s'était perdu, nous pouvons comprendre la défiance avec laquelle nous devrions affronter le texte mal corrigé.

Le préjugé humaniste de la pureté et de la correction du latin a subsisté plus longtemps que l'on ne croit. Il y a quelques décennies il était encore nécessaire de justifier la fidélité à la tradition manuscrite du latin «barbare». Je voudrais citer quelques exemples que le latiniste suédois

Dag Norberg[17] donna il y a plus de vingt-cinq ans: «Cette lecture (dans le texte de Casiodore), que l'on trouve le plus souvent et dans les meilleurs manuscrits, procède sans doute de l'archétype. Mais l'accusatif AR-BOREM éveilla la méfiance des copistes médiévaux. C'est à cause de cela qu'il fut corrigé dans quelques manuscrits moins bons. Un copiste fit une conjecture qui était bonne paléographiquement... et Mommsen la trouva tellement excellente qu'il l'accepta dans son texte. Mais une conjonction explicative n'est pas nécessaire. Et l'accusatif *ARBOREM*... est un exemple typique de l'ATTRACTIO INUERSA...».

«Souter dans son édition du Pseudo-Augustin normalise... avec une transposition un usage intéressant et surprenant d'accusatif après HOC EST et ID EST, qui demanderait une recherche plus attentive. La correction de Souter est complètement injustifiée, comme le démontrent les passages suivants...».

Traube, «qui n'avait absolument pas compris la construction, a retouché la dernière ligne... Et une telle retouche du texte transmis est en outre trop osée pour convaincre personne».

Ce fut précisément l'étude du latin tardif qui éveilla la sensibilité pour les réalités du latin classique: «De même la langue sélecte de la période classique — écrit un autre représentant de l'école suédoise, J. Svennung[18] — était loin de posséder une telle régularité mécanique: ceux qui la parlaient étaient des hommes eux aussi, et précisément de vifs méridionaux; c'est pourquoi souvent c'est du côté psychologique plutôt que logique qu'il faut chercher l'explication des anomalies.»

C'est ainsi que surgit et s'étendit peu à peu le courant de l'intérêt pour le latin non classique: Wölfflin publia son indispensable *Archiv für lateinische Lexikographie und Grammatik* et fonda le *Thesaurus,* W. Heraeus consacra de valables ouvrages aux apparentes bagatelles, qui permirent par exemple d'expliquer plusieurs obscurités dans Pétrone; des latinistes comme M. Niedermann expliquaient les gloses; en outre on commença l'étude des auteurs tardifs avec des monographies au début lourdes et un peu mécaniques, comme celle de M. Bonnet sur Grégoire de Tours; et enfin les différences régionales du latin, dont la discussion avait été amorcée par Sittl, devenaient avec le livre de F.G. Mohl[19] un problème à résoudre pour les romanistes[20].

Le travail historique et linguistique sur les textes latins n'est pas encore achevé. Malgré l'activité de plusieurs générations nous manquons

---

[17] *Syntaktische Forschungen auf dem Gebiete des Spätlateins und des frühen Mittelalters,* Uppsala Universitets Arsskrift, 1943, p. 72, 97, 101, etc.

[18] *Untersuchungen zu Palladius und zur lateinischen Fach- und Volks-sprache,* Uppsala 1936, p. 20, n. 1.

[19] *Études sur le lexique du latin vulgaire,* Paris, 1900.

[20] K.R. VON ETTMAYER, *Vulgärlatein, dans Geschichte der indogermanischen Sprachwissenschaft,* II. I, Strassbourg 1916, p. 241 et 244.

d'analyses profondes même de la langue de Virgile et d'Horace. Ainsi Bonfante put signaler brillamment les éléments vulgaires dans Horace[21].

Si nous voulons résumer les faits et nous demander qu'est-ce que la linguistique a apporté à l'interprétation des poètes et des prosateurs latins, il est évident que l'analyse historique a approfondi sur bien des aspects la compréhension des textes. Si l'on compare un commentaire moderne de l'*Énéide,* par exemple, avec celui de Heyne, on reconnaît tout de suite combien profonde a été l'influence des comparatistes. Si l'on veut ignorer l'œuvre des indo-européistes comme Delbrück ou Wackernagel, on se retrouve avec la seule et maigre doctrine syntaxique, trop liée à la logique de la tradition ancienne.

La linguistique historique et comparative découvrit dans la poésie homérique des formules qui se trouvent enracinées dans le monde des tablettes mycéniennes et qui à cause de leur concordance avec des formules des hymnes védiques pourraient être attribuées à une langue poétique indo-européenne antérieure à la fragmentation des dialectes. Dans le cas de la langue latine l'impression de toucher aux temps aussi primitifs est rare. Par contre, dans l'interprétation linguistique d'auteurs latins, on touche, plus souvent qu'on ne le pense, à la survivance romane du latin. Ainsi le poète Manzoni se trouvait sur le bon chemin lorsqu'il parlait avec le jeune philologue Ritschl de la « saveur » déjà romane de Plaute.

Pour cette raison, nous pouvons trouver dans les survivances romanes la solution de certains problèmes que les classiques nous posent, comme j'ai tâché de le démontrer à propos de quelques exemples de Caton, de Lucilius et d'Horace[22]. La survivance millénaire dans le langage ne devint claire que lorsqu'on eut commencé à travailler historiquement. Aujourd'hui on cherche avec des méthodes linguistiques nouvelles, quoique d'une façon encore assez grossière, à mesurer la vitesse du changement linguistique. C'est ainsi que la relative lenteur de l'évolution linguistique a été démontrée. Ainsi nous trouvons dans cette évolution séculaire de la langue des exemples « d'états latents » aux différents plans de la langue.

La linguistique actuelle s'est séparée complètement dans notre culture de la philologie classique. La connaissance des langues classiques n'est plus même un instrument nécessaire pour les linguistes. Comme conséquence ultérieure de l'universalité de la linguistique, la grammaire latine a cessé, avec raison, d'être la grammaire même, à laquelle on voulait ajuster toute analyse d'une langue, même des plus exotiques.

Nous ne devons pas craindre la linguistique moderne: toute nouvelle théorie représente un gain, si nous voulons être optimistes, et il est évi-

---

[21] *Los elementos populares en la lengua de Horacio,* dans *Emerita,* IV, p. 86 ss., 209 ss., V, p. 17 ss.

[22] Dans la conférence *Latín de Hispania, Aspectos léxicos de la romanización,* Madrid, Real Academia Española, 1968, inclut plus tard dans mon livre *Sprachen und Inschriften,* Amsterdam, 1973.

dent que la linguistique actuelle doit trouver des réponses à des questions qui étaient inimaginables il y a quelques décennies. Nous ne devons pas craindre non plus la linguistique qui utilise des machines, puisque les linguistes savent, et les philologues le savent aussi, que nous pouvons retirer un avantage des ordinateurs.

Mais pour la linguistique actuelle le fameux slogan de la linguistique historique, qui voulait bâtir « sur le ciment ferme de la philologie », ne vaut plus. Cependant, malgré l'indépendance mutuelle des deux disciplines, la linguistique actuelle peut offrir en plusieurs aspects des incitations à la philologie classique, et la philologie classique à son tour peut montrer à la linguistique moderne comment ordonner et traiter une quantité gigantesque de matériaux.

Pour la première fois en linguistique moderne la grammaire transformationnelle ou générative n'est plus intéressée à un *corpus* préexistant, mais elle étudie le domaine de la langue comme une capacité d'engendrer ou de produire des propositions nouvelles. Bien sûr cela signifie une séparation définitive de la linguistique par rapport à celle qui a été sa mère, la philologie. Cependant, l'application déjà réalisée des méthodes transformationnelles à certains points de la grammaire historique nous permet de reconnaître l'utilité du contact continu entre la philologie et la linguistique, contact qui aujourd'hui est plus évident que jamais.

Antonio TOVAR,
Universités de Madrid.
et de Tübingen.

Une approche stylistique
des textes littéraires

Des différentes lectures que la critique moderne, dans la diversité de ses méthodes, puisse proposer du texte littéraire la plus contestée est peut-être aujourd'hui la lecture stylistique. Après le constat de décès, quelque peu hâtif, dressé contre la stylistique par Michel Arrivé en 1969[1], le terme lui-même devenait pour beaucoup suspect, déprécié, in-signifiant[2]. S'avouer ou se vouloir stylisticien relevait de plus en plus du défi ou de la naïveté. Ce risque, fort heureusement, quelques-uns, insensibles aux modes, ont continué de l'assumer[3]. Pour eux cette stylistique que l'on enterre si vite ne demande qu'à vivre et à s'épanouir. Mais, science encore jeune, elle connaît toutes les difficultés des disciplines naissantes: imprécision de son objet[4], incertitude de ses méthodes[5], multiplicité des procédures.

Plutôt que de faire ici après d'autres[6] l'historique ou l'inventaire de ces démarches, j'exposerai ma pratique personnelle, ses principes, ses postulats, le champ d'investigation retenu, la technique d'analyse utilisée, — deux rapides illustrations finales (une page de Tite-Live, un morceau de l'*Énéide*) devant permettre à chacun de mieux se représenter la nature et la forme de notre approche des textes anciens.

* * *

---

[1] « Première constatation: la stylistique semble à peu près morte. » Cet éclat célèbre, dans le numéro de *Langue française* (3, septembre 1969, p. 3) consacré à la stylistique, procédait, croyons-nous, d'un parti pris d'école beaucoup plus que d'une analyse objective de la situation réelle.

[2] À la « stylistique » se substituerait donc « la poétique » (cf. H. MESCHONNIC).

[3] On pense en particulier à Conrad Bureau dont le récent ouvrage *Linguistique fonctionnelle et stylistique objective,* Paris (PUF, Le linguiste, 16), 1976 se réclame explicitement de la stylistique. Même revendication chez notre collègue Gilles MATHIS dans le titre de la thèse d'État, *Analyse stylistique du «Paradis perdu» de John Milton. L'univers poétique: échos et correspondances*, qu'il vient de soutenir (juin 1979) à l'Université de Provence (Aix-Marseille I).

[4] Le livre de P. GUIRAUD et de P. KUENTZ, *La stylistique,* Paris, 1970 donne quelque idée de la pluralité des conceptions et des approches.

[5] On se rappelle la brillante ouverture du *Traité de stylistique latine* (Paris, 1946) de J. MAROUZEAU: « La stylistique est une science mal définie qui porte un nom mal fait. »

[6] Outre l'ouvrage cité dans la note 4, on connaît, pour le domaine propre des langues anciennes, le travail de W. AX, *Sprachstil in der lateinischen Philologie*, Hildesheim — New York, 1976, qui propose un essai de classement systématique des différentes orientations de la recherche stylistique en latin.

L'ampleur de la tâche à laquelle, dans l'état actuel de la recherche, se trouve confronté tout stylisticien, nous faisait un devoir, si nous voulions aboutir à quelques résultats utiles, de nous plier à une double règle :

1° nous fixer des objectifs limités et simples ;
2° nous placer dans les conditions d'analyse les plus favorables possibles.

Il nous apparaissait, par exemple, qu'en dépit de l'intérêt évident des enquêtes lexicales, nous n'avions aucune chance de pouvoir mener de front avec succès une étude approfondie centrée sur le vocabulaire des auteurs, leurs mots-thèmes, leurs images dominantes, etc., et un examen systématique de la structure de leur phrase, des techniques qu'elle met en œuvre et des lois d'agencement qui les ordonnent. D'entrée de jeu un choix s'imposait : il fallait sacrifier l'une des deux directions de recherche. Nos travaux n'auraient de cohérence (tant sont différentes les procédures d'analyse que requièrent ces deux domaines d'enquête) et ne pourraient prétendre à l'efficacité qu'à ce prix. Nous avons donc opté pour la seconde voie, persuadé avec Pierre Guiraud que « si le lexique est la chair du style la structure de la phrase en est l'âme[7] » et qu'ainsi c'est ce qu'il y a peut-être de plus central dans une page, la forme et le rythme même de son déroulement, qu'il nous serait donné d'atteindre au terme de notre quête.

Mais, pour y parvenir, nous ne pouvions procéder sans méthode. Une démarche rigoureuse était nécessaire qui allait dépendre des présupposés de notre recherche. Or ils sont au nombre de trois :

1° Un grand texte doit beaucoup de sa vertu impressive à son organisation formelle, je veux dire aux *structures stylistiques* qui le soustendent.

2° S'agissant de la phrase et de ses techniques, ces structures[8] se réduisent à un petit nombre de formes ou d'*unités* centrales, communes à tous les auteurs[9] et qui s'agencent le plus souvent en un *système* homogène et construit, lié à une forme d'énonciation littéraire (discours, récit, etc.) ou *écriture* donnée.

3° Le système de cette écriture, en règle générale, ne reste pas figé, mais évolue et se transforme avec le temps d'une œuvre à l'autre et parfois chez un même auteur.

En d'autres termes, notre stylistique, d'orientation structurale, associerait étroitement les deux perspectives synchronique et diachronique

---

[7] *La stylistique,* Paris (« Que sais-je ? »), 1967, p. 61.
[8] En revanche, les structures *lexicales,* dans la mesure où elles expriment « l'univers imaginaire » de l'auteur, ont chance d'être beaucoup plus nombreuses et complexes.
[9] Il n'est évidemment pas question de nier la diversité des styles. Celle-ci ne se manifeste pas seulement dans les choix lexicaux de l'auteur, mais dans l'attitude originale de chaque écrivain à l'égard des différentes unités structurales d'une écriture donnée : v. *infra.*

comme inséparables l'une de l'autre et donnerait la priorité aux études d'ensemble, visant à dégager la typologie générale d'une « écriture », sur les monographies particulières, tendant à caractériser le style individuel d'un auteur.

Restait à décider des « écritures » qui seraient retenues. L'exigence, évoquée tout à l'heure, de conditions d'analyse simples et favorables nous commandait de choisir les plus marquées. De même qu'un visage très typé fournit une plus riche matière au talent du caricaturiste, ainsi ce sont les écritures dont les oppositions sont les plus franches et les traits les plus accusés qui offrent les meilleures prises à la description du stylisticien. Trois formes d'énonciation littéraire, qui constituent en même temps trois *écritures de base,* répondent à cette définition. Il s'agit des écritures[10] *narrative, oratoire* et *poétique*[11]. À condition d'opérer sur les modèles les plus « purs[12] » de chacune d'elles, on devait pouvoir tout ensemble reconnaître les unités stylistiques centrales composant le système de ce écritures et percevoir le sens général de leur évolution. Se trouvait ainsi tracé un vaste programme de travail dont la réalisation ferait progresser notablement le commentaire stylistique des œuvres, tout en représentant l'étape préalable nécessaire pour aborder avec fruit aussi bien l'étude des écritures « mixtes » (comme celle de l'épopée où se fondent les quatre écritures narrative, descriptive, oratoire, poétique) que les monographies portant sur un seul écrivain.

Une description synchronique et diachronique satisfaisante des trois écritures de base considérées exige, pour chacune d'elles, le dépouillement de plusieurs auteurs marquants de diverses époques, qui fourniront un *corpus* assez substantiel et étalé dans le temps pour permettre un recensement complet des pièces principales de l'écriture en jeu et une vision précise de leur histoire. Ces unités stylistiques doivent être saisies de trois points de vue différents, qui correspondent aux trois aspects essentiels de leur caractérisation. Il faut définir leur *statut,* rechercher leur(s) *fonction(s),* décrire leurs *modalités* de mise en œuvre.

L'identification correcte d'une « unité stylistique » implique évidemment une reconnaissance préalable de son *statut* propre, entendez de sa

---

[10] *Écriture* n'est pas à prendre comme un synonyme de *genre.* Un discours comme le *Pro Milone* comporte, par exemple, lors de la *narratio,* des développements qui relèvent de l'écriture narrative. Inversement, les historiens intègrent à leur œuvre de nombreux discours, mettant en jeu pour l'essentiel les structures propres de l'écriture oratoire ; etc.

[11] Ce qu'a de plus spécifique l'écriture poétique en vers régulier est mis en pleine lumière par R. CAILLOIS dans *Approches de la poésie,* Paris, 1978: « Après inventaire » dit-il, p. 146 « la métrique et l'image apparaissent les deux éléments constitutifs de la poésie, ceux qui la séparent de la prose. » Il écrit plus loin (p. 169) dans le même sens: « La poésie est à la fois l'art du vers et l'art de l'image. » Or si « l'image » relève du lexique, domaine que nous laissons inexploré, « l'art du vers » — son rythme, son organisation sonore, son harmonie — met, en revanche, en jeu, à tous les niveaux du poème, un ensemble de figures et de constructions qu'il appartient à la stylistique structurale de reconnaître et de décrire.

[12] Entendez un ensemble de textes ou *corpus* dans lequel d'autres formes d'écriture ne se mélangent pas au type étudié.

formule de base ou de ses traits distinctifs minimaux, toujours présents sous la diversité de ses réalisations particulières. La recherche de cette CONSTANTE est une étape capitale de l'analyse stylistique, cette dernière ne pouvant se développer qu'à partir du moment où l'on a appréhendé, isolé, défini le commun dénominateur d'un ensemble de faits perçus jusque là comme hétérogènes. Principe fondamental de notre méthode, cette démarche vient de trouver l'une de ses applications les plus fécondes dans notre lecture des organisateurs sonores de la poésie dactylique[13], qui procède toute d'une définition des récurrences phoniques dominantes (échos syllabiques dessinant une figure rigoureuse aux articulations structurales de l'hexamètre), ramenant à l'unité d'une formule générale, à la fois simple et opératoire, les manifestations multiples du retour des sons en poésie[14].

Mais on ne saurait déterminer le statut d'une unité stylistique sans en établir simultanément la ou les *fonctions*. Seul moyen d'apprécier les ressources d'une structure et son degré d'appropriation au texte où elle intervient, cette recherche permet, en outre, de mesurer l'exacte portée de l'évolution stylistique éventuellement constatée d'un auteur à l'autre. C'est, par exemple, pour avoir reconnu dans la phrase à rallonge et les conjonctions de rupture, deux techniques qui répondent respectivement à une volonté d'assouplissement et de dramatisation que nous avons pu interpréter leur extension continue de César à Tacite comme le fait dominant de l'histoire de l'expression narrative en latin.

Le statut et la fonction d'une unité stylistique représentent deux données CONSTANTES que partagent tous les exemples de l'unité considérée. Il en va tout autrement de ses *modalités* de mise en œuvre, c'est-à-dire du type de réalisation stylistique qui traduit en tel contexte ce qu'a de spécifique l'unité en question. Ce troisième trait constitue, par définition, l'élément VARIABLE de nos structures. En appréhender toutes les composantes conduit à ressaisir dans son individualité propre une unité stylistique que l'on s'était contenté jusqu'ici de faire rentrer, par simple identification de son statut et de sa fonction, dans une catégorie très générale, une grande rubrique de classement (phrase narrative, énoncés de rupture, etc.). Cette description du signalement particulier de l'unité retenue est une phase décisive de l'enquête. Tout, en effet, va se jouer ici, car il n'est pas d'analyse vraiment fine du fait stylistique sans un reconnaissance très précise des conditions d'emploi, des aménagements internes, bref du degré d'élaboration de la structure utilisée. Elle seule permet d'apprécier l'originalité de chaque auteur dans le maniement de cette structure et de faire apparaître de l'un à l'autre des différences interprétables et significatives[15].

---

[13]   Cf. notre communication de février 1979 devant la Société des Études latines: *Une lecture des organisations sonores dans la poésie dactylique*, à paraître dans *R.E.L.*

[14]   Cette définition s'applique également à la poésie française (v. nos travaux sur Mallarmé et Valéry) et a chance d'avoir une portée «universelle».

[15]   Ce qui revient à dégager des éléments objectifs de caractérisation dans la manière d'écrire propre à chaque auteur.

C'est proposer une application nouvelle de la fameuse méthode des «écarts[16]», application désormais réaliste et pertinente, car il ne s'agit plus d'opposer une mise en forme littéraire de la phrase à je ne sais quelle énonciation neutre et non marquée, mais, une unité stylistique centrale d'une écriture donnée ayant été préalablement reconnue et définie dans ses traits distinctifs fondamentaux, de rendre compte des traitements variables dont elle est l'objet, en un même contexte, d'un écrivain à l'autre ou en deux passages différents d'une même œuvre.

C'est aussi la meilleure procédure pour déterminer sans arbitraire le niveau stylistique d'un texte[17]. Les conjonctions de rupture (*cum, ni, donec*), avec leurs nombreuses modalités de préparation dramatique, tour à tour simple, insistante ou prolongée, donnent ici une idée assez exacte de la gamme d'effets si divers que peut produire une même unité stylistique de base, selon la mise en œuvre qu'elle reçoit[18].

Ainsi conduite, l'analyse dégagera sans peine les faits de *convergence stylistique*[19] que présente telle ou telle phrase et qui signalent toujours les grands moments d'un texte.

* * *

Cette conjonction de techniques qui se prêtent mutuellement appui est l'un des aspects les plus remarquables des deux passages très construits de Tite-Live et de Virgile, dont on va brièvement proposer en conclusion une lecture stylistique partielle, mais assez significative pour éclairer la partie théorique de notre exposé.

Le premier texte (Liu. V, 7) évoque un moment crucial du siège de Véies qui constitue lui-même, on le sait, l'un des «deux événements majeurs[20]» du livre V de notre historien. Une sortie nocturne des assiégés a détruit la totalité des ouvrages romains. Ce désastre, loin d'aggraver le conflit qui oppose à Rome Appius Claudius et les tribuns de la plèbe, y met un terme et, rendant possible une manière d'union sacrée, provoque un sursaut patriotique dont la valeur exemplaire appelait un traitement stylistique privilégié:

---

[16]   Pour un rapide historique et un examen critique de cette conception traditionnelle du style comme choix, déviation, surprise, écart, attente déçue, etc., v. en particulier G. MOUNIN, *Clefs pour la linguistique*[1], Paris, 1968, p. 174 et suiv.

[17]   On sera ainsi parfois en mesure de fonder sur des données stylistiques repérables la célèbre distinction des trois styles (*genus sublime, genus mediocre, genus humile*) qu'opérait la rhétorique des anciens.

[18]   Voir à ce sujet J.P. CHAUSSERIE-LAPRÉE, *L'expression narrative chez les historiens latins. Histoire d'un style*, Paris, 1969, p. 575-587; 609-616 et 629-632.

[19]   Sur cette notion essentielle, cf. déjà J. Marouzeau, *o.c.*, p. 339-340.

[20]   Sur cet épisode et sa place dans l'économie générale du livre, v. Jean Bayet, *Tite-Live, Histoire romaine, Livre V* (coll. des Universités de France), «Appendice», p. 94: «La vigueur de sa construction... assure [au livre V] une unité très originale. Cela tient [notamment] à ce que tous les faits se subordonnent aux deux événements majeurs: siège et prise de Véies par les Romains; prise de Rome par les Gaulois et sa libération».

Liu. V, 7:

> Par iam etiam in contionibus erat Appius tribunis plebis, CUM SUBITO, unde minime quis crederet, accepta calamitas apud Veios et superiorem Appium in causa et concordiam ordinum maiorem ardoremque ad obsidendos pertinacius Veios fecit. Nam, cum agger promotus ad urbem uineaeque tantum non iam iniunctae moenibus essent, dum opera interdiu fiunt intentius quam nocte custodiuntur, patefacta repente porta, ingens multitudo facibus maxime armata ignes coniecit, horaeque momento simul aggerem ac uineas, tam longi temporis opus, incendium hausit; multique ibi mortales nequiquam opem ferentes ferro ignique absumpti sunt. Quod ubi Romam est nuntiatum, maestitiam omnibus, senatui curam metumque iniecit ne tum uero sustineri nec in urbe seditio nec in castris posset et tribuni plebis uelut ab se uictae rei publicae insultarent, CUM REPENTE quibus census equester erat, equi publici non erant adsignati, concilio prius inter sese habito, senatum adeunt factaque dicendi potestate, "equis se suis stipendia facturos" promitunt. Quibus cum amplissimis uerbis gratiae ab senatu actae essent famaque ea forum atque urbem peruasisset, SUBITO ad curiam concursus fit plebis: "pedestris ordinis se" aiunt "nunc esse, operamque rei publicae extra ordinem polliceri, seu Veios seu quo alio ducere uelint; si Veios ducti sint" negant "se inde prius quam capta urbe hostium redituros esse". *Tum uero* iam superfundenti se laetitiae uix temperatum est; non enim, sicut equites, dato magistratibus negotio laudari iussi; neque aut in curiam uocati quibus responsum daretur aut limine curiae continebatur senatus; sed pro se quisque ex superiore loco ad multitudinem in comitio stantem uoce manibusque *significare* publicam laetitiam, "beatam urbem Romanam et inuictam et aeternam illa concordia" *dicere, laudare* equites, *laudare* plebem, diem ipsum laudibus *ferre*, "uictam esse" *fateri* "comitatem benignitatemque senatus"; certatim patribus plebique *manare* gaudio lacrimae, DONEC, reuocatis in curiam patribus, senatus consultum factum est "ut tribuni militares contione aduocata peditibus equitibusque gratias agerent, memorem pietatis eorum erga patriam dicerent senatum fore; placere autem omnibus his uoluntariam extra ordinem professis militaim aera procedere[21].

L'épisode doit son unité et sa cohésion aux techniques de rupture et de mise en scène qui en jalonnent les phases principales.

Les éléments auxquels recourt ici Tite-Live: *cum (subito)*, *cum (repente)*, *subito, donec,* assument, dans leur diversité, une fonction commune et répondent à une même intention: suggérer le jaillissement d'une péripétie décisive. Suspendant une situation en cours pour présenter avec vivacité un fait essentiel, ils entretiennent avec le mouvement qu'ils interrompent une relation stylistiquement marquée et forment tous l'articulation dramatique de la phrase[22].

La première rupture du texte (*cum subito*), tout en introduisant la péripétie initiale (*accepta calamitas apud Veios*), donne le thème général du morceau (*concordiam ordinum fecit*) et installe ainsi le lecteur dans cet état d'attente dramatique qui laisse prévoir la survenue d'événements majeurs, signe et gage de la *concordia* reconquise.

C'est aux deux moyens de rupture suivants qu'il reviendra de les mettre en scène. Coup sur coup, en deux phrases successives et selon un

---

[21]   Texte de J. Bayet.

[22]   Soit deux critères d'identification simples: l'un *formel*, l'autre de *contenu*, applicables à tous les textes narratifs et rendant compte des deux traits distinctifs minimaux qui définissent le statut de cette unité stylistique centrale du « récit dramatique » que constituent les moyens de rupture et de mise en scène.

enchaînement parfait[23], un *cum repente,* puis un *subito* vont souligner les deux initiatives parallèles — concurrentes et spontanées — des chevaliers et des plébéiens dont l'émulation va sceller l'unité nationale. Faisant acte de dévouement total à l'État devant le sénat, ils s'offrent, dans un bel assaut de civisme, à servir leur patrie à leurs frais ou comme volontaires jusqu'à la fin de la guerre.

En résultent chez les sénateurs des transports de joie, un débordement de reconnaissance et d'effusions qui se développent dans un long tableau très animé qu'ouvre un *tum uero* de présentation[24]. Une suite de sept mouvements juxtaposés à l'infinitif de narration forme une puissante séquence où tout — l'antéposition du verbe, le recours à l'anaphore, la brièveté des membres, la ponctuation rythmique[25], le relief de l'expression[26] — contribue à créer, aux deux niveaux du rythme (forme) et des sentiments (contenu), en accord avec l'intensité propre de l'infinitif historique, une *tension* et un paroxysme qui appellent, comme un terme souhaité, la *rupture* finale d'un *donec,* point d'aboutissement et conclusion nécessaire de la scène. Elle en marque, en effet, le dénouement attendu : savoir le sénatus-consulte qui, dans l'émotion et l'allégresse générales, décerne des remerciements officiels aux chevaliers et à la plèbe pour leur patriotisme et leur abnégation.

Un ensemble concerté de quatre moyens de rupture et de mise en scène[27] : *cum subito* (péripétie initiale et thème de la *concordia*), *dum repente* (civisme des chevaliers), *subito* (civisme des plébéiens), *donec*[28] (senatus-consulte final) compose, on le voit, pour l'essentiel la continuité dramatique du passage. Cette cohérence, cette unité signalent toujours un moment important du récit. Elle manifeste ici chez Tite-Live une pleine maîtrise des ressources de l'écriture narrative, au service d'une grande rigueur de composition, alliée à un sens aigu des effets de mise en scène les plus suggestifs.

---

[23]　Le sénat n'est pas plus tôt revenu de son premier étonnement que le voilà saisi d'une seconde surprise.

[24]　Sur la valeur de cette unité stylistique et le type d'emploi dont elle est ici l'objet, voir p. 519-523 de ma thèse.

[25]　On désigne sous ce terme tous les invariants lexicaux et syntaxiques dont le retour à intervalles proches institue dans le texte une cadence sensible.

[26]　On remarque notamment la forte valeur affective attachée à *pro se quisque* et *certatim,* deux synonymes très impressifs qui font entendre la même note aux deux bouts de l'évocation, en écho à la tonalité puissante du *tum uero* initial.

[27]　À quoi s'ajoute le signal propre de *tum uero.*

[28]　Les *modalités* de mise en œuvre varient, bien entendu, d'un élément à l'autre. Les différences les plus notables sont celles qui affectent la forme de *préparation dramatique* (sur cette notion, voir *L'expression narrative...,* p. 554) dont bénéficie la conjonction ou l'adverbe en jeu : 1° collaboration d'un *iam* d'ouverture et d'un imparfait de profondeur pour *cum subito* ; 2° évocation d'un abattement général (*maestitiam omnibus iniecit*) préludant, en un contraste calculé, à l'initiative inespérée des chevaliers, pour *cum repente* ; 3° irruption soudaine du *subito* (plus pathétique que *repente* : cf. ma thèse, p. 550), sans autre indice de son intervention possible que le climat d'attente dramatique où nous a plongés la première phrase du texte ; 4° *tension* prolongée annonçant la *rupture* du *donec,* en une relation de complémentarité dont on a étudié plus haut le mécanisme et qui met en place un « finale » très soutenu pour le dernier acte du récit.

Une même unité de conception et une puissance d'évocation comparable distingue l'organisation sonore du passage de l'*Énéide* (*Ae.* V, 136-150) qui va servir de seconde illustration à notre méthode d'analyse stylistique :

Ae. V, 136-150 :

> *CO*nsidunt transtris, intentaque bracchia remis ;
> Intenti exspectant signum, exsultantiaque haurit
> *CO*rda pauor pulsans laudumque arrecta cupido.
> Inde ubi clara dedit sonitum tuba, finibus omnes,
> 140 Haud mora, prosiluere suis ; ferit aethera clamor
> Nauticus, adductis spumant freta uersa lacertis.
> Infindunt pariter sulcos, totumque dehiscit
> *CO*nuolsum remis rostrisque tridentibus aequor.
> Non tam praecipites biiugo certamine campum
> 145 *CO*rripuere ruontque effusi carcere currus,
> Nec sic immissis aurigae undantia lora
> *CO*ncussere iugis pronique in uerbera pendent.
> Tum plausu fremituque uirum studiisque fauentum
> *CO*nsonat omne nemus, uocemque inclusa uo*lutant*
> 150 Litora, pulsati *CO*lles clamore re*sultant*.

Les quinze vers retenus forment en eux-mêmes un morceau complet. Ils décrivent le départ de la course de régates qui ouvre les Jeux destinés à commémorer l'anniversaire de la mort d'Anchise. Le poète ne pouvait manquer de donner l'éclat le plus vif à cette épreuve inaugurale. Le début de la joute en porte témoignage et son intensité ne le cède en rien au caractère dramatique des péripéties ultérieures.

Les forces des rameurs, concentrées et tendues, dans l'attente du signal (intenta*que*... / Intenti *exspectant signum*), se sont soudain libérées dans un déchaînement immédiat de toute leur puissance. Au milieu des gerbes d'écume, les navires s'élancent : le ciel, le rivage, les bois, les collines, tout s'emplit des cris confondus de ceux qui luttent et de ceux qui les soutiennent. Tel est notre passage, tout traversé du fracas des vagues remuées (*freta uersa*), des spasmes de la mer qui s'ouvre (*totumque dehiscit* / *Conuolsum... aequor*) et du retentissement universel d'une nature qu'ébranle l'écho répercuté des clameurs troyennes (*ferit aethera clamor*... / *Tum plausu fremituque uirum*... / *Consonat omne nemus, uocemque... uolutant* / *Litora, pulsati colles clamore resultant*).

Aucune évocation n'était plus propre à la mise en place d'une organisation phonique ambitieuse et prolongée, qui, sous-tendant l'ensemble de ces quinze vers, y fît régner le leit-motiv musical d'un thème sonore dominant, expression symbolique puissamment suggestive de tout ce que le texte comporte d'efforts cadencés, de cris, d'éclats, de résonances et de frémissements, s'appelant et s'amplifiant sans fin.

Ce thème (*ko*), donné dès l'attaque du mot initial du premier vers (*CO*nsidunt), s'associe tout d'abord à un complexe phonique *int* / *ind* (*Int*enti... / *Ind*e)[29] pour former avec lui, au longum I des quatre premiers

---

[29]   Tout signalait à l'attention le premier terme du couple *int* — *ind*, partenaire du thème *ko*, en particulier son *insistance* (*intente* reprend *intenta*, situé à l'initiale du deuxième

hexamètres du morceau, un agencement croisé *a b a b* qui, en ce repère majeur du vers, se charge d'un éclairage privilégié :

    135 a *CO*nsidunt
         b *Int*enti
         a *CO*rda
    138 b *Ind*e

Après cette brillante ouverture, la réapparition, quelques vers plus bas, du même motif *ko,* toujours à l'attaque du vers et dans une figure identique, combiné cette fois avec la négation *non* / *nec,* est immédiatement perçue par le lecteur :

    143 a *CO*nuolsum
         b *Non*
         a *CO*rripuere
    146 b *Nec*

Elle marque le début d'une série de quatre occurrences comportant la présence, un hexamètre sur deux, à l'initiale absolue du vers, de quatre verbes expressifs pourvus du même préverbe *ko*(n / r) :

    143   *CO*nuolsum
              . . . . .
    145   *CO*rripuere
          . .   . . .
    147   *CO*ncussere
            . . .   .
    149   *CO*nsonat
              . . .

La périodicité du thème dominant *ko,* intervenant sous une forme insistante unique, à la même articulation structurale de l'hexamètre, produit une construction régulière, remarquablement rythmée. Une organisation si parfaite voulait une finale à sa mesure. Il se distribue sur les deux derniers vers (v. 149-150), dont le seul contenu appelait, du reste, pour illustrer dignement le triple jeu d'échos et de résonnances infinies qu'il évoque, une mise en œuvre d'exception. Trois aménagements conjoints la distinguent :

1° Une brisure délibérée de la périodicité précédente par le retour d'une ultime manifestation du thème (150 colles) dans le vers qui suit immédiatement sa quatrième apparition (149 Consonat).

2° Un glissement simultanée de cette cinquième occurrence — qui, de surcroît, n'est plus un préverbe — au début du deuxième hémistiche.

3° Enfin, solidaire de ces deux ruptures et désignant comme elles le terme de tout le mouvement, la manière d'«accord parfait» que réalise, à la fin du morceau, au spondée sixième des deux derniers vers, l'écho des deux verbes (uo)*lutant* / (re)*sultant* où se réentend, en une ultime synthèse, l'admirable puissance rythmique et musicale du texte[30] :

----

hémistiche du vers 136) et sa *portée* (exprimant l'extrême tension physique, morale et nerveuse des rameurs avant le départ, il est un terme essentiel de ce début).

[30] D'autres organisations phoniques de moindre portée auraient mérité une mention,

143	*CO*nuolsum		
145	*CO*rripuere		
147	*CO*ncussere		
149	*CO*nsonat		uo*lutant*
150		*CO*lles	res*ultant*

* * *

Le bref commentaire stylistique de ces deux passages de Tite-Live et de Virgile permet, semble-t-il, d'affirmer que la grille de lecture mise au point pour l'écriture narrative et l'écriture poétique dégage des aspects importants des textes étudiés.

On voit, en outre, que loin de se borner à un inventaire de structures formelles dont on ne rechercherait ni la portée, ni la résonance dans le texte, une approche comme la nôtre s'interroge toujours sur la destination et la valeur esthétique de ces structures. La question fondamentale, à laquelle toute description stylistique est sommée, en dernière analyse, de répondre, reste bien celle de la pertinence et de l'efficace des unités qu'elle appréhende. C'est lorsqu'elle peut établir l'existence d'une convenance parfaite entre telle technique et tel contenu qu'elle atteint son but et remplit pleinement sa mission. Tâche à coup sûr délicate et fort longue que de dresser pareille table de concordances. Mais c'est à ce prix seulement — nos deux passages de Tite-Live et de Virgile le démontrent — qu'on se donnera les moyens d'apprécier objectivement la qualité d'un texte.

Jean-Pierre CHAUSSERIE-LAPRÉE,
Université de Provence.

---

tels, au dactyle cinquième des deux premiers vers, le couple de figures *structurantes*, phoniquement très proches: «*bracchia* — (exsul)*tantia* (que)» (...ak k. a — ta. t. a), préludant à la correspondance finale «(uo)*lutant* — (re)*sultant*»; ou encore, au vers 145, la mise en rapport insistante, aux longum I et V, repères fondamentaux de l'hexamètre, de «*cor*ripuere» et «*car*cere» que prolonge l'agencement interne très élaboré de la clausule «*carcerecu*rrus» (k.r k. r. k.r); sans parler de la figure *rythmique* «(in)*clu*sa uo*lu*tant» de la clausule du vers 149; etc. On s'en est délibérément tenu à l'essentiel. Mais une étude plus complète devrait aussi dégager les nombreux faits de convergence stylistique que contient le texte. Le plus remarquable est ici la rencontre d'une organisation phonique (la périodicité du leit-motiv *ko*) et d'une technique de mise en relief (la présence des trois verbes «*co*rripuere, *co*ncussere, *co*nsonant» en tête de vers).

Quant aux critères d'identification de l'unité stylistique centrale que forment les récurrences phoniques dominantes, on voit qu'ils sont de deux types: l'un *phonique* (il faut qu'une «séquence de rappel» reproduise au moins partiellement, par couple ou groupe de phonèmes, la structure d'une syllabe antérieure ou «séquence initiale»), l'autre *rythmique* et *architectural* (séquence initiale et séquence de rappel doivent intervenir à une crête du schéma métrique et s'intégrer à une figure construite).

The Music of the Sphinx

The Problem of Language in Oedipus Tyrannus

No play is more about language than the *Oedipus Tyrannus*. An expert at decoding difficult messages, the hero cannot decode the meaning of his own name. Human communication here parallels the communication by ritual and oracle between man and God. Continually breaking down, this communication either ceases prematurely because of fears or knowledge that cannot be spoken or runs to excess because of passion and anger. Apollo's oracles from above and the Sphinx's riddle from below provide models for human discourse, but both also short-circuit the significative function of language. The oracles are either too terrifyingly specific to be understood, or else conceal beneath apparent generality their specific purport for Oedipus' life ("Drive out the pollution nurtured in the land," 97). The riddle, with its plural meanings for each signifier, undermines the denotative and differentiating function of language. It misuses, or perhaps overuses, language, by exploiting its ambiguity rather than its precision. It thereby projects a world whose meaning corresponds to the shifting, uncertain, "enigmatic" quality of language rather than to the potential clarity, definiteness, intelligibility of language.

The play correlates personal identity, language, and the world order as multiple reflections of the hero's failure to find the mediating, ordering terms of civilized life. The oracle veers between images of the world-order as chaotic and as deterministic; the riddle-prophecies veer between the undifferentiated and the over-specific; and Oedipus, guided by both oracle and riddle, moves back to the origins of his name.

The very name of the hero links together the search for personal identity and the exploration of the limits of language as a means of interpreting the meaning or meaninglessness of life in a mysterious world. Name and oracle are analogous aspects of the ambiguities of language in its imperfect reflection of reality. In this play the archaeology of knowledge, in Foucault's sense, and the archaeology of the self coincide. Oedipus' search for himself and his origins is also a search for the origin and meaning of his name.

The play begins with Oedipus consulting the oracle on behalf of the whole city. As the action progresses, it takes us back to his lonely and private consultation of the oracle, on his own behalf, after the insult about his legitimate birth — and thereffore about his name — at Corinth. The solitary consultation of the now exiled Oedipus (794-6; cf. 787) contrasts also with the escorted visit of Laius. Soon the solitariness of that journey to Delphi becomes the crucial point in Oedipus' relation to his present city: if "one lone-girt man" met Laius in that fatal encounter at the triple roads leading from Delphi to Thebes and Corinth, Oedipus is the murderer (846-7). The prophecies to both Laius and Oedipus lead also to the wild realm outside the city: Laius exposes a son on a wild mountainside (711ff.); Oedipus leaves the shelter of Corinth for the place where the two oracles join, the desolate crossroads (787ff.).

There are three oracles in the play: one to Thebes in the present, one to Oedipus in the past, and one to Laius in the still remoter past. They come together, ironically, at the point when Jocasta, seeking to disprove the power of oracles (709-10, 723-5), inadvertently gives Oedipus the clue which proves their accuracy. Her crucial sentence about the triple roads begins, "Robbers killed him, as is the rumor ..." (175-6). But that last clause, "as is the rumor," ὥσπερ γ' ἡ φάτις, can also mean, "as (says) the oracle," for the word *phatis* means not only "rumor," but also "prophecy," "oracle," and in fact has that latter meaning in four of its five other occurrences in the play (151, 310, 323, 1440; cf. 495). Even in asserting the falsehood of the oracle, she affirms its strange truth. The "robbers" at the crossroad did indeed act in accordance with the "oracle/rumor." Public "rumor" is simultaneously one with the private "oracle" of Laius' house. Similarly the oracles that appear in the context of public cult (cf. 21, 151ff., 897ff.) show the leader of the *polis* as a lonely bull on the mountain, wandering apart in the "savage woodland" pursued by "every man" of the city (463-82).

This ode, the first stasimon, focusses a number of the central paradoxes raised by the oracles. We hear it with Teiresias' warning about his "intelligence in the mantic art" ringing in our ears (461-2). The brilliance of divine speech marked by the opening words of both strophe and antistrophe (463, 473-5) contrasts with the "unspeakable" things committed by the murderer (ἄρρητ' ἀρρήτων τελέσαντα, 465). The animal imagery and the wild setting contrast both with the human world and with the revered sanctuary: "rock" (464, 478) refers both to the sacred place and its antithesis, the savage mountain. The loneliness of the bull/murderer is literally "widowhood" (*chereuon*, 479), whereas it is just the opposite, the too close marriage of Oedipus, the *gamos agamos*, "marriage no-marriage" (1214), which makes the king his bestial opposite, the hunted animal in the savage woodland, wandering with "wretched foot" (479). The metaphor of the ode makes him both the king responsible for the oracles and the guilty criminal exposed by oracles, both a suppliant at Apollo's shrine (through his proxy, Creon) and a wanderer in the wild forest outside that shrine, both inside the city and on the mountain. Parnassus itself faces both ways. It is both a snowy mountain (473), a suggestion of desolation and remoteness, and the "mid-navel of the earth," a center of human concourse and a meeting place between man and God. Hence on the spatial axis of the ploy it occupies the place between Olympus and Cithaeron, the remote mountain of the eternal gods and the mountain which symbolizes the reduction of human life to bestial chaos.

In Oedipus' search Apollo's oracles and the Sphinx' riddles both contrast and converge. The Sphinx exalts, Apollo abases him. The victory over the Sphinx at Thebes is achieved in a lonely encounter analogous to the first visit to Delphi. This victory makes Oedipus king, but also wins him the marriage that puts him outside the human order. In his quarrel with Teiresias Oedipus contrasts his solution to the riddle with the prophetic art (techne: 390-8; cf. 380). But these prophecies of Teiresias are "riddling," ainikta (439; cf. ainigma, 393), just as the Sphinx is oracular (1200). The Sphinx propounded a riddle which required "prophecy" (manteia, 394; cf. 462). Both need "loosing" (cf. 392; also 306, 407). According to a tradition preserved in a scholion to Euripides' Phoenissae (1760), "the Sphinx was not a beast (therion), but a propounder of oracles (chresmologos) who told the Thebans prophecies that were hard to understand, and she destroyed many of them who misinterpreted the oracles." Riddle and oracle come increasingly to look like mirror-images of one another. Both, when properly "solved" ("loosed"), spell Oedipus' doom.

Oracle and Sphinx stand at the fringes of the human world, the point where divine and human and divine and bestial intersect. Whereas the oracles point upward to a divine, albeit mysterious order, the Sphinx points downward to what is dark, monstrous, subhuman. The oracles mediate between God and man; the Sphinx between man and beast. Half-bestial in form, she is described as "savage" and "raw-eating." She devours her victims and rends her human prey with talons or "savage jaws." She violates the linguistic code in her riddle, biological order in her shape, kin ties in her incestuous parentage (Hesiod, Theogony, 326ff.), the relation between city and wild in her affliction of the city from her vantage-point on the "Sphinx Mountain" (Phikeion Oros) outside or, in other versions, her position on a pillar in the heart of the city[1]. Like Oedipus, her mixed form (lion, bird, woman) involves her in ambiguous locomotion. When the riddle is solved, she plunges from a high place to her death.[2] When Oedipus' riddle is solved, he plunges from the highest to the lowest place in the city (876-9). In her connections with mountains[3], she belongs to the savage mountain world of Oedipus' exposure on Cithaeron. Yet her challenge to man is the confusion of human forms with their bestial opposites. This half-beast is a singer of oracles (1200), while the Olympian Apollo leaps like a beast. Her riddle turns man's intelligence against himself, and the solver of her riddle is the example par excellence of profound human ignorance.

As the Sphinx's riddle rests on the equation of two, three, and four, so the killing of Laius involves the coincidence of one and three at the

---

[1] See Carl ROBERT, Die griechische Heldensage, in PRELLER-ROBERT, Griechische Mythologie, II.3, ed. 4 (Berlin, 1921), pp. 892-3; see also Carl ROBERT, Oedipus (Berlin, 1915), I.517ff. and for visual representations, 48-58.

[2] See APOLLODORUS, Bibl. 3.5.8.7; A. LESKY, s.v. "Sphinx," RE, III A 2 (1929), 1723.

[3] E.g. EURIP., Phoen, 806, οὔρειον τέρας, Further references in LESKY (preceding note), 1703, 1709, 1715; see also J. C. KAMERBEEK, The Plays of Sophocles, IV, The Oedipus Tyrannus (Leiden, 1967), 4.

"triple roads," a "double goad" (*dipla kentra*, 809), and a mysterious
"equality" of "one and many" (845). This evocation of the Sphinx's
riddle, however, marks not the victory of human intelligence, but the
bestiality released at the no-man's land of the crossroads (798-813).
Oedipus now faces a numerical problem which his intelligence can solve
only to his cost.

Like Heracles in the *Trachiniae*, Oedipus protects civilized order by
defeating a bestial monster without overcoming the inward dimensions of
that monstrosity. Heracles' victory over Nessus to protect marriage ultimately reflects a defeat by his own bestial lust; Odeipus' victory of intelligence over the Sphinx plays into his defeat by his ignorance. As Heracles
is vanquished by that aspect of his victory which is still incomplete, so
Oedipus is undone by that aspect of the riddle which he has failed to
answer. Confrontation with that personal riddle calls forth the "savagery"
of his anger (344, 364) and throws him back into that confusion of god
and beast, mind and physical violence which the Sphinx herself embodies.

The Sphinx inverts the mediation between god and man effected
by oracles, especially in the realm of language. To the chorus, as we have
seen, she is a *chresmodos,* singer of oracles (1200); for presumably her
utterances, like the oracle's, are in dactylic hexameter. But she is a
"singer" who is "harsh" (36), "of tricky song" (130), a "rhapsode-dog"
(391), "hook-taloned maiden singer of riddling oracles" (1199-200)[4].
Euripides calls her songs "most unmusic" (*Phoen.* 807) and elsewhere
dwells on her "musical" aspect. In a fragment of a lost play he describes
the riddle as a horrible shrieking whistle[5]. Her song is just the reverse
of a civilized art: it enables her to prey upon and destroy a human community. And yet this perverse combination of savagery and civilization
parallels that in Oedipus himself. He is the man of intelligence and authority governed by a "savage" temper (344) and "savage" infatuation. The
"harmony" he finds in the age of the Shepherd and his own past (*xynaidei,*
1113, literally, "sings harmoniously with") leads to the dissonances of his
bestial "roar" (1265) and fulfils Teiresias' prophecy that Cithaeron will
echo in "harmony" with (*symphonos,* 421) those shouts which mark his
forfeiture of his place in the city, his loss of the right to the forms of
address from its citizens.

Choral lyric could celebrate the "concordant peace," *symphonos
hesychia,* of a coherent universe, as Pindar does in the first *Pythian*
(1-40; 71). But the tragic universe has no place for those harmonies.
Tragedy, unlike Pindar's "lordly lyre," does not celebrate the unity of
city and gods in a secure communal space. Choral song moves from the
divine and unknown to the shelter of the familiar rites at the center of
the community; tragedy moves from the ritual at the city's center outward

---

[4]   Marie DELCOURT, *Oedipe ou la légende du conquérant* (Liège and Paris, 1944),
133-35, compares the Sphinx to the Sirens as "une ogresse musicienne." See also EURIP.,
Phoen., 808ff., 1028f., 1505ff.
[5]   *P. Oxy.*, 2455.4 frag. II Austin.

to the dangerous unknown of mountain and wild. The very juxtaposition of choral song and the iambics of the suffering protagnist in tragedy sets that communal order over against something else. In like manner the myths of tragedy, unlike the myths of choral lyric, are not exemplary of the city's safe relation to its heroes and gods. The chaos or disorder viewed by Pindar of Bacchylides is itself neutralized by the implicit security of the choral setting. But the tragic performance, like the tragic hero, confronts its own negation: "Why should I dance?" this chorus asks (896). The music of this chorus too has its "bestial double," as it were, in the "harmonies" of Oedipus (421, 1113) and the choral celebration of the city's opposite, Cithaeron (1093).

Acclaimed for his victory over the "winged maiden" (508), the bird-like Sphinx, Oedipus is defeated by her Olympian opposite and analogue, the oracles which "hover" about the outcast (481-2) and their interpreter, a reader of bird signs (484, cf. 310, 395, 398). The "bird of good omen," *ornis aisios* (52), which Oedipus brought with him when he defeated the Sphinx, is actually a "bird of ill-omen" (the Greek term has both meanings). Earlier in the prologue, the Theban children are like weak fledglings (16-17); and in the parode the Thebans themselves appear as birds fleeing a vast fire (175-8).

These bird images, all underlining the helplessness of men before the supernatural, counterbalance Oedipus' victory over the bird-maiden, the Sphinx. Jubilant at the apparent failure of the oracles, he dismisses "the birds above" (963-6); but he is mistaken about the father whom he believes "below" the earth (968). His own ambiguous position between high and low, already underlined by the second stasimon, is made even more dangerous by his being "lifted too high" (914). The chorus, in the first stasimon, "flits about with uncertain hope" (486-8); but that spatial disorientation becomes more than just foreboding when Oedipus, after the peripety, does not know where he is and wonders at his voice "flitting about" as if disembodied (1308-10).

All linked with the oracles, Teiresias, the birds, and the Sphinx locate the ambiguous plane of human truth between animality (the Sphinx) and divine prophecy (Apollo and his "flitting" oracles and birds of omen). The Sphinx is a "singer of oracles" (1200), who yet points down to the beasts. Teiresias is a servant of Apollo, but, like Oedipus, is caught up in an all-too-human anger[6]. He comes in obedience to Oedipus' summons, but will not tell. He conceals as much as he reveals. He is both willing and reluctant, both majestic and irritable; both clear and mysterious; both distant and petty. The manner of his revelation cancels out its credibility. He speaks the truth, but in just such a way that it cannot be received. The context and the verbal and emotional textures which clothe his message cancel the objective truth which it contains. In him language is not simply the vehicle of truth; it contains truth in its complex, imper-

---

[6]   For the ambiguity of Teiresias' relation to truth see Karl REINHARDT, *Sophokles*[3] (Frankfurt a. M., 1947) 116ff.

fect, riddling human form (cf. 439). In him, as in all human truth in this play, reality is veiled in illusion. To tear off the veil is to bring destruction as well as "salvation"; but it is the task of the tragic hero to do exactly this, to stand at the point of "fearful hearing" and press on (1169; cf. 1312).

The two men, Oedipus and Teiresias, reinforce one another in their blindness-in-vision. They unwillingly collaborate with the god in demonstrating the imperfection and ambiguity of human truth and human speech. The shifting status of the birds between Sphinx and prophet, beastworld and Delphi, is then a function of the play's larger ambiguities of knowledge and ignorance, the intelligibility or chaos of the universe. Some of these relationships can be expressed in the following diagram:

Lower (Beast)	Oedipus	Upper (God)
pharmakos, pollution	defeated by riddles	solver of riddles
		"godlike man"
Winged maiden = Sphinx		Birds of oracles
Sphinx (beast)	riddles / oracles	Apollo (god)
anger, illusion	Oedipus and Teiresias	clarity, truth
	language as vehicle	
	of confusion / language	
	as instrument	
	of truth	
unintelligibility,	Oedipus proven / Teiresias proven	intelligible
chaos	*sophos* in *sophos* in	discourse;
	matter of birds interpreting	orderly
	(507ff.) bird-signs	universe

Convergence of oracle and Sphinx goes further still Finding his identity as both son and husband, brother and father, Oedipus finds his childhood and his maturity collapsed together — just as they are in the riddle which he solved in the past and will solve again, with a profounder and more personal answer, in the action of the play.

"Human life," to quote Geoffrey Hartman, "like a poetic figure, is an indeterminate middle between overspecified poles always threatening to collapse it."[7] Oedipus' life parallels the struggle of language in the play. He attempts to draw forth differentiating order from his world of fused polarities, to create the space or distance necessary for significance in a world where that space threatens to disappear under the threat of total nothingness, the zero of meaninglessness or the ungraspable plenum of gods who seem to direct and control everything. "The space Sophocles wrested from the gods," Hartman goes on, "was the very space of human life. That space is illusory, or doomed to collapse as the play focuses on the moment of truth which proves the oracle."[8]

Language, therefore, becomes the microcosm for all of man's means of understanding reality. It reflects the failure of the tools of his intel-

---

[7] Geoffrey H. HARTMAN, "Language from the Point of View of Literature," in *Beyond Formalism* (New Haven, 1970), 348.

[8] *Ibid.*, 350.

ligence to grasp and order world and self both, to create and maintain "difference" in the face of chaotic sameness and to assert warm familiarity in the face of coldly alien otherness. Oedipus, solver of verbal riddles, is led to defeat by the multiple riddles of his own being until he can find with his own life a deeper answer to the Sphinx's riddle, and that not with words alone.

Until that point is reached, words spoken with deliberate truth say "too much" to be understood (cf. 768-8, 841). Language is "in vain," *maten*, as characters evade or deny plain words (cf. 365 and 1057); but the dismissed *logos* returns with killing force. "Word" and "deed," *logos* and *ergon*, form paradoxical relationships (cf. 219-20, 452, 517). The confused terminology of kinship carries its grim irony throughout the play (264-5, 928, 1214, 1249f., 1256, 1403ff.). It become a matter of the first importance whether something is "speakable" or "unspeakable" (301, 465, 993, 1289). Oedipus himself, the authoritative speaker of a public proclamation (cf. 93, 236), comes to utter things unspeakable (1289, 1313-6) and falls under a ban of speaking or being spoken to (cf. 1437, 239). His first utterances after the peripety are the inarticulate cries *aiai aiai, pheu pheu* (1307-8). His own voice seems disembodied (1310). Speech is now his only means of recognizing friends or loved ones (cf. 1326, 1472f.), so that his speech too, like his relation to the rituals and the oracles, moves from the public to the personal sphere.

The basic categories of speech become confused. The riddling Sphinx is a "prophet" (1200), and the oracles are "riddles" (439; cf. 390ff.). The decree of the king (*kerygma*, 350, 450) becomes the curse on the one who has spoken it (cf. 744-5). The Corinthian's speech of congratulation (*euepeia*, 932) reveals the "reproach" of Oedipus' name and leads to Jocasta's last word of address, the "only word" of her final address, fixing Oedipus forever in his new condition, "unfortunate" (1071-2).

Logos is here not the glorious achievement celebrated in the *Antigone's* Ode on Man (353), but something "terrible," *deinon*, in an even darker sense than in the *Antigone*. At the point where "speaking" and "hearing" stand at their peak of "terror" (*deinon*, 1169-70), the *logos* seems to take over almost independently of Oedipus. Sophocles uses a dramatic device analogous to the questioning of Lichas by the Messenger in the *Trachiniae* (*Trach.* 402-33)[9]. The chief actor stands on the sidelines, a momentarily silent witness, for the most crucial *logos* of his life; and the solving of his riddle goes on, momentarily, without the direct participation of the great riddle-solver himself.

The deepest irony of Oedipus' relation to language lies, of course, in his name. That primary and fundamental act of communication, the naming of a child in the House, is not a name, a *logos*, but the scars left by his "yoking" on the mountain. His name is a reproach (*oneidos*, 1035-6). Oedipus "called the glorious"[8] will give his name to Cithaeron

---

[9] See REINHARDT (above, note 6), 135.

(1451-2), henceforth linked with him. Nothing could be less justified than this nameless ruler's pride in what he is "called" (8). To learn the truth of his name is, as he says at the end, to pronounce "the names of all the evils that there are" (1284-5).

By learning and accepting the trugh of his name, Oedipus, like the hero of the *Odyssey*, reestablishes the structures of differentiation over the randomness of the animal world. But the recreation of civilization in tragedy is far more precarious than it is in epic. The end of Oedipus' quest is to fracture the "seeming" unity of his life and his language into its bipolar reality. He is not just "king," but also scapegoat; not just husband, but also son; not just *tyrannos,* but also *basileus:* and so on. It is his tragic destiny to replace apparent oneness with binary or ternary terms. He is the quintessentially Sophoclean tragic hero in his extreme division between appearance and reality, outward and inward truth. The riddle as the cancellation or confusion of verbal differentiation parallels the other cancellations of differences which make up the moral and intellectual clarity of our world. It is the problem of the one being equel to many, as Oedipus says (845-7); and for Sophocles, as for Plato, the relation of the One to the Many is the focal point for man's understanding of himself and the universe.

Violating the limits of speech, Oedipus also violates those of silence. At the crossroads he fails to utter the humanizing word that might have saved Laius and himself. "These things will come even if I conceal them in silence," Teiresias warns. "Then should you speak to me of what will come," is Oedipus' reply (342). There are some things which are "unspeakable," but Oedipus is no respecter of these constraints. Only Creon, the man of good sense, the untragic figure, knows how "to keep knowledge where I have no knowledge" (609). He makes this remark in his futile self-defence, and repeats it, in a very different context, at the end of the play (1519). He would "give an account," *logon didonai,* in the reasonable atmosphere of forensic debate (583-4); but his attempt, like Teiresias' more spirited attempt, fails before the "savage" wrath of Oedipus.

Confounded or puzzled by silence, Oedipus forcibly elicits speech. He repeats the pattern four times: first with the chorus in his decree about keeping silent (233-43); next with Teiresias (340ff.), whom he compels to repeat his fearful words not once, but three times (359-65), "making trial of words" (360); then with Jocasta (1056ff., especially 1074-5); and finally with the old herdsman, where he actually uses physical torture (1153). Yet the mysterious silence of the gods cannot be forced before its time, and it is this which defies all of Oedipus' most strenuous efforts. "How, how could the furrows of your father have borne you in silence (*siga*), miserable man, for so long?" (1210-12).

II

With the disintegration or confusion of the communicative function of language, the basic relation to physical reality is threatened. Speaking, hearing, and seeing are no longer taken for granted. It is as if the world of Oedipus contracts from his dominion over Thebes to the mountainside where the exposed infant is doomed to cry without being heard, without learning human speech.

Early in the play "speaking" and "hearing" *(kluein, akouein)* belong to the ruler's communication with his subjects: he speaks and they hear or obey (cf. 216, 235; cf. also 84, 91, 294-5). In the encounter with Teiresias the double function of "hearing" and "speaking" as cognition and communication begins to break apart. Accustomed to having others "hear" him, he will not "hear" Teiresias (cf. 429). "Blind in ears and mind and eyes," he calls the prophet (371), but Teiresias at once turns the line back upon Oedipus himself (372-3). The three terms correspond almost exactly to Oedipus' reply to the first mention of Laius (105): "I *know* by *hearing*, but I never *saw* him." In the first stasimon striking synaesthetic imagery combines sight and sound to describe the words of the Delphic oracle: the oralce *(phama)* appears and "flashes forth" *(e-lampse*, 473-5).[10] The chorus would "see an upright word" (505; cf. also 187). But neither sight nor hearing helps Oedipus. His refusal to "hear" plays an important role in the scene with Creon (cf. 543-4). In the next scene, with Jocasta, it becomes crucial for him to ascertain just what has been heard (729, 850), until he arrives at the point of "dreadful hearing" from which there is no return (1169-70).

Having dwelt in a world of illusionary seeing and hearing, of mistaken perception as well as false or incomplete communication, Oedipus now finds that he has no desire for the organs of cognition (1224): "What deeds will you *hear*, what deeds will you *see*?" cries the Messenger at the beginning of his description of Jocasta's death and Oedipus' self-blinging. "Why then," Oedipus asks a little later, "should I want sight since when I saw there was nothing joyful to behold" (1334-5). If he could, he would have closed up the channels of hearing as well as sight "that I might be blind and hear nothing, for to house one's thought *(phrontida ... oikein)* outside of evils is sweet" (1384-90). The man who lost in infancy, and now in adulthood, the house *(oikos)* where the senses are trained to perception and communication, would now "house" *(oikein)* his mind outside of its sufferings by giving up all perception of reality. This act not only fulfils Teiresias' prophecy (cf. 371 and 1389), but also has a more fundamental meaning, referring to man's existential and cognitive reality both: cast out of the house, having no "place" among men, Oedipus does not "know where" (cf. 1309-11). His rhetoric acts out, inwardly and physically, both the parents' rejection of the child and the city's ritual expulsion of the *pharmakos* or pollution. His desire to shut out physical reality recapitulates his original expulsion from the human world and also corresponds to his newly discovered status as the pollution who cannot be shown to earth or sky (1425-8).

---

[10] For the synaesthesia see W. B. STANDORD, *Greek Metaphor* (Oxford, 1936), 56; C. SEGAL, "Synaesthesia in Sophocles," *Illinois Classical Studies*, 2 (1977), 89-91.

Yet Oedipus does not sever his bond with life. Touch and hearing remain, and are intimately linked with his human feelings of grief, pity, and joy. He can "hear" the chorus' voice in his darkness (1325-6)[11]. When he hears his "dear ones weeping," he realizes that Creon has "pitied" him "knowing," as Creon adds, his "joy" *(terpsin)* in his children (1471-7). He seems to repeat the gesture of the old servant who "touched the hand" of Jocasta in a suppliant's request to be sent away from the House, "out of sight of the town" (760-2; cf. 1437f., 1449f.). But, a little later in this scene, Oedipus, the polluted outcast, asks to "touch the hands" of his dear ones and to "weep over his woes" with them (1466f.). Reduced to this groping of hands, he hits the rock bottom of his humanity, still left to him in this relation of touch and hearing. The house is his curse, but it is the only space which can receive him now as seen and heard (1429-31); and it is still the place where he, the land's pollution, can exchange touch.[12]

Oedipus does not abandon his house as his house abandoned him. Though he is "made equal to his children" by the incest consequent on that earlier expulsion from the house (425), he asks that his children not be "made equal" to his sufferings (1507). Destroyed by the ambiguities of speech, he can now experience another quality of civilized speech in the frendly voice of the chorus who do not forsake him (1325-6) and the voices of his children whom Creon allows him to "hear" (1472). Time and knowledge, which are destructive while Oedipus was ignorant of his place in the house, can create understanding and compassion when Creon grants him the meeting with his daughters because he "knew of old" Oedipus' delight in them. Darkness and groping touch with hand (1466) or staff replace the apparent sight and "scepter" of the king. But at the same time a tender exchange of speech within a house which is now truly, if grimly, his own partially fills the gap between regal command and cry on the wild mountain-side. In the dramatic reversal from strength to weakness, from sceptred king to blind beggar with his staff, Oedipus gives his final answer to the riddle of the Sphinx. Oedipus the King becomes Oedipus the man.

Oedipus becomes a second Teiresias. Yet he has the inner sight of his blindness not as a gift of the gods, but as the hard acquisition of his human experience and suffering. In his seeing blindness he discerns not the future, like the old prophet, but the meaning of his past and the reality of his own condition of strength-in-weakness in the present.

At the end of the play Oedipus' imperfect, proud "knowing" ripens into the "knowledge that he has been set apart for a unique destiny." He discerns and responsibly accepts the fact that his life has a shape, a pattern which it must fulfil, formed by the interlocking of internal and ex-

---

[11] For these terms of perception see M. W. CHAMPLAIN, *"Oedipus Tyrannus* and the Problem of Knowledge," *CJ*, 64 (1968/69), 337-45, especially 337-41.

[12] G. H. GELLIE, *Sophocles. A Reading* (Melbourne, 1972), 102, observes that Oedipus' kingly power to serve "has shrunk to the tiny domestic circle of a ruined father and two girls born in incest."

ternal determinants, character and "chance" both. After crying out that he would dwell on the mountains which his parents chose as his tomb (1451-3), he pulls back abruptly and makes his deepest statement of "knowing" in the play (1455-8):

> But yet I know *(olda)* this much, that no disease or anything else can destroy me, for I would not have been saved from death except for some terrible suffering. Wherever my fated portion *(moira)* goes, let it go.

It is at this point, after facing the possibility that his life may be a cruel joke played upon him by malignant gods that Oedipus turns to Creon and asks about his children. In that gesture he finally leaves the bare mountainside which his own parents gave him instead of a House and turns back for the touch and the speech of those remaining to him in his own shattered house.

The pollution is still there. It is not overborne, as it is by the inward innocence of Heracles in Euripides' *Heracles Mad* or by Oedipus' own certainty of his place in the gods' will in the *Coloneus*. [13] Against the enormity of the pollution this last gesture of human contact and human love is, by its very naturalness, momentous.

Only when Oedipus joins the two ends of his life, infancy and adulthood, and becomes the incestuous parricide along with father and king, does his life begin to make sense as part of a tragic, yet intelligible pattern. At that point a design becomes visible which embraces his exposure on the mountain, his victory over the Sphinx, his consequent rule over Thebes, and his desire to be cast out upon the mountain. All the parts taken individually at any point and grasped in the totality of their interconnection exemplify his essential greatness-in-nothingness, strenght-in-weakness.

Only man spans such conflicting opposites; and only man, therefore, has a tragic destiny, which includes also the capacity to bring that coexistence of opposites to consciousness. Oedipus answers and lives out, knowingly, in his own life, the riddle of the Sphinx, which is the riddle both of man's being in time and of his paradoxical union of the one and the many simultaneously. The months which Oedipus says defined him great and small are truly proven his "kindred" (1082-3) because time and the changes which time brings not only mark man's tragic bondage to death, but also the precariousness and the painfulness of self-knowledge.

Moving from king to pollution, from seeing to blind, from rich house to the savage mountain of the monstrous birth and rejected outcast, Oedipus becomes, even more deeply than Teiresias, a constellation of contradictions and opposites. He realizes his identity not as a stable unity, but as a juncture of polarities. Replacing the blind seer as the paradigm of man's tragic knowledge, he joins these oppositions in conscious and agonized union rather than uncouscious coincidence. Oedipus seeks the

---

[13]   See Eurip., *H.F.*, 1155ff., 1214ff., 1239ff., 1399f; Soph., *O.C.*, 1130ff.; also Brian Vickers, *Towards Greek Tragedy* (London, 1973), 153-56.

murderer of Laius, whom he fears as his own, and finds himself.[14] His
sufferings in the play constitute a far more significant "answer" to the
Sphinx's riddle than the one which he so confidently gave outside Thebes
in his youth. By living out his answer, he becomes a more authentic civilizing hero, the bearer of the tragic meaning of civilization for men.
Prometheus, the archetypal culture-hero, gave men "blind hopes" along
with the arts of civilization so that they could not foresee their death. Oedipus tears away the veil and by his self-chosen blindness gives men sight.

"That we are set into a 'blind destiny,' dwell within it," Rilke once
wrote, "is, after all in a way the condition of our sight ... Only through
the 'blindness' of our fate are we really deeply related to the wonderful
muffledness of the world, that is, with what is whole, vast, and surpassing us ..."[15] For Sophocles, however, that "muffledness" is not "wonderful," but terrible-and-wonderful, *deinon*. To exemplify in his own life
the mystery of existence is not a blessing, but a misfortune, a curse. Yet
only through that blindness can the hero know the vast life of the universe
in all its strange, remote workings.

Oedipus' fate in the orchestra mirrors back to the members of the
audience their own experience, in the theater, of nothingness before time
and change. As they watch the performance, they too pass from blind
seeing to seeing blindness, from the comfortable certitudes of daily life to
the shaken awareness of how fragile these certitudes are, how thin the
film between reality and illusion. They too, in firm control of their lives,
are, like Oedipus, "struck" or "shaken", *ekpeplegmenos* (922), a word
used by Sophocles' contemporaries to describe both intense aesthetic and
emotional reactions.[16] Each member of the audience, joined but also
isolated in the silent crowd, celebrating a festival but also involved in the
sufferings of the masked actor, temporarily loses his identity, his secure
definition by house, position, friends, and becomes, like Oedipus, nameless and placeless, weighing the light accidents of birth, fortune, status
above the void of non-being. Like all tragic art this play above all reveals
the fragility of those structures — ritual, social, moral — which enclose it
and are the sources of its life. In every sense, as Knox observes, personal, historical, communal, "the audience which watched Oedipus in the
theater of Dionysus was watching itself.[17]

Yet what ultimately emerges from the *Oedipus Rex* is not a sense of
total chaos and despair, but a quality of heroism in the power of self-
knowledge. "No other mortal except myself can bear my sufferings,"
Oedipus says near the end. The verb *pherein*, "bear," "endure," is a leit-
motif of the play. Like everything which touches Oedipus intimately it
spans the two poles of weakness and strenght.[18] Both Teiresias and Jo-

---

[14] See Peter SZONDI, *Versuch über das Tragische*[2] (Frankfurt a. M., 1964), 70.
[15] Rainer Maria RILKE, *Letters*, trans. J. B. GREENE and M. D. Herter NORTON
(New York, 1948), II.308 (to Lotti von Wedel, May 26, 1922).
[16] E.g. ARISTOPH., *Frogs*, 962.
[17] Bernard M. W. KNOX, *Oedipus at Thebes* (New Haven, 1957), 77.
[18] See in general *ibid.*, chap. 5.

casta, in different ways, urge him to "bear life easily" (cf. 320-1 and 982-3). But by destiny and by temperament Oedipus does not exist in the middle ground which such "bearing" is possible. He has, as Creon tells him, a "nature most painful to bear" (675-6) and "bears ill" the half-knowledge of his encounter with Laius (cf. 770).

In a life where so much seems to have been "chance" or randomness (cf. Jocasta's *eikei* in 979), Oedipus not only discerns pattern, but creates pattern. His capacity to "bear," *pherein*, is connected with his determination to discover the shape which his life has within the mysterious order, or disorder, of the gods, to discern the coherence between the inner nature and the outward event, between the beginning and the end, the suffered and the inflicted injury. Whereas earlier Oedipus angrily rejected the "pains" (*pemonai*, 363) which Teiresias had foretold for him, at the end he "chooses" them as his own (*authairetoi pemonai*, 1230f.) and strikes with his own hand (1331ff.).[19] These "self-chosen pains' answer the "savage pain" of Jocasta (1073f.), who cannot face the suffering contained in her destiny and also the disordered pains of Oedipus' violent emotional oscillations when he "lifts up his spirit too much with pains of all sorts" (*lypai pantoiai*, 914-5).

For Oedipus, more than for any Greek hero, ontogeny recapitulates phylogeny; the hero is both individual and mythic paradigm. Oedipus does not solve the ultimate riddle, the meaning of the gods who remain as remote as the stars with which Oedipus, in the first step of the exile which will henceforth be his life's pattern, measures his distance from Corinth (779). But he follows this pattern to the end, and completes it, as symbol and paradigm, by a self-inflicted suffering. To search for and accept his hidden origins and his darker self is to essay anew the riddle of the Sphinx, that is, enter the tragic path of self-knowledge and force language too to the same tragic search and self-questioning.[20]

Charles SEGAL,
Brown University.

---

[19] On the significance of the self-blinding and its relation to the myth in earlier versions and to Greek social and ritual structures see Thalia Phillies HOWE, "Taboo in the Oedipus Theme," *TAPA* 93 (1962), 134ff.

[20] Some of this material, in altered form, will appear as part of book on Sophocles.

Contribution à l'interprétation
d'Horace lyrique
l'ode I, 22 (Integer Vitae)*

Un poème doit être étudié dans la complexité de sa texture verbale, structurale, métaphorique, symbolique pour en saisir les valeurs esthétiques et formelles. Un poème n'est pas l'expression incontrôlée d'émotions personnelles, mais plutôt un 'ensemble objectif de corrélations', un 'système organique de relations', le 'résultat d'une rencontre de forces' où « structure » (ensemble de stratifications significatives) et « texture » (trame organisée) se soutiennent et s'influencent réciproquement. D'où la nécessité pour le lecteur de concentrer son attention sur l'œuvre dans son aspect 'concret' pour en saisir l'essence par l'analyse des images, de la langue, du mètre, et aussi la signification intime par la détermination des renvois internes et des structures formelles. Une ode d'Horace n'est qu'un système de relations, à l'intérieur duquel chaque élément composant existe en fonction du « tout » dans son ensemble, mais aussi en fonction de tous les autres éléments, avec lesquels il est également mis en corrélation. Par conséquent, si l'on veut saisir le secret de ce système, on ne peut se dispenser d'examiner le poème dans sa structure statique: inutile et vaine serait donc une recherche *diachronique* de l'« intention » du poète, mais utile et nécessaire, par contre, sera une recherche *synchronique* du signe poétique (σῆμα ποιητικόν), considéré comme rapport 'nouveau' entre signifiant et signifié.

Le poème est une *forme* où chaque unité (images, sons, etc.) a la fonction de distinguer les signifiés linguistiques, puisque le but intrinsèque de la fonction poétique est de diriger l'attention vers le signe poétique ou linguistique: on met ainsi en évidence l'autonomie et l'arbitraire du signe poétique, soustrait, au moment même de la création poétique, à l'automatisme banal caractérisant la 'communication' dans son passage de l'un à l'autre, du poète au lecteur. La *forme* (c'est-à-dire la *structure*) poétique reflète l'organisation des sentiments éprouvés par le poète, grâce à laquelle celui qui lit connaît et classifie la 'réalité' poétique, la *res creata* (ποίημα, ποιεῖν). Le signe poétique (métaphore, image, etc.) devant être considéré comme rapport entre *res significans*, 'signifiant' et *res significata*, 'signifié', ce qui a le plus d'importance est alors la forme (le genre de l'organisation poétique), le système de signes. C'est justement ce système de signes qui doit être interprété par le critique: parce que chaque texte littéraire

* Cet article est d'abord paru en italien dans le volume *Studi in onore di V. De Falco*, Naples, 1971, pp. 393-407. La traduction française par Mlle Olympie Cupaiuolo est revue par E. Gareau.

constitue un tout dont les parties-membres-éléments reçoivent leur pleine signification de leurs rapports avec l'ensemble.

Il est caractéristique de la Muse d'Horace que le poète parle essentiellement de lui et de ses affaires : cela, dans les satires, dans les épodes, dans les épîtres, constitue l'histoire intime d'Horace. Dans les Odes, pourtant, ce *modus* poétique ne prend pas l'aspect d'une confidence lyrique, au sens moderne (ce qui, par contre, est très fréquent, dans la poésie ancienne, chez Catulle et Properce) : au contraire, lorsque dans les odes Horace parle de lui, il semble presque qu'il parle pour que cela serve de leçon aux autres (cf. III, 4). C'est que la poésie lyrique d'Horace est en grande partie conditionnée par le souci de se refléter dans le milieu et pour ainsi dire de s'extérioriser. Les odes d'Horace supposent une scène, un auditeur : il aurait accueilli cette forme de lyrisme dialogique, cette «fiction dialogique» (avec un interlocuteur que l'on suppose présent et intimement lié à l'action mimétique de la poésie) afin d'imiter certaines qualités formelles de ses modèles lesbiens[1]. Ce n'est que partiellement, et en rapport avec cette situation, que l'ode révèle le sentiment intime du poète : elle prend forme, substance et rythme dans un dialogue fictif et idéal avec un personnage représentant l'*alter ego* dialectique, plutôt que de s'intérioriser dans un soliloque[2]. En conséquence, la structure de l'ode exige une série d'opérations techniques se rapportant d'abord au rôle du poète-personnage principal et à la fonction de l'interlocuteur-destinataire de l'œuvre. On se demande ce que peut signifier le fait que deux odes, qui ont en commun l'élément du βεβιωμένον, l'expérience d'Horace et un épisode de vie réelle, l'ode I, 22 et l'ode I, 34, présentent l'une la « Du-Form» et l'autre l'« Ich-Form». Doit-on pour cette raison attribuer à l'ode I, 34 une note de plus grande participation lyrique ? La nature de l'interlocuteur-destinataire, choisi comme *alter ego* dialectique dans l'ode I, 22, appartient-elle au «système» du poème, selon lequel la *Weltanschauung* d'Aristius Fuscus, à qui s'adresse Horace, en conformité avec son «caractère», appartient à la figure qui agit à l'intérieur d'un système de relations, essentiellement 'déterminée' par la place que lui attribue la structure même du récit poétique ? Par conséquent, découvrir l'unité de l'ode I, 22 revient à rechercher le schéma d'association poète-interlocuteur, à saisir comment la personne à laquelle le poète fait le récit de l'expérience vécue s'insère dans le système. Or, pourquoi Horace, pour raconter ce cas bizarre qui lui est arrivé (le cas du loup qui, dans le bois de la Sabine, s'enfuit dès que le poète paraît), pour faire cette confidence, aurait-il choisi justement Aristius Fuscus, l'ami blagueur qui dans *Sat.* I, 9, 74 abandonne le poète *sub cul-*

---

[1]	Pour les lois formelles auxquelles la poésie d'Horace obéit, cf. R. HEINZE, *Die horazische Ode*, dans «Neue Jahrbb. f. Klassische Alt.». 1923, p. 153 et suiv.; F. CUPAIUOLO, *Lettura di Orazio lirico*, Napoli, 1967, p. 32 et suiv.

[2]	Cependant, III, 12, le soliloque de Néobule, est un très beau monologue (d'imitation alcaïque en ce qui concerne le mètre — qui est l'ionien —, le «motto» du début [fr. 123, I D, 10 L.-P.] et le contenu). L'obligation d'introduire des éléments manifestement autobiographiques dans la poésie — de laquelle, pourtant, celui qui écrit aspire à tirer une gloire nouvelle, celle du «poète-amant» — deviendra essentielle dans la poétique de l'élégie latine.

tro, aux prises avec le fâcheux, l'ami très cher, mais de type plaisant et *Urbis amator* (*epist.* I, 10)? Le choix de cet interlocuteur-personnage nous fait penser que le poète veut maintenir son propos sur un plan mi-badin mi-humoristique: ce que confirme l'impression produite par la lecture de l'ode[3], avec sa fin plutôt inattendue. Le ton badin de l'ode résulte d'un humour plus accentué si l'on songe à la solennité[4] du début: *Integer vitae scelerisque purus ...* un vers qui trouve son équivalent dans le schéma lexical du premier vers *(Parcus deorum cultor et infrequens)* de l'ode I, 34, qui, comme nous le verrons, a avec l'ode I, 22 des liens formels et substantiels. On serait même tenté de croire que dans l'ode I, 22 Horace épicurien se moque pour ainsi dire du pouvoir miraculeux que les Stoïciens attribuent à la vertu; la première strophe de l'ode I, 22 et la première de l'ode I, 34 seraient en nette opposition (I, 34 serait sur un ton sérieux et, de façon idéale, la palinodie, la *retractatio* de ce qu'on affirme en I, 22)[5], mais il ne faut pas exclure, bien que peut être peu probable, que le ton de la première strophe de l'ode I, 34 soit, lui-aussi, humoristique.

Donc, si le fait que le poète parle essentiellement de lui et de ses affaires se réalise dans l'ode grâce au stylème, presque constant de la fiction dialogique, si bien que le sentiment lyrique ne se révèle qu'indirectement, presque comme une vision reflétée par un miroir oblique, cependant, dans le recueil lyrique d'Horace il y a un motif, plusieurs fois récurent, plus intime et subjectif: le miracle de son existence de poète, qui se manifeste dans la protection dont il bénéficie en différentes occasions de la part des Muses, de la part de Mercure, de la part de Faune. Le motif de la divinité protectrice, du miracle est cher à Horace. Les divers moments de son existence sont présentés et caractérisés par l'intervention divine, dès son enfance (III, 4, 9-20 *Me fabulosae ... fronde nova puerum palumbes / texere ...*) jusqu'à son expérience de Philippes (II, 7, 9-16 *... sed me per hostis Mercurius celer / denso paventem sustulit aere*): et, encore, jusqu'au jour où un arbre, qui aurait pu le tuer, tomba sur lui mais sans le blesser (II, 13, I-13; II, 17, 27-30: *me truncus inlapsus cerebro / sustulerat, nisi Faunus ictum / dextra levasset*). Miraculeux doivent être considérés les deux cas racontés dans l'ode I, 22 et dans l'ode I, 34 (le

---

[3] Il faut remarquer que l'épisode du loup s'enfuyant à l'arrivée d'Horace est vu avec des tons excessifs (v. 13 et suiv.: *Quale portentum neque militaris / Daunias latis alit aesculetis / nec...*). D'ailleurs il peut s'agir d'une simple invention, *fictio poetica*: déjà Porphyre, dans les temps anciens, demeure hésitant sur l'apparition réelle du loup *(et haec dubito utrum ioculariter dicantur an vero, quoniam lupi dicuntur solere singulares homines invadere)*.

[4] C'est qu'Horace aime soit un début solennel (cf. par exemple I, 27, 1 et suiv. *Natis in usum laetitiae scyphis pugnare / Thracum est...*) soit une fin d'un ton estompé, ainsi qu'en cette ode (cf., p. ex., *epod.* 14, 15 et suiv. *gaude sorte tua: me libertina, nec uno / contenta, Phryne macerat; carm.* I, 5, 13 et suiv. *... Me tabula sacer / votiva paries indicat uvida / suspendisse potenti / vestimenta maris deo;* I, 7, 32; etc.).

[5] Cela ne nous oblige pas à croire que l'ode I, 34, ait été forcément composée après I, 22. Nous ne possédons pas d'indices pour établir l'année de la composition de I, 22 (si ce n'est le détail qu'Horace, lorsqu'il écrivait l'ode, devait déjà posséder la villa de la Sabine): généralement, d'ailleurs, on pense que cette ode est de 25, mais cette supposition se base sur des éléments très faibles et assez discutables (v. 15).

loup qui s'enfuit dès que, dans le bois de la Sabine, il se trouve en face d'Horace et l'insolite éclat d'un éclair dans un ciel serein, suivi du tonnerre). Le motif de la protection divine atteint encore le sommet lyrique dans l'ode I, 17 (vers 13 et suivants):

> Di me tuentur, dis *pietas* mea
> et *Musa* cordi est.

Ces vers revèlent deux symboles, *pietas* et *Musa (poetica)*, qui sont à la base de l'ode I, 22 ainsi qu'il apparaît à travers le vers 1 *Integer vitae scelerisque purus* et à travers le vers 10 ... *meam canto Lalagen*. Mais la base littérale du sens d'un poème étant la structure intime des motifs liés entre eux, pour comprendre littéralement un poème (le comprendre dans sa totalité globale, c'est-à-dire comme poème et comme il se présente à nous) il faut coordonner tous les symboles. Donc, pour une perception simultanée de l'unité structurale de l'ode I, 22, il nous faudra d'abord nous assurer qu'il n'y a pas en elle d'autres symboles liés les uns aux autres. Or, au vers 23 *dulce ridentem Lalagen amabo* revient le même nom Lalagé qui appartient, comme on l'a déjà vu, au deuxième symbole (v. 10 *canto Lalagen*): ce nom fait partie — lui aussi — du troisième symbole en concaténation avec les deux autres *(Lalagen amabo)*. Il est évident alors que dans l'ode I, 22 il y a concaténation de trois symboles *(pietas, Musa poetica, amor)* chacun desquels appartient d'une façon essentielle à l'une des trois sections, qui se succèdent dans l'œuvre, mais pas seulement à elle: a) vv. 1-8: *propositio* (l'homme à la vie intègre et sans tache, l'homme *pius*, est en sûreté et protégé); b) vv. 9-16: *exemplum*, παράδειγμα de ce qu'on a précédemment affirmé *(namque me silva lupus in Sabina | dum meam canto Lalagen ... fugit inermem)*; c) vv. 17-24 conclusion et épilogue (a + b): j'aimerai toujours et en tout lieu Lalagé *(... dulce ridentem Lalgen amabo | dulce loquentem)*.

Si l'on considère la structure de l'ode I, 22 et de l'ode I, 34 on remarque une analogie de construction non seulement dans la tripartition (des parties parfaitement symétriques[6] de huit vers chacune dans I, 22; des groupes de vers où il n'y a correspondance numérique et technique que dans la première et la dernière section de l'ode dans I, 34: vv. 1-5; 5-12; vv. 12-16). À la partie centrale, de ces deux odes est assignée la fonction qui, dans un poème parénétique d'Alcée ou d'un autre poète lyrique grec, revient au παράδειγμα, à l'*exemplum* tiré de la mythologie ou de l'histoire: mais Horace dans l'ode I, 22 et dans l'ode I, 34 puise dans son expérience personnelle, dans le βεβιωμένον (et en cela il innove). Comme καὶ γάρ, venant après une maxime générale où un avertissement ou une admonition (παφαίνεσις), servait dans la lyrique grecque ancienne[7] à introduire ce qui prouvait la validité de la maxime ou ce qui devait

---

[6] Il y a une symétrie parfaite, même si ce n'est pas celle de III, 9, *Donec gratus eram tibi* ...

[7] Cf. dans le chant d'Alcée à Mélanippe 73 D., 38 L.-P.: ... ᾽all᾽ ἄγι μὴ μεγάλων ... καὶ γὰρ Σίσυφος Αἰολίδαις βασίλευς.. Le stylème καὶ γὰρ ... introduisant dans le chant des références à des exemples illustrés remontait déjà à l'époque d'Homère (cf. E. FRAENKEL, *Horace*, Oxford, 1957, p. 186).

renforcer l'admonition, de la même façon *namque* dans I, 22, 9 et dans I, 34, 5 commençait le récit. Dans l'ode I, 34 le παράδειγμα, l'*exemplum* est constitué par la narration du cas insolite d'un éclair qu'Horace a vu resplendir dans un ciel serein: ce phénomène est présenté comme une explication de ce qui est affirmé dans la *propositio* (vv. 3 et *suiv. ... nunc retrorsum | vela dare atque iterare cursus | cogor relictos*). Dans l'ode I, 22 *namque* introduit, avec valeur explicative, le récit d'un cas arrivé au poète, un cas décrit par des couleurs et des tons de miracle[8]. Les odes présentent donc toutes deux une structure tripartite et circulaire *(Ringkomposition)*, avec un retour plus ou moins explicite et direct, dans la partie finale, au motif du début[9]: les vers 17-22, en effet, sont parallèles aux vers 5-8 et les deux groupes de vers se complètent réciproquement (Fraenkel).

Mais comment alors dans l'ode I, 22 Horace a-t-il pu soutenir avec une sorte de transposition que celui qui aime est en sûreté? Il ne faut pas penser que, par une espèce de romantisme *ante-litteram*, le poète chercher à spiritualiser, à élever ce moment particulier de la vie d'un homme, qui consiste à être amoureux, c'est-à-dire à vivre comme dans un état de béatitude et d'enivrement, indifférent à toute chose et, à cause de cela, en sûreté (*tutus*). On retrouve ici à vrai dire un motif conventionnel, un *topos* de la poésie hellénistique, suivant une formule que nous retrouvons chez Tibulle[10], chez Poperce[11], chez Ovide[12]: *a)* l'amant est sacré; *b)* protégé par les dieux, par Vénus; *c)* grâce à cette protection il n'est molesté par les voleurs, ni par des brutes[13]. Mais Horace, selon sa nature et comme il a souvent l'habitude de faire, a, par goût de *variatio*, contaminé le *topos* hellénistique par le recours à une idéologie d'origine différente: d'un côté l'homme qui aime est *tutus*, étant protégé par la divinité, de l'autre poète, par tradition (que l'on se rappelle les légendes relatives à Arion, à Ibicus, à Simonide, etc.) était considéré, comme *sanctus*, selon

---

[8]   Une fonction en partie analogue ont, par exemple, le discours du Centaure Chiron à Achille dans l'épode 13, vers 12-18 et le discours de Teucer dans I, 7, 21-30: mais l'*exemplum* avec fonction parénétique est tiré de la tradition mythologique, c'est-à-dire grecque.

[9]   Pour la structure de l'ode chez Horace cf. N. E. COLLINGE, *The Structure of Horace's Odes*, Londres, 1961; F. CUPAIUOLO, *op. cit.*, p. 32 et suiv.

[10]   TIBULL., I, 2, 27 et suiv.:
        Quisquis amore tenetur, eat tutusque sacerque
        qualibet: insidias non timuisse decet.

[11]   PROP., III, 16, 11 et suiv.:
        Nec temen est quisquam sacros qui laedat amantes:
        Scironis media sic licet ire via.
        Quisquis amator erit, Scythicis licet ambulet oris:
        nemo adeo ut feriat barbarus esse volet.
        Luna ministrat iter, demonstrant astra salebras;
        ipse Amor accensas percutit ante faces.
        Saeva canum rabies morsus avertit hiantis;
        huic generi quovis tempore tuta via est.

[12]   OVID., *am.* I, 6, 13 et suiv.:
        Nec mora, venit amor; non umbras nocte volantis,
        non timeo strictas in mea fata manus.

[13]   Cf. aussi Philodème *A.P.* V, 25.

l'expression d'Ennius et de Cicéron. Le personnage poétique créé par Horace est unique: il est *integer vitae* (v. 1); en tant que 'poète' (v. 10), il est *sanctus, vates*[14]; il est amoureux (v. 10 et v. 23) et, par le fait qu'il aime, il est *sacer*, protégé des dieux. Or, le symbolisme de ce poème n'est qu'une structure ambigue de motifs, de *symboles connexes* entre eux; à côtés des trois symboles, ou signes poétiques, principaux, il y a des 'séries contextuelles' de la culture de l'âge d'Auguste (idéologie de la fonction éducatrice de la poésie; idéologie du poète vu comme *vir bonus, integer, magister*, etc.) et de la *Weltanschauung* d'Horace (désir d'idéaliser la figure du poète; ambition du poète *doctus* de joindre des événements personnels à des exemples illustres transmis par la tradition littéraire; cf. par ex. III, 4, 9 et suiv. les colombes sur le Volture Apulien couvrent de tendres rameaux l'enfant Horace, réminiscence et réadaptation de la légende de Iamus de Pind. *Olymp.* VI, 52).

Comme une critique 'ouverte' doit converger, au delà de la différence de goût et de culture, vers une phénoménologie de l'œuvre d'art, c'est-à-dire vers une analyse rationnelle des procédés expressifs, à la découverte de l'objet poétique dans la totalité de son être, notre regard doit, bien sûr, se tourner, vers les centres affectifs et spirituels de l'œuvre poétique, en avançant d'un esprit analytique et spitzérien qui va de la partie au tout et du tout à la partie, mais il ne peut pas omettre de situer au premier plan l'unité organique de l'œuvre littéraire. S'il est vrai, donc, que trois symboles (*pietas*, v. 1; Muse poétique = ποιεῖν, 'faire de la poésie', *cantare*, v. 10; *amor*, v. 23) gouvernent le système poétique de l'ode I, 22, nous ne devons pas moins oublier qu'une œuvre résulte toujours d'un contexte complexe de signifiés: en tant que telle, l'ode I, 22 est une réalité autonome douée d'une cohérence intime. La tâche du critique est de rechercher si, ou jusqu'à quel point, dans cette réalité autonome les paroles s'enrichissent réciproquement, compte tenu du fait que, à l'intérieur de la totalité de la structure, les parties opèrent sur plusieurs niveaux différents. Puisque aussi une ode d'Horace, bien que brève, se présente comme une multiplicité de niveaux, il nous reste alors à compléter la découverte des différents niveaux qui, par leurs mouvements intérieurs, produisent l'harmonie polyphonique de l'ode I, 22 et la description des mécanismes et des effets littéraires, c'est-à-dire la décomposition de l'ode dans les éléments qui en constituent la synthèse artistique, et la recherche des relations idéologiques et culturelles qu'ils contiennent, en un mot, rechercher à côté des symboles ou des motifs successifs qui en constituent la trame, les 'séries latérales linguistiques', les 'séries latérales hétérogènes' (en relation avec la biographie du poète, la signification de son poème pour l'histoire de son âge; etc.), les 'séries contextuelles' (de la culture d'un âge ou de

---

[14] On peut voir en cela l'adhésion d'Horace au credo esthétique, dominant pendant l'âge d'Auguste, selon lequel le poète a la fonction de *vates, magister populi, Musae sacerdos*, d'«éducateur», (cf. HOR., *ad Pis.* 391 et suiv.; *Epist.* II, I, 126 et suiv.). Cf. à ce propos F. CUPAIUOLO, *Tra poesia e poetica*: Su alcuni aspetti culturali della poesia latina nell' età augustea, Naples, 1966, p. 165 et suiv.; ainsi que le beau livre de E. PARATORE, *Poetiche e correnti litterarie nell'antica Roma*, Rome, 1970.

la manière de voir du poète), etc.[15] Et il sera plus aisé et plus simple d'examiner une section à la fois, parce que, comme on l'a déjà vu, dans chacune d'elles figure un « symbole », lié l'un à l'autre.

Certes, on ne peut pas dire que le symbole de la *pietas*, aux vers 1-8, représente un 'ressort poétique' heureux : l'image, l'idée dans ces deux premières strophes se perd et se brise en des images complémentaires (flèches de la Mauritanie, arc, flèches empoisonnées, carquois et, encore, les Syrtes, le Caucase, l'Idaspe) qui n'appartiennent pas à la 'poésie', mais qui font partie d'un bagage rhétorique et culturel. On remarque des *topoi* conventionnels évoquant des échos littéraires. Voir à ce propos les vers 5 et suiv. :

> sive per Syrtis iter aestuosas
> sive facturus per inhospitalem
> Caucasum, vel quae loca fabulosus
> lambit Hydaspes

qui, par un écho allusif si cher au poète de l'âge d'Auguste, font revivre Catuelle (II, 2 et suiv.) :

> sive in extremos penetrabit Indos
> ....
> sive in Hyrcanos Arabasve molles
> seu Sagas sagittiferosque Parthos,
> sive quae septemgeminus colerat
> aequora Nilus
>
> sive trans altas gradietur Alpes[16].

mais qui sont aussi une *variatio* de *loci* semblables (HOR., *epod.*, I, 11 et suiv. : *te vel per Alpium iuga | inhospitalem et Caucasum | vel Occidentis usque ad ultimum sinum | forti sequemur pectore;* — carm. II, 6, 1 et suiv. : *Septimi, Gadis aditure mecum et | Cantabrum indoctum iuga ferre nostra et | barbaras Syrtes ubi Maura semper | aestuat unda*)[17].

Aux vers 9-16 le motif, le symbole est la sûreté qui accompagne le poète. À partir du vers 10 *dum meam canto Lalagen*, une sorte de centre lyrique de l'ode, le vers se colore de temps en temps de quelques notes

---

[15]   Qu'on nous permette d'énoncer ici une prémisse préjudicielle : nous considérons l'œuvre d'art comme une 'forme' qu'il faut saisir dans ses structures intimes, mais nous n'allons pas jusqu'à rechercher dans cette 'forme' une expérience sous-jacente, parce que cette recherche nous conduirait au-delà du texte et au-delà de l'espace du langage (métalinguistique). On ne doit pas oublier que chaque œuvre est un produit où se règlent, se gouvernent, s'harmonisent les rapports difficiles, non prévisibles et non évaluables, d'une opération et d'une expérience linguistique (conception dynamique de l'œuvre = vie, mouvement vers l'inconnu). Cette dynamique interne appartient soit à la création de l'œuvre de la part de l'artiste, soit à sa révélation à chaque lecteur. Il s'ensuit que les analyses des structures d'un texte ne sauraient procurer qu'une vérité partielle, si elles prétendent enfermer dans un schéma ce qui est la source même des possibilités expressives de ce texte. D'ailleurs chaque critique doit toujours être modeste et reconnaître que, dans la dynamique des recherches, la critique ne peut pas ne pas être partielle, hypothétique, provisoire.

[16]   Sur les rapports Horace-Catulle, cf. le beau livre de D. GAGLIARDI, *Orazio e la tradizione neoterica*, vol. 10 de la « Collana di studi classici », Naples, 1971.

[17]   Cf. encore HOR. III 4, 29 et suiv. ; PROP., I 6, 1 et suiv. ; III 22, 7 et suiv.

profondes, mais de sens plus ou moins voilé[18], sans que cependant à cause de ces notes on ne découvre jamais derrière l'image le mystère, et sans qu'on ne fasse allusion au grand mystère que constitue l'imprévisible dans la vie de l'homme. Et il n'est guère de pauses lyriques qui, s'ouvrant à l'improviste, ne revèlent une note secrète de l'âme du poète: au contraire, aux vers 13-16 idées et images s'accumulent d'une façon dispersive l'une après l'autre. De plus, relativement au motif de la fuite du loup, il est facile d'imaginer[19] qu'à un poète savant, tel qu'Horace, soit venue à l'esprit la tradition suivie et acceptée par Pindare (*Pyth.*, V, 57) là où l'on fait allusion au mythe de Battos, fondateur de Cyrène, devant lequel par volonté d'Apollon les lions s'enfuirent. Il faut remarquer aussi une correspondance qui se reflète sur le plan linguistrique, entre l'épisode de I, 22 et III, 4: cf. I, 22, 9 *me silva lupus in Sabina* et III, 4, 9 *me fabulosae Volture in Apulo (palumbes)*; I, 22, 10-11 *ultra terminum vagor* et III, 4, 10 *nutricis extra limina Pulliae*; I, 22 12 *(me) fugit inermem* et III 4, 11-12 *fronde nova puerum (me) ... texere*; etc.

> Dans la troisième partie, v. 16-24:

> *Pone me* pigris ubi nulla campis
> arbor aestiva recreatur aura,
> quod latus mundi nebulae malusque
> Iuppiter urget;
> *pone sub* curru nimium propinqui
> solis in terra domibus negata;
> dulce ridentem Lalagen amabo,
> dulce loquentem

apparaît un stylème *(pone me ... ubi; pone ...)* qui devait appartenir à un bagage de rhétorique, tant il est vrai que nous le retrouvons plus tard chez Sénèque *Dial.*, VII, 25, 1-2 *(De vita beata): pone in opulentissima me domo, pone aurum argentumque ubi in promiscuo usu sunt: non suspiciam me ob ista quae, etiamsi apud me, extra me tamen sunt...; pone in stramentis splendentibus et delicato apparatu: nihilo me feliciorem credam, quod mihi mille erit amiculum*[20]. Et, pour ce qui concerne la dynamique des mécanismes et des effets littéraires, on ne peut passer sous silence l'imitation, qui appartient à une tradition saphiquo-catullienne *dulce ridentem Lalagen...dulce loquentem*[21]: également, pour ce qui concerne la résolution du poète d'aimer Lalagé, où qu'il se trouve dans le monde, on a pensé[22] que le motif pourrait remonter à la poétique hellénistique dont

---

[18] Il est peut-être excessif de donner une interprétation symbolique de l'épisode (comme le voudrait E. CASTORINA, *La poesia di Orazio*, Rome, 1965, p. 133): le loup représenterait le mal, la douleur mise en fuite par l'amour).

[19] Cf. G. PASQUALI, *Orazio lirico*, Florence, 1920 (réimp. anastatique, avec une introd. et App. bibl. de A. LA-PENNA, Florence, 1964), p. 471.

[20] Par contre, le schéma artificiel et rhétorique sur lequel est construite l'œuvre de Pétrarque (145) remonte à l'exemple de l'ode d'Horace, avec une accentuation évidente de la virtuosité: en somme, l'œuvre de Pétrarque est une amplification rhétorique d'un seul des motifs d'Horace *(pone me... Lalagen amabo)*.

[21] SAPPHO, 31, 3 et suiv. L.-P. πλάσιον ἇδυ φωνείσας ὑπακούει / καὶ γελαίσας ἱμέροεν et CATULL., 51, 4 *spectat et audit / dulce ridentem*.

[22] G. PASQUALI, *op. cit.*, p. 474.

les traces et les reflets se trouvent encore dans un épigramme d'Asclé-
piade (*AP* V, 64) et dans un épigramme anonyme (*AP* V, 168).

Horace, poète doué d'un esprit vigoureux, mais d'une imagination assez frêle, voit le prototype, le modèle parfait de la poésie lyrique dans une
œuvre qui se distingue par son admirable équilibre d'éléments réels et
imaginaires. C'est à cet idéal poétique que se conforme l'ode I, 22, bien
que dans la dimension et avec les limites qu'au passage nous avons signa-
lées. Il y a lieu de louer ici les vertus stylistiques d'Horace. Cette ode, à
sa manière, est aussi un poème et, sous certains rapports, peut plaire ;
ça et là, cependant, elle déçoit le lecteur moderne car il n'y trouve ni
richesse, ni profondeur d'inspiration, mais seulement forme artistique, simplicité et ordre de composition[23]. Nuisible pour la poésie est la tendance
évidente à exprimer des pensées plutôt que des sentiments, la tendance à
la « description » : la poésie, au contraire, est expression, non description,
de sentiments. Si l'on veut en saisir l'unité poétique, on ne peut la trouver que dans une certaine note de sérénité qui se dégage du poème[24] et
qui produit chez le lecteur un sens de tranquilité, et qui procure aussi le
calme du rythme et du mètre saphique, souligné par le manque d'enjamb-
ements d'une strophe à l'autre. Oeuvre toute particulière : on ne peut pas
dire, comme le voudrait Commager[25], une ode sur la poésie, ni une ode
d'amour. La *qualitas* la plus frappante en est l'articulation du poème en
des modules quelquefois très proches de ceux de la poésie élégiaque[26].

Fabio CUPAIUOLO,
Université de Naples.

BIBLIOGRAPHIE de l'Ode I, 22

E. CASTORINA, *La poesia di Orazio*, Rome, 1965, pp. 130 et suiv.
P. S. COMMAGER, *The Odes of Horace: A Critical Study*, New Haven and London, 1962,
    pp. 130-136.
F. CUPAIUOLO, *Lettura di Orazio lirico*, Struttura dell'ode oraziana, Naples, 1967.
E. FRAENKEL, *Horace*, Oxford, 1957, pp. 184-188.
M. HADAS, *Class Journ.*, 31 (1935), pp. 17 et suiv.
G. L. HENDRICKSON, *Class. Journ.*, 5 (1910), pp. 250-258.
A. W. I. HOLLEMAN, *Latomus*, 28 (1969), pp. 575-582.

---

[23]   Le *lucidus ordo* était pour Horace, poète et théoricien de la poésie, un don essentiel ; cf. F. CUPAIUOLO, *Lettura di Orazio lirico, op. cit.*, p. 39 et suiv.
[24]   Cf. v. 10 *dum meam canto Lalagen* ; v. 11 *curis vago expeditis* ; v. 12... *fugit
(me inermem* ; v. 23-24 *dulce ridentem Lalagen amabo / dulce loquentem* ; etc.
[25]   S. COMMAGER, *The odes of Horace : A Critical Study*, New Haven and London,
1962, p. 342. — Une ode célébrant le pouvoir régulateur de la poésie est la III, 4.
[26]   Pour les rapports thématiques qui lient Horace à la poésie élégiaque cf. B.
OTIS, *Horace and the Elegists*, « Trans. Am. Philol. Ass. », 76 (1945), p. 177-190 ; V.
Leonard GRANT, *Elegiac Themes in Horace's Odes*, dans « Studies G. *Norwood* », Toronto,
1952, pp. 194-202 (qui cependant ne parlent pas de I, 22).

C. JOSSERAND, *Ant. Class*, 4 (1935), pp. 357-363.

R. M. HAYWOOD, Integer vitae and Propertius, *Class. Journ.*, 37 (1941), pp. 28-32.

A. LA PENNA, *Orazio e la morale mondana europea*, Florence, 1968, p. 88.

G. PASQUALI, *Orazio lirico*, Florence, 1920 (réimp. anastatique, avec une introd. et App. bibl. de A. LA PENNA, Florence, 1964), pp. 470 et suiv.

J. PERRET, *Horace*, Paris, 1959.

R. REITZENSTEIN, *Hermes*, 57 (1922), pp. 357-365.

P. SHOREY, *Class. Journ*, 5 (1910), pp. 311 et suiv.

E. TUROLLA, *Orazio*, Florence, 1931, pp. 121 et suiv.

L. P. WILKINSON, *Horace and his lyric Poetry*, Cambridge, 1951[2], p. 62.

E. WISTRAND, *Eranos*, 29 (1931), pp. 81-86.

Textes des odes d'Horace établis, présentés et annotés par:

F. ARNALDI, Milan, 1966[5].

A. KIESSLING-R. HEINZE, Berlin, 1960.

R. G. M. NISBET-M. HUBBARD, Oxford, 1970.

O. TESCARI, Turin, 1948[3].

V. USSANI, vol. 1. Turin, 1940[2], vol. II, 1942[3].

Les rets d'Aphrodite
Interprétation de la première ode de Sapho*

Omai veggio la rete
che qui v'impiglia e come si scalappia.

DANTE, *Purg.* XXI 76-77.

L'interprétation de la première ode de Sapho est beaucoup plus ardue qu'on ne le croit habituellement. Il n'y a pas que les deux passages où la leçon est incertaine qui soient obscurs, ou bien encore la signification de certaines expressions ou l'accord de quelque adjectif, mais, après les interprétations divergentes et parfois opposées auxquelles elle a donné lieu, il résulte que le sens même de l'ode, dans son ensemble, apparaît obscur.

Jusqu'à quel point reproduit-elle le schéma de la prière? Est-elle animée par un véritable sentiment religieux? L'épiphanie est-elle authentique? Quelle fonction ont les épithètes dans les deux premiers vers? Que promet Aphrodite? Pourquoi sourit-elle?

Il suffit de choisir les fiches et de les regrouper: on en dégage rarement deux jugements semblables. *Schéma rituel.* Wilamowitz (p. 42): «Nur die Form des Einganges schliesst sich... an die rituellen Hymnen an». Perrotta (p. 56): «l'ode finisce con un tono inatteso di confidenza ... tra il ritornare delle forme rituali». Bowra (p. 200): «The poem is cast in the form of a prayer». *Sentiment religieux.* Bowra (p. 204): «no Greek would dispute their seriousness». Cameron (p. 15): «an exercise in the style of prayer». Schadewaldt (p. 87): «sie betet wirklich». *Epiphanie.* Bowra (p. 202): «The appearance of Aphrodite must be treated as a genuine experience». Schadewaldt (p. 94): «sie hat im Traum wie Wachen dergleichen Gesichte gehabt und ist mit den Göttern umgegangen». Fränkel (*Dicht.*, p. 201): «Aber eine Vision würde sich auf das beschränken, was für Sappho sichtbar und hörbar gewesen wäre».

On pourrait facilement poursuivre le *collage*, et ce jusqu'à l'ennui; les jugements varient sur chaque détail, même secondaire. Mais ils varient aussi sur la signification même de l'ode, sur le sens de la prière et de la promesse. Après l'interprétation de Page, à la gradation, à la diversité a succédé la cassure. D'un côté l'interprétation traditionnelle qui diffère dans les détails mais qui est foncièrement unitaire: Aphrodite promet à Sapho qu'elle sera encore aimée; elle lui promet le bonheur. De l'autre, Page: les rôles seront inversés — c'est ce qu'assurerait la déesse. Son sourire serait aussi celui de Sapho (p. 16): «This everlasting sequence of pursuit, triumph, and ennui is not to be taken so very seriously.»

---

* Cet article parut d'abord en italien, en une version détaillée, dans *Quaderni Urbinati di cultura classica*, 1967, pp. 1-58. La traduction française, fournie par l'auteur, fut revisée par M. Yvan LePage.

Les égarements de la critique n'ont des causes différentes qu'en apparence. Au delà des excès de psychologisme et en dehors d'une pris en considération insuffisante des données culturelles et religieuses ainsi que du tissu linguistique même, il n'est pas difficile de découvrir, à l'origine de toutes les divergences, une conscience peu claire de la *structure*.

Les essais, les chapitres, les articles même les plus subtils, sur la première ode, éludent le problème: ils sont riches en intuitions souvent très fines, mais fragmentaires et même contradictoires. Ils concordent toutefois sur deux points: l'architecture de l'ode est en anneau; le ton est différent dans l'invocation et dans la conclusion. Ces deux circonstances sont trop évidentes pour qu'il faille admirer la sagacité des interprètes: il est permis, par contre, de s'étonner que ces deux observations n'aient pas été approfondies et rapprochées pour formuler une hypothèse de travail unitaire.

Constater que la composition en anneau constitue un procédé stylistique qui, comme l'a montré van Groningen, était fréquent dans la poésie archaïque et dans la prose ionique, n'explique rien. L'explication pertinente est différente: l'ode a la forme d'une prière et la prière n'a aucune validité sans la reprise finale et symétrique de l'invocation. La tripartition observée par Bowra (p. 200 ss.) est une conséquence: elle découle du rapport entre les termes extrêmes qui, précisément parce qu'ils correspondent entre eux, isolent la partie centrale.

D'autre part, les termes extrêmes de la prière ne sont pas une simple copie l'un de l'autre: et ils le sont encore moins dans l'ode où le ton confiant de la conclusion inverse et renverse le ton angoissé du proème. La disposition cyclique ne comporte donc pas une répétition, mais un retour enrichi de nouveaux aspects: elle comporte une progression jusqu'au rôle opposé, orientée sur un même axe.

La disposition, d'une clarté évidente, fournit la base pour une hypothèse opérationnelle centrée sur ces questions: l'architecture en anneau n'est-elle qu'une enveloppe élusive ou est-elle la manifestation d'un principe qui sélectionne et organise constamment à tous les niveaux? qui organise aussi le rapport des phrases entre elles et des mots entre eux à l'intérieur des phrases? le rapport Sapho-Aphrodite et la manifestation de leur être? l'expérience que Sapho a de l'amour et la loi qu'Aphrodite déclare être propre à chaque amour?

En somme, le caractère cyclique bipolaire est-il occasionnel ou structural? La vérification se trouve dans l'étude qui suit.

Sapph. 1 L. P.

πο]ικιλόθρο[ν' ἀθανάτ'Ἀφρόδιτα,
παῖ] Δ[ί]ος δολ[όπλοκε, λίσσομαί σε,
μή μ'] ἄσαισι [μηδ' ὀνίαισι δάμνα,
πότν]ια, θῦ[μον,
4
—]

ἀλλ]ὰ τυίδ' ἔλ[θ', αἴ ποτα κάτέρωτα
τὰ]ς ἔμας αὔ[δας ἀίοισα πήλοι
ἔκ]λυες, πάτρο[ς δὲ δόμον λίποισα
8 χ]ρύσιον ἦλθ[ες

—]

ἄρ]μ' ὑπασδε[ύξαισα· κάλοι δέ σ' ἄγον
ὤ]κεες στροῦ[θοι περὶ γᾶς μελαίνας
πύ]κνα δίν[νεντες πτέρ' ἀπ' ὠράνωἴθε-
12 ρο]ς διὰ μέσσω·

—]

αἶ]ψα δ' ἐξίκο[ντο· σὺ δ', ὦ μάκαιρα,
μειδιαί[σαισ' ἀθανάτῳ προσώπῳ
ἤ]ρε' ὄττ[ι δηῦτε πέπονθα κὤττι
16 δη]ῦτε κ[άλ]η[μμι

—]

κ]ὤττι [μοι μάλιστα θέλω γένεσθαι
μ]αινόλᾳ [θύμῳ· τίνα δηῦτε πείθω
.].σάγην [ἐς σὰν φιλότατα; τίς σ', ὦ
20 Ψά]πφ', [ἀδικήει;

—]

κα]ὶ γ[ὰρ αἰ φεύγει, ταχέως διώξει,
⟨αἰ δὲ δῶρα μὴ δέκετ', ἀλλὰ δώσει,⟩
⟨αἰ δὲ μὴ φίλει, ταχέως φιλήσει⟩
24 ⟨κωὐκ ἐθέλοισα.⟩

—]

⟨ἔλθε μοι καὶ νῦν, χαλέπαν δὲ λῦσον⟩
⟨ἐκ μερίμναν, ὄσσα δέ μοι τέλεσσαι⟩
⟨θῦμος ἱμέρρει, τέλεσον, σὺ δ' αὔτα⟩
28 ⟨σύμμαχος ἔσσο.⟩

Trône orné, immortelle Aphrodite, fille de Zeus, qui ourdis les filets, je t'en supplie: par des angoisses et des tourments, ô toute-puissante, ne dompte pas mon cœur, mais viens ici, si jamais en d'autres occasions aussi en entendant de loin mon cri, tu m'écoutas, et quittant la maison de ton père, tu vins sur ton char attelé. Beaux et rapides, les passereaux t'emportaient sur la terre noire, battant vite des ailes, du ciel à travers l'éther. Ils arrivèrent tout de suite: et toi, ô bienheureuse, souriant dans ton visage immortel, tu demandas ce qui m'affligeait à nouveau et pourquoi à nouveau j'appelais et que désirait encore mon cœur fou: «qui encore... a ton amour? qui t'offense, Sapho? Car si elle te fuit, bientôt elle te cherchera; si elle ne veut pas de tes dons, elle t'en offrira; et si elle ne t'aime pas, bientôt elle t'aimera, quand même elle ne le voudrait pas». Viens à moi cette fois encore, libère-moi de mes lourds tourments, et ce que mon cœur désire, accomplis-le. Toi-même sois mon alliée.

L'épithète ποικιλόθρονος évoque les épithètes homériques εὔθρονος et χρυσόθρονος, qui se rapportent le plus souvent à l'Aurore. Il s'agit

de deux adjectifs purement conventionnels qui ont perdu presque complètement leur force évocatrice. Il est difficile de croire que l'image de la
déesse sur son trône, comme la représente l'art archaïque, ait traversé
l'esprit du poète et des auditeurs quand ils entendaient que l'Aurore « au
beau trône » ou « au trône d'or » montait de l'Océan dans le ciel.

Les deux épithètes homériques, plutôt que de *dépeindre* la déesse,
en ennoblissent l'évocation. À l'origine il y a probablement eu l'image de
la dame mycénienne assise sur son trône, entourée de ses servantes. Par
la suite l'expression « sur son trône » attribuée à une personne a voulu
en affirmer la supériorité. Le premier élément de ces adjectifs composés
tend à accentuer cette idée de noblesse: parce qu'il est beau ($\dot{\epsilon}\acute{v}$- « bien
fait ») ou précieux ($\chi\rho\upsilon\sigma o$- « d'or »), le trône se distingue des autres sièges
et distingue la personne qui l'occupe. Il y eut certainement une époque
où « Aurore au beau trône » ou « au trône d'or » n'était qu'une métaphore
pour dire « noble », « royale Aurore », métaphore que l'on retrouve encore
chez Homère, mais qui est désormais usée par la manière conventionnelle
dont l'ont utilisée les aèdes.

En substituant $\pi o\iota\kappa\iota\lambda o$- à $\dot{\epsilon}\acute{v}$- ou à $\chi\rho\upsilon\sigma o$-, Sapho a vivifié l'épithète,
mais non au point de lui redonner sa force primitive. C'est précisément
parce qu'il rappelait $\dot{\epsilon}\acute{v}\vartheta\rho o\nu o\varsigma$ et $\chi\rho\upsilon\sigma\acute{o}\vartheta\rho o\nu o\varsigma$, fréquents chez Homère,
que l'adjectif $\pi o\iota\kappa\iota\lambda\acute{o}\vartheta\rho o\nu o\varsigma$ restait encore dans le domaine opaque de la
tradition: il n'évoquait pas l'image de la déesse sur son trône, il en exal-
tait seulement la royauté. La notion même du trône $\pi o\iota\kappa\acute{\iota}\lambda o\varsigma$ n'était pas
nouvelle: elle était homérique elle aussi. Le premier élément, avant même
encore d'évoquer des ornements et des polychromies, fait plus généralement allusion à sa facture complexe et ingénieuse, née de l'esprit astu-
cieux de l'artiste. Le modèle sémantique en est l'homérique $\delta a\iota\delta\acute{a}\lambda\epsilon o\varsigma$
$\vartheta\rho\acute{o}\nu o\varsigma$: $\dot{\epsilon}\acute{v}\vartheta\rho o\nu o\varsigma$ et $\chi\rho\upsilon\sigma\acute{o}\vartheta\rho o\nu o\varsigma$ n'en sont que le modèle morphologique. L'équivalence entre $\pi o\iota\kappa\acute{\iota}\lambda o\varsigma$ et $\delta a\iota\delta\acute{a}\lambda\epsilon o\varsigma$ est affirmée de la manière
la plus explicite par les scholiastes et les lexicographes. $\Pi o\iota\kappa\iota\lambda\acute{o}\vartheta\rho o\nu o\varsigma$ reprend synthétiquement les différentes expressions homériques, mais en les
reprenant l'épithète apporte un élément nouveau. À la différence de
$\delta a\iota\delta\acute{a}\lambda\epsilon o\varsigma$, qui indique uniquement le produit artistiquement élaboré,
$\pi o\iota\kappa\acute{\iota}\lambda o\varsigma$ implique aussi bien l'effet que l'agent: l'objet $\pi o\iota\kappa\acute{\iota}\lambda o\varsigma$ rappelle
la $\pi o\iota\kappa\iota\lambda\acute{\iota}a$ de l'artiste lui aussi $\pi o\iota\kappa\acute{\iota}\lambda o\varsigma$.

C'est à ce point qu'à côté de l'axe diachronique on commence à
entrevoir l'axe synchronique: la réalité expressive $\pi o\iota\kappa\iota\lambda\acute{o}\vartheta\rho o\nu o\varsigma$ résulte
de leur rencontre. Dans la succession diachronique, l'épithète est con-
ventionnelle comme chez Homère, mais par rapport à Homère elle amplifie
la notion contenue dans $\delta a\iota\delta\acute{a}\lambda\epsilon o\varsigma$ de façon à entraîner la $\mu\tilde{\eta}\tau\iota\varsigma$ de l'agent.
Ce très léger écart suffit à indiquer la ligne de corrélation, c'est-à-dire
la position de l'épithète dans l'ode: la correspondance est avec $\delta o\lambda\acute{o}\pi\lambda o$-
$\kappa o\varsigma$, qui se situe explicitement dans le champ de la $\mu\tilde{\eta}\tau\iota\varsigma$ et qui a évidemment influencé la formation du néologisme, jouant à son égard le rôle
de *telos*.

Que l'écart ait été nettement perceptible, c'est ce que montrent les fréquentes variations des composés en -ϑρονος, efffectuées dans le sillage de Sapho au cours des premières décennies du Ve siècle. La technique de formation est identique, mais elle est reproduite parfois extérieurement, par force d'inertie, et rarement par nécessité dynamique. Calqué sur l'homérique χρυσόϑρονος est ἀγλαόϑρονος attribué par Pindare aux Muses (ol., XIII, 96) et aux Danaïdes (Nem., X 1 + Schol.) et par Bacchylide aux jeunes filles qui étaient destinées au Minotaure (XVII, 124 ss. L'or, qui chez Homère était le signe de la richesse, n'est considéré que pour son éclat. L'épithète perd ses connotations économiques et sociales. L'équilibre entre les deux éléments qui la composent est renversé: ἀγλαόϑρονος n'est pas différent de ἀγλαός. L'évolution confirme qu'il est juste de voir déjà chez Sapho un renforcement du premier élément, suffisant pour en assurer le relief par rapport au modèle homérique (c'est-à-dire suffisant pour éviter que sa réduction entre les limites du modèle se fasse sans résidus). Les adjectifs pindariques ὁμόϑρονος et ὑψίϑρονος, qui se rapportent l'un à Héra *égale* de Zeus (Nem., XI, 2), l'autre a Klotho (Isthm., VI, 16) et aux Néréides (Nem., IV, 65), confirment que dans leur aspect conventionnel les composés en -ϑρονος étaient perçus comme des équivalents de « noble » : les deux épithètes ne signifient pas autre chose que « d'égale noblesse », « de haute noblesse ».

Eschyle est le seul qui, en variant ce terme, lui ait restitué son caractère concret. En définissant λιπαρόϑρονοι les ἐσχάραι des Euménides (Eum., 806), non seulement il en a vanté l'éclat, mais il a aussi affirmé que les autels étaient le siège royal des divinités : en outre, grâce au premier élément, il a rappelé l'usage qui consistait à les enduire d'huile. D'autre part, en appelant δίϑρονον le κράτος des Atrides (Ag., I09), il a créé une expression complexe, dans laquelle le sentiment de la royauté et son image symbolique se renforcent réciproquement grâce à une forte tension entre abstrait et concret.

Une nouvelle preuve que ποικιλόϑρονος est lié à δολόπλοκος est donnée par la disposition en chiasme des éléments. Le nom de la déesse sert de pivot, et il est symétriquement en corrélation, à son tour, avec λίσσομαι qui le reprend en lui opposant le sujet, Sapho. C'est une structure en chaîne dont les éléments sont disposés en anneau.

La corrélation est visuelle ('Αφρόδιτα, et λίσσομαι, à la fin du vers) et rythmique (tous les deux -◡-◡). Mais elle est surtout structurale. Aphrodite et Sapho représentent en tant que protagonistes les deux pôles de l'ode: le pôle haut et le pôle bas. La déesse de l'amour que l'on supplie est à la femme amoureuse suppliante (sur des plans différents) ce que le générique ἀϑανάτα est au spécifique παῖ Διός (sur le même plan). On peut maintenant se demander si cette même relation n'existe pas également entre ποικιλόϑρονος et δολόπλοκος.

La traduction usuelle de δολόπλοκος par « trameuse de ruses » est plus qu'approximative: elle est « désagrégeante ». Elle altère l'image concrète qui était encore perceptible pour Sapho dans δόλος. L'interprétation de l'épithète dépend de la reprise de cette image. Une fois encore ce sont les passages où le terme apparaît en opposition qui en indiquent avec évidence le champ sémantique.

La corrélation est chez Homère avec λάϑρη et ἀνωϊστί: l'opposition avec κράτος, βίη, ἀμφαδόν: δόλος c'est l'embûche où l'on attire l'adversaire pour l'éliminer. L'équivalence apparaît évidente dans un passage de l'*Iliade* (VI, 187 ss; cf. aussi *Od.*, VI, 529 ss.; Hes. *Theog.*, 173 ss). À Bellérophon qui revient vainqueur de la Chimère, des Solymes et des Amazones, le roi de Lycie, qui lui avait imposé ces expéditions comme autant d'embûches mortelles, πυκινὸν δόλον ἄλλον ὕφαινε: ayant choisi ses meilleurs guerriers, il lui dressa une embûche (ἑῖσε λόχον). L'équivalence n'est pas seulement entre δόλος et λόχος mais aussi entre Homère et Sapho. Le δόλος que le roi de Lycie sait *ourdir* n'est pas différent de celui qu'Aphrodite sait *tramer*: πλέκω, dans le δολόπλοκος de Sapho, et ὕφαίνω, dans le passage d'Homère, indiquent une même action. À l'origine de la métaphore, il y a les rets, d'autant plus inévitables qu'ils sont plus serrés (πυκινός). L'allusion est encore plus évidente dans un passage de l'*Odyssée* (VIII 272 ss.) où le sens de δόλος oscille entre les deux extrêmes « rets »/« ruse ».

Quant aux liens préparés par Héphaïstos (il les avait forgés sur l'enclume: c'étaient donc des chaînes en métal indestructibles), leur forme n'est pas indiquée: à moins que δόλον (v. 276) n'ait un sens concret, comme pourrait le suggérer le verbe technique τεῦξε qui désigne essentiellement la production de choses matérielles. Dans le doute on peut le traduire par « piège » qui est un terme concret mais générique, avec une ample fonction métaphorique. Ce mécanisme qu'il avait forgé, le dieu l'installa tout autour des montants et le fit tomber d'en haut, le suspendant en l'air sous le toit, exactement *comme* une toile d'araignée. La comparaison éclaire, d'un seul coup, trois aspects: *a*) les liens se croisaient en forme de filet, *b*) ils étaient suspendus en l'air, *c*) ils étaient si fins qu'ils semblaient invisibles. À cause de cette dernière caractéristique, ils pouvaient être vraiment définis δολόεντα (la valeur du prédicat-adverbe est sans aucun doute abstraite), car ils permettaient la surprise, qui est la condition même de toute embûche.

En terminant le récit des préparatifs, le poète dit: ἐπεὶ δὴ πάντα δόλον περὶ δέμνια χεῦεν. Auquel des deux substantifs se rapporte πάντα? certainement pas à δέμνια! Mais s'il qualifie δόλον, quel sens aurait l'expression « car il étendit *toute* la ruse sur le lit »? L'interprétation «*tout* le filet» est alors inévitable, et l'acception concrète ne saurait scandaliser. Dans un autre passage de l'*Odyssée* δόλος est le nom d'un objet, non plus du filet mais l'appât (XII, 251 s.).

Si au lieu de faire un filet, Héphaïstos avait fabriqué une cage ou une trappe (comme celle dont fut victime, par exemple, l'Andreuccio de Pérouse de Boccace, *Déc.*, II, 5), le terme dans ce contexte aurait eu la valeur de « cage » ou de « trappe ». Autrement dit, la comparaison entre les différents passages d'Homère conduit à un seul résultat sûr: outre le sens (abstrait) de « ruse », δόλος a aussi le sens (concret, mais générique) d'« instrument de ruse ».

Grâce au second élément, le saphique δολόπλοκος précise la valeur concrète du mot jusqu'à évoquer l'image spécifique du filet. Cette évocation est cependant le résultat secondaire d'un processus métaphorique qui va de l'abstrait au concret (et non inversement) à travers les étapes suivantes :

δόλος « ruse »   « instrument de la ruse »   « appât » « filet ».

À ce point il est déjà possible de tirer une conclusion suffisamment bien fondée sur le type de rapport qui lie ποικιλόθρονος et δολόπλοκος. Ils apparaissent tous les deux pour la première fois chez Sapho. L'hypothèse selon laquelle il s'agirait d'une création de sa part est renforcée par leur extrême rareté. On ne peut naturellement en être sûr: il est cependant très significatif que ces deux termes se comportent, par rapport à la tradition homérique, d'une manière tellement identique qu'ils semblent sortis de la même matrice.

Il existe chez Homère un certain nombre de composés avec δολο- qui ont une signification semblable à celle de δολόπλοκος, comme δολομήτης, δολόμητις, δολοφραδής, δολοφρονέων. Ils signifient que la divinité ou le mortel auxquels ils se rapportent sont capables de *concevoir* des ruses. Il y a pas ailleurs un passage déjà analysé (Od., VIII, 272 ss.) où la structure de la métaphore confère à δόλος une valeur concrète, en lui donnant le sens de « filet ». Le terme δολόπλοκος a les premiers comme modèle morphologique et le second comme modèle sémantique: de la même manière, ποικιλόθρονος est construit comme εύθρονος et χρυσόθρονος, mais équivaut à δαιδάλεος θρόνος. Mais le comportement de deux composés est semblable pour une autre raison encore. De même que l'un, au moyen de ποικιλο-, dilate la notion matérielle jusqu'à entraîner la valeur abstraite (si bien que le trône, qui était « beau », « d'or », « dédaléen » chez Homère, en devenant « ingénieusement construit » évoque aussi l'ingéniosité de l'artiste), de même l'autre, au moyen de -πλοκος, délimite la notion abstraite jusqu'à suggérer l'acte concret (si bien que la ruse, qui chez Homère n'était que conçue, évoque, lorsqu'elle est matériellement tramée, un objet spécifique, c'est-à-dire le filet).

Une métaphore comporte diverses phases qui, en se succédant, pâlissent jusqu'à devenir sans couleur. Une ruse tramée est un filet, mais à son tour le filet est lié à des situations qui en permettent l'usage. Leur identification, décidée par la sensibilité du lecteur, est souvent *viciée par une syntonie imparfaite*. Il arrive en effet qu'une image légèrement esquissée ne soit pas du tout perçue par le plus grand nombre, parce qu'elle est trop évanescente, et qu'elle soit au contraire enrichie par certains, précisément parce qu'ils l'ont perçue, au delà de ses limites originaires. Dans ce cas, l'imagination de celui qui lit opère sur l'image comme pourrait opérer sur une cellule un stimulus cancérigène: elle la développe au détriment du tissu contextuel, altérant ainsi l'équilibre de tout l'organisme.

Puisque la capture au moyen du filet est un moment de la pêche ou de la chasse, Aphrodite δολόπλοκος pourrait apparaître, aux yeux d'un tel lecteur, comme une pêcheuse ou une chasseresse, et la victime comme un poisson ou une bête féroce. C'est un danger que court habituellement la critique sémantique toutes les fois qu'elle considère les mots d'une manière abstraite, en les surchargeant des significations qu'ils ont dans d'autres textes, que ceux-ci soient antérieurs, postérieurs ou contemporains. Pour être fructueuse, au contraire, la comparaison doit avoir pour but de définir uniquement la limite extrême où, à l'intérieur d'une même aire culturelle homogène, l'image a été développée.

Quelques générations après Sapho, Ibycos, qui est vieux désormais, se plaint d'être tombé amoureux à nouveau (fr. 287 P.): Eros l'avait une fois encore poussé irrémédiablement dans les rets (ἐς ἄπειρα δίκτυα) de Cypris. Aussitôt après, le poète se compare à un vieux coursier, éliminant ainsi la possibilité de s'attarder sur l'image qu'il offrait comme victime et sur celle d'Aphrodite comme chasseresse. Dans le même temps, Anachréon (fr. 346/4 P., 65 Gent.) se réjouissait d'avoir échappé à Eros (en évitant) les lourds liens (δεσμῶν ... χαλεπῶν) d'Aphrodite. Le texte, qui présente des lacunes, ne révèle pas si la métaphore était en quelque sorte libre de certaines références allogènes. Mais cela aurait-il été vraiment nécessaire? Certainement pas, car δεσμός est un terme générique qui sert à indiquer ce qui retient ou empêche: du câble qui retient un bateau au mouillage (Od., XIII, I00) à la petite corde ou à la lanière en cuir qui tient la porte fermée (Od., XXI, 241) et aux chaînes qui retiennent Prométhée prisonnier (AESCH., Prom., 509, 770). La métaphore est réalisée grâce à la mention d'un objet trop générique pour évoquer une image circonstanciée.

Dans aucun de ces passages les connotations humaines ne disparaissent. C'est ce qui se passe aussi chez Sapho. Il est permis d'entrevoir le filet (et δάμνα, au vers 3, permet de ne l'entrevoir que comme filet de chasse) mais pour voir en Aphrodite une chasseresse et en Sapho une bête féroce, il faudrait que notre sensibilité esthétique nous pousse en dehors des limites de la métaphore, dans le domaine dangereux de la spéculation. Cette déviation est exclue par les vers 3-5:

μή μ' ἄσαισι μηδ' ὀνίαισι δάμνα,
πότνια, θῦμον,
ἀλλὰ τυίδ' ἔλθ' κτλ.

Le filet grâce auquel la déesse a raison du cœur de Sapho est un tissu d'angoisses et de tourments (ἄσαισι ... ὀνίαισι): les deux mots constituent la limite infranchissable de la métaphore et la confinent dans le domaine humain. L'ambigu δάμνα, semblable à une clef de voûte, renferme trois valeurs:

1° il s'adapte à l'image de la chasse avec un filet. Les animaux sauvages, une fois pris, étaient domptés. La représentation la plus ancienne se trouve sur les deux tasses mycéniennes de Vaphio. Sur la première un taureau sauvage est tombé dans un filet tendu entre deux arbres ; sur l'autre un taureau est capturé et dompté ;

2° c'est un verbe typique de la sphère érotique ;

3° comme verbe usuel du vocabulaire de la guerre, il oriente de plus en plus nettement la métaphore vers son résultat définitif (la guerre) qui apparaîtra clairement dans la conclusion, mais qui est déjà formulé dans le « viens ici » adressé à la déesse au vers 5.

Contre cette ruse d'angoisses et de tourments par laquelle Aphrodite dompte (en l'enveloppant comme dans un filet) son cœur, Sapho invoque comme remède (ἀλλά est fortement adversatif) la présence de la déesse auprès d'elle, son assistance (dans le double sens du mot de : *être auprès de* et *aider*) dans ce duel d'amour. Que ce soit là le champ de la progression fantastique, cela est confirmé avec exactitude et sans équivoque par les vers de la conclusion. Le parallélisme est parfait : la structure aux anneaux enchaînés réapparaît, avec les membres du chiasme rangés selon l'opposition habituelle (générique/spécifique ; négatif/positif).

Une structure aussi solidement eurythmique est rare dans la lyrique archaïque et peut-être même chez Sapho (l'état fragmentaire des autres odes impose le doute). Mais c'est précisément pour cette raison qu'il auraut fallu en expliquer les causes. Observer que l'ode est une composition en anneau et que par sa forme elle rappelle la prière, ne signifie pas grand-chose si l'on ne spécifie pas qu'elle est en anneau *parce qu'*elle a la forme d'une prière. C'est justement parce qu'il existait d'anciennes normes de la tradition cultuelle qui imposaient une technique rituellement déterminée, que Sapho a construit un organisme achevé : elle n'a pas inventé, mais elle a fait revivre intégralement un schéma. C'est dans cette perspective historique et culturelle que l'ode doit être placée et c'est ce que postule la pleine fonctionnalité de chaque élément du poème.

Pour qu'une prière fût efficace, il fallait invoquer la divinité avec des épithètes qui proclamaient qu'elle était en mesure de satisfaire à la requête : à l'origine on leur attribuait le pouvoir magique d'en déterminer l'intervention et l'action. Quand Chrysès prie Apollon de le venger, il l'appelle simplement « Arc d'argent », en parfaite cohérence avec la requête finale qui est que le dieu frappe les Danaens de ses flèches (Hom., *Il.*, I, 37-42).

La prière de Chrysès et l'ode de Sapho ont un schéma commun : invocation, rapports précédents du « priant » avec la divinité et requête (anticipée par Sapho après l'invocation et reprise plus longuement à la fin). Mais qu'elle peut être dans l'ode l'épithète-clé si ce n'est δ·ολόπλοκος, considérée généralement, mais à tort, comme conventionnelle ? Sa réalité fantastique a son origine dans l'émotion religieuse de Sapho et dans sa conception sacrale de l'amour. Ces conclusions peuvent être tirées facilement d'après l'analyse comparée du poème et de la conclusion.

J'ai déjà souligné la forte opposition qui lie les deux membres de la requête (vv. 3-5) : « ne me vaincs pas par des angoisses et des tourments, *mais* viens ici ». La disposition d'Aphrodite peut donc être double : défavorable ou favorable, selon que la déesse est loin (v.6 πήλοι) ou près (v.5 τυίδε) de celle qui la prie. Quand elle est près, elle assiste, elle est alliée: σύμμαχος (v.28) rend explicite la valeur de ἔλθε μοι καὶ νῦν (v.25) mis en corrélation avec τυίδ᾽ ἔλθε (v.5). À la base du terme — comme de δάμνα aussi en partie — il y a la métaphore qui fait de l'amour une bataille. On la perd quand on est seul, sans l'aide d'Aphrodite: alors on tombe dans un amas d'angoisses, de douleurs et de profonds tourments (v.3 ἄσαισι ... ὀνίαισι v.25 χαλέπαν ... μερίμναν), tendu, comme un piège, par la lointaine et hostile déesse. Il n'y a que celle qui a dressé le piège qui peut le défaire (v.25 λῦσον). D'où la nécessité de l'invoquer rituellement comme δολόπλοκος.

Autrement dit, le λῦσον du v.25 («défais» «démêle» moi, indiqué par μοι, dans le même vers et dans le suivant) est parallèle à μή με ... δάμνα du vers 3, et est «polairement» opposé au deuxième élément de δολόπλοκος. Dans les deux grâces que Sapho demande, l'épithète est jointe à la première, négative: «ne me dompte pas» «libère-moi». La deuxième grâce, positive, ne se situe plus dans le domaine du δόλος, mais dans le domaine opposé de la μάχη.

Sapho prie: en tant que δολόπλοκος libère-moi de ces liens; en tant que σύμμαχος aide-moi dans ma bataille d'amour. Si elle avait invoqué la déesse comme δολόπλοκος pour obtenir non seulement sa libération mais aussi la prise au piège amoureux de son adversaire, elle n'aurait rien demandé d'autre que l'inversion des rôles. Elle aurait demandé vengeance et non un amour partagé: de même que j'aime et ne suis pas aimée en retour, ainsi, que celle qui maintenant ne partage pas mon amour m'aime alors que je ne l'aimerai plus. Interprétation impossible, exclue — surtout par le rapport d'opposition implicite qui existe dans les deux termes δολόπλοκος et σύμμαχος, et plus précisément dans leurs noyaux constitutifs δόλος et μάχη.

On a déjà parlé de l'équivalence entre δόλος et λόχος «piège». Ils désignent tous les deux, une des deux manières possibles d'anéantir l'adversaire: l'autre manière est la bataille à visage découvert, la μάχη. Dans aucun passage l'opposition n'apparaît plus clairement que dans Il. I 226-28. En l'insultant, Achille fait un reproche à Agamemnon: «jamais tu n'as eu le courage de t'armer pour une bataille (ἐς πόλεμον) avec ton peuple; jamais celui de partir te poster aux aguets (λόχονδ᾽ ἰέναι) avec les Achéens les plus valeureux». Le fait que, dans ce passage, πόλεμος figure à la place de μάχη ne présente pas de difficulté. Les deux termes sont considérés comme synonymes par Homère: ils sont même unis plusieurs fois en hendiadys. Il est intéressant, par contre, de relever que μάχη et même, dans certains cas πόλεμος, indique la manière ouverte de combattre, opposée à l'autre, sournoise et insidieuse, exprimée par δόλος et par λόχος: σύμμαχος c'est l'allié en rase campagne.

Il suffit pour s'en convaincre de relire deux passages des Choéphores, fondés sur la même opposition. En invoquant son père, Électre dit (Aesch. Cho. 492 ss.): «souviens-toi du filet (ἀμφίβληστρον) et comment ils l'inventèrent». Oreste: «avec des chaînes sans airain tu as été fait prisonnier (πέδαις ... ἐθηρεύθης), ô mon père». Électre: «dans d'infâmes et insidieux complots» (αἰσχρῶς τε βουλευτοῖσιν ἐν καλύμμασιν). Quelques vers plus loin Oreste prie (vv. 497-98): «envoie la Justice livrer, à côté des tiens, une bataille ouverte; ou bien laisse que nous usions des mêmes ruses contre eux». Le texte est moins ample mais il n'est pas moins explicite que la traduction:

Ἤτοι δίκην ἴαλλε σύμμαχον φίλοις,

ἢ τὰς ὁμοίας ἀντίδος λαβὰς (Canter: βλάβας codd.) λαβεῖν.

Un autre passage est complémentaire de celui-ci. Oreste (vv. 555-58): «j'ordonne à ces jeunes filles (celles du chœur) de garder secrets mes projets, afin que ceux qui par ruse (δόλῳ) ont tué un roi révéré, soient pris par la même ruse et le même filet (δόλῳ γε καὶ ληφθῶσιν ἐν ταὐτῷ βρόχῳ) et tués».

Du point de vue sémantique le parallélisme est parfait. Comme chez Sapho, chez Eschyle *la ruse* est un piège avec un filet, auquel est opposée la bataille ouverte, l'unique type de lutte où le compagnon peut être défini vraiment σύμμαχος. L'appréciation du δόλος est naturellement différente: chez Eschyle elle est crûment négative, parce que la ruse a été tramée contre un roi vénéré, dans sa propre maison; contre l'époux par l'épouse; contre le père par la mère. Au contraire, en temps de guerre, sur le plan de l'*areté* héroïque, ruse et combat dans un champ de bataille ouvert sont également positifs (et ils le sont aussi pour Sapho), mais ils indiquent toujours des actions différentes. Que signifie, alors, dans la prière, ce passage d'un terme à l'autre (de δολόπλοκος à σύμμαχος), tous les deux appropriés à une même expérience, la guerre, et tirés de celle-ci métaphoriquement? Il signifie, avant tout, une rigoureuse cohérence fantastique: c'est-à-dire, entre autres, une adhérence à l'occasion concrète où l'ode aurait été chantée, et une adhérence, sur le plan expressif, au mécanisme de la métaphore choisie.

C'est Schadewaldt (p. 87 ss) qui a souligné le fait que la prière est une «verhüllte Liebeswerbung»: Sapho l'aurait chantée dans la thiase, devant les jeunes filles, au cours peut-être d'une des cérémonies en l'honneur d'Aphrodite; la jeune fille aimée aurait été présente et aurait compris. Il ne fournit cependant aucune preuve de cette juste intuition. La preuve est précisément dans cette opposition entre l'Aphrodite σύμμαχος du v.28 et l'Aphrodite δολόπλοκος du v.2. Par sa prière Sapho a déclaré qu'elle est désormais ouvertement amoureuse. La bataille pour conquérir la personne aimée sera dorénavant à visage découvert et elle sera victorieuse si l'invincible Aphrodite est près d'elle comme une alliée et l'aide de sa force et non de ses ruses. Mais en quoi consistaient les ruses que Sapho exclut? Il conviendra de le répéter: en attirant la victime dans un amour qui prend son âme dans le filet des angoisses et des tourments, parce que précisément il n'est pas payé de retour. Et que demande Sapho? J'aime et je ne suis pas aimée en retour: libère-moi de cette situation, ô déesse, et aide-moi à conquérir le cœur de la personne que j'aime, *afin que notre amour soit réciproque et heureux.*

Au moment même où elle l'invoque non plus comme δολόπλοκος mais comme σύμμαχος, Sapho exclut la ruse: c'est-à-dire qu'elle exclut de ses vœux que la personne aimée soit enveloppée elle aussi dans ces mêmes peines et qu'elle l'aime elle aussi mais sans être aimée en retour. Si nous n'avions eu que l'introduction et la conclusion de l'ode, leur analyse seule aurait été suffisante pour faire comprendre le motif et le but de la prière: mais la partie centrale a également survécu, qui confirme les deux autres d'une manière catégorique.

Sous son double aspect de déesse qui sait tromper, mais qui sait aussi contraindre par la force, Aphrodite était déjà représentée par Homère. Dans le livre III de l'*Iliade,* après avoir soustrait Alexandre à la fureur de Ménélas, elle va appeler Hélène, sur la tour, et, pour allumer son désir, elle lui parle de celui qui l'attend dans la chambre, sur le lit resplendissant, rayonnant de parures et de beauté, comme un homme qui ne revient pas d'un duel mais qui s'en va danser, ou vient de danser. Bien qu'elle se fût présentée sous l'apparence d'une vieille femme, Hélène la reconnaît et résiste (v. 399 ss.): «Malheureuse, pourquoi veux-tu me séduire?» Parce que Ménélas veut m'emmener chez lui» te voici encore ici, en train de préparer tes ruses?» (νῦν δεῦρο δολοφρονέουσα παρέστης). Puis elle l'insulte. Aphrodite lui répond en colère, menace de l'abandonner, de semer une haine funeste entre Troyens et Danaens, de la destiner à un sort malheureux. Alors Hélène, saisie de peur, se dirige en silence vers la chambre. La déesse la précédait.

Le parallélisme, partiel, est entre Hélène et la personne aimée par Sapho. Comme Sapho, Alexandre aussi est en proie au désir d'amour: il attendait en effet Hélène dans la chambre, sur le lit, quand Aphrodite est allée la chercher. Hélène est coupable, avant tout, parce qu'elle refuse de satisfaire à ce désir: ses insultes sont l'extériorisation de son cruel refus. À la fin de l'épisode, Aphrodite est une déesse terrible, comme dans l'*Hippolyte* d'Euripide, inexorable et funeste, et qui peut entraîner à la ruine un mortel et des nations entières. Non moins inexorable apparaît la déesse qui en d'autres occasions avait promis catégoriquement à Sapho, dans des situations identiques à la situation actuelle, que la personne qu'elle aimait l'aimerait en retour à tout prix. Elle demande maintenant de l'aide à cette déesse: c'est le souvenir qui la pousse à oser et à avoir confiance.

Pour pousser Aphrodite à lui porter secours, Sapho a recours à un argument traditionnel, d'origine probablement magique. Ma situation — dit-elle — est aujourd'hui semblable à celle qu'elle a été en d'autres occasions, lorsque tu n'as pas manqué de m'aider: tu peux et tu dois donc m'aider maintenant encore. C'est un moyen presque mécanique de déterminer l'intervention divine. La formule du début «si jamais» équivaut à un «comme», même chez Sapho, comme déjà dans la prière de Chrysès (de même que moi je t'ai honoré, ainsi toi exauce-moi). Mais tandis que Chrysès rappelait tous ses actes de constante vénération, Sapho présente le fait de tomber amoureuse et d'être aidée par la déesse comme une expérience qui se répète. Présent et passé étaient simplement superposés chez Chrysès, alors que chez Sapho ils sont scandés dans une fuite temporelle indéfinie: dans son évocation il y a un sens de la perspective qui manque totalement dans celle de Chrysès.

Pour symboliser ces innombrables fois il n'y a que trois moments expressifs, mais qui sont organisés et développés successivement: 1) aide-moi *maintenant* (que l'on déduit d'après le contexte et qui est repris explicitement au v. 25 καὶ νῦν; 2) comme *en d'autres occasions* aussi (v. 5 κἀτέρωτα), quand tu es venue pour m'aider et que tu m'as demandé: 3) quoi / qui *à nouveau, encore* (δηὖτε répété trois fois, vv. 15, 16, 18). Cette notion d'identité qui se répète est la notion même que Sapho eut de l'amour; symétriquement la déesse de l'amour revient elle aussi de façon identique et sans fin. Elle est en somme *éternelle* et comme «immortelle»; elle doit être invoquée ἀϑανάτα (v. I) a la même fonction rituelle que δολόπλοκος.

Que ce soit aussi une épithète-clé, cela est prouvé par les vv. 13-14. C'est le moment suprême de l'épiphanie, quand la déesse, arrivée bientôt à travers les airs», révèle son visage. L'invocation initiale est reprise par le vocatif ὦ μάκαιρα et développée analytiquement dans le μειδιαίσαισ' ἀϑανάτῳ προσώπῳ suivant: sa condition de «bienheureuse», Aphrodite la manifeste «en souriant dans son visage immortel», c'est-à-dire «dans son visage qui sourit éternellement». Par rapport à μει-διαίσαισα et à προσώπῳ, qui évoquent seulement une image immobile, ἀϑανάτῳ joue un rôle dynamique et imprime à l'image une durée qui va au delà du temps humain. Les termes des deux premiers vers sont donc disposés non seulement en forme de chiasme, en anneau, mais aussi parallèlement, selon l'ordre visuel même:

ποικιλόϑρονε / παῖ Δίος = Royauté d'Aphrodite
ἀϑανάτα / δολόπλοκε = caractéristiques de son mode d'opérer.

L'expression παῖ Δίος mérite qu'on s'y arrête. Les deux figures du proème (en anneau, en chiasme; linéaire, par séries parallèles) contribuent certainement, en se croisant, à rendre plus vive l'expression «fille de Zeus»: elles ne sont pas en mesure toutefois d'en prouver la fonctionnalité. Et l'on pourrait être amené à nier qu'il en ait une, si le πάτρος du v. 7, en insistant sur le rapport d'Aphrodite avec Zeus, n'imposait un examen plus attentif du contexte. La comparaison avec Homère offre encore une fois une direction valable.

Dans le livre XIV de l'*Iliade*, Héra, pour éviter que Zeus n'empêche les dieux de secourir les Grecs qui se trouvaient en mauvaise posture, décide de le séduire (v. 159 ss.). Elle va dans sa chambre, prend son bain, s'oint d'huile, se vêt de ses plus belles robes et, prenant à part Aphrodite, lui demande de l'aider (v. 197 ss.):

Τὴν δὲ δολοφρονέουσα προσηύδα πότνια Ἥρη·
 '' δὸς νῦν μοι φιλότητα καὶ ἵμερον, ᾧ τε σὺ πάντας
δαμνᾷ ἀϑανάτους ἠδὲ ϑνητοὺς ἀνϑρώπους ''.

Elle lui cache cependant son dessein et donne comme motif son
désir de vouloir réconcilier Océan et Téthys en les invitant à s'unir dans
l'amour. La φιλομμειδής Aphrodite répond: il est impossible d'opposer
un refus à l'épouse de Zeus. Elle parle ainsi et détache de sa poitrine
le bandeau qui donne l'amour (vv. 214-24):

Ἦ, καὶ ἀπὸ στήθεσφιν ἐλύσατο κεστὸν ἱμάντα
ποικίλον, ἔνθα τέ οἱ θελκτήρια πάντα τέτυκτο·
ἔνθ' ἔνι μὲν φιλότης, ἐν δ' ἵμερος, ἐν δ' ὀαριστύς,
πάρφασις ἥ τ' ἔκλεψε νόον πύκα περ φρονεόντων.
τόν ῥά οἱ ἔμβαλε χερσὶν ἔπος τ' ἔφατ' ἔκ τ' ὀνόμαζε·
" τῆ νῦν, τοῦτον ἱμάντα τεῷ ἐγκάτθεο κόλπῳ,
ποικίλον, ᾧ ἔνι πάντα τετεύχαται· οὐδέ σέ φημι
ἄπρηκτόν γε νέεσθαι, ὅ τι φρησὶ σῇσι μενοινᾷς ".
Ὣς φάτο, μείδησεν δὲ βοῶπις πόντια Ἥρη,
μειδήσασα δ' ἔπειτα ἑῷ ἐγκάτθετο κόλπῳ.
Ἡ μὲν ἔβη πρὸς δῶμα Διὸς θυγάτηρ Ἀφροδίτη,
κτλ.

> Elle dit et, de sa poitrine, elle détacha le bandeau brodé, artistement
> travaillé, où tous les charmes se trouvaient enfermés: là se tenaient l'amour,
> le désir, la séduction, flatterie qui captive l'esprit de celui-là même qui est
> sage. Elle le posa entre ses mains et prenant la parole, s'adressa à elle en ces
> termes: «Tiens, mets sur ta poitrine ce bandeau, artistement travaillé, où tout
> a été préparé, et je t'assure que tu ne reviendras pas sans avoir accompli
> ce que ton cœur désire». Ainsi parla-t-elle. La souveraine Héra aux yeux de
> génisse sourit et en souriant elle posa le bandeau sur son sein. Alors, la fille
> de Zeus, Aphrodite, vers sa demeure se dirigea.

Dans cet épisode Aphrodite est la grande déesse qui rend possible
la ruse d'amour. Mais la ruse est différente de celle dont est victime
Sapho. Toute la situation est même complètement différente: une comparaison approfondie ne pourrait avoir d'autre résultat que l'exclusion d'un
quelconque rapport de dépendance de Sapho par rapport au passage d'Homère. Mais c'est précisément pour cette raison que sont encore plus sur-
prenantes les correspondances ponctuelles et partielles ainsi que les résonances lexicales qui unissent les deux textes.

L'homérique δολοφρονέουσα (v. 197) rappelle le saphique δολόπλοκος (v. 2). Il importe peu que les deux termes réfèrent l'un à Héra, l'autre à Aphrodite: du reste Héra assume dans cet épisode la fonction
d'Aphrodite. En revanche il est important de remarquer que, dès que l'on
pénètre dans l'aire d'Aphrodite, la ruse réapparaît. Le renversement des
positions ne peut surprendre: c'est un renversement polaire, structurale-
ment inhérent à la conception même du divin. Elle réapparaît également
dans le passage déjà cité de l'*Odyssée* (VIII 272 ss.), où la victime de la
ruse et du filet est Aphrodite elle-même, qui savait si bien tramer des
ruses. La confirmation de cette oscillation est représentée ici par l'opposition entre la φιλομμειδής Aphrodite (v. 211) et Héra qui rit, après l'avoir
trompée, et qui, en riant, ceint sa poitrine du bandeau (v. 222 s.).

Chez Sapho, c'est Aphrodite qui rit (v. 14). Le rapprochement est révélateur: évidemment *ruse* et *rire* étaient étroitement liés dans la sphère amoureuse. De même que la δολοφρονέουσα Héra rit lorsque, après avoir trompé Aphrodite, elle se prépare à tromper Zeus, de même la δολόπλοκος Aphrodite rit lorsqu'elle a enveloppé Sapho dans le filet d'amour. Dans les deux textes le verbe δαμνάω et le substantif φιλότης sont identiques. Il est très intéressant de remarquer avec quelle insistance Homère qualifie de ποικίλος le bandeau d'Aphrodite: c'est donc un adjectif qui se trouve dans le domaine de la déesse. Le bandeau est ποικίλος parce qu'il est fait *ingénieusement*. La proposition relative qui suit, aussi bien au vers 215 qu'au vers 220, a une valeur causale cachée et explique dans quel sens ce vêtement était ποικίλος: non seulement parce qu'il était artistement brodé (κεστός ne réapparaît pas au v. 220), mais plus particulièrement à cause de tous les charmes qui y avaient été tissés. C'est une confirmation de mon interprétation de ποικιλόθρονος.

Ces correspondances, dans deux textes probablement indépendants, sont la preuve d'une manière d'être fondamentale de l'imagination et du langage qui correspondent entre eux et qui se présentent habituellement à la sensibilité sélective du sujet, non pas de manière fragmentaire mais en bloc, comme un agrégat d'images et de mots, que le poète a le rôle d'agencer. Si cela est vrai, il n'est pas surprenant que Sapho ait invoqué Aphrodite comme «fille de Zeus». Homère ne procédait pas différemment. Mais le parallélisme est encore plus convaincant: Aphrodite vint vers Sapho «quittant la maison de son père» (v. 7); chez Homère elle s'éloigne d'Héra «vers la maison de Zeus» (v. 224). Le rapport étroit qui existe, chez Sapho, entre l'allusion «à la maison paternelle» et l'invocation «fille de Zeus» est aussi confirmé par Homère chez qui Διός est carrément ἀπὸ κοινοῦ (v. 224): ἣ μὲν ἔβη πρὸς δῶμα Διὸς θυγάτηρ Ἀφροδίτη.

Naturellement, Sapho n'opère pas mécaniquement en utilisant au hasard, jusqu'à épuisement, le bagage lexical que la situation (la ruse d'amour) comportait. Elle a invoqué Aphrodite comme «fille de Zeus», poussée par la norme culturelle qui réclamait une allusion généalogique; mais également et surtout pour obéir à un autre motif, car l'obligation d'introduire le transfert ultérieur de la déesse auprès de son père a été déterminante pour elle. Même si cela lui était suggéré par la tradition, il y avait chez elle un autre but: celui d'exprimer visuellement une des deux manières d'être d'Aphrodite, être loin. L'autre manière, être près, est représentée par son sourire immédiat et immortel. Entre les deux moments se place l'évocation du voyage qui commence par ἀλλὰ τυίδ'ἔλθε au début de la deuxième strophe et qui se termine par αἶψα δ'ἐξίκοντο au même endroit, au début de la quatrième strophe.

La venue de la déesse est tout d'abord évoquée dans ses différentes phases et ensuite observée attentivement. Dans la deuxième strophe se déroulent deux mouvements opposés sur un même axe: d'abord du bas vers le haut («ma voix — que tu entendis de loin — tu écoutas») puis en sens inverse («la maison paternelle — quittée — tu vins»). Dans la troisième strophe l'image l'emporte sur le mouvement, l'adjectif sur le verbe:

la tension se relâche et s'apaise dans la vision du miracle. Les vers 8-9 servent de liaison, avec les verbes en position inverse («tu vins, ayant attelé»), précédés de χρύσιον, la première d'une insistante série d'épithètes: *beaux* et *véloces* les passereaux, *noire* la terre, *rapides* les ailes. L'image est suspendue entre ciel et terre, dans les airs: γᾶς, ὠράνω, αἴθερος se succèdent dans cet ordre, qui est celui de la perspective qu'a la personne qui regarde et attend, depuis la terre. Enfin l'arrivée et l'épiphanie: αἶψα qualifie la première de soudaine et, par suggestion, la seconde d'imprévue (bien qu'attendue).

Dans les trois strophes suivantes (vv. 13-24) la polarité qui oppose symétriquement les termes dans le reste de l'ode, se réalise dans la confrontation directe entre Aphrodite et Sapho. Au début, le discours se développe par séries d'oppositions: dans la première prévalent encore les éléments nominaux, dans la seconde les éléments verbaux. L'une est la sphère sereine de la déesse, l'autre la sphère agitée de la femme:

μάκαιρα	πέπονθα
μειδιαίσαισα	κάλημμι, θέλω γένεσθαι
ἀθανάτῳ προσώπῳ	μαινόλᾳ θύμῳ.

Il serait inutile de tenter de réduire en deux formules les termes de l'opposition: on perdrait les indications les plus valables, que seule l'analyse est en mesure de révéler.

Nous voyons le visage de la déesse et nous connaissons les sentiments de la femme. Aphrodite s'identifie à son sourire «épiphanique», qui n'est pas la manifestation non plus que l'expression d'un sentiment particulier donc changeant, que l'on pourrait rechercher ailleurs et identifier: elle *est* ce sourire immortel de bienheureuse, tout comme elle est δολόπλοκος. Sourire et ruse d'amour se correspondent et sont la déesse même, dans un de ses aspects fondamentaux. En revanche nous connaissons les mouvements les plus secrets de l'âme de Sapho, ses souffrances, ses cris, ses désirs, mais non son image. Au visage immortel de l'une est opposé le cœur fou de l'autre.

Les valeurs de μαινόλας sont les mêmes que celles de μαίνομαι d'où le mot dérive. La notion de temporaire est fondamentale. Le cœur de Sapho n'est pas toujours fou, mais il l'est toutes les fois qu'elle est prise par l'amour: de la même manière les mains de Patrocle μαίνονται quand, avec Achille ou tout seul, il se jette dans la bataille (Hom. *Il.* XVI 244 s.). À cette notion est liée l'autre notion, à savoir que la folie, en tant que *raptus* temporaire, est causée par une divinité. C'est Dionysos qui provoque la manie bachique qui prend les Ménades et qui a pris le scythe Skylas (Hérodt. IV 79); c'est Athéna qui provoque la folie meurtrière d'Ajax (Soph. *Ai.* 59 s.). Même le μάντις vaticine quand il est possédé par Apollon, comme Cassandre chez Eschyle (*Ag.* 1275).

L'expression μαινόλᾳ θύμῳ non seulement s'oppose à ἀθανάτῳ προσώπῳ comme la temporalité intermittente s'oppose à la continuité immuable, mais elle suggère aussi que la folie est infligée par un dieu, c'est-à-dire par Aphrodite, et qu'elle est faite des angoisses et des tourments qui accablent Sapho. De même que l'expression ἀϑανάτῳ προσώπῳ rappelle l'ἀϑανάτα du 1, ainsi μαινόλα ϑύμῳ rappelle le μή μ'ἄσασι μηδ'ὀνίαισι δάμνα, πότνια, ϑῦμον des vv. 3-4: la répétition de ϑῦμος (aux vv. 4 et 18) et les deux invocations parallèles πότνια / μάκαιρα (aux vers 4 et 13) en sont la preuve. Dans cette perspective, Sapho apparaît comme le témoin de la déesse et l'amour comme une expérience religieuse, digne d'inspirer une ode qui est une prière, mais qui est aussi un hymne à la souveraine et bienheureuse puissance d'Aphrodite.

La manière dont Sapho conçoit l'amour résulte des questions mêmes que la déesse lui pose. Les éléments fondamentaux sont les deux éléments sur lesquels on a le plus insisté: δηὖτε, répété trois fois, et les groupes φεύγει — διώξει, μὴ δέκεται — δώσει, μὴ φίλει — φιλήσει. D. Page, à qui revient le mérite de les avoir découverts, en a proposé une interprétation suggestive mais insoutenable (p. 12 ss.). Après avoir opportunément précisé (contre Wilamowitz) que ce n'est pas la déesse qui demande à nouveau mais Sapho qui souffre à nouveau, il voit en δηὖτε une nuance d'indignation et d'impatience. Aphrodite reprocherait à Sapho de prendre au sérieux sa passion qu'elle sait pourtant inconstante et passagère comme les précédentes: demain c'est elle qui fuira la même personne aimée qui la fuit aujourd'hui. C'est ainsi que s'expliquerait son sourire. La déesse serait amusée: un peu impatiente mais tolérante, «as a mother with a troublesome child».

Pour poser correctement le problème, il faut partir des vers 18-20. Le sens n'est pas entravé par la situation en partie désespérée du vers 19. Aphrodite demande: « qui à nouveau = cette fois (dois-je amener) à ton amour? qui te fait du tort, ô Sapho?» Évidemment l'expression ἐς σὰν φιλότατα, qui équivaut à εἰς φιλότητα σου, n'indique pas l'amour de Sapho pour une autre personne, mais l'amour d'une autre personne pour Sapho. L'adjectif possessif (ou le génitif du pronom) a une valeur objective et non subjective. La question «qui dois-je amener à t'aimer» n'exclut pas cependant que Sapho aurait été encore amoureuse quand son antagoniste aurait commencé à l'aimer. Cette perspective est celle de toute histoire d'amour. Une personne souffre parce qu'elle n'est pas aimée et elle désire que l'autre l'aime en retour: elle désire recevoir de l'autre cet amour qu'elle lui offre, selon le *juste* principe de la réciprocité. C'est à cette supposition que se rattache la deuxième question d'Aphrodite: «qui te fait du tort, ô Sapho?». La déesse vient pour mettre fin à une situation qu'elle juge injuste.

Ce nouvel aspect d'Aphrodite, qui de δολόπλοκος est devenue juge, a une profonde signification. L'amour, qui pourtant vient d'elle devient une duperie s'il n'est pas partagé: la responsabilité du malaise qui en dérive retombe cependant sur la personne qui, aimée, n'aime pas en retour. La non-observation de la réciprocité est une faute dont est juge la même divinité qui a fait naître le processus.

Si la déesse est juge, l'autre personne est l'accusée et Sapho est l'accusatrice. Le grec exprime ce rapport par δικαστής, ὁ φεύγων, ὁ διώκων. Ces mêmes termes, avec une signification différente, se rencontrent également chez Sapho. On comprend clairement quel est le domaine qui les lui a suggérés. Un mot (ἀδικήει) est suivi automatiquement par les autres (φεύγει, διώξει) auxquels il est lié habituellement: à cet instant même, cependant, la valeur juridique du groupe est remplacée en partie par la valeur érotique. Les conséquences sont décisives. La notion de dualité dans un mouvement interdépendant, qui dans le domaine juridique était intériorisée et ne survivait que métaphoriquement (devant le juge, l'accusé « qui fuit » et l'accusateur « qui poursuit » sont tous les deux immobiles), n'existe pas du tout dans la sphère affective. Non seulement le mouvement est métaphorique, mais c'est une seule personne qui l'accomplit: elle évite ou cherche quelqu'un ou quelque chose qui ne fuit pas mais qui se présente comme un but.

Grâce à une différente orientation du lien qui les unit, φεύγειν et διώκειν se dégagent du rapport d'équidistance: le premier reprend son entière autonomie; le second en acquiert une pour la première fois. Que l'on cherche l'amour furtif (λαθραίαν κύπριν ... διώκειν, EUB, fr. 67, 8 s.), que l'on coure après le plaisir (ἡδονὴν δ. PLAT., *Phaedr.*, 251 a); que l'on aime la vérité (τὴν ἀλήθειαν δ., PLAT. *Gorg.*, 482 e) ou que l'on suive le bien et le beau (τὸ ἀγαθὸν καὶ καλὸν δ., *ib.*, 480 c), l'objet vers lequel on tend ne fuit pas, mais il attire et dirige vers lui. Certes, même dans le rapport entre celui qui guide et celui qui est guidé il y a une idée de mouvement, mais c'est un mouvement d'accord et non d'hostilité. Personne ne fuit et personne ne poursuit, mais l'un guide et l'autre suit.

Quelle a été alors la promesse d'Aphrodite? Non que la situation se renverserait dans un mauvais sens, mais que Sapho serait aimée de nouveau: une promesse de réparation et non de vengeance.

Comme les autres fois, cette fois aussi. Ainsi ce n'est pas en une seule occasion mais en chaque occasion que Sapho a connu l'amour: comme une progression dialectique de la passion. Un *partner* cherche impatiemment l'autre, lequel le cherche ensuite. Ces deux dimensions temporelles (les différents épisodes de l'amour dans le temps et les moments de chaque épisode d'amour) sont exposées dans les vv. 15-18: la première par δηὖτε, la seconde par les trois verbes conjugués précisément au passé, au présent et au futur (πέπονθα, κάλημμι, θέλω γένεσθαι).

Dans l'interprétation de δηὖτε il ne faut pas pousser trop loin les spéculations psychologiques. La structure polaire, selon laquelle l'ode est agencée, atteint son plus haut degré d'évidence dans les vers où Sapho invoque la déesse et où la déesse vient jusqu'à elle. C'est à ce moment-là que la tension entre la béatitude divine et éternelle, d'une part, et la nature humaine passionnée et changeante d'autre part, est à son maximum? Mais c'est à ce moment précis que se produit le miracle de l'identification: la déesse s'humanise, parle le langage angoissé de Sapho; et Sapho se rassérène, voit en elle la compagne d'un combat victorieux. Séparer la sphère de l'une et de l'autre devient dès lors impossible et serait arbitraire. Il ne faut pas oublier que les vv. 15-20, hérissés et contractés par la foule des verbes qui expriment la condition endurée par Sapho en d'autres occasions, font partie des propos que la déesse lui a tenus alors et que Sapho revit à présent. Les trois δηὖτε se trouvent au confluent de ces plans et de ces moments différents. Leur polyvalence même nous interdit de les interpréter d'une manière unique, et il en va de même pour les passages d'Homère, qui en plus comportent des situations tout à fait hétérogènes. En revanche, on peut faire une comparaison avec la poésie lyrique d'amour, où δηὖτε revient souvent, comme une formule rituelle, pour indiquer la manifestation «à nouveau» de la passion: et c'est un δηὖτε de constatation, sans aucune valeur propre, mais qui est chaque fois chargé des nuances prédominantes du contexte.

L'individuation de δηὖτε sera d'autant plus exacte que l'on tiendra davantage compte de son ambiguïté et de ses degrés d'oscillation sémantique. Le «à nouveau» d'Aphrodite (compréhension, affection) répète le «à nouveau» qui était chaque fois dans les prières de Sapho (souffrance, espérance confiante). Le troisième δηὖτε a un coloris différent, car il n'indique pas une *même* chose endurée ou accomplie à nouveau, mais un nouvel amour pour une personne *différente*: «tu as demandé ce que j'ai souffert *à nouveau,* et pourquoi *à nouveau* je t'ai invoquée... qui (dois-je amener) de nouveau» c'est-à-dire «*cette fois* à t'aimer?». L'écart dépend du changement du sujet: la personne est toujours la première personne du singulier (de même que l'adverbe est toujours δηὖτε); le sujet cependant n'est plus Sapho (comme elle l'était de πέπονϑα, de κάλημμι et de ϑέλω γένεσϑαι), mais Aphrodite (comme le prouve le possessif ἐς σὰν φιλότατα). Depuis τίνα δηὖτε du vers 18 jusqu'au v. 24 les paroles de la déesse sont rapportées dans la forme directe.

Les deux questions «qui (dois-je amener) à ton amour? qui te fait du tort, ô Sapho?» constituent une limite: elles concluent et ouvrent. D'exécutrice affectueuse qu'elle était, Aphrodite devient juge. Le mouvement est énergiquement relevé par l'*hysteron proteron*: c'est la deuxième question qui aurait dû précéder l'autre. L'élément nouveau, polarisant, est le pronom interrogatif: la personne aimée est enfin introduite dans le tableau. D'abord elle est évoquée simplement comme quelqu'un (τίνα) qui doit être amené à Sapho; aussitôt après elle est citée comme étant la responsable de sa souffrance. Placée au premier plan, promue au rôle de sujet (τίς), elle acquiert une stature, mais reste anonyme et sans visage. C'est la structure même de l'ode qui lui refuse toute identité: d'un côté, il y a Sapho, liée à Aphrodite comme le témoin à son dieu; de l'autre, comme une ombre, se trouve quiconque l'a emflammée d'amour. Ce qui donne une réalité à l'antagoniste, c'est uniquement la passion de la protagoniste. Une personne qui possède une pleine individualité existe aussi peu que ce cas particulier: quelle autre fonction ont, en effet, κἀτέρωτα et δηὖτε sinon celle de dissoudre personne et circonstance en les multipliant indéfiniment (il en est de celle-ci comme des autres mentionnées les fois précédentes) et de les réduire à des indices d'une fréquence indéterminée?

Conséquemment les paroles qu'Aphrodite prononce aussitôt après ont le caractère absolu qui convient à l'affirmation d'une loi générale. Plusieurs siècles après, Dante inclura la même loi dans ce vers essentiel et inéluctable de l'*Enfer* (V, 103): «Amour, qui contraint à aimer qui est aimé». Cette citation a la valeur que prend n'importe quel appel à des *loci similes*. C'est un point, choisi par approximation, qui ouvre un arc de perspective; un réactif qui met plus nettement en évidence les différentes caractéristiques du texte-base. Le vers de Dante a le ton paisible et raisonnable d'une énonciation: Francesca voit dans son obéissance passionnée à l'amour de Paolo la vérification d'une norme inévitable. Les paroles d'Aphrodite sont différentes: elles sont pressantes, résonnent comme des menaces et sont prononcées par une déesse, après que *sa* norme a été foulée aux pieds. Elles n'énoncent pas, mais réaffirment: elles reprochent d'un côté et promettent de l'autre. Plus qu'une promesse, elles sont un verdict. Aphrodite ne vient pas seulement pour exaucer un être qui lui est cher. Ce n'est pas seulement l'affection qui la pousse à écouter Sapho, mais aussi ce sentiment particulier de solidarité jalouse qui impose au chef de secourir les membres de son groupe: la volonté de rétablir l'ordre dans la sphère de sa compétence.

À ce point, les considérations d'ordre historique ne peuvent plus être repoussées. Comme presque toute la poésie archaïque, comme les autres odes de Sapho, celle-ci aussi était destinée à un groupe: dans ce cas spécifique, avant d'être destinée à un plus vaste auditoire anonyme, elle s'adressait aux jeunes filles du thiase. À l'égard de cet auditoire concret l'ode a des fins pratiques qui accompagnent le but principal qui est celui d'obtenir par des prières l'aide divine. Parmi ces fins pratiques l'une est pédagogique: l'histoire de Sapho qui se répète est paradigmatique et sert à consolider le principe — fondamental pour le fonctionnement ordonné de la vie du thiase — que celui qui est aimé doit aimer à son tour. Une autre fin est psychagogique et représente l'aspect individuel de l'autre fin, qui est générale: Sapho veut persuader son antagoniste de l'aimer en retour.

On a coutume de répéter que le point culminant de l'ode est l'apparition d'Aphrodite. Cette affirmation est vraie mais à condition que l'épiphanie ne soit pas coupée des vers qui l'introduisent: sans αἴ ποτα κἀτέρωτα du v. 5, on ne pourrait pas comprendre non plus les δηὖτε des vers 15-18. Si on les considère globalement, les cinq strophes enchâssées entre la première et la dernière, révèlent une *Stimmung* qui n'évolue pas de façon linéaire mais cyclique. Le souvenir des épiphanies passées change l'angoisse initiale de Sapho en une attente confiante. Le schéma de l'apparition est gradué en sens inverse: Aphrodite qui lors de sa rapide apparition sourit avec béatitude dans son visage immortel, s'anime graduellement, pose des questions pressantes, et, menaçante, prononce son verdict nu et inexorable. Ainsi, même la partie centrale est agencée selon le même principe qui dispose de façon cyclique les éléments constitutifs du proème et de la conclusion et oppose symétriquement les deux strophes.

Le miracle de l'identification des deux sphères, la sphère humaine et la sphère divine, se réalise selon un mouvement de compensation que reflète clairement et fidèlement le tissu stylistique. La correspondance, qui est donc structurale, se retrouve aussi au niveau des contenus. Sapho déclare que l'amour est une expérience qui se reproduit d'une manière identique; Aphrodite le confirme et proclame que sa loi est la réciprocité. Le résultat de ces deux déclarations complémentaires est un message, une sorte de code (destiné avant tout aux jeunes filles du thiase) qui sanctionne ce principe fondamental: l'amour se manifeste selon un rythme cyclique qui comporte deux phases antithétiques et alternées: d'opposition et d'angoisse qu'on est aimé en retour. La déesse en est la garante et le juge, elle « qui abat et ranime, qui tourmente et qui console » et dont Sapho est le témoin privilégié, elle qu'Aphrodite prend au piège et visite.

En face d'une si haute tension spirituelle, d'une conception du caractère sacré de l'amour aussi douloureusement vécu, il est superflu de se demander si elle a vu la déesse et si elle lui a parlé véritablement. Entre les trois possibilités: qu'elle ait eu réellement des visions ou qu'elle ait feint d'en avoir comme peut le faire un imposteur ou comme a coutume de le faire un poète, la moins vraisemblable est précisément la deuxième. En réalité nous n'avons personnellement aucun motif pour douter qu'elle ait *vu*.

Évidemment l'épiphanie est la projection d'un état émotif: celui qui la subit agit comme dans les rêves, utilisant les expériences dont il dispose, quelle que soit leur origine, littéraire, populaire ou rituelle. Dans ce cas, plus que dans tout autre, soustraire les composantes d'origine littéraire ne sert ni à retrouver les composantes d'origine rituelle (qui étaient souvent à la base des premières) ni à établir l'authenticité de la vision. Cela sert par contre à mieux définir la culture de Sapho et à situer historiquement sa spiritualité. Dans ce sens l'enquête n'est pas seulement légitime mais elle doit être étendue aux contenus du message: d'où provient la conception selon laquelle le rythme de l'amour serait cyclique et que l'amour serait juste quand la réciprocité en équilibre les phases alternées? Répondre à la première question est plus facile une fois qu'on a répondu à la seconde.

La norme de la réciprocité n'est pas originale: c'est l'habituelle « règle d'or » de l'éthique commune. Dans sa forme la plus élémentaire elle apparaît déjà chez Archiloque (fr. 54, 14 T.). Les variations chez Homère (*Od.* VI 184 s.), chez Alcée (fr. 341 L.P.) et chez Solon (fr. 1, 5 D.), outre qu'ils en montrent la validité dans les domaines les plus divers, prouvent encore qu'à l'époque archaïque, elle était acceptée par les classes aristocratiques. Son application présupposait une claire distinction entre ce qui est bien et ce qui est mal, selon l'opinion commune dans une société déterminée.

Le Grec du VIIe siècle croyait qu'il était possible de réaliser cette norme comme il ne le croira plus un siècle plus tard: la problématique de la faute et du châtiment chez Eschyle porte les signes d'une crise grave. L'élargissement temporel, le transfert de la contrepartie dans les générations successives et l'idée, qui en découle, des réactions en chaîne, avaient semé le doute sur le rôle de la divinité, au moment même où l'on tentait de sauvegarder l'efficacité de sa garantie, en avertissant qu'elle ne récompense ou ne châtie pas immédiatement.

En revanche, la foi que le monde homérique a dans cette norme est assez solide. Dans l'*Iliade*, Agamemnon et les Grecs sont aussitôt punis par Apollon pour avoir outragé son prêtre. Et ils sont punis ensuite par Zeus en subissant de graves défaites pour avoir offensé Achille en lui enlevant Briséis. Cet abus de pouvoir de la part d'Agamemnon avait été le dernier d'une série : Achille avait été offensé en d'autres circonstances, lorsque, après la bataille remportée surtout grâce à sa bravoure, il avait reçu des dons inférieurs à ses mérites. Le don ($\gamma\acute{\epsilon}\rho\alpha\varsigma$), qui n'était pas en rapport avec son *areté* blessait son *honneur* ($\tau\iota\mu\acute{\eta}$) devant tout le monde (*Il.*, I, 163-171). L'équilibre ne pouvait être rétabli que par les dieux (en somme c'est ce que lui rappelle Athéna quand elle l'arrête au moment où il va se précipiter sur Agamemnon) ; c'est pourquoi il prie sa mère d'intervenir auprès de Zeus en sa faveur. Son retour sera déterminé par un fait nouveau, le meurtre de Patrocle, qui inaugure une nouvelle série, mais qui comportera quand même la restitution de Briséis de la part d'Agamemnon.

Les éléments fondamentaux de cette conception (en confrontant les différents textes il est facile d'extrapoler un paradigme) reviennent aussi dans la prière d'Aphrodite. En ne partageant pas son amour, son antagoniste a piétiné la norme : Sapho, offensée, invoque la déesse pour qu'elle impose la réparation promise et réalisée en d'autres occasions. La dimension sociale est représentée par les jeunes filles du thiase : elle n'est pas explicite mais on la présuppose. En disant sa prière devant elles, elle annonce sa prochaine victoire et le recouvrement de sa $\delta\acute{o}\xi\alpha$: joie à qui lui « veut du bien », chagrin à qui lui « veut du mal ». Les $\delta\tilde{\omega}\rho\alpha$ qu'elle recevra seront le signe tangible de sa $\tau\iota\mu\acute{\eta}$, comme le $\gamma\acute{\epsilon}\rho\alpha\varsigma$ l'était de la $\tau\iota\mu\acute{\eta}$ d'Achille ; $\delta\tilde{\omega}\rho\alpha$ et $\tau\iota\mu\acute{\eta}$ sont des termes étroitement liés, comme le montre Théognis dans un passage inspiré non seulement d'Homère, mais justement de Sapho : « à toi, ô Aphrodite, en plus Zeus donna, en signe d'honneur, ce don » (*Théogn.*, 1386 s. $\tau\acute{o}\delta\epsilon$ $\tau\iota\mu\acute{\eta}\sigma\alpha\varsigma$ $\delta\tilde{\omega}\rho o\nu$ $\acute{\epsilon}\delta\omega\kappa\epsilon\nu$ $\acute{\epsilon}\chi\epsilon\iota\nu$). De même qu'Achille, en battant les Troyens, procurait de l'honneur à Agamemnon (*Il.*, I, 159) qui devait donc l'honorer, ainsi Sapho, en aimant son antagoniste, l'honore et exige donc d'elle un pareil honneur. D'ailleurs, le sentiment de jalousie qu'elle éprouva envers elle-même est explicite dans de nombreuses odes, même à propos de l'amour : « Les Muses m'ont donné tous les honneurs ($\tau\iota\mu\acute{\iota}\alpha\nu$) en me faisant don de leur œuvre », dit-elle dans le fr. 32 L.P. ; et dans le fr. 58 L.P. elle déclare : « moi j'aime l'*abrosyna* ». Elle considéra la poésie et le raffinement comme deux signes distinctifs de son *areté*, comme le confirme, dans le fr. 55 L.P., le mépris qu'elle éprouva pour une rivale qui « ne participe pas des roses de la Piérie » ; et dans le fr. 57 L.P., pour une autre (ou pour la même) qui « ne sait pas porter ses robes au-dessus des chevilles ». La circonstance du fr. 57 L.P. est justement instructive : Sapho réprimande une jeune fille dont une inélégante rivale a séduit l'esprit (ϑέλγει νόον), comme la rivale Andromède séduisit l'esprit d'Atthis, qu'elle Sapho avait jadis aimée.

L'orgueil est une composante secondaire, mais non absente de son amour. Si le fait de ne pas aimer est une injustice, une plus grande injustice est le fait de ne pas l'aimer : car plus haute est son *areté* et plus précieux est son amour. C'est une nuance qu'il ne faut pas négliger quand on lit le v. 22 : δῶρα a une signification érotique et des nuances éthiques.

On se souvient qu'Achille abandonne sa colère et retourne au combat parce que Patrocle a été tué : et malgré tout, Agamemnon lui donne des présents et lui rend Briséis. De la même façon, selon le principe de la réciprocité, l'antagoniste doit aimer Sapho à son tour, quand bien même Sapho ne l'aimerait plus : la leçon proposée pour le v. 24 paraît plus claire et plus plausible si elle est projetée sur le fond de la conception éthique archaïque.

Les passages analysés montrent que la loi du talion, entre le VIIe et le VIe siècle, commençait à être dépassée, dans la mesure où l'individu ne rendait pas toujours directement le bien ou le mal qu'il avait reçu, et où il transmettait à la divinité cette tâche, demandant pour lui *olbos* et réputation — dans le domaine de sa propre *areté* de guerrier, de femme, d'aristocrate et de poète comme moyens pour réjouir ses amis et affliger ses ennemis. Cette fonction régulatrice et distributrice de la divinité fait mieux comprendre l'autre aspect que Sapho a vu dans l'amour, considéré comme une histoire réglée par un rythme cyclique.

J'ai répété plusieurs fois déjà que l'ode se termine sur un ton confiant ; opposé au ton angoissé du début. Les explications divergent parce qu'on en a cherché chaque fois le motif à des niveaux différents : sur le plan émotionnel, par une réduction draconienne des diverses dimensions temporelles ; ou sur le plan de l'analogie entre présent et passé, comme source d'une espérance et d'un bonheur futur, réservé uniquement à Sapho. Implicitement les deux positions nient toute valeur paradigmatique et toute fonction psychagogique à l'expérience chantée par Sapho : elles ne tiennent pas compte du troisième point de référence, qui est l'auditoire formé par les jeunes filles du thiase et surtout par l'antagoniste.

L'expérience de Sapho est certes privilégiée, mais dans des limites bien définies : elle est privilégiée, non pas parce qu'Aphrodite l'écoute, mais parce qu'elle se manifeste à elle et réaffirme la norme par une promesse directe ; parce que, en la faisant tomber souvent amoureuse, elle la choisit comme témoin et instrument de sa puissance (ce n'est pas par hasard qu'au v. 4 Sapho l'invoque comme πότνια). La norme en elle-même n'est pas valable que pour Sapho, mais pour tous, dans tous les domaines, comme un pacte qui règle l'ordre entre les hommes et leurs rapports avec les dieux. La religion de Sapho est construite précisément sur ce fondement commun.

L'équivalent, pour ainsi dire, « laïque » de la prière à Aphrodite est la virile apostrophe d'Archiloque à son propre cœur (fr. 67a D.) : « quand tu es vainqueur, ne te réjouis pas ouvertement, et si tu es vaincu ne t'afflige pas et ne te décourage pas à la maison ; mais avec mesure sois gai dans les joies et triste dans les malheurs : sais reconnaître quel est le rythme qui dirige les hommes ». Comme Archiloque, Sapho aussi reconnaît qu'à la douleur d'aujourd'hui fera suite la joie comme par le passé. La ressemblance est plus forte si l'on songe que la parénèse d'Archiloque n'est « laïque » qu'en apparence. Dans l'élégie à Périclès (fr. 7 D.) l'allusion aux vicissitudes des destinées humaines (ces malheurs sont vécus tantôt par les uns, tantôt par les autres) est introduite par une affirmation animée par un sentiment religieux authentique : « mais les dieux, ô mon cher, contre les malheurs irréparables ont mis comme remède une forte endurance » ; et dans un autre passage (fr. 11 D.) ces mêmes infortunes (sur mer) sont considérées comme un don de la divinité : « cachons les *dons* douloureux de Poséidon, Seigneur » (δῶρα indique des choses différentes chez Archiloque et chez Sapho, mais il a des nuances éthiques chez l'un et chez l'autre).

Le mérite d'avoir identifié la composante gnomique et parénétique de l'ode revient à B. Snell (p. 99) : « Dass dem Menschen in diesen Wechselfällen des Lebens nichts bleibt, als standhaft zu dulden, hat sie (Sappho) also ebenfalls von Archilochos gelernt ». Son affirmation doit être retouchée sur deux points : la sententia ne remonte pas nécessairement à Archiloque, mais ce fut plus probablement un élément de l'éthique commune ; Sapho en a modifié radicalement l'aspect (ou si l'on veut, elle a pris la norme dans sa version la plus rigide et la plus rigoureusement précise) car elle a considéré la souffrance et la joie non comme des moments, dans le rythme des vicissitudes humaines, indépendants l'un de l'autre et qu'il faut supporter avec modération, mais comme deux moments dialectiques d'une même aventure d'amour qui doit être revécue globalement, avec confiance, comme un cycle complet. À la différence d'Archiloque, elle ne dit pas : tant pis si je souffre aujourd'hui, cela se passera mieux la prochaine fois. Mais elle dit : tant pis si je souffre maintenant ; bientôt certainement (vv. 21, 23 ταχέως ... ταχέως) mon amour sera partagé. L'amour n'est pas pour elle tantôt doux, tantôt amer, mais il est toujours doux et amer à la fois, comme elle le déclare explicitement dans le fr. 130 L.P. : « À nouveau Eros qui assouplit les membres m'agite, irrésistible fauve doux et amer » (γλυκύπικρον) .

Le changement de perspective dérive d'une union plus étroite des deux conceptions, celle du rythme cyclique avec celle de la réciprocité. C'est un écart significatif qui implique une vision unitaire et une foi totale en Aphrodite comme gardienne *hic et nunc* de son destin.

L'épuisante recherche des sources est certes utile mais elle est insuffisante pour éclairer le texte de l'ode : elle est surtout vraiment indispensable pour définir la culture de Sapho. Les paroles et les images, isolées ou groupées, les situations et les conceptions, peuvent être nouvelles ou traditionnelles, sans pour autant être poétiques ou antipoétiques. Ce qui peut indiquer que l'appréciation a pour objet non la provenance des matériaux mais leur utilisation, c'est précisément la différence qui existe entre le jugement sur les éléments particuliers, qui entrent dans la composition et qui sont souvent connus, et la conscience claire que l'ode même, dans sa totalité, est nouvelle et incomparable. Au milieu il n'y a pas le vide, mais quelque chose qui explique le résultat: il y a un principe dynamique qui peut être constant chez un poète ou commun à plusieurs poètes, mais qui produit, dans chaque cas, des résultats différents, parce que les conditions sur lesquelles il opère sont chaque fois différentes. Le rôle de la critique (et que le fait de répéter des choses anciennes ne soit pas trop ennuyeux: trop souvent, en effet, on continue à les oublier) est de le rechercher et de l'identifier dans un texte particulier, et ultérieurement dans les autres textes du même auteur ainsi que chez différents auteurs, de la même ou de diverses aires culturelles.

Les études faites jusqu'à présent sur la première ode de Sapho s'appuient sur la conviction que la fonction et la signification de chaque élément résultent d'une interprétation globale de ces éléments, car c'est un principe unique qui les choisit, les dispose et les rend significatifs. Le schéma de la prière voulait que le proème et la conclusion correspondent entre eux dans une progression polaire: Sapho a adopté ce plan traditionnel comme principe organisateur, comme chiffre et forme des différents contenus. Son ποικιλόθρονος variait et renforçait les modèles homériques et préparait en même temps l'épithète δολόπλοκος: sa validité ne dérive pas de sa nouveauté, de sa rareté ou de sa diversité (qui lui donnent seulement un plus grand relief) mais de sa fonction suggestive, de sa destination hiérarchique, qui agissent sur le lecteur à un niveau plus secret. Ἀθανάτα et παῖ Δίος seraient évidents et presque superflus, s'ils ne correspondaient pas entre eux, annonçant πότνια et le déplacement futur de la déesse lointaine. Dans la conclusion l'ordre est le même et prend une signification s'il est vu comme un reflet ou un développement précis des éléments du proème. La conclusion a un ton tout à fait différent, un ton confiant, parce que la déesse est déjà venue; mais elle est cependant un reflet du proème, parce que la déesse n'est venue qu'en apparence: il ne s'agit pas d'une épiphanie mais seulement du souvenir des épiphanies passées, au cours desquelles Aphrodite imposait à l'antagoniste les mêmes actes que Sapho avait accomplis pour conquérir son amour.

Ces correspondances, et les nombreuses autres correspondances, font de l'ode un ensemble solidement articulé: l'ordre des strophes, le choix et la valeur des mots, le tissu syntaxique, la structure des métaphores, la conception sacrale de l'amour, le rapport avec Aphrodite, la signification de la prière et de la promesse, la validité du message et ses données culturelles et éthiques, sont le résultat d'une dynamique qui opère d'une manière constante, en incluant tous les matériaux, sans résidus, pour un résultat unitaire. La prière, comme un cristal rigoureusement géométrique, révèle dans chacun de ses aspects une même structure.

Son unité ne provient pas de rapprochements, non plus que d'un style qui se développe par séquences associatives périphériques, mais d'un principe qui opère selon des hiérarchies, qui connaît la perspective, qui réalise l'œuvre non pas comme une figure picturale, mais comme un organisme architectural pourvu d'une dimension temporelle. Cette caractéristique a échappé à Fränkel, qui, en la considérant comme un exemple (même s'il s'agit d'un exemple tout à fait particulier) de « schildernder Stil », l'a située dans un domaine stylistique archaïque. En réalité, l'ode dépasse ce domaine. Sa structure aurait été différente — plus faible — si, tel un bloc, elle n'avait pas eu les articulations nombreuses et savantes qui en font un organisme complexe : articulations plus efficaces alors, quand elles sont moins apparentes et évidentes.

G. Aurelio PRIVITERA,
Université de Messine.

ABRÉVIATIONS BIBLIOGRAPHIQUES

BOWRA	C.M. BOWRA, *Greek Lyric Poetry*, Oxford, 1961[2].
CAMERON	A. CAMERON, « Sappho's Prayer to Aphodite », *Harv. Theol. Rev.*, 32 (1939), pp. 1-17.
FRÄNKEL	H. FRÄNKEL, *Wege und Formen frühgriechischen Denkens*, Müchen, 1960[2].
FRÄNKEL, *Dicht.*	FRÄNKEL, *Dichtung und Philosophie des Frühen Griechentams*, München, 1962[2].
GENTILI	B. GENTILI, « La veneranda Saffo », *Quad. Urb. cult. class.*, 2 (1966), pp. 37-62.
PAGE	D. PAGE, *Sappho and Alcaeus*, Oxford, 1955.
PERROTTA	G. PERROTTA ,*Saffo e Pindaro*, Bari, 1935.
SNELL	B. SNELL, *Die Entdeckung des Geistes*, Hamburg, 1955[3].
VAN GRONINGEN	B.A. VAN GRONINGEN, *La composition littéraire archaïque grecque*, Amsterdam, 1958.
WILAMOWITZ	U. VON WILAMOWITZ-MOELLENDORFF, *Sappho und Simonides*, Berlin, 1913.

Helen's «Good Drug»:
Odyssey IV 1-305

I

duo ta polla ton anthropon.

ALCMAEON.

Were someone to try to formulate for archaic Greece what Foucault calls the *episteme,* it would likely be some version of "polarity."[1] Or so we would predict, judging from what is regularly said about this period, when Greek texts first appear. To begin to study Greek is to learn of its pervasive antitheses, built around the particles, *men,* "on the one hand," and *de,* "on the other hand." Supported by such syntax are the dualities of myth, philosophy and social organization, pairs so various, subtle and interconnected by opposition and analogy that the principle of analogous bi-polar oppositions would seem to be the mental paradigm of the age. Life is conceived and arguments are made, to cite the text of G.E.R. Lloyd that charts this phenomenon best, in terms of *Polarity and Analogy.* For example, the Pythagorean "Table of Opposites:" "one group of Pythagoreans apparently referred to ten definite pairs of opposite principles: limited and unlimited, odd and even, one and plurality, right and left, male and female, at rest and moving, straight and curved, light and darkness, good and evil, square and oblong."[2] The working of the principle is especially clear in the theories by which some Presocratics accounted for the differentiation of the sexes. Parmenides claimed the sex of the child depended upon the position in the womb (right for males, left for females), Empedocles, upon the temperature of the womb at conception (hotter for men, colder for women), and Anaximander, the side from which the father's seed came (right for males, left for females).[3] And the medical texts of the Hippocratic corpus illustrate again and again that disease is caused by an imbalance in a pair of opposites and that, as a result, counter-balancing opposites effect cures: ta enantia ton enan-

---

[1] That "someone" would not be Foucault himself. Apparently on the basis of *Les maîtres de vérité en Grèce archaïque* of M. DETIENNE (Paris, 1967), although it is not cited, Foucault closes off archaic Greece from his "archaeology" of western knowledge as the primordial time and place in which language, truth and power were as yet undifferentiated, *L'ordre du discours* (Paris, 1971) pp. 10-11. For Foucault's use of *episteme* to designate the mental paradigm of a period, see *Les mots et les choses* (Paris, 1971).

[2] G. E. R. LLOYD, *Polarity and Analogy, Two Types of Argumentation in Early Greek Thought* (Cambridge, 1971) p. 16.

[3] LLOYD, p. 17, with bibliography.

tion estin hiemata, "opposites are cures for opposites."[4] Believing that
such polar classification is relatively lacking in early poetic texts, Lloyd
concentrates on the evidence from philosophy and science, but as recent
work, based in the propositions of structuralist linguistics and anthropology, richly shows, Greek epic is equally constituted by this structure of
mind.

Informed, sometimes indirectly, by the models of Saussure, Jakobson, Levi-Strauss and Dumezil, many classicists have shown the language
and culture of the epics to operate in accordance with structuralist theory,
as systems of analogical oppositions. Indeed, the fruitfulness of the
lexicologies structurales of myth and ritual of Vernant and Detienne and
the Homeric anthropology of Vidal-Naquet, Redfield and Foley would suggest that it is only now, through a methodology designed to appreciate
structures of mediated oppositions, that we can do justice to the polarities
that have always been seen in early Greece.[5] In the fullest application of
structural anthropology to Homeric poetics Norman Austin declares
that "whatever the original impulse, it is clear that Homeric man sees the
world through the structure of polarity" and that "analogical thought
is fundamental to Homer; it is through analogy that the various phenomena
and experiences are attributed to one or the other of the polar oppositions."[6] This declaration rings true not only by virtue of Austin's own
demonstration of it in the language and action of the *Odyssey*, but also
by virtue of several, somewhat more technical studies of the Homeric
Kunstsprache, the artificial and traditional diction of which the epics are
composed. Here formulations of structuralist linguistics, such as marked
vs. unmarked pairs and the fundamental tenet that the meaning of a word
resides in its differential relations with other words, intersect with such
insights of Milman Parry as the economy of formulas (the tendency to
use only one form to fill a given metrical and semantic function) and the
generation of formulas by analogy. To cite one particularly elegant instance, Leonard Muellner demonstrates in the economy of their formulaic
usage a marked vs. unmarked pair of the verbs, *phemi*, "to say," vs
euchomai, "to say with sacral, legal or heroic force."[7] At all levels, from

---

[4]　Lloyd, pp. 20-23.

[5]　In *Les maîtres de vérité en Grèce archaïque, op. cit.*, p. 5, n. 6 Detienne describes
his method: "déterminer les lignes de force d'un système lexical, atteindre les rapports d'opposition et d'association, bref, appliquer les méthodes de la lexicologie structurale, essayer
dans le domaine de la Grèce archaïque les possibilités de la théorie du 'champ semantique'."
See also, M. Detienne, *Les jardins d'Adonis* (Paris, 1972), *Dionysos mis a mort* (Paris, 1977),
M. Detienne and J.-P. Vernant, *Les ruses de l'intelligence. La metis des Grecs* (Paris,
1974), J.-P. Vernant, *Mythe et pensée chez les Grecs* I, II (Paris, 1965). For Homeric
anthropology see P. Vidal-Naquet, "Valeurs religieuses et mythique de la terre et du sa-
crifice dans l'Odyssée," *Annales Économies-Sociétés-Civilisations*, 25 (1970), 1278-1297; J.
Redfield, *Nature and Culture in the Iliad, The Tragedy of Hector* (Chicago, 1975) and H.
Foley, "'Reverse Similes' and Sex Roles in the Odyssey'," *Arethusa*, 11 (1978), 7-26.

[6]　N. Austin, *Archery at the Dark of the Moon, Poetic Problems in Homer's
Odyssey* (Berkeley-Los Angeles-London, 1975), pp. 90, 105.

[7]　L. Meullner, *The Meaning of Homeric euchomai Through its Formulas* (Ins-
bruck, 1976). Among other studies that combine the methodology of comparative structural
linguistics with the formulaic analysis pioneered by Parry, see especially D. Boedeker,

diction to theme, Homeric epic reveals its constitution of and by analogous polarities, and nowhere more so than in the opening of *Odyssey* IV.

II

I'm a man of medicine, not a medicine man.

The Wizard of Oz.

If we do not already know that in archaic Greece, life and language are made up of alternating opposites, the *Odyssey* itself will accomplish the education of its audience — especially in the Telemachy, where it educates the hero's son in *xenia*, the exchanges that make up culture. When with him at the start of Book IV we come to the palace of Menelaus and Helen, we enter a world of dualities. The first evening there is divided into two movements: one, extending from the opening at the banquet up to Menelaus' attempt to put an end to the speeches, (1-218), and two, from Helen's re-introduction of speeches up to the retirement of everyone for the night (219-305). Each of these divisions is itself divided into two. The first section, presided over by Menelaus, begins as a wedding feast for his children and ends as a funeral with eulogies and lamentation for the Greek losses, chiefly the absent Odysseus. In the second section, governed by Helen, her story of Odysseus is matched by one from Menelaus. And within these units the polarities proliferate.

The wedding celebration keynotes this evening in Sparta. With it we encounter the original locus of the Trojan war, the marriage of Menelaus and Helen, encounter it now as re-formed, and, it would seem, about to reduplicate itself in the marriages of its children. For this is a double wedding. Not only are there two weddings — that of Hermione, the daughter of Helen and Menelaus, to Achilles' son, Neoptolemus, and that of Megapenthes, the son of Menelaus and a slave woman, to the daughter of Alector — but one is present, taking place in Sparta, and one is absent, taking place at Achilles' home (3-14). The existence of war is acknowledged — it was at Troy that Menelaus promised Hermione to the son of "man-breaker" Achilles — but it is kept absent, in the past.

Aphrodite's Entry into Greek Epic (Leiden, 1974); M. NAGLER, *Spontaneity and Tradition, A Study in the Oral Art of Homer* (Berkeley-Los Angeles-London 1974); G. NAGY, *Comparative Studies in Greek and Indic Meter* (Cambridge, Mass., 1974), R. SHANNON, *The Arms of Achilles and Homeric Compositional Technique* (Leiden, 1975); L. CLADER, *Helen: The Evolution from Divine to Heroic in Greek Epic Tradition* (Leiden, 1976); D. FRAME, *The Myth of Return in Early Greek Epic* (New Haven, 1978). See also now G. NAGY, *The Best of the Achaeans, Concepts of the Hero in Archaic Greek Poetry* (Baltimore, 1979); this magisterial text, which reconstructs the relations between archaic epic and hero cult through a vast network of close analyses of diction, theme and ritual practice, is based throughout upon the assumption that early Greek language and cult is structured by stable oppositions. For the distinction, "marked vs. unmarked," see N. S. TRUBETZKOY, *Principles of Phonology*, tr. C.A.M. BALTAXE (Berkeley and Los Angeles, 1969) and for its status as a "language universal" that applies to both phonology, grammar, semantics and kinship terminology, see J. H. GREENBERG, *Language Universals* (The Hague and Paris, 1966).

Now Neoptolemus has returned home from Troy (8-9) and is joined not in battle but in marriage to the lovely (erateine) Hermione, the incarnation of golden Aphrodite (13-14). The erotic reigns, and amid the banqueting neighbors and the dancer-acrobats, the poet stations another poet singing what must be epithalamia (15-19). Then upon a declaration of the function of *xenia*, this marriage song changes into a funeral dirge.

In the midst of the wedding feast arrive Telemachus and Peisistratus, two who are *xeinoi*, that is, foreign or "other" than those who belong at Sparta. This fundamental opposition of "own" vs. "other" (*philos* vs. *xeinos*) is mediated by the principle and practice of social exchange. Menelaus' reply, when asked if the two strangers should be received, encapsulates the norm.

> Eteoneus, son of Boethous, you were never a fool before, but now indeed you are babbling nonsense, like a child. Surely we two have eaten much hospitality (*xeineïa*) from other folk before we came back here. May Zeus only make an end of misery hereafter (31-36).[8]

Because he has received hospitality when he was a wanderer, he, too, should give it, now that he is home. His suffering may recommence at any time, whenever Zeus — the order of things — so moves. Life oscillates between suffering and safety, and to counterbalance the system for all, those in times of good fortune must aid those who are not by treating them as "own" (*philein* = *xeinein*: "to treat the *xeinos* as a *philos*").[9] Such aid consists, as we notice, of a bath by servant women and a generous share of the feast (48-67).

By mediating between social opposites, Menelaus' act of *xenia* moves his portion of the evening from one ritual with its particular kind of song to the opposite. For it is Telemachus, the admitted guest, who initiates the modulation from marriage song to funeral dirge by comparing the gleam of the gold and silver around him to the palace of Zeus on Olympus (71-75). Menelaos replies with the first of two speeches (another doublet) that end by arousing lamentation. He acknowledges his riches, but then exposes the economy by which they were bought with irremediable loss: his brother murdered while he was away, wandering and collecting the wealth, and before that, the deaths of the Greeks who fought at Troy (80-99). Thus he has no joy in his wealth, but only the pleasure of lamentation, lamentation that alternates with its opposite, the surfeit of lamentation.

> Still and again mourning and sorrowing over and over as I sit in our palace at one time (*allote*) I delight (*terpomai*) my heart in lamentation and at another time (*allote*) I stop.

For surfeit of gloomy lamentation comes quickly (100-103). In particular he laments for Odysseus, who, when remembered, divides Menelaus'

---

[8]   The translations are mine and more literal than felicitous.

[9]   For the opposition between *philos* and *xeinos* and this meaning of the verb *philein*, see É. BENVENISTE, *Le vocabulaire des institutions indo-européennes* I (Paris, 1969), pp. 341-342.

life into food and sleep, on the one hand, and mournful recollection on the other (104-107). Even so now, by recollecting these sorrows of the past, Menelaus arouses in the son of Odysseus the *himeros gooio*, "desire for lamentation" (113). A few minutes later Menelaus answers his first eulogy with another memory of the war gone by, how he wanted to settle Odysseus upon their return in one of his client cities, where "we would mix together, and nothing would separate us, loving and delighting ourselves as a unit of two, until the blood-dark cloud of death covered us over" (178-180). Again his recollection excites the *himeros gooio*, and all weep, even Peisistratus who remembers his brother killed at Troy (183-188).

It is now Peisistratus, however, who moves to close the occasion, to switch it back from funeral to feast. He takes, he says, no delight (*terpomai*) in dinner mixed with tears, since dawn comes ever new (193-195). The alternation of night and day forbids suspending animation in prolonged mourning. Menelaus readily acceeds: he and Telemachus can exchange more stories in the morning (212-215). Upon his direction, water is poured and all the men, their hands now washed of these Iliadic recollections of war, turn back to the feast (216-218).

In its two-part structure, in its contrary rituals and in its detailed dualities, this first portion of the evening at Sparta enacts, it would seem, the working of the world and of language as mediation or exchange or alternation of opposites. It is in this way a clear instance of the categorization by polarity that seems to constitute Homeric thought and of meaning made, as structuralist theory maintains, by those polar relations. Two rituals, wedding/funeral; two poetic genres, epithalamium/dirge; two sexes, male/female; two times, past/present; two places, present/absent; two categories of person, own/other; of economy, gain/loss; of activity, remember and weep/sleep and eat. Between the members of each pair there exists a relation variously named in this portion of the text as marriage (*gamos*), exchange (*xenia*) and alternation (*allote...allote*). Such is the constitution of both cosmos and logos here. And when Helen intervenes, inaugurating the second half of the evening and delaying the closure upon speeches, this character of the Homeric logos is initially confirmed.

III

> Si dans les deux cas, ce qui est censé produire le positif et annuler le négatif ne fait que *déplacer* et à la fois *multiplier* les effets du négatif, conduisant à prolifération le manque qui fut sa cause, cette nécessité est inscrite dans le *signe pharmakon*.
>
> Jacques DERRIDA.

In opposition to her husband's attempt to regulate the production of speeches, Helen "intellected otherwise" (219). Her counter-action divides this evening into two parts, but parts that match, insofar as each is made up of speeches and actions that exemplify a world of polarities.

It is to continue the exchange of *mythoi* that Helen intervenes, to imitate her husband's portion of the evening. Her action differs from that of her husband by being described in terms that cast the wife as a poet, but one working, like the poet of the *Odyssey,* within a poetics of analogous oppositions. For tracing the connections between the terms of her action and the rest of hexameter diction reveals a classification of two contrary poetic genres as parallel to two contrary kinds of drugs. Here is what the poet says:

> Into the wine of which they were drinking she cast a drug (*pharmakon*), grief-less (*a-penthos*), without anger, a forgetfulness of all sorrows, and whoever should drink it down, once it was mixed in the bowl, for that day would not drop a tear on his cheeks, not if his mother and father should die, not if men should slay with the bronze before him his brother or his own son, and with his eyes he should see it. Such were the crafty drugs (*pharmaka*) the daughter of Zeus possessed, good ones, given to her by the wife of Thon, Polydamna of Egypt, where the fertile earth bears the most drugs, many good in mixture (*memigmena*) and many wretched (*lugra*), and every man there is a doctor, knowledgeable beyond all people. For indeed they are of the race of Paeeon. Now when she put in the drug and ordered the wine to be poured, beginning again the stories (*mythoi*) she spoke (220-234).

The contexts of the word *"pharmakon"* in hexameter diction depict drugs in their capacity to cure or to destroy as analogous to two faces of epic poetry. Parallel terminology displays the following corresponding doublets: [10]

	two genres of *pharmakon*
Helen's *pharmakon*	Circe's *pharmakon*
grief-less (*a-penthos*)	
a forgetfulness of all eveils	a forgetfulness of the fatherland
good (vs. *lugros* "wretched")	wretched (*lugros*)

	two genres of epic poetry
kleos "fame"	*lugros* "wretched" [11]
about *klea* ("famous deeds, victories")	about *lugra* ("wretched deeds, defeats
gives forgetfulness of cares	gives unforgettable
delight (*terpsis*) vs. *penthos*	grief (*penthos*)

Epic diction attempts to divide poetry and *pharmaka* into two mutually exclusive kinds.

Mediator between drugs and poetry is Paeeon, once a god and later an epithet of Apollo, as dispenser of healing and song. Indeed, the god, Paeeon, is himself a type of song, the so-called paean, sung to Apollo. [12]

---

[10]   It is not possible here to examine all the usages from which this set of oppositions is derived. The most relevant texts are: for *kleos*, Hes. *Th.* 96-103, Nagy, op. cit., pp. 244-261; for *lugros* and poetry, *Od.* I 326-327, 337-342, III 87, 92-93, 132-133, 194-198, 203-235-241, 287-292, 391-394; for the collocation of all these terms, *Il.* XV 390-394. This categorization of drugs and poetry in hexameter diction is analyzed fully in my forthcoming text, *Textures of Time, A Study in the Poetics of the Iliad and the Odyssey.*

[11]   There is an a-symmetry here in that *kleos* is a noun and *lugros* is an adjective. The poetic connotation of *kleos*, "fame in song," is a marked instance of its unmarked meaning, "fame." The adjective, *lugros*, "wretched," designates a song by modifying either *aoide*, "song," or any event that as a subject of song produces *penthos*, "grief," e.g., the *lugros nostos*, "wretched homecoming," of the Greeks, the title of the song by the bard, Phemius, at *Od.*, I, 326-327.

[12]   NAGY, *op. cit.*, pp. 136-137, 231.

By citing this Paeeon and by calling Helen's drug "griefless," and a "forgetfulness of all evils" and "good" as opposed to "wretched," the poet's description implies that her mixture of wine and a "good drug" is something analogous to the poetry of *kleos*, the poetry that is the antidote of "grief" and a "forgetfulness of cares." By this description the poet makes Helen a reflection of himself.

Helen's drug is, then, like *kleos*. It is so effective an antidote to pain that at the tragedy of your family, you would sense only glory and would not weep. With this drug Helen will supply what the banquet has lacked heretofore, re-presentation of the past without pain. For just as she adds a "good drug" with the power of *kleos*, so she will now add a speech with the properties of her *pharmakon*. [13] Unlike Menelaus' recollections, Helen's *mythos* will be a painless painful memory. By her medical supplement, events naturally tragic for some of the audience will be detoxified. A song of the *lugros-* genre for some will sound like *kleos* and will be heard by all without loss or pain. By this description of her action, the poet casts Helen in the role played by himself and by the Odyssean tradition he repeats: the role of making past deeds present, with *kleos* for the actors and oblivious delight (*terpsis*) for all the audience.

Helen's *pharmakon-mythos* is, therefore, the opposite of Menelaus' part of the evening — just as female is the opposite of male, wife of husband and *Odyssey* of *Iliad* — but it is the equal of its mate in constitution. Both are based upon the assumption of analogous polarities, controllable and mutually exclusive, to which poetry and drugs offer no exception.

At least initially, the content of Helen's *pharmakon-mythos* maintains this identity. After naming her audience, she abruptly invokes the alternation of opposites at the heart of the universe.

> Son of Atreus, god-nourished Menelaus, you and these children of good men. But the god Zeus gives both good and evil at one time to one man (*allote*) and at another to another (*allote*). For he has all power (235-237).

After this invocation, she declares herself a bard.

> Now indeed feast yourselves, seated in the hall, and delight yourselves (*terpein*) in stories (*mythoi*). For I will narrate *eoikota* ("things like, fitting, probable") (238-239). [14]

Her tale will be *eoikota*: like to the truth, fitting for the occasion and not hard to believe. The truth meant is, presumably, this dispensation of Zeus, but it is also the heroism of Odysseus.

> I could not tell you all the number nor could I name how many are the struggles of enduring Odysseus, but such a thing as this the strong man endured

---

[13]   The identification of Helen's *mythos* with her *pharmakon* is an ancient interpretation found in PLU., *Quaest. Conv.*, I 1 4, 614 and MACR., *Sat.* VII 1 18; see R. DUPONT-ROC and A. LE BOULLUEC, "Le charme du récit (*Odyssey*, IV, 218-289)," *Écriture et Théorie Poétiques, Lectures d'Homère, Eschyle, Platon, Aristote* (Paris, 1976) p. 35.

[14]   For these meanings of *eoikota* see Dupont-Roc and Le Boulluec, op. cit., p. 37, n. 13.

and accomplished in the Trojans' country, where you Achaeans suffered
miseries. He beat himself with unseemly blows, then threw a cheap sheet
around his shoulders, and in the likeness of a servant, he crept into the wide-
wayed city of the enemy men. By hiding himself he looked like another man,
a beggar. Never was there such a man beside the ships of the Achaeans.
Like to this one he crept into the Trojans' city, and they were all taken in.
I alone recognized him even so disguised, and I questioned him. But he by
his craftiness eluded me. But after I bathed him and anointed him with
olive oil and put some clothing on him, after I swore a great oath not to
reveal to the Trojans that this was Odysseus until he reached the swift ships
and the shelters, at last he told me the whole plan of the Achaeans. Then after
killing many Trojans with the thin-edged bronze, he returned to the Argives
and brought back much intelligence. At that the other Trojan women cried out
shrill, but my heart was happy, since my heart had turned to going back home,
and I mourned over the delusion that Aphrodite gave, when she lead me there
from my own fatherland, forsaking my child and my bedroom and my husband,
a man who lacks nothing either in sense or in appearance (240-264).

Helen is a poet of the *kleos* of Odysseus. And indeed, as is often noted,
her tale, while concerned with the Trojan War, also forecasts the "epic
fame" Odysseus will attain later in the *Odyssey* itself, when he will again
enter a city covertly and kill those he succeed in tricking with his disguise
as a beggar.[15]

In addition, Helen's story is perfectly concocted to present an image
of herself that will impress and delight her audience of Greek partisans.
As the only one to have recognized Odysseus, she shows herself even
more than he, a master of disguise. The revelation of her heart's own
reaction to the murder of the Trojans sets her apart as a true ally of the
Greeks, only an apparent collaborator with their enemy. How appealing
for Menelaus, Telemachus and Peisistratus to be able to see Helen, the
object of all the sacrifices they were just lamenting, as a victim of Aphrodite's machinations. How flattering to her husband to conclude with these
compliments. Her aim, it appears, is not only the *kleos* of Odysseus,
but also her own "fame" among the assembled men.

Yet Helen's recollection is oddly elliptical and when questioned,
its foundations slip.[16] How did this mendicant Odysseus come to be
received in the royal house and bathed by none other than Helen herself?
Earlier it was servant women who bathed Telemachus and Peisistratus.
What was Helen doing bathing a naked beggar? Why did Odysseus permit
himself to be bathed, anointed and clothed by a woman whose earlier
recognition and questioning he had to elude? Why is it necessary to omit
the answers to these questions, if Helen's "good drug" can cure any
negative side-effects of the story? And, indeed, what in Helen's story
would be *lugros* without the "good drug" and for whom? Would Odysseus' victory by violation of *xenia* be shameful to Telemachos? Would

---

[15] See O. ANDERSEN, "Odysseus and the Wooden Horse," *Symbolae Osloenses*,
52 (1977), pp. 5-18, with bibliography.

[16] DUPONT-ROC and LEBOULLUEC, *op. cit.*, pp. 31, 37, n. 11, correlate this
speech with the rhetorical figure of "enigma;" specifically, of the kinds of enigma listed
in the ancient treatise of Trypho, "la seconde, *kat' enantion*, pourrait s'appliquer à Hélène,
amie des Achéens tout en étant leur ennemie."

Helen's intimacy with Odysseus be painful to Menelaus? And if so, why does she include it? Is she trying not only to enhance her glory and to flatter her husband, but to seduce her young guest with glimpses of a sexual scene with his father? Recollections in the *Odyssey* are modes of characterization. Is the poet here showing how Helen does it, how she once seduced Paris, another young guest, and can ever re-seduce her husband by representing reality as these men want to hear it? This would be a magnificent *kleos* for Helen, comparable to Odysseus' victories through deceit.

If such a *kleos* is the aim of Helen and of the poet, too, it does not last for long. It is as brief as Menelaus' previous attempt to end the recollections of the past, for to the supplement of Helen's *pharmakon-mythos* comes the supplement of Menelaus' antiphonal reply. The "good drug" of Helen's representation of the past engenders a doublet that is also a rival. Menelaus' *mythos* is a product of the same *pharmakon*, the same power to recall the past without pain, but now by its very working, this drug loses its positive valence and poisons the "fame" of Helen that it has just produced.[17]

Menelaus' tale is clearly marked as the doublet of Helen's. He opens by repeating her line, "but such a thing as this the strong man endured and accomplished." (271=242). His tale, too, is a glorification of Odysseus, another victory through disguise.

> Inside the wooden horse we who were greatest of the Argives were all sitting and bringing death and destruction to the Trojans. Then you came there; you will have been ordered by some divine spirit, who wished to extend glory to the Trojans. And Deiphobus, a godlike man, followed beside you as you came. Three times you walked around the hollow ambush, feeling it, and you called out to the best of the Danaans, naming them by name, and likened your voice to the wives of all the Argives. Now I myself and the son of Tydeus and shining Odysseus were sitting in the middle of them and heard you as you shouted. Diomedes and I started up, both determined to go outside or to answer at once from inside, but Odysseus pulled us down and held us, for all our desire. Then all the other sons of the Achaeans were silent; only Anticlus wanted to answer you, but Odysseus pressed his mouth mercilessly with his strong hands and saved all the Achaeans, until Pallas Athena led you away (272-289).

In this addition to the addition, however, the element of disguise has reduplicated, for now Helen, too, is an imitator and Odysseus, the one who sees through the ruse. Here the bi-polar opposition collapses, as both Odysseus and Helen fill the same category disguiser (he by the horse and

---

[17] DUPONT-ROC and LE BOULLUEC, *op. cit.*, p. 37, n. 13, claim that the force of Helen's drug applies only to her tale and not to that of Menelaus, but do not explain why. The two speeches are clearly marked as a doublet by the same opening line (242=271) and by similar themes of role-playing, unmasking and divine manipulation of Helen. There is no reason to think that Menelaus did not drink the wine Helen mixed. What is true is that the drug does not work as intended in Menelaus' speech and that this disfunction then claims Helen's speech as well. As a result of this basic difference in the interpretation of Menelaus' speech and its relation to Helen's "good drug" the analysis of Dupont-Roc and Le Boulluec reaches substantively different conclusions than those presented here.

she by the voices), while Odysseus simultaneously occupies the contrary category, discerner.

Similarly, the sign, "recollection without pain", slips from the status of a "good" producer of *kleos* to that of a *kleos*-deconstructor, for it permits Menelaus to recall the one fact that belies Helen's self-portrait and retroactively renders her *mythos* yet another fictitious imitation of the voice of a Greek wife. As if he caught it from the end of her tale, Menelaus opens his own with the same explanation for Helen's anti-Greek activity, the interference of a god. But inserted between this defense and his full account of her trick, as if recollected by accident along the chain of associations, is the crucial detail: "and Deiphobus, a godlike man, followed beside you as you came" (276). This Deiphobus is, of course, Helen's second Trojan husband, the man she married after the death of Paris, a figure who belies her claim that even back when Odysseus infiltrated the city, her allegiance was already with the Greeks.[18] Helen's *pharmakon* has recoiled upon its practitioner. By permitting Menelaus to recall without pain, what pain might have kept beyond recall, Helen's "good drug" and her "good tale" have reminded Menelaus of another, similar feat of Odysseus, one that violates her claim to *kleos* and to being *eoikota*.

Yet by counter-acting the effect of Helen's *mythos*, Menelaus also de-activates his own, for they share the same pharmacology. Both result from the same attempt to recall the past without pain, to divide drugs and poetry into governable opposites. But the opposite of Helen's *pharmakon-mythos* is a double with a difference, both drug and antidote (just as inside Menelaus' tale Helen is disguiser and Odysseus both disguiser and discerner). Once invoked, the power of drugs and poetry defeats all attempts to divide and control it, in a manner that forecasts the patterns of tragedy: in both speeches by its successful operation the "good drug" fails. Here the recollection of Iliadic traditions about Odysseus in order to produce Odyssean pleasure imperfectly represses Iliadic pain. Such is the testimony of our counterpart, Telemachus.In response to both tales he says, "It is all the more painful (*algion*), for even these exploits did not guard my father from wretched (*lugros*) destruction" (293). Come, he says, let us turn to sleep. And with that, the couples return to the earlier polarities and sleep apart, the men outside and the man and woman inside, beside one another (295-305).

IV

Who knows if life is death, or death life.

EURIPIDES.

Is such a return to the earlier model of meaning by polarity open to the audience? We have seen Helen attempt to apply to painful recollection

---

[18] See ANDERSEN, *op. cit.*, pp. 10-12; DUPONT-ROC and LE BOULLUEC, *op. cit.*, pp. 30-31, and J. KAKRIDIS, *Homer Revisited* (Lund, 1971), p. 45.

a remedy defined, according to an ontology of governable opposites, as "good" (vs. "wretched") and watched the drug (re)assert its pharmacology against this attempt at logical domination. We have seen Homeric language change from a structure of analogical opposites into differing doublets, whose difference is not stable. The "good drug" of Helen's speech becomes the "good-wretched drug" of its non-identical twin; in repeating itself it reverses itself, leaving each tale an indistinct "gain-loss." With such a constitution Helen's half of the evening no longer appears to be the equal opposite of her husband's. Rather, like Menelaus' complement to Helen's speech, Helen's half of the evening comes as a double with something different, something in excess. It now appears that the text has changed from working according to Saussurean semiotics to enacting the operation of the sign described by Derrida.[19] Yet, this appearance is deceiving. No such change could occur, or at least not in these terms. If it ever worked by pure oppositions, no text can be an allegory of *le style derridean*.[20] If the polarities of Menelaus' part of the evening are mutually exclusive, all we may see after Helen adds her "good drug" to the wine, is a temporarily inebriated text. For it to exemplify the Derridean analysis of language, a return to the earlier polarities must reveal them to have been "*toujours déjà*" imperfect.

After observing the effects of Helen's *pharmakon,* we notice its traces in the first part of the evening. None of the earlier terms now gives the impression of unalloyed identity. First, marriage. In the names of the couples, this union is occupied by adversaries. War is not successfully kept in the past, for even as a groom, "Neoptolemus" is the one to whom not a wedding, but "*polemos is new.*" To his marriage "Megapenthes" contributes "great grief," that *penthos* supposedly absent from Helen's drug (*a-penthos*) and forgotten upon hearing a song of *kleos*. This double wedding does and does not reproduce the marriage of Menelaus and Helen, for "Great-Grief" is the child of Menelaus and a slave woman, a union within and without the legitimate family.[21] While uniting opposite sexes for legitimate procreation, marriage imperfectly excludes death, grief and illegitimate intercourse with an extra female. Within the epithalamimum sound the notes of a dirge.[22]

---

[19] For the critique by Derrida of Saussure see *De la grammatologie* (Paris, 1967) pp. 46-64. The version of DERRIDA's own views most relevant to this Homeric text is "La pharmacie du Platon," *La dissémination* (Paris, 1972), pp. 71-197.

[20] In *Éperons, Les styles de Nietzsche* (Paris, 1978) Derrida develops the operation of the text as "style" and of literary style not as "l'homme," but as "l"operation' feminine" (p. 44).

[21] The instability of the opposition, within/without, is treated by DERRIDA in the essay, *Fors,* tr. B. JOHNSON, *Georgia Review,* 31 (1977) 64-116; the translator notes: "the word *fors* in French, derived from the Latin *foris* ('outside, outdoors'), is an archaic preposition meaning 'except for, barring, save.' In addition, *fors* is the plural of the word *for,* which, in the French expression, 'le for interieur,' designates the inner heart, 'the tribunal of conscience,' subjective interiority. The word *fors* thus 'means' both interiority and exterriority..." (p. 64). This pun applies to the psychoanalytic topography traced in this essay, a topography that is akin to the confusion of boundaries in the *himeros gooio.*

[22] Other archaic Greek wedding songs fail to suppress the war and death that counteract marriage. Sappho 44 LP, the Wedding of Hector and Andromache, ends with indirect

The funeral that follows this marriage is similarly impure. Here terms belonging to the discourse of sexuality and the *kleos*-genre of poetry are coupled with the language of lamentation. In the phrase, *gooi terpomai* (102), Menelaus says that he gains from mourning the delight produced by *kleos* or by "golden Aphrodite". [23] In his second recollection Menelaus applies the diction of sexual intercourse to the relationship he longed for with Odysseus, but he limits the relationship to life: "and going there we would mix together (*emisgometh'*), and nothing would separate us, loving and delighting ourselves as a unit of two (the duals, *phileonte* and *terpomeno*), until the blood-dark cloud of death covered us over" (178-180). [24] Yet by the litany that follows each of Menelaus' speeches, "and he aroused in them the *himeros gooio*" (120, 183), this separation between sex and death is bridged. For in addition to its unmarked sense of "desire", *himeros* bears in hexameter diction the marked meaning of "sexual urge," a meaning brought to mind now by the earlier emphasis on marriage and by Menelaus' own use of erotic terminology and, in retrospect, by the sexual relations in the speeches of Helen and Menelaus. [25] In this context *himeros gooio* becomes, like *gooi terpomai*, an oxymoron. Just as Helen's imitation of the voices of the Greek wives aroused in the Greeks the sexual urge to break open the horse and meet certain death, so Menelaus' bard-like recollections arouse "the lust for lamentation." As a ritual to separate opposite states of being, this funeral imperfectly repres-

---

allusions to the death of Hector in the *Iliad* through the agency of Apollo and Achilles; see Nagy, op. cit., pp. 135-139. Similarly, in Alcaeus' hymn to Helen and Thetis, 42 LP, the wedding of Peleus and Thetis is framed by descriptions of the deaths in the war at Troy over Helen, the losses that result from and include the child of that marriage, Achilles.

[23] For *terpein/terpsis* in hexameter diction as the "delight" effected by poetry see, e.g., *Od.*, I 346-347, 421-422, VIII 45, 91, 367-368, 429, XII 52, XVII 385, XXII 330; *Il.*, IX 186-189, XVIII 603-604; *h.Ap.*, 169-170; HES., *Th.*, 36-37, fr. 274 MW; for the sexual sense, see, e.g., MIMNERMUS, 1.1 West: *tis de bios ti de terpnon ater chruses Aphrodites*, "what is life, what is delightful without golden Aphrodite?" For the opposition between *terpein* and mourning, see *Od.*, XIX 513.

[24] While being the regular term for sexual intercourse, the verb, *meignesthai*, "to mix," also is used of "mixture" in battle (*Il.*, XV 510) or in *xenia* (*Od.*, XXIV 314). The point is that in context with *phileonte, terpomeno, gooi terpomai* and *himeros gooio* the audience is reminded of the erotic as well as the social sense of the word (there is no textual support for the military, as applied to Odysseus and Menelaus). Note that in Menelaus' memory, the Trojan war was the Greeks fighting for him (170), "men and a man," while to Helen it was "men and a woman," the Greeks fighting for her (145-146). Love among men who fight together is not un-Homeric; Achilles and Patroclus are the paradigm, as Plato recalls in the *Symposium*.

[25] When Hera begs from Aphrodite the zone with which she can seduce Zeus, she says, *dos nun moi philoteta kai himeron*, "now give me love and sexual desire," and the same terms are used by the poet to describe what the love charm contains (*Il.*, XIV 198, 216). Compare also the Homeric Hymn to Aphrodite (2, 45, 53, 57, 73) where the essential nature of the goddess is the power to arouse *himeros*, a power that threatens Zeus and that he must reappropriate. The adjective, *himeroeis* modifies *choros*, "dancing place," when it is the scene of sexual arousal or rape, BOEDEKER, *op. cit.*, pp. 46-48, 50-51. For the collocation of *himeros* and death, compare Sappho 95 LP, evidently concerning the beloved Gongula (4), in which the speaker says, *katthanen d' himeros tis [echei me]*, "a kind of sexual urge to die possesses me" (11). Note also the adjective modifying the face of a groom suffused with *eros* in her epithalamium 112. 4 LP.

ses the erotic bond between the living and the dead. Within this dirge are heard the sounds of *terpsis*.

Within the first half of the banquet, and particularly within Menelaus' two speeches of funereal recollection, therefore, the oppositions are as unstable as they are within the second half. The terms are in motion, with one temporarily inhabiting the territory of the other. After the operation of Helen's *pharmakon-mythos*, it is not possible to see exclusive polarities in the earlier part of the evening. Were we deceived to see them there in the first place or to see them in Homeric diction as a whole? And was I deceiving to describe the passage at first only in terms of polarity and analogy? In each case, no. For it is not that there are no analogous polarities. It is rather that they are not fixed and that we notice their movement and admixture only through the effect of Helen's "good drug." We are not mistaken to see Homeric language and thought in structuralist terms. The "post-structuralist" theory of language supplements rather than cancels Saussure. The structures of oppositions should be discovered, and their movements, as well. Just as the structuralist methodology elucidates the one, so the Derridean critique uncovers the other.

V

> Some of the Homeridae also recount that, coming to Homer by night, she ordered him to compose an epic on those who fought at Troy, wishing to render their death an object of greater envy than the life of others, and that thus, partly through the craft of Homer but chiefly through her this poem became so enchanting and known by all.
>
> ISOCRATES.

Through the action of Helen's "good drug," this banquet in Sparta becomes an allegory of the movement of opposites within two opposite forms of relationship, "marriage" and "funeral." By neither of these forms, either marriage that joins or death that separates, are countervalent forces excluded. Neither unification nor division is final. Marriage and the marriage song include *polemos* and *penthos*; in funeral and dirge there is *himeros* and *terpsis*. The lamentation and its poetic counterpart, Menelaus' painful, Iliadic recollections, do not expel their erotic impulses and satisfactions. And when Helen attempts to separate recollection from pain by the dividing of drugs and of poetry, her "good" *pharmakonmythos* moves against her, (re)forming itself as "good-wretched." Her erotic impulse toward creating a pure *kleos* from the mixed past results in erotic, comic, Odyssean tales that do not exclude pain.

When it (re)turns upon Helen, the text turns upon itself, for the division of drugs and of poetry belongs, as we have seen, to Homeric diction as a whole.[26] Indeed, the words that attempt to separate drugs belong

---

[26] By Derrida's designation of the textual activity as female and the effort to control it as male, the woman, Helen, is vindicated, when the text (re)turns against the "male" structure of oppositions that she has been forced to assume.

not to a character, but to the poet alone, and, like Helen's *mythos* they contain their own contradiction:

pharmaka, polla men esthla memigmena polla de lugra

drugs, many one hand good mixed, many on the other wretched (230)

Despite the construction with *men...de*, the order of words imitates what the operation of Helen's *pharmakon-mythos* proves: between the two kinds of drugs there is not exclusive division, but mixture that moves with its semantic force in either direction. The two are opposites, but the relationship between them is one of potential movement and combination.

Ann L. T. BERGREN,
Princeton University.

Synchronic and Diachronic Aspects of Some Related Poems of Martial

One of the most important insights of contemporary Hermeneutics, particularly in the theories of H.-G. Gadamer, is that all understanding of literary and other texts must involve *interpretation* and *application*. Informal versions of this view may be seen in the slogans of some, though not all, literary critics of ancient literature. An obvious example is to be seen in Ezra Pound's advice to translators, *Make It New*; to which H.A. Mason's corollary was that the Classics survive only in translation.

I propose here to examine cursorily a neglected series of Martial's epigrams, which until recently were usually left in the obscurity of a learned (or unfamiliar) tongue in the Bohn and Loeb translations, just as they were segregated to an appendix in the monumental Delphin edition. These are Martial's epigrams on various aspects of Roman sexual habits and attitudes. One should add immediately that these constitute a very small proportion of Martial's work and by comparison with recent English, French, and American pornography, indeed by comparison with English Restoration literature, and nineteenth century French literature, they are very small beer indeed. Yet it was this set of short poems which made it difficult to approach Martial from a critical and literary viewpoint and serves to explain why there is not standard book in English on Martial and why he is read in schools and universities, if he is read at all, in harmless and unrepresentative selections. Yet his corpus is many times larger than that of Catullus, also best known for his short poems; it is larger than that of Tibullus or Porpertius, who, despite their erotic character, have certainly not been neglected in the twentieth century. Can it be that Martial's flattery of Domitian, a supposedly bad Emperor, is more distasteful to us, though not to Jacobean and Restoration poets, than Horace's flattery of Augustus, who is traditionally regarded as a "good Emperor"? Does this aspect of his poetry, along with the element of obscenity, discourage serious literary and historical criticism of his extensive *œuvre*? It would appear that the synchronic view normally taken by classical philologists and historians of literautre is largely responsible for the low estimation and neglect of our author. None of them, in the last three centuries at least, have been able, to use Gadamer's terminology, to open up a "dialogue" with him. These two prominent aspects of Martial's work have blinded the supposedly neutral and value-free interpreter presupposed by objectivist criticism and prevented a proper appreciation of Martial's value as a poet and a witness of his times. Objective criticism, in practice a chimaera, as the case of Martial proves, is the implicit or explicit philosophical founda-

tion of most classical philology that concerns itself with literary or historical texts from the ancient world. (I note here the honorable exception of
Nietzsche.) Yet although unconscious moral values affect the study of
Martial, and remain unquestioned, the conscious and sophisticated deploy-
ment of the insights of modern psychoanalysis, for instance, whose
founder after all declared that he was but formalizing scientifically the findings of poets and other writers, ancient and modern, is an object of
suspicion to these would-be neutralist critics. Similarly a Marxist might
with good reason deduce from the criticism of Martial that this supposedly
"objective" interpreter of classical texts comes to his subject laden with
unexamined romantic and bourgeois values. An examination of his popularity and influence in earlier times, particularly in England in the sixteenth
and seventeenth centuries, would suggest a totally different picture of
Martial and a radically different set of critical values and presuppositions.

In such an investigation, the logic of hermeneutic theory would be
vindicated. As D.C. Hoy, discussing Gadamer's theories, pointed out in
The Critical Circle (Berkeley, 1978), "the most influential aspect of hermeneutical theory is its emphasis on influence, on the tradition of the
reception of literary works as a constituent of the understanding of these
works and of literature per se" (p. 150). Similarly, Hans Robert Jauss, in
his book *Literaturgeschichte als Provokation der Literaturwissenschaft*
plausibly suggests that the proper method "not only pursues throughout
history a poet's success, posthumous fame, and influence, but also inves-
tigates the historical conditions and modifications of his comprehension"
(p. 183).

One might add, therefore, parenthetically, that one subsidiary function of hermeneutics is that of "rescuing" certain authors, such as Martial,
who have been downgraded or denigrated in the supposedly "objectivist"
literary histories, whose values in fact reflect the moral and critical, even
political, climate of their own times. A Gadamerian dialogue with some of
the more obscure authors, unnoticed or disregarded for various reasons
in other periods, would involve an attempt to harmonize their horizons
with ours (John Donne is a salutary case in point in the twentieth century).
Martial's impact on English literature in the 16th and 17th centuries, his
responsibility for the vogue of epigram among a large number of poets:
John Owen, Henry Parrot, Thomas Bastard, Sir John Davies, Sir John
Harington, Ben Jonson, Robert Herrick, and many others, his responsibility for sharpening the wit and point of English poetry after the almost
shapeless luxuriance and experimentation of Elizabethan verse style, must
affect at least the English interpreters of Martial. Indeed it would be little
of an exaggeration to claim that Martial's effect on English poetry culmi-
nates in Dryden and Pope, the two masters of English Augustan literature.
If the scholarly interpreter of Martial is unaware of Martial's imitators
and unpredictable influence, unpredictable certainly by his contemporaries,[1] then is he really a scholarly reader of Martial? Or a serious reader

---

[1]   Cf. PLINY, *Epistulae*, 3.21.6.

of epigrammatic poetry at all? For his synchronic critical purposes, he would need a thorough knowledge of the Greek epigram and its influence, along with that of earlier Roman epigrammatists, on the Flavian poet; why then should he be absolved from a more than perfunctory acquaintance with Martial's *Nachleben*? Can we take seriously a critic of Greek Tragedy who is not familiar with modern as well as ancient discussions of that genre, and with modern examples of tragedy from Shakespeare's time to our own?

It is possible also that the hermeneutic critic has accidentally discouraged serious attention to poets of the range and rank of Martial by his emphasis in metacritical discussion on the high linguistic and ontological status that must be granted to "poetry", which is generally defined in the highest possible value terms and thus sharply distinguished from mere communication, assertion, historiography, criticism and other complex uses of words. This obfuscates matters. Minor poets, poets in the standard sense of the word, are then either denied their status as "makers", or are elevated to impossible heights of impersonnality, to be adjudged context-free when their petty talents were all to bound up with their personalities, their financial circumstances, their love affairs, their confessions, and their infantile problems. T. S. Eliot, for instance, follows this tendency in judging that Rudyard Kipling was not a poet: he chose, successfully, by Eliot's lights, to write "verse".

These then are the problems that confront one in dealing with a poet such as Martial: the unconscious modern (moral) values brought to the work by the "objectivist" interpreter along with the lack of a diachronic perspective, and then the sharp distinction drawn by the hermeneutic critic between poetic and non-poetic discourse, even though prose poems and poetical prose are automatically brought across the magical dividing line. Perhaps a more Wittgensteinian concern with contextuality, the important concept of "Family Ressemblances" may help solve, or rather dissolve, many of the problems that beset us in the definitional areas both of practical criticism and hermeneutical methodology. Martial did not often write context-free poems: many of his epigrams were written for patrons, or derived from situational pressures and *ex tempore* exercises, or were merely "fillers", translations perhaps directly dependent on his Roman or Greek models, and so to be regarded as instances of witty adaptation rather than original poems. Yet these too are surely to be described as poetic also. And here I would agree with Stanley Fish, when he argues in "Literature in the Reader: Affective Stylistics"[2] that the attempt to find specific linguistic features that distinguish poetry from other nonpoetic language is based on a misconception; ordinary language may involve, to a greater or lesser degree, similar complexity — the language of lovers, for instance. Observely, poetry that is more akin to ordinary language, not very complex or apparently interesting — and here Martial would be a case

---

[2]   See *Self-Consuming Artifacts: The Experience of Seventeenth Century Literature* (Berkeley, 1972), pp. 383-426.)

in point — should not be denied its poetic claims, given the agreement of literary history and tradition that the epigram is a legitimate poetic form.

We are not dealing then with timeless lyrics or self-explanatory epics which create their own world, when we endeavor to interpret and evaluate those poems of Martial's that I have selected. For these we would look in vain for the objective and neutral reader. As these poems deal exclusively with sexual matters, is the reader supposed to be sexless? Then he will have little understanding of the point of many of epigrams presented to him, if not in the *literal*, then certainly in the *affective* sense. From a synchronic viewpoint, Martial could rely on his reader's responses and indeed expectations, which would be far different from the responses of the next one and a half millennia, which were to be dominated more and more by Christian assumptions and expectations as well as by other social and intellectual changes. Only a diachronic analysis can do any sort of justice to the very fact that Martial survived so handily, when large portions of Livy and Tacitus and countless other more important poets were lost, since a synchronic analysis of these epigrams will do no more than relate them to the ancient literary tradition of erotic epigram and to their contemporary social and sexual *mores*.

A hermeneutic interpretation then of the material must, if it is to be valuable, reveal far more about Martial, his society, his audience, and about the whole Western attitude to sex than a synchronic interpretation possibly can. We cannot, after all, recreate the impact of an homosexual epigram, say, on Martial's audience. How can we expect to divine, over a period of nearly two thousand years, the real intentions of the poet and the probable reaction of his audience, even when we use all recoverable evidence and exclude all absurd interpretations. Consequently, no critical judgment here can be context-free, synchronically or diachronically, since Martial's work is dependent on almost irrecoverable psychological effects and we are conditioned by our education, traditions, personal (if trained) preferences, or by our Arnoldian "touchstones." When therefore we shine a light from the present to illuminate objects from the past (and the lighting effects will differ from century to century), the light is focused on the same objects, the same texts, but the total impression will be naturally and inevitably different. A dialogue with Martial, then to use Gadamer's metaphor, will reveal much about his own society, about the poet's *persona*, if not his personality, but it must also reveal much about our own changed, or rather different, ways of thinking.

The hermeneutic approach I am advocating is the search for a meaning and significance in Martial in the light of *later*, not just contemporary history, society, and thought. Just as in biblical hermeneutics, the Old Testament took on fresh meanings because of the statements and "facts" recorded in the New Testament, so Martial's suppressed poems regain a coherence, even if a sinister coherence, in the light of our modern attitudes towards women and sexuality in general. This is consonant with what I take to be Gadamer's view that we cannot understand an ancient author's text better, only differently. Martial did intend to denigrate those women

— and men — whom he feared and despised, but he was unaware in his writing of the broader social and psychological context that we can now interpret more clearly if we adopt a modern feminist perspective and bring to the work an understanding of the socio-economic dynamics of ancient society which so rightly concern J. Habermas in his book *Erkenntnis und Interesse* (1968).

Let us turn now to the epigrams of Martial that I have selected for examination. The pederastic bias of Martial's *persona*[3] for handsome slave boys in obvious (1.58, 2.49, 11.23, 11.26, 11.43, 12.75). The preferred method of intercourse with them is anal sodomy and mutual masturbation would be frowned upon because of Martial's superstition that this would cause premature maturity in the slave (11.23). Except for variety or proof of extreme lasciviousness (3.67, 11.104), Martial regards such sexual practices with females, e.g. with his imaginary wife, as distasteful and, in his eyes, subersive of customary sexual roles (11.43, 12.96), a factor of great importance, as we shall see, to the poet as he represents himself in his work. Despite the minor problems individual temperaments present (12.75), slave boys do not remind the fastidious poet of his mortality nor increase his client's sense of social, and so psychological, insecurity. The preferred method of sexual intercourse and the status of his partners would naturally reinforce his sense of power. Not unexpectedly then, Martial is extremely condemnatory of other forms of male homosexuality, most notably, *fellatio* by a male (2.28, 2.54, 2.61, 2.72, 2.88, 11.45), and playing the passive role in sodomy (2.54, 2.62, 3.62, 3.71, 12.35). Possibly because of the male passivity involved, he is equally hostile to *fellatio* by females (1.94, 2.50, 2.87, 3.87, 4.84, 6.69), although there are some traces in him of ambivalence on the issue (cf. 3.67). Many of his witticisms therefore revolve round the Roman belief that people addicted to such practices developed halitosis (e.g. 2.50) and an unhealthy pallor (e.g. 7.4).

Since active pederasty with beautiful boys is his favored form of sex, he sneers at *verpi*, slaves who have been circumcised by their masters in order to gratify their perverse sexual tastes (e.g. 7.82.6, 11.9.4); at infibulation (11.75, 14.215); and at castration (11.75.6, 3.91), which to him was a sign of sexual depravity (6.2). The loss of masculinity involved (11.75) goes against Martial's strong genital orientation, witness the frequent epigrams involving the penis (e.g. 2.51, 6.16, 6.23) and the jokes deriding old age and impotence (2.45, 3.70, 73, 75).

Martial's attitudes to women in general and to female sexual *mores*, indeed to the female libido in general, are consistent with such a pederastic orientation, although there is much more to the question than that. He does

---

[3]   Since poetry is not autobiography, of course, however consistent and apparently realistic the attitudes that emerge from a given *oeuvre*, it must be assumed that where I speak of the poet or Martial, I refer only to the personal image depicted in the writing. To dispense with a lengthy discussion of this concept, the reader is referred to I. EHRENPREIS, "Personae" in *Restoration and Eighteenth Century Literature: Festschrift A. D. McKillop* (Chicago, 1963) and the further discussion in *Satire Newsletter*, 3.2 (Spring 1966) 89 ff.

not disapprove of prostitutes (1.34, 2.53) and admires exemplary widows and matrons, such as Lucan's relict, Polla Argentaria (7.21, 23, 10.64), Porcia and Paeta (1.42, 1.13), who were *univirae*; he can even be movingly affectionate about the pretty young slave girl, Erotion (5.37). Psychologically, none of these present any threat to his masculinity or his sexual image of himself.

The number of savage satiric epigrams which concern themselves with sexually aggressive females is revealing. These attack unconventional older women (e.g. 3.32, 10.90, etc. — although Roman notions of "older women" would differ considerably from ours); Lesbians (1.90, 3.67), and serial polygamists such as Telesilla (6.7). There are over a dozen of these, a small number in comparison with the whole corpus of Martial's work, but they constitute a significant presence in the epigrams generally reckoned to be obscene.

To understand fully this group of epigrams, we must put them in their contemporary sociological context and examine them with insights derived from modern feminist theory.

The evidence indicates that between the closing years of the Republic and the years when Christianity gained social, and then official, influence in Roman society, the female sex, at least in the social strata most visible in our documents, enjoyed a personal, sexual and economic liberation unparalleled in civilized states before the latter half of the twentieth century in America, England, and some parts of Europe. The causes of this phenomenon are complex, but testimony is to be found not only in the voluminous pagan and early Christian literature, but also in such works as the *Digest* (in its discussions of guardianship and property ownership) and in the fragmentary history of imperial legislation regulating civic morality. This relative freedom for women sprang from a number of causes. Firstly, there was the growing instability and casualness of marriage, in particular the decay of the type of marriage where the legally absolute rights *(manus)* of the father, the *paterfamilias*, were handed over to the husband. Concomitant with this there were the legal developments concerning a wife's dowry. For all practical purposes a husband had little more than the right to the income from it so long as the marriage lasted. The dowry, in the event of divorce or the husband's death, could be sued for and so it belonged in substance to the wife and in form only to the husband. The wife's property was thus a trust made over for a certain time to the husband. This state of affairs gave Roman women of substance the same sort of power over their husbands that the fear of heavy alimony might inspire in men today.

Another factor was the matter-of-fact, even cynical, view the Romans adopted towards multiple divorce and *mariages de convenance*, whether for political or financial reasons; the matrimonial adventures of such Roman worthies as Cicero and Cato Uticensis are worthy of note in this regard. Again, the Romans' attitude towards their offspring, which ties in with their attitudes towards abortions, suppositicious babies, foundlings, and natural children by female slave, was considerably different from that of later Western cultures. To the modern, to whom the bloodlink between parents and progeny is of overwhelming importance, the frequency, indeed the apparent desirability among upper class Romans, of adoption must seem surprising, a good example being the willingness of Claudius to make Nero his almost certain successor instead of his own son, Britannicus. Concern then over a cuckoo in the nest, the chauvinist desire to be the first and only man in a woman's life, would appear to have been minimal in well-to-do Roman males. Indeed the recorded eulogies to *univirae*, wives who had had but one husband, which would be a phenomenon generally unremarked in most later European societies, point to the rarity of this status in Rome at this period. A number of Martial's epigrams, for all their epigrammatic hyperbole, make a similar point, as 6.7, where the epigrammatist jeers at Telesilla who has just married for the tenth time: this is merely legalized adultery.

There would have been other factors contributing to this emancipation, such as the frequent absence from home of the male on business, military, or civic duties, and contact with the more matriarchal cultures of the East, particularly Alexandria. Of course, Republican and Imperial Rome in turn produced striking examples of women who were distinguished or notorious for their "unfeminine" or "overly feminine" behaviour or character; such were Clodia, Fulvia, Porcia, Julia, Agrippina and Messalina.

Again, just as the Roman male attitude towards adoption is almost incomprehensible to the modern guardians of the Judaeo-Christian nuclear family tradition, so too, even in these times, it is impossible to imagine the enormous accessibility to all varieties of sex that is possible in a slave society, such as that of Rome or the American South before the Civil War. There are in Martial such revealing epigrams as 1.84, directed against a member of the equestrian order who could not be bothered with the problems of a wife, but preferred to produce sons, home-bred knights, with the help of female slaves, which jibes with Pliny's mention of a praetor who kept several concubines. The point of Martial's epigram depends rather on social snobbery (he might free these servile sons and adopt them) than on any questioning of Quirinalis' abuse of his power. It is most unlikely that Roman women did not take surreptitious advantage of this servile availability for sexual services. This may be deduced not just from the evidence of Petronius, Martial, and Juvenal, but also from the complex and often penal legislation governing the relationships, legal status and offspring of free women and male slaves. A typical, if hyperbolic, epigram to illustrate this whole topic is 6.39, in which Martial claims that Cinna's wife, Marulla, has made Cinna seven times a father — not of free children, for neither friends nor neighbours nor he were involved. No, the curly-haired brat is the son of the North African cook; the negroid child is the offspring of a local wrestler; the third belongs to the baker; the fourth has inherited the homosexual traits of Cinna's own catamite; the fifth was clearly fathered by the village — or house — idiot; the girls, one dark, one redhead, spring form the loins of a local musician and Cinna's own farm manager; and there would be more if two of Cinna's slaves were not eunuchs. Another more humorous squib (7.14) retails a female friend's recent calamity: she has lost her plaything, which is not Lesbia's sparrow or Violentilla's dove, but a twelve year old slave whose tool had not yet reached 18 inches.

This then is the background against which these epigrams must be read. Women were claiming equal rights also in the most intimate areas of their personal lives. What Ovid had advocated as properly thoughtful behaviour, perhaps even as a method of control, by a sensitive and self-confident male, mutual pleasure, women at this period were now demanding as standard behaviour in their menfolk: sauce for the gander was now seen as sauce for the goose, also. It is true that Roman women did not develop an ideological consensus in these areas, although Plato's *Republic* could hardly have been lost to sight by this time. There was no Fanny Wright, no Mary Wollstonecraft, no Betty Friedan nor a Shulamith Firestone to articulate their aims or enunciate a coherent philosophy. Personal and sexual freedom seems to have been gained circumstantially and unsystematically by individually determined women. In Juvenal's words, wrenched from a different and more hostile context, the Roman wife said *hoc volo, hoc iubeo; sit pro ratione voluntas*. The effects on some males in a fundamentally patriarchal society, as documented in our literary and non-literary evidence, would be easily predictable by any sociologist or feminist. Martial's record of the male reaction may be paralleled in many private and public documents of the reaction of men in the twentieth century to the Women's Liberation Movement, with all that this entails in personal relationships and domestic life. The subsequent jealousy and spying are humorously recorded in such epigrams as 1.73, as is the complaisance and acceptance of this freedom by some husbands (cf. e.g. 5.61).

Martial provides us with additional, if derogatory, evidence about the sexual freedom exercised by the women of his time or earlier. One need not dwell on the frequent references to unpunished adultery committed by women (cf. 2.39; 2.56); this is an age-old theme. But consider in particular Martial's confirmation of recent modern studies that the preferred position in Roman heterosexual intercourse was the male supine with the female on top, whether in the position known as *Venus aversa*, with no eye contact, or, as in some of the Pompeian brothel paintings, with the femal above, and facing the male. This contrasts with the Greek preference for vaginal entry from the rear, and with the modern Anglo-American preference, now being rapidly overtaken by other preferences, for the so-called "missionary position" with the male superior and the female supine. (The statistics, of course, are only reasonably reliable, due to the fragmentary nature of the pictorial and literary evidence from ancient times and the mendacious and changing responses to sexual questionnaires in the modern era.)

Now, as any careful reader of Dr. Alex Comfort or Masters and Johnson knows, the female superior positions give greater powers of control, and therefore enhanced means of sexual gratification, to the woman, as well as slowing down the ejaculation time of the male, which is again in the interest of the more sexually capable female. That the ancients were aware of the female's greater sexual capacities is clear from the myth of Teiresias, who stated that a woman derived nine times more pleasure from the sexual act thant a man did. [4] It could be argued that these positions project the image of the male being taken care of, the inert *dominus* being tended by the industrious *serva*, but the physiological facts militate against this theory, inasmuch as these positions are somewhat harder to sustain by an unenthusiastic or lazy male partner, and the loss of physical control would, in any case, point to a passive attitude inconsonant with any theory of domination by the supine participant in the act.

In further evidence may be adduced Martial's strong dislike of oral sex and in particular of that frequently mentioned, and, in the eyes of Martial (and presumably his audience), that most detestable sexual practice, cunnilingus, to which he devotes several epigrams (2.28, 3.80, 81, 84, 96, 4.43, 11.45, 47, 61). Now this is hardly a sexual technique that would establish itself spontaneously in societies where women were *not* accustomed to demand and receive extensive foreplay, orgasm, and indeed sexual satisfactions comparable to those of males. Female sexual exhibitionism is another of Martial's butts for ridicule (1.34). Such shamelessness in a free woman might indicate an emancipated disregard for social conventions or the liberated gratification of her unnatural sexual needs. In either case Martial would have strong objections to it.

More of Martial's animus is directed against older women who are still gratifying their sexual urges. Biting barbs are directed at aged widows hoping to remarry (3.93) or aging Lady Chatterleys, who buy their sexual pleasures by purchasing handsome young slaves (2.34). He also, expresses dismay at blatant and excessive sexuality in any female, whatever her age or social status (4.12). A particular target, as was noted above, is fellation performed by females. Several criticism is directed also at the non-servile lovers of such aging women (cf. e.g. 3.76, 4.5.6, 4.28, 5.45).

His general cynicism, then, about contemporary female chastity comes as no surprise to the reader; it is no more than a variation on Ovid's dictum: *casta est quam nemo rogavit* (*Am.* 1.8.43, cf. Ma. 1.62, 4.71, 4.81, 7.30). Martial doubtless shared this point of view with most of his audience and certainly with his younger friend Juvenal and his Neronian contemporary Petronius. Not surprisingly, we may divine in Martial (and Juvenal) a pervasive fear and resentment of female sexuality and of the personal liberty that women now claimed and obtained for themselves, whatever their official legal status. This is then expressed in an almost Swiftian disgust at female body odours (4.4; 6.93) and stinks (4.87), as well as the scents and other subterfuges used to disguise the symptoms of our animality — this extends, as we have seen, to similar signs which

---

[4]   Cf. OVID, *Met.*, 3.316-38.

Martial associates with oral sex of any kind, homosexual or heterosexual (6.55).

In sum, Martial displays in his work, a patent fear of women, particularly of rich and therefore more liberated women, whose status cannot be gainsaid by an indigent poet, even though a male. One of his more revealing epigrams, whether it be more revelatory of himself or his audience, is perhaps 8.12, which concludes with the ringing chauvinist sentiment:

> inferior matrona suo sit, Prisce, marito: non aliter fiunt femina virque pares (3-4).

In Fletcher's version:

> Let matrons to their spouse inferior be, Else man and wife have no equality.

We must remind ourselves again that what we are constructing here is a sort of psychohistory, not necessarily of the poet Martial himself, but rather of his poetic *persona*, which may be conditioned not just by his fantasies and experiences, but also by the epigrammatic tradition he is following and by the expectations of his audience. With this caveat, one may now summarize our findings. In conformity with ancient thinking on the subject, as seen in most Greco-Roman authors, the poet assumes that most men, including himself, are bisexual, but the orientation of the epigrams examined is predominantly pederastic, although the poet may at times have appeared to satisfy his sexual urges with prostitutes (about whom he is somewhat fastidious). He has nothing but contempt for older passive male homosexuals, in accordance with standard Greco-Roman thinking; he is in no way sexually exclusive, his more complimentary remarks on female sexuality being however reserved for prostitutes and similar loose women of the lower classes, who present no threat to his virility. Despite some devastating epigrams on a fictitious wife, he presents himself as a well set-up bachelor with a strong dislike of domineering, oversexed, ugly or, much the same thing, older women. He dislikes and jeers at all sorts of deformity and practices that seem aberrant from his social and sexual norms: circumcision, infibulation, fellation and cunnilingus (by either sex), lesbianism, masturbation, sexual hypocrisy, particularly when practiced by frequently married women or Stoic philosophers. His preference for young and handsome males leads him to hate smells and the perfumes used to disguise them, which he associates with pathic homosexuality; consequently he dislikes social kissing ("where have those lips been?"), whereas he enjoys kissing pubescent slaves. He is defensive about pornography, while believing it a reflection of reality, and in a literary tradition to which some of the most famous figures in Roman social and literary history have contributed. The picture presented is generally consistent, once we discount the contradictory evidence in the epigrams about his marital status. His nauseating epigrams on his non-existent wife must be seen as the ancient equivalent of the jokes told about their wives by burlesque comedians; he was also witty at the expense of women who *want* to marry him. His reverence for domestic bliss which was somewhat broader than our definition includes young boy and girl slaves who would be their master's favourites; new brides; *univirae* who died before, or with, their husbands (Arria Paeta, for example), as opposed to the rich and many-times divorced women of the time. He praises devoted widows who revered their husbands' memories long after death. We find therefore, to our surprise, that Martial, was really, by the lights of his age, fairly conventional, if not prudish, in his sexual values, indeed in everything except his frank language, which was hallowed by literary tradition and contemporary practice.

J. P. SULLIVAN,
University of California,
Santa Barbara.

Odi et Amo

Une lecture linguistique du c.LXXXV de Catulle*

Ódi ét ămó. | quāre íd făciám, // fōrtássĕ rĕquíriś.
néscĭŏ, sĕ́d fĭĕrī́ // sĕ́ntĭo ĕt ĕ́xcrŭtĭŏ́r.

Après les études pénétrantes et exhaustives dont le c. 85 de Catulle
a fait l'objet[1], il est bien malaisé d'en pouvoir encore dire quelque chose.
Il n'a pas de sens non plus d'allonger la liste de caractérisations comme:
« unnachahmliche Schönheit, einzig in der ganzen römischen Literatur; in
einem Distichon ein ganzes Menschenleben» (M. Haupt); « eines der kost-
barsten Kleinodien her gesamten römischen Dichtung, ja der Epigrammatik
aller Zeiten» (O. Weinreich); « sa dureté cristalline» (J. Bayet); « l'esplo-
siva drammaticità del c. 85» (E. Paratore). Ce que nous tenterons ici c'est
juste une mise au point par le remplacement d'interprétations déjà propo-
sées dans un cadre plus uniforme et tant soit peu doctrinal.

Ce qui ne laisse pas d'impressionner de prime abord dans ce petit
poème c'est qu'il est dépourvu d'images. Mais Roman Jakobson nous met
en garde à ce propos: « As a rule, in imageless poems it is the figure of
grammar which dominates and which supplants the tropes[2]. » Voici en
quels termes il parle des figures grammaticales (*figurae verborum*), autrement dit de la « poésie de la grammaire», constitutive, avec les tropes
lexicaux, de la « grammaire de la poésie» :

> Any unbiased, attentive, exhaustive, total description of the selection, distri-
> bution and interrelation of diverse morphological classes and syntactic construc-
> tions in a given poem surprises the examiner himself by unexpected, striking
> symmetries and antisymmetries, balanced structures, efficient accumulation of
> equivalent forms and salient contrasts, finally by rigid restrictions in the re-
> pertory of morphological and syntactic constituents used in the poem, elimina-
> tions which, on the other hand, permit us to follow the masterly interplay of
> the actualized constituents[3].

Si l'on envisage sous l'angle de sa texture grammaticale, on remarque tout de suite que notre distique ne contient pas de substantifs; pour

---

* La première partie de cet article a été d'abord publiée dans les EMC/CNW,
XIII (1969), pp. 65-68, sous le titre «Grammaire et poésie: Catulle 85». La seconde partie
(après les astérisques) contient des réflexions complémentaires.

[1] Nous n'en citons que deux, des plus importantes: O. WEINREICH, *Die Distichen
des Catull*, Tübingen, 1926, pp. 32-83; E. PARATORE, «Catullo e gli epigrammisti dell'
Antologia," *Miscellanea di studi Alessandrini*, Torino, 1963, pp. 572-581.

[2] R. JAKOBSON, «Poetry of Grammar and Grammar of Poetry », *Lingua*, 21 (1968),
p. 604.

[3] *Ibid.*, pp. 602-603.

employer l'expression de Jean Bayet, qui s'y réfère[4], « les verbes domi-
nent ». Ce sont des verbes simples, communs, familiers, qui dénotent des
procès fondamentaux du cœur et de la pensée. Deux d'entre eux, *faciam*
et *fieri*, qui équivaut ici à *me id facere* selon Kroll[5], fonctionnent comme
des substituts abréviatifs ou « verbes pronominaux[6] », dont l'un accompagne le pronon *id* et l'autre le sous-entend. Il y a en tout huit verbes,
quatre dans chaque vers, distribués en sens inverses : la paire *odi et
amo* correspond à *sentio et excrucior, faciam* à *fieri, requiris* à *nescio*.

Mais c'est par les catégories grammaticales qui s'y rattachent qu'on
voit à l'œuvre les verbes du c. 85. Elles sont articulées en paires d'opposition : « personnel »/« non-personnel » (et à l'intérieur du « personnel » :
« première »/« deuxième personne »), « actif »/« passif », « verbum finitum »/
« verbum infinitum », perfectum »/« infectum » (bien que la différence entre
odi et *amo* soit neutralisée sur le plan du signifié), « indicatif »/« sujonc-
tif ». En plus de ces oppositions morphologiques, on a les oppositions
syntaxiques : « proposition énonciative »/« proposition interrogative » (et à
l'intérieur de la première : « affirmation »/« négation »), « proposition indépendante »/« proposition dépendante ».

Ces oppositions sont distribuées de telle sorte que chaque vers en
contient le même nombre. Cinq dans le premier vers : « première personne »/« deuxième personne », « perfectum »/« infectum », « indicatif »/
« subjonctif », « proposition énonciative »/« proposition interrogative »,
« proposition indépendante »/« proposition dépendante ». Cinq aussi dans
le second : « personnel »/« non personnel, » « actif »/« passif, » « verbum
finitum »/« verbum infinitum », « affirmation »/« négation », « proposition
indépendante »/« proposition dépendante ».

Le cas de *faciam/fieri* présente un intérêt particulier. Tout en s'opposant l'un à l'autre au point de vue de la voix et de la personne et sous
les rapports de la distinction « verbum finitum »/« verbum infinitum » et
du type d'énoncé où ils sont situés (interrogation/assertion), *faciam* et
fieri ont, en même temps, des traits communs prononcés : ils se trouvent
à l'intérieur du vers, ils appartiennent à des propositions subordonnées qui
précèdent leurs principales[7], ce sont des verbes pronominaux à racines
différentes mais de même sens. C'est par ce qui distingue et rapproche la
forme, la fonction et la syntaxe de ces deux verbes que les vers du distique, en partie, se ressemblent et diffèrent.

Nous avons mentionné plus haut la distribution des huit verbes
dans les deux vers. Les verbes indicatifs du dialogue dans le distique
(*requiris* et *nescio*) occupent des positions diamétralement opposées, d'où
leur proximité. Quant aux verbes pronominaux *faciam* et *fieri*, le premier

---

    [4] J. BAYET, « Catulle, la Grèce et Rome », Fondation Hardt, *Entretiens*, t. II, p. 33.
    [5] W. KROLL, *Catulli Liber*, 2e éd., 1929, p. 259.
    [6] Cf. E. BENVENISTE, « La nature des pronoms », *For Roman Jakobson*, La Haye,
1956, p. 37.
    [7] Voir E. PARATORE, *op. cit.*, p. 573.

suit *odi et amo* et le second précède *sentio et excrucior,* ces deux paires occupant elles aussi des positions diamétralement opposées.

Ce parallélisme inverse est un seulement des schèmes structurels de notre poème. D'autres divisions aussi s'y laissent voir, dichotomiques ou trichotomiques. J'en suggère deux : une dichotomie, qui isolerait *odi et amo* et *nescio* par rapport au reste du vers respectif ; une trichotomie, consistant à *odi et amo /quare id faciam / fortasse requiris* d'un côté, à *nescio / sed fieri sentio / et excrucior* de l'autre.

Dans cette structuration à plusieurs variables, il y a une seule constante : le couple *odi et amo,* pivot et arête, pour ainsi dire, du distique. C'est sur lui qu'est, en grande partie, modelé le reste du c. 85, qui en est aussi un commentaire et une interprétation. Il réunit les deux termes, grammaticalement différenciés, d'une opposition sémantique qui traduit l'état d'âme déraisonnable, toutefois réel, puisque vécu, du poète. Examinons, par rapport à *odi et amo,* la texture du second vers. *Odi et amo* y est relayé par trois, au moins, équivalents notoires. La coordination au moyen d'une copulative est reprise par *sentio et excrucior.* L'opposition sémantique est transposée sur le plan syntaxique par la coordination au moyen d'une adversative : *nescio, sed ... sentio.* La même opposition se retrouve condensée dans le seul (et crucial) *excrucior* où l'idée de la *crux* est ainsi remise en relief. Comme dit Jakobson : « In poetry the internal form of a name, that is, the semantic load of its constituents, regains its pertinence[8]. » Si cette interprétation est valable, il y aurait dans notre distique, après tout, un terme imagé.

Le second vers, tout en étant un pendant ou un supplément du premier, s'en distingue aussi par ce qu'il a en propre, en plus de sa forme métrique. C'est ici uniquement que l'on trouve, comme déjà indiqué, la voix passive, un verbum infinitum et un énoncé négatif. Sur le plan phonémique, on remarque tout d'abord l'absence de /a/. Les temps marqués des quatre dactyles sont tous occupés par /e/[9]. À la tête des deux hémistiches, le triphone *sen* est un anagramme de *nes.*

C'est le jeu de ces correspondances phonémiques et grammaticales qui donne à notre distique de la consistance et en fait, comme dirait Jakobson, « an enduring thing[10] ». Qui plus est, l'entrelacement des divers éléments mis en jeu a comme résultat un ensemble non seulement consistant, mais aussi dynamique. Il aurait suffi à Catulle d'exprimer son état par les simples mots *odi et amo.* Ce qu'il a accompli c'est la conversion du message en poésie. Dans l'espace exigu de deux vers, un chemin sinueux mène du début à la fin. À l'intérieur de la tautologie *odi et amo... fieri sentio* s'implante un dialogue et à sa fin se greffe *et excrucior.* On passe successivement de l'assertion à l'interrogation, de l'interrogation à la négation, de la négation à l'affirmation. Le premier vers commence

---

[8] R. JAKOBSON, « Linguistics and Poetics », *Style in Language,* ed. by T. SEBECK, New York, 1960, p. 376. Ce qui est valable pour le nom l'est aussi pour le verbe.

[9] Voir E. PARATORE, *op. cit.,* p. 574.

[10] R. JAKOBSON, *op. cit.,* p. 371.

par un verbe à la première personne et finit par un verbe à la deuxième, le second commence par un verbe à la première personne et à l'actif et finit par un verbe passif. Le passage au passif se fait immédiatement après la réponse négative en tant que sa contrepartie. L'aveu
d'ignorance déclenche un retour aux procès que dénote la paire verbale
initiale et, en même temps, un revirement dans la relation de ces procès
au sujet. L'action est sentie et présentée comme subie. Ceci vaut aussi
pour le verbe final *excrucior,* qui suggère par son sémantème le caractère
antinomique des sentiments de Catulle et indique par sa désinence la con-
trainte qui en résulte.

* * *

Je croyais avoir réglé mes comptes avec le *c.* 85 de Catulle par l'article que je viens de citer en entier. Mais une lecture plus attentive du
livre d'Otto Weinreich, *Die Distichen des Catull,* m'a fait changer d'avis.
Pour apprécier à sa juste valeur le rôle de la question (*quare id faciam,
fortasse requiris*) au milieu du *c.* 85, on ne doit pas perdre de vue, selon
Weinreich, qu'il s'agit dans ce distique d'une allocution. « Nun, wenn
das Gedicht Ansprache ist », dit Weinreich, « einen inneren Zusammen-
hang wecken will zwischen dem lyrischen Ich und einem anderen, schliess-
lich dem Leser schlechthin, der Anteil am Dichter nimmt, dann hat das
zur begreiflichen Folge, dass das Gedicht auch Antwort sein kann auf
eine gestellte oder gedachte Frage dieses anderen Ich[11] ». Le mérite de
l'approche de Weinreich est d'attirer l'attention sur le statut linguistique de
notre épigramme. L'allocution s'y exprime sous forme de réponse susci-
tée par une interrogation.

Le schéma « question — réponse » n'est pas l'apanage du *c.* 85. On
le retrouve dans le *c.* 7 (*quaeris, quot mihi basiationes*) et le *c.* 72 (*qui
potis est? inquis*), tous les deux cités par Weinreich (cf. aussi *c.* 24:
qui? non est homo bellus? inquies). Catulle exploite ici ce qu'Émile Benveniste appela « le cadre figuratif de l'énonciation », décrit en ces termes:
« deux figures en position de partenaires sont alternativement protagonistes de l'énonciation[12] ». En faisant intervenir son allocutaire, réel ou
imaginé, par une question ou une objection, le poète s'offre l'occasion de
souligner ce qu'il veut dire par une forte assertion. L'effet poétique est
ainsi produit par le jeu de ce que Benveniste appela « les grandes fonctions syntaxiques[13] ».

Pour revenir à *Odi et amo,* le schéma « question — réponse » n'est
pas le seul angle sous lequel on peut l'envisager. Si on le compare avec
les autres distiques, on voit qu'il ressemble davantage au *c.* 94:

> *Mentula moechatur. 'moechatur mentula'. certe.*
> *'hoc est quod dicunt, ipsa olera olla legit'*

---

[11]   Cf. WEINREICH, *op. cit.,* pp. 44-45.
[12]   Cf. É. BENVENISTE, *Problèmes de linguistique générale,* II, 1974, p. 85.
[13]   Cf. BENVENISTE, *op. cit.,* p. 84.

et au *c.* 112:

> *Multus homo es Naso, neque tecum multus homo est qui*
> *descendit: Naso, multus es et pathicus.*

Tous les trois commencent par une assertion (*c.* 85: *Odi et amo*; *c.* 94: *Mentula moechatur*; *c.* 112: *Multus homo es Naso*). Ce qui suit, dans les trois cas, est un développement interprétatif de l'affirmation initiale[14]. Il s'agit, en fait, de ce que Roman Jakobson a appelé une opération métalinguistique[15].

Le *c.* 94 constitue le cas le plus évident, le cas modèle. On y est en présence d'une double élucidation: une nouvelle assertion, *moechatur mentula,* précise le sens de *Mentula moechatur*; le proverbe *ipsa olera olla legit* explicite le rapport entre les deux assertions. D'une élucidation à l'autre, il y a, certes, développement, mais le contexte demeure, pour employer une autre expression de Jakobson, «équationnel». Toutefois, l'«usage séquentiel d'unités équivalentes[16]» remplit ici, en même temps, la fonction métalinguistique et la fonction poétique. L'opposition diamétrale entre la poésie et le métalangage, dont parle Jakobson, s'y neutralise.

Dans le *c.* 112, l'imprécision du premier *multus* entraîne, sous le couvert d'une identification psychosociologique, un commentaire sémantique[17]. Catulle passe du général au particulier par une spécification négative d'abord (*multus homo* peut signifier, selon le contexte, des choses différentes); par une spécification positive ensuite (avec l'adjonction de *pathicus,* on apprend en quoi consiste l'«abondance» de Naso). Ici aussi, «l'usage séquentiel d'unités équivalentes» est, à la fois, au service du métalangage et de la poésie.

Comme dans les cas précédents, où ce qui est mis en question est l'assertion initiale, *Mentula moechatur* et *Multus homo es Naso,* c'est du paradoxe *odi et amo* que veut s'enquérir le destinataire du *c.* 85. Le paradoxe résulte du fait que les deux verbes, *odi* et *amo,* se contredisent l'un l'autre. Il s'agit d'un non-sens. Comme s'il n'en croyait pas ses oreil-

---

[14] Comme autres exemples de poèmes chez Catulle qui commencent par une affirmation, on peut citer *c.* 57: *Pulcre convenit improbis cinaedis; c.* 79: *Lesbius est pulcer; c.* 89: *Gellius est tenuis; c.* 110: *Aufillena, bonae semper laudantur amicae.*

[15] Cf. JAKOBSON, *op. cit.,* p. 356.

[16] Cf. JAKOBSON, *op. cit.,* p. 358.

[17] Cf. K. QUINN, *Catullus: The Poems* (1970), p. 451: «Apparently a pun on two (or more) meanings of *multus*», et S. Reisz DE RIVALORA, *Poetische Äquivalenzen,* 1977, p. 60: «In den Fällen, in denen das wiederholte Wort polysemisch ist und dementsprechend der Kontext jeweils bestimmt, welche der verschiedenen Bedeutungen des Wortes in der Aussage aktualisiert wird, kann die Wiederholung zum Wortspiel dienen. So in *c.* 112.» Il faut ajouter que ce livre important représente la première application d'envergure de la poétique linguistique moderne à l'œuvre d'un auteur de l'antiquité classique. Mais c'est John P. Elder qui traita pour la première fois une poésie de Catulle à la façon de Roman Jakobson dans un article intitulé «The Figure of Grammar in Catullus 51», *The Classical Tradition: Literary and Historical Studies in Honor of Harry Caplan,* Ithaca, New York, 1966. Sur les rapports entre la philologie classique et les approches récentes dans les sciences littéraires, cf. K. STIERLE, «Klassische Literatur, moderne Literaturwissenschaft und die Rolle der Klassischen Philologie», *Gymnasium,* 85 (1978), pp. 289-311.

les, le destinataire demande : « Comment est-ce possible que tu fasses une telle chose ? » Cette question, qui porte sur le plan de l'action, recouvre la question métalinguistique : « Je ne te suis pas — qu'est-ce que tu veux dire ? » Le destinateur répond par un aveu d'ignorance. Le non-sens persiste en tant que tel, mais il est résolu sur le plan de la réalité psychologique. Le verbe crucial *excrucior,* qui décrit l'état d'âme de celui qui aime et déteste à la fois (« langage-objet »), traduit, en tant que signe linguistique, le sens de *odi et amo* ; reproduit, en le résumant, le contraste entre les deux verbes et leur croisement (« métalangage »). *Excrucior,* jouant ici le rôle du proverbe dans le *c.* 94, conclut le contexte équationnel.

Si, comme il vient d'être proposé, le modèle selon lequel sont structurés les trois distiques est une opération métalinguistique, le schéma « question — réponse » dans le *c.* 85 cesserait d'avoir l'importance capitale que lui attribuait Weinreich et apparaîtrait comme un moyen dont se sert Catulle pour agencer son poème. Si ce schéma est présent dans le *c.* 85 et, peut-être, dans le *c.* 94[18], il ne l'est pas dans le *c.* 112. Bien que similaires du point de vue de leur structure de base, les trois distiques suivent des voies diverses quant à leur réalisation.

Le caractère spécial des distiques qu'on vient d'examiner devient plus apparent si on les compare avec les trois autres distiques de Catulle :

(93)

Nil nimium studeo, Caesar, tibi velle placere
nec scire utrum sis albus an ater homo.

(105)

Mentula conatur Pipleum scandere montem :
Musae furcillis praecipitem eiciunt.

(106)

Cum puero bello praeconem qui videt esse,
quid credat, nisi se vendere discupere ?

Dans ceux-ci il n'y a pas de constatation initiale, mise en question ou discutée. L'énoncé y va de l'avant, par progression en sens unique. Les trois distiques « métalinguistiques », au contraire, sont rétrospectifs et se replient sur les assertions : *Odi et amo, Mentula moechatur, Multus homo es Naso.* Ils s'organisent autour d'une equation : *odi et amo = excrucior, Mentula = mentula, multus = pathicus,* qui s'irradie en variations (c'est le cas de *c.* 94) ou qui les enclôt (c'est le cas de *cc.* 85 et 112). On a dans *c.* 94, par exemple, l'inversion de *Mentula moechatur* en *moechatur mentula* et la conversion de leur interdépendance en une locution proverbiale, tandis que dans *c.* 85 on trouve emboîtés, entre l'assertion initiale et le verbe final, deux substituts pronominaux de *odi et amo,* un *id* explicite avec *faciam* et un *id* implicite avec sa variante passive *fieri.* On a de même dans *c.* 112, entre le premier et le dernier *multus,* de sens identique, l'insertion d'un *multus* de sens différent et l'emploi de *descendit* (verbe à valeur lexicale) par opposition à la copule (à valeur simplement

---

[18]   Comme on sait, certains éditeurs voient dans *moechatur mentula* une interrogation.

grammaticale). On pourrait y ajouter comme élément de variation le changement de position de *Naso* par rapport à *multus*. On voit ainsi à l'œuvre,
dans les distiques « métalinguistiques », un principe de compensation : la
simplicité de l'équation de base est contrebalancée par la complexité des
variations.

Pierre COLACLIDÈS,
Université de Californie à Irvine.

Language, Structure, and the Son
of Oedipus in Aeschylus'
Seven Against Thebes*

> One great part of every human existence is passed in a
> state which cannot be rendered sensible by the use of
> wideawake language, cutanddry grammar and goahead
> plot.
>
> James JOYCE

> The lord, who has the oracle in Delphi, neither discloses
> nor hides his thought, but indicates it through signs.
>
> HERACLITUS.

I. — NARRATIVE, TIME, AND REPETITIVE FORM

The *Seven Against Thebes,* like its protagonist, Eteokles, is an
orphan twice over, for it has lost both of its predecessors in Aeschylus'
Theban trilogy, in which each of the dramas corresponded to one generation of the accursed Labdacid family. Our difficulties in interpreting this
last and single play are compounded not only by the probable spuriousness
of the ending,[1] but by the prestige and hence priorization of its successors on the tragic stage — the *Oresteia* in the matter of trilogic form,
and Sophocles' *Oedipus Tyrannos* and *Antigone* in the development of
the Theban myth.

In the *Oresteia,* time brings change that will rupture the chain of
hereditary guilt so that child need no longer replicate parent but will be
judged instead on action and intention. In Sophocles' *Oedipus,* the oracles
to father and son need no causal necessity to justify them. They meet
and collide in the anguished consciousness of Oedipus to give him the

---

* This essay is the introduction to a detailed semiotic study of the seven paired
speeches exchanged by the scout and Eteokles in the shield scene which is the central
section of the drama. Space does not permit the inclusion of the full text which will be
published elsewhere. My intention here is to establish the principles by which that analysis
will operate.
  [1] The problem of the ending will never be fully resolved, nor is the appropriate
forum for airing the debate. My study of the logic of the text may add, perhaps, another
argument against the authenticity of those passages directly concerned with the city's
unmotivated intervention in the matter of the brothers' burial.
  All references will be cited from the Oxford Classical Text, 2d ed., ed. PAGE.

full meaning of his name and the identity of the stranger he met and killed at the crossroads long before. Sophocles' Creon and Antigone act out their conflict of values and language on a more universal plane, unburdened by an explicit predictive design.

The *Seven Against Thebes* is a drama concerned too with oracles, seers, and identity, with self and other, family and city, doubleness of language and of human existence. But it is the third act of a drama in which Oedipus served as the middle term, the receiver and transmitter of a destiny which began with the transgression of the unnatural law of sterility imposed upon Laios, and which passed through parricide and incest, only to end in this play with the cancellation of progeny as a reflexive and reciprocal action when brothers, now indistinguishable from each other, meet and slay one another at the seventh gate of Thebes.

Triadic structure in the *Seven* does not offer the third term as a synthesis which, as in the *Oresteia,* mediates and transcends the dialectic of two opposing terms. In that trilogy, the last play, the *Eumenides,* puts an end to repetition and recurrent crimes within the family as it breaks out of the genealogical frame of the house of Atreus in Argos into the civic space in Athens. Only with the change of venue and its attendant implications can the family be saved from the ill-fated autonomy of its vendettas which consumes its own progeny. Athena, herself the arbiter now in the dispute, installs the permanent principle of mediation in the city by establishing the law court, protecting it at the outset from a relapse into hopeless equality/division by a procedure for breaking a tie vote. Retrospectively, the *Oresteia* is an aetiological drama which opens out at its end upon a prospective future in creating a new founding myth by which city and family might both endure [Zeitlin 1978].

But the *Seven,* as the third term, moves towards closure in the working out of its plot — a closure that is the cumulative end of a series — the end of the story which is the double end of the two brothers, at once closing play, trilogy, myth, and genealogical sequence. The downward pull towards the final and irreversible end is doubly determined as the fulfillment of not one, but two predictive utterances. For the two brothers have not only incurred the curse of the father, but they still bear the burden of the unfulfilled oracle given to Laios in the first generation that dying without issue, he would save the city (745-49).

For the *Seven*, the possibility of mediation is, in fact, the the sustaining fiction of the play. On the level of plot, its false promise is vitiated, as events will prove, once Eteokles, the director of operations in the defense of beleaguered Thebes, enters into the drama by placing himself as a participant at the seventh gate (282-86). On the level of language, that hope of mediation equally fails. For the threat of the father's curse that the brothers would divide his goods by the sword seemed to be mitigated by the message of the dream to which Eteokles, at the moment of recognition, will refer (710-11). The dream proposed that a Chalybian stranger would peacefully arbitrate the fraternal quarrel over the patrimony

[Burnett 1973]. But the dual messages of curse and dream proved only an illusory set of alternatives. Each was, after all, only the restatement of the other, Chalybian stranger being in reality the riddling equivalent of the sword of Ares (727-33). To the matching of the two antithetical meanings that were one, corresponds the matching of the antithetically named brothers, Eteokles and Polyneikes, in reciprocal slaughter. Each serves as the instrument/agent of arbitration/division against the other, the only true means for resolving the intestine violence of the family.

If the irreversible movement of linear time brings together the first and second dramas in the fulfillment of oracle (Laios) and curse (Oedipus), the sequence of events likewise involves repetition and condensed reenactment. When Eteokles, in his misogynist tirade against the unruly Theban women of the chorus in the first scene of the play, declares his desire never to live with a woman (187-90), his refusal of cohabitation might be construed as a reaction against the excessive sexual intimacy of his father's crime of incest [Méautis, 1936: 108, Caldwell, 1973]. Yet by this act of negation, Eteokles would also seem to counter Laios' original violation of the injunction against begetting progeny and thus perhaps to protect his personal destiny from the ominous terms of the prophecy concerning that violation. By the fact of refusing the role of genitor, Eteokles would indeed die childless and, as patriotic ruler of Thebes, he would pose no threat to the city — quite the contrary. But oracles only predict an event, not the time, place, or mode of fulfillment. After all, the father's curse spoke only of hostility between the brothers, while the remoter oracle to Laios spoke of the family's threat to the city's safety. Thus, retrospectively, when, in the context of an Argive attack on Thebes, Eteokles and his brother slay one another in combat according to the prescription of the *curse* of Oedipus, Eteokles' status as *ateknos*, childless (828), now also fulfills the terms of the *oracle* given to Laios. The encounter between the brothers marks, in fact, the perfect coincidence of oracle and curse. The movement away is inevitably the movement towards, even as Oedipus himself at the crossroads turned from Corinth to Thebes.

Likewise, in the play itself, Eteokles' various strategies for avoiding the compulsion to repeat the family history also fail. For in the shield scene that justifies the fated outcome, he reenacts and condenses his father's and his father's father's experiences by treating the emblems of the shields as riddles and by converting these riddles into curse and oracle. That reenactment, in fact, becomes more specific as the sequence of the shields progresses towards its climax with Polyneikes revealed at the seventh gate. For at the fifth gate, Eteokles confronts the riddle again in the emblem of the sphinx on Parthenopaios' shield and at the sixth, he tests his wits against the oracle, when he counters Amphiaraos, the seer of the Argive host.

The brothers, in their encounter, also repeat and condense the acts of the preceding generations: first, in the mutual desire to expel the other from the city, as Laios expelled Oedipus, and second, in their slaughter of one another. In one single moment, they reproduce the incest/parricide of the father in their struggle for hegemony and their desire to take possession of their father's goods and the mother earth of Thebes, while their "autoktony," their reflexive attack upon themselves and each other, recapitulates Oedipus' mutilating self-punishment of putting out his two eyes. [2]

Thus time in its forward movement is also regressive. The *telos*, therefore, that is completed, is also the *telos* of the circle, as past imposes its patterns on the present, as each resistance to the past and its implications only encourages and justifies the return of the past. There is no escape, for present is at the same time enacted as the fulfillment of an already predicted futurity. The triadic structure of the play itself reflects this forward and backward movement. The first and third sections are mirror images of one another in the structural correspondence of their parts [Thalmann 1978: 26-29], a device which frames the peripeteia of the drama with formal symmetry in the balance of first against last.

But the peripeteia, the pivotal point of the play, is more inclusive, as it extends beyond its own praxis to embrace all three generations. On the one hand, reversal and regression lead to a larger reordering, when the chorus contemplates in its grief the death of the two brothers. For the lament that constitutes the last third of the play brings all the generations together in the linear sequence of their family history by which each event is shown as causally connected to the next (734-91, 832-47). But this recapitulation is also a regression of another sort, when the identities of the two brothers merge, and they lie bedded beside their father in the earth (1004), thus effecting a return to a point anterior to the founding of the family and the prediction of its demise. This is the final reduction of diachrony to synchrony, the effacement of all differences upon which identity through time is maintained and social communication and continuity made possible.

From this brief overview, several significant features emerge. First, an analogical relationship can be posited between the genealogical triad and the narrative structure, both as to the trilogic form of the whole, and as to the triadic pattern of the last play itself. Second, the effacement of difference works on two levels; one, on the level of action, as the dramatic event of isomorphic death which levels all distinctions of position and priority; the other, on the level of language, the speech act by which

---

[2] Greek does not distinguish lexically between violence against the self and violence against kin. The word *autos*, as in *autocheir* and *authentes*, refers both to suicide (reflexive violence) and to kin murder, an indication of the archaic solidarity of the family. See Gernet, 1955, "La désignation du meurtrier." The use of *autos* in this text in describing the simultaneous death of the two brothers exploits the ambiguity (e.g., 681, 735, 734, 805, 850). Thus Oedipus' violence against himself would be equivalent to the brothers' violence against each other, equal crimes against the self. The text at 782-86 seems to express Oedipus' self-blinding in terms that suggest the two brothers, but the textual corruption of the passage makes an identification unsure.

the identities of the brothers become one, even as curse and dream (Oedipus) become one, even as oracle (Laios) and curse (Oedipus) coincide. Furthermore, the levelling of these distinctions is the direct result of the opposite action — namely, Eteokles' performance in the central scene of the shields, where he establishes distinctions; i.e. the antitheses between enemy and defender, where antagonists are named and matched against each other, and where the enemy's shields are reinterpreted to deflect their evil import.

What then is the significance of language and structure in relation to the family history of the house of Laios? What relation exists between language and identity, between self and other? What connects the ambiguities of speech posed by oracle and riddle with Eteokles' status as son of Oedipus, i.e. a child of an incestuous union? Why, in short, does everything in the play happen as it does and in the way it does? To begin the hermeneutic task, I turn to an examination of the correlation of kinship and language systems.

II. — *GENOS:* SYSTEM OF FAMILY/SYSTEM OF LANGUAGE

Modern structuralist theory postulates that language stands in a direct relationship to the social order, both as its reflection/distortion and as its maker/unmaker. From this point of view, language is understood as "a system of relations and oppositions defined in formal differential terms" which operates according to rules that govern the proper selction and combination of its elements [Culler 1975:11]. Furthermore, this model of language serves as the model for the functioning and intelligibility of each of the systems that inheres in the culture, whether social, political, psychological, or literary/mythic. And finally, the linguistic model works as the model of and the medium for the relations among the systems. It is the master code which communicates meaning and legitimates communication among the other coded languages which constitute the complex text of our experience.

The structuralist view of language is especially relevant to the understanding of the structure/language of kinship systems which regulate marriage and other family ties and ensure the proper relations of reciprocity and exchange among the members of a given human community. Marriage, the system of relations and oppositions, is the "archetype of exchange," of the "gift and counter-gift," in which women function as "signs... which are to be communicated" [Lévi-Strauss, 1947: 1969, 483, 496]. Women serve as "the mediating factor... circulated, like words, between clans, lineages, or families" [Lévi-Strauss 1963: 60]. As language operates according to the rules of its grammar, the rules of the circulation of women obey the grammar of the social system. Marriage, which is the "dramatic encounter between nature and culture, between alliance and kinship" [Lévi-Strauss, 1947: 1969, 489], together with language itself, are the two most distinctive marks of human societies for the Greeks as for others. That the taboo against incest, i.e., the breaking of the rules, is universal to human culture and that the Oedipus myth stands as the paradigm of its transgression for Western culture needs, of course, no demonstration in the wake of Freud and Lévi-Strauss.

Regulated endogamy-exogamy within a society prevents the isolation and solipsism of the biological family. It maintains the separate identities of families, but also defines through the rules of permissible combination the collective identity of the group and marks the difference of that group from those outside its boundaries. From the point of view of the family, this exogamy inscribes the child in the household and the city and socializes him through the rules which permit or forbid transactions of reciprocity and exchange within and without.

Marriage as an alliance of affines (non-kin) and of opposites (male-female) teaches the child the relations of difference. As the institution of kinship, it teaches him the relations of similarity. But his position as child in the family also teaches him how to manage the necessary rapports between the relations of difference and relations of similarity in still another way. For through rules of nearness and distance and through the subordinating hierarchy of age he learns the crucial difference between parents and child and observes the structure which confers upon him his distinct but related social and biological identity.

The orderly line of generations creates a vertical spacing which operates on the principle of difference-in-sameness and sameness-in-difference, exemplified by the Greek notion that in the lawful family and the lawful society women bear children who resemble but are not identical to their begetters (Hesiod, *WD*, 235) in order to continue the family line and to inherit its goods. On the horizontal level, proper exogamy is necessary to maintain the vital difference among the several children of the same generation, if there are more than one. For children are the smallest units of repetition in the family sequence with the least difference among them [Girard 1972: 1977, 61-64].

In the logic of Greek myth, incest, which violates all the rules of difference in the interests of obsessive sameness, either produces no progeny (sterility) [Delcourt 1938, 97], or, as in the case of Oedipus and Jocasta, it reproduces its own redundancy by the begetting of a double progeny (excessive fertility). This reduplication subverts the ideological unity of the *oikos* by generating two sons instead of one to inherit a single patrimony, sons who demonstrate their sameness (not their resemblance) by their struggle for the same object which they cannot share [Girard 1972: 1977, 63]. Two sons must "fight not so much to settle the differences between them... but instead to establish through violence a definitive difference — victor-vanquished — by means of which they can be distinguished each from each" [Fineman, 1977, 238, on Girard]. But Eteokles and Polyneikes, by their mode of death, which I have termed reciprocal and reflexive, fail to establish that difference between victor and vanquished, for each is victor over the other but each is also vanquished by the other. This is exactly the meaning of their conflict, unlike other conflicts between brothers in Greek myth, namely, that issue from an incestuous union cannot establish any difference between its offspring, but can only produce sons who embody the principle of difference, unreconcilable except through their inevitable identical end.

Here, more precisely for the Greek context, we can point to the logical economy of the *lex talionis* to explain the phenomenon of the enemy brother. This law of retaliation decrees that one extreme provoke its opposite. Thus excessive sameness, which violates the law of difference, must generate excessive difference as its response, in this case, in the form of antithetical opposites which cannot be mediated. The rigor by which the *lext talionis* operates here situates the purest representation of difference, i.e., the truly radical. Other, the enemy, within the entity of the homogeneous group instead of without and, by necessity, produces the hostile antithesis of Eteokles and Polyneikes. Unmediated antitheses in the incestuous family therefore can only shuttle between radical division or drastic fusion, as the action of the play shows, between polarized duality or a doubled unity, like the *symbolon*, that token of recognition which can be viewed both as two divided halves or as a doubled whole [Lallot, 1974, 39-40; Froidefond, 1977, 217-21; cf. Plato, *Symp.*, 191d].

But as this law of exacting compensation is worked out, the result, paradoxically, is a closed economy of self-sufficiency, a totality into itself. For excessive closeness (union) and distance (division) turn full circle upon themselves and prove in the end to be really homologous, parallel to the two transgressions which engendered the two brothers, namely, incest and parricide, each only a different side of the same coin.

This autonomous system monopolizes function and role in relation to the family, the city, and those outside the city by absorbing the hierarchy of social relations into itself since it cannot properly distinguish between same and different. And the system is, by its nature, imperialistic, as Eteokles' verbal actions in the play will demonstrate when he aims to appropriate all the discourse of the other, whether that of the women of the city or that of the enemy outside the gates. The double issue from a single origin offers a model both of exclusive commonality and of exaggerated antithesis, but it cannot provide a viable pattern for relations of union and separation between two terms which could engender a third one in time.

This synchronic system then cannot extend itself into temporal progression, and, in its entropy, it can end only in sterility, like all contradictions in terms (or hopeless ambiguities). Such a system poses, in fact, a contradiction in terms for the city, a radical menace to its continuation, as the oracle to Laios implies, and as the play, in conflating the roles of ruler and son of Oedipus in the character of Eteokles, acts out. For Eteokles can move only between the common collective of the city (in his unitary allegiance to the state) and the radical antithesis of combat with his brother who is placed against him at the seventh gate. Just as the city was first founded by the survivors of the Spartoi, after the rest of them in their common autochthonous origin, slew one another, the city can now be saved again only by the reciprocal destruction of the brothers, the last of the line of Laios, in order to expel from Thebes the subversive principle of "no difference."

But the various elements of the system of the text must demonstrate the necessity of this expulsion: its themes, events, structure, and, above all, its language. The conclusion is more accurately an end which Eteokles himself as the sole protagonist on stage will justify with exacting precision during the course of the drama created expressly and only for him, a text where all his defenses against the end are, at the same time, symptoms of the family legacy which insure the inevitability of that end. But before analyzing those defensive strategies which Eteokles deploys, I turn to examine in more detail the thematics of the play which devolve upon the special relationship between family and city in Thebes.

III. — *MYTHOS: POLIS/GENOS:* AUTOCHTONY/INCEST

The climax of the drama, after the seventh shield, when the two codes: that of the city and that of the family, diverge, does not constitute a sudden reversal, as many have suggested, a substitution of one set of terms for another, but is rather the culmination of a process which has governed the logic of the text from the beginning. The relations of oppositions and homologies which underlie the text are strained to their limits by the inherent but unnatural contradiction of *genos* and *polis* exemplified in the person of Eteokles, who is always both the ruler of Thebes and the son of Oedipus. Thus the text resonates throughout in both registers, each voice now dominant in one part and recessive now in another. At times these voices reply to each other antiphonally, at times they join in unison. This tension between the two codes is demonstrated on the structural level of plot in the complex relationship between the two major episodes, that with the *women* of Thebes *inside the city and that involving the shields of the men outside*. These two scenes are both opposites and doublets of each other, the first a rehearsal for and a dynamic mover of the second.

Limitations of space do not permit the analysis of the role of the women of the chorus who carry the largest burden of the text, with whom and through whom Eteokles activates the doom which awaits him.[3] Here I would point only to the operation of the sexual code, which, through its various inversions, establishes the proper norm for the city. That norm insists upon a dual allegiance — to the general collective of the group as exemplified in the unifying myth of autochthony (Origin from one, the mother earth) and to the individual family in its exogamous union of male and female (origin from two). The women in the parodos speak both for

---

[3] This material will be published as part of a forthcoming book on male and female polarities in Aeschylean drama. The first stasimon is of special importance.

the city and for the family, sanctioning the norm by the nature of their appeals to the gods of both genders who hold sway in Thebes [Benardete, 1967, 22-30].

Eteokles, however, invokes only the myth of the autochthonous origin of Thebes (10-20). On the one hand, he appeals to this myth, as a good general might, to serve the interests of patriotic ideology. For the resort to the myth of birth from the mother earth serves as a reminder of the absolute duty of her hoplite sons to defend their city [Loraux 1979]. On the other hand, autochthony is a dangerously seductive model for Eteokles: first, he is not truly a Spartos, but the son of Jocasta and Oedipus, hence not fully an insider in the city (679-80). His identification with the Spartoi then implies a potential misrecognition of himself and his own origins. Second, and conversely, since autochthony, like incest posits a single undifferentiating origin, Eteokles all too easily transposes the pattern from one domain to the other and runs the risk of contaminating the city's myth of solidarity with the negative import of his own story.

For the city, single autochthonous origin is only a point of origin, one which precedes the next stage when different families are founded in Thebes. Ares, as the chorus indicates in the parodos, is the deity who makes this transition possible. For he faces in both directions, first, as the founder of Thebes through his connection with the Sown Men (104-05); second, as the consort of Aphrodite (135-40) with whom he united to engender Harmonia who, in turn, was given to Cadmos. [Benardete 1967, 27-28]. For the chorus, on the other hand, the city has two primordial mothers: Gaia (earth) and Aphrodite *promator* (140).

Return to the notion of a single origin excludes the circulation of females as signs of exchange who guarantee continuing differentiation within the system. Eteokles, when he attempts to silence the unruly women at the altars (*siga*: 232, 250, 262, 263) and insists on the rigid antithesis between the sexes, is perhaps performing his proper role as general in the interests of group morale and demanding from the women only what the social conventions expected from them. But the addition of his misogynistic tirade against *all* women for *all* time (181-202) demonstrates precisely the status of Eteokles as child of an incestuous union, who knows only how to repress the "speaking signs"[4] that are essential to the city for its genealogical diversity, in favor of a homogeneous commonality ruled by a single principle.

---

[4] "The emergence of symbolic thought must have required that women, like words, should be things that were exchanged... But woman could never become just a sign and nothing more, since even in a man's world she is still a person, and since in so far as she is defined as a sign she must be recognized as a generator of signs. In the matrimonial dialogue of men, woman is never purely what is spoken about; for if women in general represent a certain category of signs, destined to a certain kind of communication, each woman preserves a particular value arising from her talent, before and after marriage, for taking her part in a duet. In contrast to words, which have wholly become signs, woman has remained at once a sign and a value" [LÉVI-STRAUSS, 1949: 1967, 496].

In the context of the play, the ill-omened words are dangerous to the city, dangerous to the evocation of the curse in its riddling ambiguity [Cameron 1970, 98-99,

The import of this repression is emphasized when the chorus in the first stasimon evokes the polar opposite of incest/autochthony, namely, the vision of the forcible rape and abduction of the city's women by the alien attackers (321-35, 363-68). This is exogamy in its most negative form as unlawful appropriation of women which accompanies and is homologous with the pillaging of the goods of the city and its homes (352-62). When the violence of strife has entered the city, both extremes, that of excessive distance and that of excessive closeness, are correlated in the hidden mantic message of the choral ode (cf. e.g., 291-92, 352-55). For war and incest both interrupt the normal exchange of women, one in excessive exogamy, one in excessive endogamy.

ENDOGAMY	ENDOGAMY/EXOGAMY	EXOGAMY
within city	within city/without city	without city
autochthony/incest	orderly exchange	rape/abduction
single origin: same	same/other	other
unlawful appropriation	lawful marriage	unlawful appropriation

Eteokles' flight from woman, a refusal both of genealogy and generation, substitutes asexual autochthony for hypersexual incest, and replaces the biological mother with the symbolic mother of the collective city.[5] But his antithesis of either/or cannot stand. Polarity is also analogy, for in the language of the Greek city, the woman imitates the earth and the earth imitates the woman (e.g., Plato, *Men.* 238a). Each terms lends to the other the appropriate metaphorical quality by which literal and symbolic stabilize one another in an integrative system of values, an attack upon one equivalent to an attack upon the other. Eteokles' dissociation of the two is paradoxically only the sign of their inherent relationship, for incest is the hidden paradigm of autochthony. The denial of this analogical connection between mother and earth can only encourage a false claim to autonomy and will therefore establish a system in which reciprocal relations must take the form of antithetical violence, whether with the women inside or the warriors outside.

116], and dangerous to Eteokles' name, dependent as it is for its positive meaning on a Theban victory. (see *infra*). That Eteokles reveals his more absolute misogyny under the pressure of their inauspicious language, the source of his deepest dread, is consistent with principles of Aeschylean dramaturgy.

[5] Benardete, 1967, 29, points out that Eteokles uses the word *meter* four times, twice for the mother earth, 16, 416, once in a significant metaphorical context, 225, and only in his reply to his brother does he refer to the biological mother, 664. Benardete remarks further that, in contrast to the chorus' emphasis on the sexual categories of male and female in their prayer to the gods in the parodos, Eteokles in the shield scene refers only to the virgin goddesses, Artemis, Athena, Dike (450, 501, 662). In the case of the iconic emblem of Dike (Justice) on Polyneikes' shield, the scout calls her a *gyne*, woman, but Eteokles, in his reply, subtly changes the term to *parthenos*, virgin (645 vs 662). Oddly enough, Benardete misses the crucial opposition to Ge, earth, as mother in the mythology of the city, namely, the choral allusion to Aphrodite as the *promator* (ancestral mother of the *genos*, 145) who with Ares bore Harmonia to be wife to Cadmos.

Similarly, Eteokles uses the word *genos* for women as a group (188, 256) or for gods (236) or for the company on board a ship (604), and only afterwards for the race of Oedipus (654) and the race of Laios (691).

That analogy is already at work, for the curse of Oedipus was precipitated by the sons' neglect of *trophe* (735-37), the nurture they owed in return for their *trophe* [Cameron 1964, 1-8; 1971, 85-95, 103-04], the same *trophe* owed in the language of autochthony to the mother earth as her *Dike* (16, 477, 548). The terms of the father's curse, when fulfilled, will perfect the paradigm, for the sons, as citizens of Thebes, will repeat the violation of *trophe*, this time against the mother earth, by Polyneikes' attack against it (580-85, 668) and by Eteokles' willingness to pollute the earth with fratricidal blood (680, 734-41).

Eteokles' single adherence to *polis* in his appeal to the myth of the city's single origin can and does confirm a positive political ideology for the group. But when construed also as a defense against *genos*, Eteokles appeal also reconnects *genos* to *polis* by invoking now the negative paradigmatic force implied by the terms of the origin myth. For when the brothers reenact the crimes of the father against one another for possession now of their father's goods and of his city, they are, at the same time, reenacting the regressive aspect of the city's founding myth, which first led to destruction before it culminated in solidarity. The fratricide of the sons of Oedipus follows the model of the Sown Mean, who, springing up in autochthonous birth form the dragon's teeth in the soil of Thebes, slew one another in mutual combat, with the exception of five who survived to establish families in Thebes and to profit from the prestige of their indigenous origins [Petre, 1971; Cameron, 1971, 85-95]. The city is saved, not for the first time, but for the second, when Laios proves to have died without issue. And the second time proves a repetition of the first time, when Eteokles is enrolled at last among the Spartoi only after his death [Dawson, 1970, 21]. Autochthony, in its ambiguities in the political and mythic codes, is therefore the sign that Eteokles will function as the bridge between a defective model of city and a defective model of family, a negative mediator between the two. His is a monocular gaze whose partial vision will betray him in the reading of the signs on the warriors' shields.

IV. — HERO: STRUCTURE, SIGN, AND IDENTITY

If we can speak of the power of the family over its offspring as a "genealogical imperative," in the case of the family of Laios we can speak of a negative "genealogical imperative" [Tobin 1978, 3-28], which now decrees not life but death to its progeny and which regulates the text from its beginning to its end. From this perspective, Eteokles' defensive strategy, one might say, is dedicated both to preserving the integrity of the walls that protect the besieged city of Thebes and to preserving his unique singular identity. The encroachment of "no difference" heralds the fall into plurality with his brother (829-30) and hence back into genealogy as the son of Oedipus.

On the one hand, Eteokles, who characterizes himself as s "one" (*heis*), at the opening of the play, only to juxtapose the term with *polus* ("many", 6), prophesies more truly than he knows that he alone, as the son of Oedipus, will be separated out from the many (679-80, 720-21), the citizens of Cadmos' city whom he addresses (1). On the other hand, once the distinction between the two brothers fails, so does the line between singular and plural. Thus Eteokles will quite literally be absorbed into the pluralizing name of *Poly*-neikes (829-30).[6] In other words, he will prove to be singular with regard to his fellow citizens and plural with regard to his brother when the two identities merge.

The potential loss of Eteokles' name carries a double jeopardy. In general terms, a name is the guarantee of identity and of existence, of difference from others in the world at large and at home. Surrendering one's name is a dangerous act, even in the interests of survival, as Odysseus well knows when he reasserts his name at his peril after he names/unnames himself as Outis, "No One", in the cave of the Cyclops [Dimock 1956; Austin 1973]. The name also attests to the legitimacy of the father's prerogative to name his progeny and to inscribe the bearer of that name together with his patronymic in the continuing line of the family.

In specific terms, maintaining a stable relation between signifier and signified in the name, Eteokles (truly famed, full of *kleos*), offers another hope in the face of the shadow of negation that broods over the family. For the alternative to generation as the guarantee of immortality through the continuance of *genos* is the winning of individual *kleos*, of singular heroic renown in battle so as to survive through the memory of tradition on the lips of men. In the economy of praise and blame which structured archaic Greek society, Eteokles (*kleos*-fame × praise) and Polyneikes (*neikos* × strife × blame) are lexical signs of the opposition itself. This dichotomy opposes positive (presence of praise) to negative (absence of praise), memory to oblivion, clarity to obscurity, the brightness of fame (to be named) to the darkness of ill repute (anonymity); in short, opposes immortality to extinction [Detienne 1973, 18-252]. But the fulfillment of the curse through fratricidal combat must inevitably defeat Eteokles' claim to moral and personal identity which his name represents and which he had hoped his virtuous allegiance to the city would protect. Instead, the deflection of heroism to fratricidal combat fulfills the hidden, sinister signifier of his name, i.e., "truly bewept," or "true cause of weeping" (*klaio* × weep, lament). Thus, as Bacon persuasively argues, Eteokles' own name, like that of his father, functions as a riddle and prophecy of his fate, namely a death without *kleos* that will be truly bewept.[7] The

---

[6] For Sophocles' Oedipus, fate also hangs on the distinction between the singular and plural — one murderer of Laios or many, as the witness had reported, *OT* 842-47.

[7] These two stages may be simultaneous, depending on the reading of the text at 829-30. As the text stands, the chorus laments: truly (*orthos*) and literally, i.e., etymologically (*kat'eponumian*) they perished *Polyneikeis* (plural). In this reading Eteokles can also mean "truly called (*klezomenos*) [Verrall 1887, 98; Sheppard 1913, 78] and his name, therefore, descends from the autonomy of noun to the status of an adverbial modifier. If a lacuna is proposed, as many have suggested, to be filled with a parallel plural of

last stage of the drama will efface his name when both brothers are jointly characterized as Polyneikeis (829-30), the plural form of the singular, Polyneikes. The name, *Poly*neikes, already contains within itself the notion of plurality, and the grammatical plural redoubles, as it were, the annulment of Eteokles' name and identity.

Thus in broadest terms, Eteokles' best defense against the curse of his father and on behalf of his own name is attention to language and control of the discourse. The best defense against the collapse into "no difference" is attention to the maintenance of the binary opposition. And, in thematic terms, as we have seen, the best defense against *genos* is exclusive adherence to *polis*.

No other play is as generous and as repetitive in establishing the competing codes and values at work in the system according to the fundamental dichotomies which regulate Greek thought: male/female, enemy/friend, Greek/barbarian, inside/outside, self/other, man/god; and there is none that specifically elevates the task of making and unmaking binary oppositions to the level of a crucial and explicit action of the drama.

Binary opposition informs both the structure and content of the two major episodes in the play, the first when Eteokles counters the unruly Theban women of the chorus, the second, the centerpiece of the drama, the shield scene. There, through seven paired speeches between himself and the scout, Eteokles seven times pairs enemy with defender until the barrier of the antithesis that guarantees the opposition begins to break down when brother faces brother at the seventh gate. Polarized difference then yields to doubling homology, as the doubly progeny of a doubly seeded womb meet in a duel and collapse their single selves into the grammatical category of the dual.[8] The enemy brothers thus act out on the synchronic level of fraternity (i.e., of the same generation) their status as offspring of the diachronic collapse of generational distinction that the two original acts of the father represented, i.e., parricide and incest. The erotic vocabulary of passion (*eros*) and desire (*himeros*) used to characterize Eteokles' eagerness to confront his brother in mortal combat (687-88,

---

Eteokles' name (=*Eteokleis*), the meaning "truly bewept," which Bacon (1973, 14-15) suggests, is in my opinion indisputable. Her brilliant observation (to the elaborated further in work not yet published) provides the key to Eteokles' urgency in regard to the ill-omened prayers of the chorus, the particular nature of his response to the revelation of his brother's identity at the seventh gate, and the specific terms of the choral lament. The pluralizing of Eteokles' name would parallel the pluralizing of Polyneikes' name, each reciprocally depriving the other of unique identity.

[8] Dual forms: 811, 816, 863, 922, 932 [and 681]. Words of doubling: *diplai, diduma, dimoira, disso*: 782, 849, 972, 816. Play on words with *di-* prefixes, the phonic oxymoron of *dai-, di-*, and *dia-*, involving the twin notions of dividing and doubling, prefigured 735, and dispersed throughout 811-960. Antiphonal divided chorus, 961-1005; See especially 971, 984, 985. *Koinos* (common): 812; *ison* (equal) 908, 945. Reciprocal compounds in *autos*: 681, 734, 735, 917 (twice). *Homaimon*, 940; *homosporoi* (of the same seed): 804, 820, 932, 933; *homosplanchnon*, 889; *homonuma* (of the same name) 984.

692-94), suggests the merger of Eros and Thanatos — the conflation of
the two transgressions that engendered the two brothers.

The shield scene, located strategically at the midpoint of the drama,
acts as a model system that condenses, climaxes, and hypostasizes the
problems of structure and language that inform the play from the beginning
when war establishes the legitimacy of the polar opposition, and Eteokles,
as the ruler of Thebes, determines to speak the proper words (*legein ta
kairia,* 1). Throughout, the privileged field of combat is the semantic field.
The speech act is truly performative.

Semiotics, the study of the system of signs and how they communicate, can provide a hermeneutical tool for analysis of the synergetic
system of relations that comprises Aeschylus' distinctive world view. In
Aeschylean drama nothing can come into existence before its name has
been uttered, concept is fully embedded in image, and figure is inseparable
from idea. Conflict in the *Seven* is literally war, the antithesis is a pair-
ing of opponents with antithetical names. Homology is the identity of kin
(*homoios/homaimon*), the oxymoron is the enemy brother. *Moira* as fate
is literally *moira* as portion, since the destiny of the brothers is the ap-
portioning of the father's patrimony, and the equal *moira* of death will
prove to be the equal *moira* of land for their interment (733, 947). Above
all, the shield devices, *semata,* are signs, iconic emblems, that speak and
move within a system that is not only tactical (military) but syntactical
(linguistic). Language is therefore action and action is language through
which the "genealogical imperative" of the accursed family at last asserts
itself. Eteokles will create a text which claims linguistic competence in
the "langue," i.e., the public language of civic values, which will insure
the victory of Thebes over Argos, but through which his own "parole"
will "speak itself," the language upon which his personal identity rests,
and which once discovered in its signification, will constitute the language
of curse and oracle.

Here then in the shield scene is a coded demonstration of the science
of signs and how they operate within the social system in regard both
to the special status of tragic language in its necessary and intrinsic
ambiguity and to the more general question of problems of language as a
means of communication and as a guarantee of identity and truth. Literature has been defined as a "language, but a language around which we
have drawn a frame" by which we "indicate a decision to regard with
a particular self-consciousness the resources language has always possessed" [Fish 1974:52]. From this formalist point of view, the language of
the shield scene is doubly marked: first, by the artful frame of formal
design which characterizes the scene within the larger structure of the
literary text of the play, and second, by reason of its explicit oracular
activity.

Oracles, by their nature and the mode of their operation, inevitably
direct attention to the problematics of language and reality and point to
the potential slippage in the sign between signifier and signified. Once

personal identity becomes equivalent to the proper name and once oracle and riddle, as forms of speech, translate the problems of personal identity into those of the linguistic sign, the decipherment of language claims first priority as the hermeneutic way into those issues which, whenever they concern Oedipus (or his progeny), always reside at the core of human existence. In a semiotic perspective, the case of Eteokles to an even greater extent than that of Oedipus, exemplifies the "power of the signifier to be both instrument of power and through the deception inherent in it, a cause of misfortune" and destruction [Green: 1969; 1979, 221]. What then are the rules of the semiotic game? How and why do they function as they do?

V. — RIDDLE AND ORACLE: READING THE SIGNS BY THE RULES OF THE GAME

In tragedy, the economy of thought, word, and deed dictates the correlation of character with destiny/plot by the terms of which one *is* what one *does*, and the doing reveals *what* and *who* one is. If Agamemnon's trespass upon the crimson carpets which Clytemnestra has prepared for him upon his homecoming reenacts on stage his earlier transgressions and paves his own way to the destiny which awaits him in the house, what are we to say of Eteokles' actions on the stage? Eteokles, true to his family tradition, reverses omens, poses and solves riddles, and utters curses and predictions in a repetitive series. His task is hermeneutical, based on a semiotic skill which constructs and justifies a system of relations. He acts by the reading and re-reading of signs in order to make opposites and doubles in paired antitheses. He decompose and recomposes the elements of the coded messages which he selects, transposes, and rearranges, according to the conventions of the kledonomantic system of divination, in order to turn them against their senders. Accordingly, he must also exercise a rhetorician's talents for figures of speech (e.g., metaphor, metonymy, simile, paronomasia, oxymoron, litotes, negation, irony, euphemism). Above all, he must demonstrate his capacity over and over again for distinguishing between same and different in a classificatory system which assigns the appropriate values on each side.

Eteokles meets the enemy one by one through the scout's report which names and describes each warrior together with his shield in the sequential order of their placement at the gates. Eteokles, for his part, answers, reversing and returning to them the ill omens of their shields and verbal threats, naming and justifying a defender to match the opponent, his own place at the seventh gate already determined in the preceding scene (282). On the Argive side, the attackers have been selected by lot for their respective posts; the Thebans, on the other hand, by Eteokles' choice.[9] All the moves are mapped in the symbolic system of

---

[9] The mechanics of Eteokles' choice are still disputed, whether he selects all the champions before his return, or some then and some during the shield scene itself. I agree with Wolff's arguments [1958] for the unitary consistency of choices completed before the

language; the object is to overcome and capture the enemy's verbal and iconic signs in advance of their persons when the battle is joined. The shield system itself functions as a model language system, the axis of selection corresponding to the choice of antithetical pairs of warriors and the axis of combination to the sequential order on the separate sides. Each paradigmatic set of attacker and defender is part of a syntagmatic series of Thebans and Argives and each set is framed as a synchronic unit within the diachronic narrative of the scout's report.

The defense Eteokles deploys against the enemy and their shields is that of kledonomancy, a system of divination which operates on the conviction that language possesses an enigmatic oracular capacity to bear an unexpected meaning not intended or even understood by the speaker. Words, once uttered, can be rearranged, reinterpreted, and accepted by another in their new meaning so as to function as an irrevocable omen, which not only predicts future events, but actually has the power to effect what it predicts. That person who has taken control of the other's language can be said even to "force his own meaning upon the omen," twisting it for his own advantage [Halliday 1913, 47; Peradotto 1969, 2-10; Cameron 1970]. For everyone can speak more truly than he knows and his own words may prophesy against him without his knowledge (406), the only protection of one's utterance being the euphemism of silence. The rules apply to all utterances, even without another to accept them, and the more unconscious they are, the more effective they are felt to be. Thus even the kledonomantic reply is available for the status of *kledon*. If Eteokles receives the messages of the shields and, in an apotropaic gesture, sends them back, he is also a potential receiver of his own message. The master troper cannot prevent the palintropic drift of his own utterance from working as a *kledon* against him and his name.

The operation of a kledonomantic system attests to the basic instability and ambiguity of language, where one discourse can lie concealed behind another. It attests to the arbitrary character of signs in the signifying system whereby meaning can shift, gaps can open up between signifier and signified, and new sequences of signs can be created and recreated. Yet once the sign is seized as a *kledon,* it loses its indeterminacy and gains instead a dynamic power to determine the future. Like Proteus, when captured, the sign can and does yield up irreversible and unequivocal truths, the hidden relations of signifiers and signifieds, of signs and referents. [10]

What distinguishes the shield scene from other literary examples of kledonomantic play is first, the overt purposivenes of its word play set within a highly regulated structure; second, the sheer extension and

---

scene takes place. The problems of the verb tenses are less daunting than an unexplained failure on Eteokles' part to complete the task he had set out to do (282-84). Cf. also Burnett [1973, 347], Manton's argument [1961, 77-84], and Maltomini [1976, 65-80].

[10] I am especially indebted here to Rebecca Bushnell for her share in an arduous dialogue on the nature of the *kledon*.

complexity of that structure in its various interrelations; thirdly, the dynamic incremental effect of the series as it builds to a climax; and, finally, the double and divergent functioning of the *kledon* itself, by which the capturing of the *kledon* each time opens out into a new one. This sharp cleavage in Eteokles' replies marks him, in the most thoroughgoing irony, as the best interpreter with regard to the defense of the city and the worst in regard to himself, an exact replication of the double bind of his own nature.

A semiotic analysis can uncover the fearful precision of this intricate text as it progresses from shield to shield. All the issues raised in the introduction — the narrative pattern of trilogy and play as repetitive form, *genos* and *polis* and the problematics of their correlation and conflict as they meet in the figure of Eteokles, structures of antithesis and the notion of the self and the double, and finally, the formal composition of the shield scene as a dynamic semiotic system which works through the coded ambiguities of the oracular utterance — all these issues will come into play during the actual analysis.

No summary, however extensive, could hope to lay out in advance the operation of this system and the working of its parts through which Eteokles the semiotician will be judged. But to anticipate a conclusion, I might say that Eteokles will prove to be better at a structuring of parts into antithetical categories than at perceiving a complex system of inter-relations, better at classification (the axis of selection) than at sequence (the axis of combination), more concerned with the synchronic moment (present time) than with the diachronic dimension. Against Eteokles' resistance to time and hence to inscription in the family's *history,* the narrative of the *story* presses *forward* to bring *back* the brother at the last and with him the memory that links one to the other so as to make an end.[11]

Froma I. ZEITLIN
Princeton University.

REFERENCES

AUSTIN, N., 1973, "Name Magic in the *Odyssey,*" *Cal. St. in Class. Ant.,* 3, 1-19.

BACON, H., 1973, Introduction to *Aeschylus, Seven Against Thebes,* tr. Anthony HECHT and Helen BACON, New York.

BENARDETE, S., 1967, 1968, "Two Notes on Aeschylus' *Septem,*" *Wiener Studien,* 80, 22-30; 81, 5-17.

---

[11] Parts of this study were prepared under the auspices of an NEH Fellowship in 1975-76. I wish to thank Helene Foley, Georgia Nugent, and James Zetzel for helpful criticism. Inexpressible gratitude to Marylin B. Arthur, Ann L. T. Bergren, Rebecca Bushnell, Richard Goodkin, Alexander Nehemas, and Patricia Tobin, who each gave so generously and so fully of themselves and to whom I owe so much.

BURNETT, A., 1973, "Curse and Dream in Aeschylus' *Septem*," *Greek, Roman, and Byzantine Studies*, 14, 343-368.

CALDWELL, R. S., 1973, "The Misogyny of Eteocles," *Arethusa*, 6, 197-231.

CAMERON, H. D., 1964, "The Debt to Earth in the *Seven Against Thebes*," *Transactions of the American Philological Association*, 95, 1-8.

——, 1970, "The Power of Words in the *Seven Against Thebes*," *Transactions of the American Philological Association*, 101, 95-118.

——, 1971: *Studies on the Seven Against Thebes of Aeschylus*, The Hague.

CULLER, J., 1975, *Structuralist Poetics*, London.

DAWSON, C., 1970, *Aeschylus, The Seven Against Thebes*, tr. and comm., Englewood Cliffs, N. J.

DELCOURT, M., 1938, *Sterilités mystérieuses et naissances maléfiques dans l'antiquité classique*, Paris.

DETIENNE, M., 1973, *Les maîtres de vérité dans la Grèce archaïque*, Paris.

DIMOCK, G., 1956, "The Name of Odysseus," *Hudson Review*, 9, 52-70.

FINEMAN, J., 1977, "Fratricide and Cuckoldry: Shakespeare's Doubles," *Psychoanalytic Review*, 64, 409-453.

FISH, S., 1974, "How Ordinary is Ordinary Language?", *New Literary History*, 5, 41-54.

FROIDEFOND, J., 1977, "La double fraternité d'Etéocle et de Polynice (*Les Sept Contre Thèbes*, v. 576-579)," *Revue des Études grecques*, 90, 211-222.

GERNET, L., 1945, *Droit et société dans la Grèce ancienne*, Paris.

GIRARD, R., 1977, *Violence and the Sacred*. tr. P. Gregory. Baltimore.

GREEN, A., 1969, 1979, *The Tragic Effect: The Oedipus Complex in Tragedy*, tr. A. SHERIDAN, Cambridge.

HALLIDAY, W. R., 1913, *Greek Divination*, London.

LALLOT, J., 1974, "*Xumbola kranai*: Réflexions sur la fonction du *sumbolon* dans l'Agamemnon d'Eschyle," *Cahiers internationaux de Symbolisme* 26, 39-48.

LÉVI-STRAUSS, C., 1949, 1969, *The Elementary Structures of Kinship*, Boston.

—— 1963, *Structural Anthropology*, New York.

LORAUX, N., 1979, "L'autochthonie: une topique athenienne," *Annales ESC*, 3-26.

MALTOMINI, F., 1976, "La scelta dei difensori delle sette porte nei *Sette a Tebe* di Eschilo," *Quaderni Urbinati di Cultura Classica*, 21, 65-80.

MANTON, G. K., 1961, "The Second Stasimon of the *Seven Against Thebes*," *Bulletin of the Institute of Classical Studies*, London, 8, 77-84.

PERADOTTO, J. J., 1969, "Cledonomancy in the *Oresteia*," *American Journal of Philology*, 90, 1-21.

PETRE, Z., 1971, Thèmes dominants et attitudes politiques dans les *Sept contre Thebes* d'Eschyle," *Studii Clasice*, 13, 15-28.

SHEPPARD, J. T., 1913, "The Plot of the *Septem Contra Thebas*," *Classical Quarterly* 2, 73-82.

THALMANN, W. G., 1978, *Dramatic Art in Aeschylus' Seven Against Thebes*, New Haven.

TOBIN, P. D., 1978, *Time and the Novel: The Genealogical Imperative*, Princeton.

VERRALL, A. W., 1887, *The Seven Against Thebes*, London.

WOLFF, E., 1958, "Die Entscheidung des Eteokles in den *Sieben gegen Theben*," *Harvard Studies in Classical Philology*, 63, 89-95.

ZEITLIN, F. I., 1978, "The Dynamics of Misogyny: Myth and Mythmaking in the *Oresteia*," *Arethusa*, 11, 149-84.

Structures temporelles dans
le De Rerum Natura*

1. *Du paradigme au plan syntagmatique*. On sait que le poème de Lucrèce se compose d'une partie théorique, absolument prédominante, et d'une partie qui sert d'exemple, riche en images, reliée à la première de façon directe et fonctionnelle[1]. Ces sections explicatives sont ordinairement constituées de narrations-descriptions dont il est souvent possible de reconnaître la structure. Mais il y a une partie du poème où la narration prévaut entièrement, si bien que la partie théorique qui en résulte, est même placée en rapport de subordination fonctionnelle. Il s'agit de la célèbre 'histoire du genre humain' qui se trouve au livre V (nous en plaçons le début au v. 772 et la fin au v. 1457, lorsque le chant se termine). Dans cette longue section, Lucrèce se fait narrateur et, par un procédé opposé à celui qu'il emploie dans les autres livres (où l'exposition didactique est entrecoupée d'exemples), il interrompt ici la narration pour se livrer à des considérations théoriques. Nous aimerions parvenir à déterminer le schéma constitutif (ou le *pattern*, qui est d'ailleurs un « modèle » culturel) de cette narration, non seulement en l'insérant dans le contexte général du livre, mais surtout en procédant à un examen des « structures » temporelles qui sont immanentes à la narration même.

En tant que « narration », l'« histoire du genre humain » aura évidemment une temporalité à elle, une progression, ou une évolution dans le temps. L'étude attentive de cette dimension temporelle, particulièrement à travers les interruptions relatives à une succession donnée dans le temps, nous permettra de saisir le caractère spécifique — au plus large sens socio-culturel non moins que littéraire — de la narration de Lucrèce. Il est certain qu'on peut identifier dans les traits essentiels une ligne d'évolution, dans la narration de Lucrèce, qui va de la description de la vie des hommes primitifs (vv. 925 s.: *At genus humanum multo fuit illud in arvis/ durius...*) jusqu'aux conquêtes les plus marquantes de la civilisation et du progrès (qu'on songe aux célèbres deux derniers vers du livre: *Namque alid ex alio clarescere corde videbant/artibus ad summum donec venere cacumen*) qui seront après couronnées par les découvertes spirituelles du maître, Epicure (cf. le proème du livre VI, dialectiquement mis en corré-

---

* Cet article est paru d'abord dans *Bulletino di Studi Latini*, 9 (1979), pp. 5-24. Il est traduit par l'auteur. La traduction est revue par M. Pierre Brind'Amour.
  [1] La tension dialectique entre les deux parties a été bien saisie et illustrée par E. PASOLI, « Ideologia nella poesia: lo stile di Lucrezio », *Lingua e stile*, 5 (1970), pp. 367 ss.

lation avec *le final* du Ve)[2]. Mais dans cette ligne temporelle essentiellement en évolution, nous remarquons différentes anachronies[3] relatives à
un hypothétique degré zéro de la narration. En d'autres termes, il existe
une *erzählte Zeit*, qui est le temps de l'histoire racontée, et une *Erzähl-
zeit*, le temps de la narration. Le degré zéro est la coïncidence éventuelle
entre le temps de l'histoire et le temps du récit. Il est évident, à ce point,
que des discordances significatives entre les deux types de temps auront
une importance particulière pour la compréhension d'un texte. Dans notre
cas, nous le verrons, Lucrèce, en racontant l'histoire primitive de l'humanité, interrompt souvent la gradation temporelle par des intrusions relatives au présent: c'est là un exemple où ce que nous appelons le « degré
zéro» ne se réalise pas, car il est bien clair que le temps de la narration
(à cause de ces intrusions) *ne* coïncide pas avec celui de l'histoire racontée (mais ce sera justement l'opposition entre le « passé» de l'histoire et
le « présent» de l'actualité qui nous fera découvrir le « modèle» qui est
au fond de tout). La question préalable est de déterminer les unités narratives, les segments du discours le long d'un axe syntagmatique (nous
emploierons souvent cette expression: elle indique simplement une ligne
dans laquelle les événements, contrairement à ce qui arrive dans le moment
du paradigme, sont exposés dans leur enchaînement). Il est facile de comprendre que le poète n'indique pas explicitement le temps à l'intérieur de
sa narration. C'est nous qui devrons, après la segmentation, déduire une
ligne chronologique intérieure.

A   vv.772-82: Reprise de la matière précédente et propos de traiter de l'his-
     toire de la terre (v. 780 *nunc redeo ad mundi novitatem*). C'est un seg-
     ment clairement didactique qui annonce la narration proprement dite.
B   vv.783-825: Début de la narration. La terre engendra les plantes, les ani-
     maux et enfin les hommes: c'est la mère de tout (v. 795 s. *linquitur ut
     merito maternum nomen adepta/terra sit, e terra quoniam sunt cuncta
     creata*). Les temps prédominants sont l'imparfait et le parfait, comme
     dans toute la narration. Malgré des oscillations, d'ailleurs peu importantes,
     relatives à la qualité de l'action verbale, le temps est donc essentiellement
     passé et l'action trouve ici on premier moment évolutif.
C   vv. 826-27: Deux vers qui annoncent toute une unité successive: comme
     une femme âgée et fatiguée, la terre, à un certain moment, a cessé d'en-
     fanter.

---

[2]   P. GIUFFRIDA («Il finale [vv. 1440-1457] del V libro di Lucrezio», *Epicurea in
memoriam Hectoris Bignone*, Genova, 1959, pp. 129 ss.) met le poème du VIe livre en continuité idéale avec le final du Ve livre dans le sens que toutes les conquêtes de l'humanité
exposées au cours du Ve livre aboutissent à Athènes, mais il considère à tort les éloges
d'Athènes comme sarcastiques. Pour F. GIANCOTTI (*L'ottimismo relativo nel «De rerum natura» di Lucrezio*, Torino, 1960) le poème est optimiste du moment qu'il semble fondé sur
une « visione unamistica dell'uomo protagonista del proprio destino» (p. 183); à son encontre Giuffrida considère sarcastiques les éloges d'Athènes à cause du pessimisme qu'il relève
dans le final du livre V et de l'ironie qu'il croit déceler dans l'expression de 5,1457 ...*ad
summum domec venere cacumen*.
[3]   Pour la technique de l'analyse et de la terminologie cf. G. MUELLER, «*Erzähl-
zeit und erzählte Zeit*», *Festschrift Kluckhorn*, 1948; T. TODOROV, «Les catégories du récit littéraire», *Communications*, 8 (1966); C. SEGRE, *Le strutture e il tempo*, Torino, 1974;
surtout G. GENETTE, *Figure*, III, tr. it., Torino, 1976. Les discordances entre l'ordre du
récit et celui de l'histoire racontée sont des anachronies.

D   vv. 828-36: Pause dans la narration au cours de laquelle est exposé le
    principe que toute chose s'affaiblit et décline. Comme on peut remarquer,
    les parties didactiques représentent autant de corollaires à la narration.

E   vv.837-81: La narration recommence; c'est le deuxième segment narratif,
    interrompu seulement par une courte parenthèse didactique (vv.849-54):
    la terre, fatiguée, produisit des monstres avant la constitution des races
    actuelles, monstres qui détruisirent les uns les autres. Toutefois ni les
    Centaures, ni d'autres êtres mythiques n'existèrent.

F   vv.882-924: Large pause didactique où l'impossibilité de l'existence d'êtres
    mythiques monstrueux est démontrée.

G   vv.925-1010: L'emploi du passé recommence, de préférence l'imparfait, et
    la véritable histoire du genre humain prend son essor. Cette section dé-
    crit la vie absolument sauvage des premiers hommes, souvent comparée
    par le poète avec son âge propre: il s'agit de comparaisons qui présentent
    un grand relief et sur lesquelles nous reviendrons (vv.940-42; 988-89; 999-
    1010).

H   vv. 1011-27: Segment narratif de synthèse, clairement proleptique: on y
    trouve en effet l'annonce d'événements qui seront développés diachronique-
    ment par la suite et qui représentent les différentes étapes de l'histoire du
    genre humain.

I   vv.1028-90: Après deux seuls vers (1028 s.), qui s'insèrent à nouveau dans
    la narration et qui mentionnent l'origine du langage (*At varios linguae
    sonitus natura subegit/mittere, et utilitas expressit nomina rerum*) Lucrèce
    ouvre une section à la fois didactique et polémique sur le problème du
    langage[4].

L   vv.1091-1135: La narration recommence: Lucrèce expose comment naquit
    l'emploi du feu et le besoin d'édifier des villes. Il s'en suivit la découver-
    te de l'or et la course au pouvoir de la part des hommes. C'est un seg-
    ment riche en pauses didactiques (que nous ne croyons pas devoir isoler
    comme de véritables segments, du moment qu'elles sont complètement rat-
    tachées à la partie narrative. Nous citons seulement le passage significatif
    du parfait au présent (cf.vv.1124-25): un autre déphasage temporel, avec
    une application au présent, sur lequel nous reviendrons.

M   vv.1136-60: Origine de l'État de droit (après l'élimination des rois et le
    début de l'anarchie, on éprouva le besoin de magistrats et de lois). Le
    segment, essentiellement narratif, se termine (vv.1151-60) sur une pause
    didactique qui précise la signification du passage. Celui qui viole les lois
    et qui se met en dehors de la légalité ne peut pas vivre une existence
    tranquille.

N   vv.1161-97: Origine de la religion, avec une allusion finale à la situation
    présente.

_____

    [4]   Pour le langage, Lucrèce comme Épicure postule une origine naturelle et exclut
qu'un maître ait imposé le nom aux choses: outre Lucrèce cf. aussi Dem. Lac. *Pap. Herc.*
1012 col. XLV, 9-12 et Diog. de En. fr. X, col. II-IV, fr. XIW.; N. CASINI, « Diogene di
Enoanda e Lucrezio », *Riv. di storia della filosofia*, 4 (1949), pp. 287 ss., ainsi que *Pap.
Herc.* 1479/1417 (*peri physeos* d'Epicure). À ce sujet cfr. C. GIUSSANI, *Studi lucreziani*,
Torino, 1896, pp. 267 ss. (sur la position d'Épicure cf. aussi G. ARRIGHETTI, dans EPICURO,
Opere, Torino, 1960, p. 476, mais, déjà auparavant, cf. R. PHILIPPSON, « Platons Kratylos
und Demokrit », *Philol. Wochenschrift*, 1929, p. 923); Ph. DE LACY, « The Epicurean Analysis of Language », *Am. Journ. Philol.*, 60 (1939), pp. 85 ss. (en général J. H. DAHLMANN,
De philosophorum Graecorum sententiis ad loquellae origines pertinentibus capita duo, Leipzig, 1928); E. CHLUMSKA-J. KABRT, « Quid Lucretius de origine orationis eiusque incrementis
senserit », *Latinitas*, 16 (1968), pp. 189 ss.; P. H. SCHRIJVERS, « La pensée de Lucrèce sur
l'origine du langage (De rerum natura V 1019-1090) », *Mnemosyne*, 27, 1974, pp. 337 ss.
(l'auteur met en évidence les aspects purement physiologiques de l'acquisition du langagage,
tandis que la *ratio* ne semble avoir aucune fonction dans la conception de Lucrèce); D.
SKILJAN, « Lucrèce sur le langage », *Latina et Graeca*, 6 (1975), pp. 5 ss. (slov. avec ré-
sumé français; Lucrèce aurait vu la distinction moderne entre *langue* et *parole*).

O   vv.1198-1240: Polémique didactique sur l'origine de la religion[5].
P   vv.1241-1457: Nous regroupons dans une seule grande unité narrative pres-
    que deux cents vers: ils sont proprement narratifs et montrent la montée
    progressive de l'humanité, à travers des étapes différentes, vers des for-
    mes de plus en plus évoluées de civilisation. Les hommes découvrirent et
    travaillèrent les métaux pour faire des armes (vv.1241-96); de là on imagi-
    na des techniques d'art militaire toujours plus atroces (vv.1297-349). Les
    hommes apprirent à s'habiller et à cultiver la terre (vv.1350-78); enfin la
    musique, les arts, l'écriture, la poésie, virent le jour, jusqu'à ce qu'on
    atteigne le dernier faîte du progrès à Athènes, symbole de la civilisation
    la plus adroite, fameuse pardessus tout pour avoir vu s'épanouir le mes-
    sage de libération d'Épicure (début du livre VI). Le segment n'est pas inter-
    rompu de pauses didactiques (que nous aurions placé comme des segments
    à part, dans le cas contraire). Toutefois il ne manque pas de quelques dé-
    phasages temporels significatifs: des relations passé/présent (vv.1275-80;
    1423-35) comme nous en avons déjà vu paraître précédemment.

Nous nous sommes efforcés de rendre notre segmentation objective
dans toute la mesure du possible, la plus neutre (comme le lecteur a compris, nous appelons segmentation le dégagement des différentes unités
narratives — ou segments —; nous emploierons sous peu le terme « sous-
segmentation», qui, évidemment, indiquera un dégagement ultérieur, toujours sur la base des unités fondamentales). Nous ne pouvions pas nous
passer de cette première partie explicative mais, essentiellement, nous
nous en sommes tenus au dégagement de la syntaxe conceptuelle et logique proposée par le poète lui-même. En d'auters termes, nous avons suivi
les divisions du texte. Après cet examen nécessaire nous devons toutefois
revenir à la question préliminaire: quelles sont les structures temporelles
de la narration? De la segmentation proposée nous pouvons seulement déduire ceci: *a*) qu'il existe une progression dans le temps; *b*) que cette progression est interrompue, assez fréquemment, par des digressions ou des
pauses de nature didactique. Nous avons donc deux lignes temporelles:
l'une, qui se projette dans le passé (cf. l'emploi de l'imparfait ou du parfait), l'autre, dans le présent (à titre d'exemples de passages exprimés au
présent didactique, citons vv.772-82, 828-36, 849-54, 882-924, 1030-90
1091-1100, 1115-19, 1161-68, 1198-1240). Pourtant nous sommes encore
éloignés de notre objectif: le présent examiné jusqu'ici est le présent didactique, le présent de l'activité théorétique qui fait absolument abstraction
de n'importe quelle relation de temps. De plus les parties didactiques vi-
sent à donner une valeur de paradigme aux parties narratives, dans ce sens

---

[5]   Pour le passage nous renvoyons à G. BARRA, «La polemica antireligiosa nel V
libro di Lucrezio», *Rend. Acc. Arch. Lett. Belle Arti Napoli*, 29 (1954), pp. 141 ss. (Lucrèce emploie les arguments qu'Épicure avait employés contre Aristote en polémique avec les
Stoïciens aussi); pour la défense de l'unité du morceau dans le contexte du V⁰ livre cf.
J. H. WASZINK, «Zum Exkurs des Lukrez über Glaube und Aberglaube (v 1194-1240)»,
Wien. Stud., 79 (1966), pp. 308 ss. Pour A. O. MAKOVERLSKII («K voprosu ob ateizme Lu-
kretsiia», *A.N.S.S.S.R. Muzei istorii religii i atteizma, Ezhegodnik*, 3 [1959], pp. 372 ss.)
le morceau témoignerait de l'athéisme du poète (contre ces thèses historiquement et philo-
sophiquement absurdes cf. au moins R. MARTINI, «La religione di Lucrezio», *Giorn. ital.
filol.*, 7 (1954), pp. 142 ss., et L. PERELLI, «Epicuro e la dottrina di Crizia sull'origine della religione», *Riv. Filol. Class.*, 82 (1955), pp. 29 ss.). Des divergences avec Épicure selon
L. PERELLI, «Lucrezio contro Epicuro in V, 195-234», *Riv. Filol. Class.*, 39 (1961), pp. 239
ss.

qu'en partant de la *narration* de l'*histoire* du genre humain, on tend chaque fois à une *didactique* atemporelle. Dans ce sens, cette didactique a une
certaine fonction «détemporalisante» par rapport à la structure proprement narrative. Pourtant, puisque le présent de la didactique est «achronique», il est clair qu'il ne parvient pas à entamer la projection temporelle de la narration entière qui est nettement orientée dans le sens d'une évolution progressive qui appartient au passé. Les «emboîtements» n'altèrent
pas le niveau temporel de la narration car ils sont toujours fonctionnelle-
ment reliés à elle. Devrions-nous en conclure que ce niveau temporel ne
connaît pas de déphasages et qu'il se meut finalement sans écarts de relief
par rapport à une rigoureuse gradation dans le temps? C'est ici qu'il semble urgent de faire une «sous-segmentation» qui puisse considérer des unités narratives n'étant plus reliées à la disposition évidente du texte, mais
suivant plutôt comme critère de division et de différenciation un saut, un
véritable déphasage dans l'ordre temporel.

Il y a dans la narration de Lucrèce — nous l'avons déjà remarqué —
une opposition entre les temps au passé et les temps au présent. Cette
alternance peut être d'une aide considérable si nous abordons notre recherche à la lumière d'une «grammaire du récit». Nous avons exclu de notre
perspective le présent de la narration pure, comme essentiellement atemporel. Si Lucrèce, par exemple en D (vv.828-36), dit que toute chose doit
subir la déchéancé et la ruine, en faisant abstraction de la précédente partie narrative, il dit quelque chose qu'il entend comme valable toujours et
de toute façon, et le présent employé dans les vers en question (cf. *mutat,
debet, manet...)* non seulement ne crée pas d'opposition avec l'emploi du
parfait (employé dans la principale de C: v.827 *destitit*), mais au contraire
en renforce la dimension temporelle. Alternances et oppositions de temps,
nous les avons quand la projection temporelle enregistre des déphasages
d'une façon explicite. Ces «coupures temporelles» sont expressément
introduites par l'auteur lorsque, dans la gradation temporelle de sa narration (essentiellement tournée vers le passé), il introduit des passages d'exposition *simultanée*. En d'autres termes: à une narration de type *ultérieur*
(c'est-à-dire qui est faite *après* les événements racontés) succèdent signi-
ficativement des passages narratifs de type simultané, c'est-à-dire en rapport avec le présent. Dans ce complexe, donc, «maintenant» s'oppose à
«avant» et la gradation verbale au présent indique une contemporanéité
chronologique authentique, qui s'oppose à l'anteriorité des événements
narrés. C'est à ce point alors qu'il faut proposer une sous-segmentation
axée sur ces «écarts temporels», en tenant compte du fait que c'est Lucrèce lui-même qui nous met sur la voie, lorsqu'il souligne ces déviations
temporelle par l'emploi de *nunc* (parfois opposé à *tunc*):

    a. Dans G, unité essentiellement narrative, la narration pure est interrompue
    trois fois par ordre croissant d'importance:
    1.vv.940-42: les arbousiers d'aujourd'hui sont inférieurs comme volume à
    ceux d'autrefois;
    2.vv.988-89: comme maintenant, autrefois aussi les hommes quittaient la
    lumière de la vie au milieu des lamentations;
    3.vv.999-1010: autrefois les hommes n'étaient pas envoyés par milliers, com-
    me aujourd'hui, à l'extermination, et l'art de la navigation n'était pas connu;

alors on mourait par faute de nourriture, aujourd'hui par abondance ; alors, sans le savoir, il arrivait que, par inadvertance, ils s'empoisonnaient eux-mêmes, tandis que maintenant ils administrent le poison aux autres par méchanceté ;

b. P constitue une autre ample unité narrative, marquée par deux coupures significatives et temporelles :

1.vv.1273-80 : alors le bronze avait une valeur et l'or était considéré un vil métal ; aujourd'hui c'est au bronze à être négligé, tandis que l'or est en vogue : chose naturelle — comme l'affirme Lucrèce — du moment que ce que nous apprécions hier, nous avons l'habitude de le mépriser aujourd'hui.

2.vv.1423-35 : alors la possession d'une peau pour se vêtir, maintenant la possession de l'or et de la pourpre angoissent la vie des hommes, plus coupables aujourd'hui, dans le sens que les métaux précieux et les pourpres raffinées sont des plaisirs superflus, tandis que l'usage d'un vêtement de peau pouvait, autrefois, être considéré nécessaire : ce qui démontre l'éternelle impossibilité pour le cœur humain d'être content.

Comme on peut facilement s'en rendre compte, tandis que dans l'ensemble du morceau Lucrèce *narre*, et par conséquent projette sa narration le long d'un axe syntagmatique, ces rappels introduits par *nunc*, en coupant la continuité temporelle du discours, constituent d'authentiques sauts, même qu'il y a une tendance à instituer une articulation d'opposition binaire *(tunc...nunc)*. La linéarité temporelle enregistre donc quelques flexions, presque des intermittences, momentanées cependant, puisque le discours dans le temps est toujours aussitôt repris. De toute façon, les segments rapportés au présent, tout en créant une nette opposition par rapport à ceux où la gradation temporelle est au passé (un « avant » opposé à un « ensuite », à un « maintenant ») restent tout de même assimilés dans la narration ; bien plus ils sont insérés dans un plan proprement syntagmatique. Autrement dit : le long morceau de l'histoire du genre humain, essentiellement narratif, se dispose sur un axe d'enchaînement (syntagmatique) « dans le temps » (les « structures temporelles ») ; les quelques écarts de cette cohérence temporelle (les unités narratives au « présent ») ne sortent pas de manière essentielle, même dans leur rapport non équivoque à l'actualité (le *nunc* opposé au *tunc*), du plan du syntagme, de l'enchaînement dans le contexte. Or, cette opposition (qui est en effet une structure intérieure, profonde) semble être une caractéristique du monde de Lucrèce. Dans la célèbre conclusion du IIe livre (vv.1157 ss.)[6], Lucrèce se rappel-

---

[6] W. M. GREEN examine ce paysage (« The Dying World of Lucretius », *Amer. Journ. Philol.*, 1942, pp. 51 ss.) et met en évidence particulière les contributions de Lucrèce aux concepts de fond qui sont tout de même épicuriens. Le processus de décadence est expliqué par Lucrèce en ces termes : le monde, dans sa phase de croissance, reçoit des atomes en nombre plus grand qu'il ne les expulse, jusqu'à ce qu'il se consolide dans sa forme adulte ; mais à l'arrivée de la vieillesse, les atomes dépérissent tandis que le monde n'arrive plus à assimiler la nourriture : voilà alors que sous les coups provenant de l'extérieur il périt et se dissout (pour cette théorie cf. déjà DEMOCR., *Vors.* 68, A 40, 4). Il est clair que le poète tire un parallèle entre le monde inorganique et le monde organique (c'est-à-dire qu'il compare le cosmos à un organisme biologique). On aperçoit déjà chez Épicure « the parallel between the Cosmos and an organic body » selon F. SOLMSEN (« Epicurus on the Growth and Decline of the Cosmos », *Amer. Journ. Philol.*, 74 (1973), pp. 34 ss.), qui fournit des comparaisons avec le *Tim.* de Platon et, surtout, avec les écrivains médicaux (mais voir aussi, pour la comparaison entre le monde physique et le vie humaine, J. BAYET, « Lucrèce devant la pensée grecque », *Musc. Helv.*, 1954, p. 97). On trouve une discussion

le des temps où la terre produisait d'elle-même des moissons et des vignobles, dans sa fervente exubérance; maintenant, au contraire, la charrue est inférieure au travail, et malgré tant de sueurs, les récoltes sont pauvres et grêles. Aujourd'hui le paysan secoue la tête et soupire en comparant les temps actuels avec les anciens; même le vigneron regrette les générations passées, tellement plus heureuses, *nec tenet omnia paulatim tabescere et ire/ad capulum, spatio aetatis defessa vetusto* (vv.1173 s.). L'allusion est très claire: Lucrèce *ne* narre pas; il se rapporte à une histoire passée, mais entre celle-ci et le présent il n'y a aucune liaison fonctionnelle de temps. Et cette «façon» de disposer et d'opposer deux âges entre eux n'est pas seulement une structure mentale ou technique ou littéraire de Lucrèce: c'est un authentique «modèle culturel», une véritable marque de l'univers sémiologique. Seulement si nous comparons les modules dispositifs dans le IIe dans le Ve livre, nous devons conclure que le ésultat est essentiellement différent: dans la conclusion du IIe livre les structures se détemporalisent dans une dimension absolument achronique (et toute la conclusion de ce livre — comme nous le constaterons — se révèle d'importance capitale pour la compréhension du V), tandis que dans le Ve livre le schéma fondamental de l'opposition des âges est inséré dans un contexte «temporel».

L'opposition au niveau emblématique est un «modèle» de notre culture occidentale. Elle se présente chez quelques auteurs comme «thème» de l'âge d'or[7], ou, plus simplement, «motif des âges». Maintenant, ce se-

---

plutôt sommaire de la conclusion (mise en relation structurelle avec la conclusion du Ve livre) chez W. R. NETHERCUT («The conclusion of Lucretius' fifth book: Further remarks», *Class. Journ.*, 63 [1967], pp. 97 ss.), tandis que la meilleure étude sur le morceau reste celle de F. KLINGNER («Philosophie und Dichtkunst am Ende des zweiten Buches des Lukrez», *Hermes*, 80 [1952], pp. 3 ss.) où il est démontré que Lucrèce, tout en respectant pour l'essentiel la philosophie épicurienne, a orienté son intérêt vers le concept du cataclysme final de notre monde.

[7] Le morceau d'Hésiode sur le thème des âges est célèbre: cf. à ce sujet les études de psychologie historique de J. P. VERNANT, *Mythe et pensée chez les Grecs*, Paris, Maspéro, 1967 (*Mito e pensiero presso i Greci*, tr. it., Torino 1970, pp. 13 ss.). Mais déjà Hésiode recevait ce motif de traditions préexistantes et le reprenait d'une manière originale. Le mythe primitif, hérité par Hésiode, s'insère dans une vision cyclique du temps, tandis qu'il nous semble que Lucrèce insère le motif dans une conception linéaire (*cf. infra*), parce que — pour lui comme pour son maître — l'histoire humaine est insérée dans l'histoire du monde: et le monde s'achemine vers une fin totale (remarques pénétrantes sur le temps cyclique et le temps linéaire chez S. MAZZARINO, *Il pensiero storico classico*, II 2, Bari, 1974, pp. 412 ss., qui fournit aussi un examen approfondi des études à ce sujet). Ce thème, chez Lucrèce, a été comparé au passage des *Géorgiques* de Virgile (1,118-59) par G. CASTELLI («Echi lucreziani nel brano delle età: Verg. Georg. 1, 118-59 e nella concezione virgiliana del destino umano e del lavoro», *Riv. St. Class.*, 17 [1969], pp. 20 ss.) et E. CASTORINA («Sull' et à dell' oro in Lucrezio e Virgilio», *Studi di storigrafia antica in memoria di Leonardo Ferrero*, Torino, 1971, pp. 99 ss.): les deux critiques relèvent des concordances de fond et, en même temps, des discordances, surtout dans le détachement de Virgile vis à vis du «pessimisme» de Lucrèce et dans l'adjonction de l'élément divin qui est propre à Virgile (les innovations introdutes par Virgile — avec leurs connotations politiques aussi — deviendront institutionnelles chez les poètes impérieux successifs: cf. F. CUPAIUOLO, *Intinerario della poesia latina nel I secolo dell'impero*, Napoli 1973, pp. 191 ss.) . Des affinités et des divergences sont aussi soulignés par W. LIEBESSCHNETZ, «The Cycle of Growth and Decay in Lucretius and Virgil», *Proc. Virg. Soc.*, 7 (1967-68), pp. 30 ss. (Virgile, dans le cycle de la naissance et du déclin, met au centre l'homme et a une con-

rait trop peu que de reconnaître qu'en Lucrèce reparaît ce thème (qui,
d'ailleurs, ne décrit pas un authentique âge d'or). Disons plutôt, que ce
motif reparaît selon un schéma déterminé (la nette, achronique opposition)
qui en constitue le *signifiant*. Ce point une fois reconnu, à savoir qui ce
signifiant est présent chez Lucrèce, nous n'avons encore rien dit sur le
signifié qu'il prend. Tandis que le signifiant reste presque inaltéré dans le
cours des siècles (c'est une structure mentale, socio-anthropologique, liée
à des contextes culturels précis), le signifié change continuellement selon
les circuits dans lesquels le schéma compositif est introduit. Le circuit,
dans notre cas, est le contexte du poème de Lucrèce, dans sa riche, vitale
articulation, soit interne, soit dans ses rapports plus d'une foi détermi-
nants avec les destinataires de l'œuvre (il s'agit, en d'autres termes, de déterminer quelle fonction a, dans le contexte précis de Lucrèce, la structure
fondamentale, le schéma primitif — que pour abréger nous appelle-
rons communément *pattern* — de l'opposition des âges).

Quelle signification prend ce schéma dans le contexte de Lucrèce ?
Quelles connotations nouvelles devaient saisir en lui les lecteurs du premier siècle avant J.Ch. ?

Commençons par dire que le schéma fondamental revêt une fonctionnalité différente selon que nous nous trouvons dans le IIe ou dans le Ve
livre[8]. Comme nous le dirons par la suite, nous considérons la conclusion
du IIe presque comme un préambule poétique du Ve. Ce qui, dans la conclusion du IIe est seulement esquissé, sera repris, en essentielle conformité
de structures, dans le Ve livre. Or, nous pouvons remarquer une évolution
dans l'application du schéma original. Dans le IIe livre, l'«avant» et
l'«après» sont perçus comme deux moments tout à fait autonomes, sans
aucun rapport fonctionnel de temps. Les deux moments sont donc considérés dans leur portée purement emblématique: c'est la façon dont nous
pouvons, pour le moment, définir l'application du motif traditionnel des
âges, qui sont réduits par Lucrèce essentiellement à deux, un passé fécond
et heureux opposé à un présent aride et triste. Tout en traitant d'histoire
passée, les observations de Lucrèce se révèlent tout à fait atemporelles,
introduites comme elles le sont dans un axe exemplaire rigidement achronique. Et l'opposition binaire est une caractéristique de la façon dont on
a traité de toute antiquité — le thème des âges. Qu'est-ce qui arrive dans
le contexte du Ve livre ? Il arrive que l'opposition — comme on l'a déjà

---

ception tout à fait différente, par rapport à Lucrèce, des dieux et de la mort) et par E. M.
STEHLE, « Virgil's Georgics: the Threat of Sloth », *Trans. Am. Philol. Ass.*, 104 (1974),
pp. 347 ss., qui voit une ligne évolutive du matérialisme de Lucrèce au spiritualisme et pro-
videntialisme de Virgile. Sur le thème de l'âge d'or on peut utilement consulter R. H. MAR-
TIN, « The Golden Age and the κύκλος γενέσεως (Cyclical Theory) in Greek and Latin
Literature. Notes on the influence of Lucretius », *Greece and Rom.*, 1942-43, pp. 62 ss.;
H. REYNEN, « Ewiger Frühling und goldene Zeit: Zum Mythos des goldenen Zeitalters bei
Ovid und Vergil », *Gymnasium*, 72 (1965), pp. 415 ss.; pour le moyen-âge cf. les excellen-
tes remarques chez D'A.S. AVALLE, « L'età dell'oro in Dante », dans *Modelli semiologici
nella Commedia di Dante*, Milano 1975, pp. 77 ss.

    [8] Les rapports entre la conclusion du IIe livre et le Ve dans son complexe avaient
déjà été entrevus par Klingner (*Philosophie und Dichtkunst, etc.*, p. 8).

pu relever — reste essentiellement inaltérée *(tunc...nunc)*, mais, fait excep-
tionnel en égard à ce qui s'était toujours passé à l'endroit de ce *pattern*,
elle est temporalisée et introduite dans un circuit temporel. Nous pourrions
comparer la structure qu'on trouve chez Lucrèce avec toutes les autres
qui, plus tôt ou plus tard, ont accueilli le même *pattern*[9]. Mais il nous a
suffi de la comparer avec une structure analogue contenue chez Lucrèce
même, essentiellement identique au *pattern* traditionnel. Au Ve livre Lucrèce prive le schéma originaire de sa connotation fondamentale, qui était
d'opposition paradigmatique et catégorielle, en l'insérant dans un plan
syntagmatique. En d'autres termes, il ne suffit pas au poète d'opposer simplement la société primitive à la société contemporaine: il veut, par une
puissante structure narrative, éclairer le *pourquoi* du changement et de la
dégénération. Pour Lucrèce, il faut que ces motivations soient aperçues
dans l'histoire primitive de l'homme: seulement de cette façon pourra-t-on
comprendre l'origine des fausses terreurs, de la superstition religieuse, de
toutes ces pseudo-convictions qui ont amené la décadence morale et sociale. C'est ainsi que cette décadence n'est plus simplement opposée à un
âge passé et heureux (comme il arrive dans toutes les structures, y compris
celle du IIe livre du même Lucrèce, qui ont accueilli le thème des âges),
mais elle se dispose le long d'un axe *linéaire dans le temps*. Or, ce n'est
pas que cet axe enregistre ce degré zéro de la narration dont nous avons
parlé précédemment (= coïncidence absolue entre l'histoire narrée et la
narration en question) du moment que les «écarts» temporels sont présents dans le discours de Lucrèce; mais il s'agit, en ce cas, seulement
d'anachronies, c'est-à-dire de discordances entre l'ordre du récit et l'ordre
de l'histoire narrée (à cause des intrusions répétées du présent dans un

---

[9]   Le problème des sources de tout le morceau est extrêmement complexe et on ne
peut affirmer avec certitude qu'il ait, au moment actuel, trouvé une solution définitive. On
est parti souvent de la surprenante affinité entre Lucrèce et Diodore de Sicile (cf. 1,8,11
ss.), au siècle d'Auguste, pour aboutir à une source commune qui serait Démocrite (K.
REINHARDT, «Hekataios von Abdera und Demokrit», *Hermes*, 47 (1912), pp. 492 ss.; sur son
sillage, mais avec de nombreux apports personnels, I. LANA, «Le dottrine di Pitagora
e di Democrito intorno all'origine dello Stato», *Atti Acc. Lincei*, 1950, pp. 184 ss.), lequel
aurait influencé, naturellement, même Épicure (cf. Cens., *de die natali* fr. 161 Arr. = 329
Usen.: *Democrito Abderitae ex aqua limoque primum esse homines procreatos. Nec longe
secus Epicurus: is enim credidit limo calefacto uteros nescio quos radicibus terrae cohae-
rentes primum increvisse et infantibus ex se editis ingenitum lactis umorem natura minis-
trantem praebuisse, quos ita educatos et adultos genus humanum propagasse*). W. SPOERRI,
croit devoir rapporter la *Quellenkunde* aux thèmes en vogue à l'époque hellénistique, *(Spä-
thellenistische Berichte über Welt, Kultur und Götter. Untersuchungen zu Diodor von Sizi-
lien*, Basel, 1959). Des points de contact ont été relevés aussi entre Lucrèce et Diogène
de Enoanda (A. GRILLI, *I frammenti dell'Epicureo Diogene da Enoanda, Studi di filosofia
greca*, Bari, 1950, pp. 379 ss.). On trouve une analyse soignée des sources chez A. GRILLI,
«La posizione di Aristotele, Epicuro, e Posidonio nei confronti della storia della civiltà»,
Rend. Ist. Lomb., 86 (1953), pp. 3 ss. Sur tout le livre, cf. ensuite A. DYROFF, *Zur
Quellenfrage bei Lucretius (5 Gesang)*, Bonn 1904 (mais, du même, cf. aussi «Das 5. Buch
des Lukrez. Bericht über einen Vortrag», *Jbüch. f. d. Gymnasialwesen*, 1905, pp. 184 ss.)
et W. LUECK, *Die Quellenfrage im 5 und 6 Buch des Lukrez*, Breslau 1932. Intéressant
pour l'accent mis sur les précédents latins, il y a T. MANTERO, *L'ansietà di Lucrezio e il
problema dell'inculturazione dell'umanità nel «De rerum natura»*, Genova 1975, pp. 167 ss.
Consulter T. COLE, *Democritus and the Origins of Greek Anthropology*, 1967.

tissu grammatical essentiellement et toujours exprimé au passé) qui ne compromettent pas la dimension temporelle du fond des structures.

2. *Pour une «grammaire» de la narration : entre «achronie» et temporaiité*. — Axe linéaire, donc ; mais le terme «linéaire» implique une succession, un avancement progressif, dans le temps, des actions décrites. Et, en réalité, du v.295 (*At genus humanum multo fuit illud in arvis/durius*) jusqu'au vers 1457 (*... ad summum donec venere cacumen*) nous trouvons un compte-rendu continu des étapes progressives parcourues par l'humanité primitive jusqu'à la fin (mais l'«histoire» commence déjà bien avant, aux vv.783 s.: *Principio genus herbarum viridemque nitorem/terra dedit circum collis*). Toutefois, à la lecture immédiate du morceau, on reste sans aucun doute perplexe devant l'alternance du parfait avec l'imparfait, comme si le poète avait voulu laisser planer une certaine «confusion» temporelle. En particulier, le grand nombre d'imparfaits, dans une narration fondée sur la succession chronologique, a de quoi surprendre. C'est donc la notion d'aspect verbal qui nous intéresse. Et avant tout nous distinguons une action singulative (= raconter une seule fois ce qui se passe *n* fois) Quand, par exemple, Lucrèce écrit: *Nec robustus erat curvi moderator aratri* (v.933), ou *Glandiferas inter curabant corpora quercus* (v.939) ou encore (mais les exemples pourraient se multiplier) *At sedare sitim fluvii fontesque vocabant* (v.945), il est clair que *erat, curabant, vocabant* expriment des actions qui se déroulaient en se répétant, même si le poète les énonce une seule fois. Au contraire quand nous disons: «César passa le Rubicon», il est clair que nous énonçons d'une manière tout à fait singulative un événement qui s'est passé une seule fois.

La narration classique, traditionnelle, prévoit la fréquence de segments itératifs, mais le plus souvent d'une façon subordonnée par rapport aux segments singulatifs qui en constituent le nécessaire «espace» et, en même temps, garantissent la temporalité de l'événement (end'autres termes, raconter des événements en succession au parfait équivaut à narrer un événement en succession temporelle). Examinons plus directement ce qui se passe chez Lucrèce. Le morceau présente des alternances parfait/imparfait, mais, il *ne* semble pas présenter une nette opposition singulatif/itératif (de là les conséquences intuitives : s'il n'existe pas un véritable singulatif, où se trouve la progression temporelle de l'action ?). Nous ne pouvons pas, évidemment, citer ce long morceau tout entier. Nous nous limiterons à examiner quelques cas plus significatifs, qui fournissent clairement un cadre applicable à tous les vers en question. Nous citons les vv.925-47 :

> At genus humanum multo *fuit* illud in arvis
> durius, ut decuit, tellus quod dura creasset,
> et maioribus et solidis magis ossibus intus
> fundatum, validis aptum per viscera nervis,
> nec facile ex aestu nec frigore quod caperetur
> nec novitate cibi nec labe corporis ulla.
> Multaque per caelum solis volventia lustra
> volgivago vitam *tractabant* more ferarum.
> Nec robustus *erat* curvi moderator aratri
> quisquam, nec *scibat* ferro molirier arva,

nec nova defodere in terram virgulta, neque altis
arboribus veteres decidere falcibus ramos.
Quod sol atque imbres dederant, quod terra crearat
sponte sua, satis id *placabat* pectora donum.
Glandiferas inter *curabant* corpora quercus
plerumque; et quae nunc hiberno tempore *cernis*
arbita puniceo fieri matura colore,
plurima tum tellus etiam maiora *ferebat*.
Multaque praeterea novitas tum florida mundi
pabula dura *tulit*, miseris mortalibus ampla.
At sedare sitim fluvii fontesque *vocabant*,
ut nunc montibus e magnis decursus aquai
claricitat late sitientia saecla ferarum.

Nous nous trouvons devant deux parfaits: *fuit* (v.925) et *tulit* (v. 944). Il est évident (ici comme dans tout le morceau) qu'il ne s'agit pas d'actions instantanées, singulatives. Ce sont au contraire des parfaits atemporels[10], dans le sens qu'ils établissent un clair rapport chronologique entre le moment de la narration et celui de l'histoire narrée, en plongeant la narration dans un passé atemporel — et il s'en trouve qui ont nié à ce type de passé toute connotation de temps[11]. De toute façon, le premier parfait *(fuit)* détermine un premier segment: «les hommes primitifs furent bien plus résistants». Quand? Nous ne pouvons pas préciser: ils furent, ils étaient, ils avaient l'habitude d'être. Une série de six imparfaits *(tractabant, nec erat, nec scibat, placabat, curabant, ferebat)* suit jusqu'au v.942, série interrompue par un présent, *cernis*. L'action des imparfaits est clairement itérative, mais ce caractère itératif, même s'il ne s'oppose pas au parfait *fuit* (il n'est pas singulatif), quant au contenu, est intimement «subordonné» au parfait. En effet les différentes actions exprimées par les imparfaits doivent être toutes subordonnées (quant au concept exprimé) au premier segment: la plus grande résistance des hommes primitifs. À tel point que le parfait suivant, *tulit* (v.944), même s'il n'est pas singulatif, établit un nouveau segment («la terre fournit une nourriture suffisante aux hommes») auquel il faut subordonner l'imparfait suivant, *vocabant*, suivi à son tour d'un présent. Nous avons, alors, dans les deux segments, la succession temporelle suivante:

fuit	/tractabant		tulit /vocabant /claricitat
	/nec erat		
	/nec scibat		
	/placabat		
	/curabant	/cernis	
	/ferebat		

Il s'agit d'un schéma (parfait/imparfait/présent) qui peut être aisément répété plusieurs fois tout le long du morceau (nous avons déjà discuté la fonction et la différente gradation des présents), mais qui n'apparaît pas toujours d'une manière aussi simple. Nous citons ici un cas où Lu-

---

[10] Des remarques très fines, à ce sujet, chez A. RONCONI, *Il verbo latino*, Firenze 1968, pp. 79 ss.

[11] K. HAMBURGER, *Die Logik der Dichtung*, Stuttgart, 1957 (chez GENETTE, *o.c.*, p. 268).

crèce semble avoir donné libre cours à sa fantaisie dans ce «jeu avec le Temps» (vv.1379-1415):

> At liquidas avium voces imitarier ore
> ante *fuit* multo quam levia carmina cantu
> concelebrare homines possint aurisque iuvare.
> Et zephyri, cava per calamorum, sibila primum
> agrestis *docuere* cavas inflare cicutas.
> Inde minutatim dulcis *didicere* querellas
> tibia quas fundit digitis pulsata canentum,
> avia per nemora ac silvas saltusque reperta,
> per loca pastorum deserta atque otia dia.
> Haec animos ollis *mulcebant* atque *iuvabant*
> cum satiate cibi; nam tum *sunt* omnia cordi.
> *Saepe* itaque inter se prostrati in gramine molli
> propter aquae rivom, sub ramis arboris altae,
> non magnis opibus iucunde corpora *habebant*,
> *praesertim cum* tempestas *ridebat* et anni
> tempora *pingebant* viridantis floribus herbas.
> Tum ioca, tum sermo, tum dulces esse cachinni
> *consuerant*: agrestis enim *tum* Musa *vigebat*.
> *Tum* caput atque umeros plexis redimire coronis
> floribus et foliis lascivia laeta *monebat*,
> atque extra numerum procedere membra moventes
> duriter, et duro terram pede pellere matrem;
> *unde oriebantur* risus dulcesque cachinni,
> omnia quod nova *tum* magis haec et mira *vigebant*.
> Et vigilantibus hinc *aderant* solacia somno
> ducere multimodis voces et flectere cantus,
> et supera calamos unco percurrere labro;
> unde etiam vigiles *nunc* haec accepta *tuentur*,
> et numerum servare genus *didicere*, neque hilo
> maiorem interea *capiunt* dulcedini' fructum
> quam silvestre genus capiebat terrigenarum.
> Nam quod *adest* praesto, nisi quid cognovimus ante
> suavius, in primis *placet* et pollere *videtur*,
> posteriorque fere melior res illa reperta
> *perdit*, et *immutat* sensus ad pristina quaeque.

Il y a avant tout une succession de trois segments, déterminés par *fuit, docuere, inde didicere*. Subordonnés à *didicere* il y a deux clairs ité-ratifs: *mulcebant, iuvabant*; suit un présent *(sunt)*, mais qui est entre parenthèses. À ce point s'ouvre une «spécification»: *saepe habebant* («la spécification» est une indication du rythme de répétition d'une action dé-terminée), par rapport à laquelle les actions qui suivent *(praesertim cum… ridebat; pingebant)* sont des spécifications ultérieures et intérieures, qui se poursuivent avec *tum consuerant, tum vigebat, tum monebat, unde orie-bantur, tum magis vigebant, aderant*. Il s'agit d'une riche série d'itératifs qui n'ajoutent rien à la temporalité de l'action, dans le sens qu'ils se dé-veloppent à l'intérieur d'*une seule* action. Suit *(nunc… tuentur)* une série de présents (avec fonction, évidemment, de propositions principales; il est inutile de remarquer que *didicere* est un parfait logique) qui, comme d'ha-bitude, clôt le segment. Nous avons alors:

fuit	/mulcebant	/nunc tuentur
docuere	iuvabant	didicere
inde didicere	saepe habebant	capiunt

praesertim cum ridebat	adest
pingebant	placet
tum vigebant	videtur
unde oriebantur	perdit
aderant	immutat

Le schéma est sans doute plus ardu et complexe que le précédent (peut-être est-il le plus complexe de tout le morceau), mais il en répète la même essentielle structure temporelle. La plus importante articulation dérive du fait que l'unité narrative développe une puissante *diachronie intérieure*, qu'il faut ensuite mettre en relation avec la *diachronie extérieure* au segment, celle qui lie, en succession temporelle, les segments entre eux. Or, il est clair que, sans cette ossature, sans ces « structures temporelles », le morceau de Lucrèce, avec son caractère narratif, n'existerait même pas, et c'est justement dans l'approfondissement de cet échafaudage que nous en apercevons la richesse et les articulations intérieurs.

Certes, le texte de Lucrèce présente, par rapport à une narration commune, quelques caractéristiques de base : l'emploi d'un parfait non singulatif, mais le plus souvent atemporel, devant lequel s'impose l'emploi d'un imparfait clairement itératif ; la répétition du présent à plusieurs reprises et à plusieurs niveaux. L'absence de caractère franchement singulatif dans l'image des parfaits fait qu'ils ne sont que les indicateurs des segments : en d'autres termes, ce sont justement les parfaits qui déterminent la division en segments temporaux. À l'intérieur de chaque segment on peut démêler toute une série d'actions plus immédiatement itératives qui, dans des cas particuliers, donnent lieu à des séries riches et articulées de spécification intérieure. En marge, plusieurs fois, le présent ; ça et là, des pauses amples (avec le verbe toujours au présent).

Singulière façon de narrer, donc, que celle de Lucrèce : les puissants écarts le long de l'axe temporel, comme l'absence d'un authentique singulatif, d'un côté nous laissent apercevoir la technique compositive du poète, complexe et adroite, de l'autre côté documentent une sûre, paradoxale *achronie* des structures temporelles dans le *De rerum natura*.

3. *Les structures et la réalité sociale.* — L'axe syntagmatique demeure donc, mais son déroulement se produit le long de parfaits atemporels (presque épiques). Et l'opposition se dessine entre un présent, avec sa triste réalité, et un passé où les arts et la culture étaient, il est vrai, extrêmement rudimentaires, mais où le progrès et la technique et la civilisation n'avaient pas encore ouvert de blessures profondes dans la vie morale de l'homme. L'application du *pattern* traditionnel du thème des âges, apparaît avec évidence même s'il est interprété dans son processus historique, même s'il est introduit dans un contexte diachronique aux amples articulations. Le tout dans le cadre puissant du Ve livre, avec son *Leitmotiv*, la mortalité du monde, sa fin, le cataclysme qui l'anéantira (c'est un thème qui apparaît déjà dans la section préliminaire, et qui se déroule, à part quelques digressions, à travers un grand nombre de vers : 91-415). Le « pro-

grès[12]» du monde humain (même si seulement technique, du moment qu'au point de vue moral les choses semblent empirer par rapport aux premiers âges) doit donc être inséré dans le cadre du cataclysme final : concordance singulière avec la conclusion du IIᵉ livre, où le thème des âges est précédé du cadre de la fin graduelle du monde. En ce sens, la clô-

---

[12] On sait que la critique a exprimé des avis très discordants sur l'interprétation globale du passage : certains ont voulu voir l'exaltation du progrès humain, d'autres au contraire, y ont découvert la représentation du déclin. Un des premiers apports est celui de L. ROBIN, « Sur la conception épicurienne du Progrès », *Rev. de Métaphys. et de Morale*, 1916, pp. 679 ss., à l'encontre duquel M. TAYLOR (« Progress and primitivism in Lucretius », *Amer. Journ. Philol.*, 68 (1947), pp. 180 ss.) a confirmé le concept que l'épicurisme n'excluait pas l'idée de progrès, puisque la parole du maître aussi est un instrument d'espoir. Pour P. MERLAN « Lucretius, primitivist or progressivist ? », *Journ. of the History of Ideas*, 11 [1950], pp. 364 ss.), Lucrèce n'entend pas écrire une véritable histoire de l'humanité : l'intention du poète serait de montrer que les découvertes qui ont déterminé le progrès de l'homme se sont produites sans le concours des dieux (dans cet article — mais aussi dans un article précédent : « The composition of Lucr. V, 925-1459 », *Trans. Am. Philol. Ass.*, 78 (1947), pp. 437. — Merlan discute des problèmes relatifs à la composition du livre en invoquant la possibilité de doubles rédactions (il considère par exemple que les vers 1440-57 et les vers 1105-1389 sont des versions d'un même argument ; une double rédaction des vv. 925-1457 est aussi supposée par G. JELENKO, « Die Komposition der Kuulturgeschichte des Lucretius », *Wien. Stud.*, 54 (1936), pp. 59 ss. ; pour ces questions nous préférons renvoyer au traité équilibré de K. BARWICK « Kompositionsprobleme im 5. Buch des Lukrez, *Philologus*, 95 (1943), pp. 193 ss.) qui montre — contre Lachmann — l'essentielle cohérence des vv. 925-1457. Pour P. GIUFFRIDA (*L'epicureismo nella letteratura latina nel I secolo av. Cr.*, II, Torino, 1950, p. 24, n. 31) l'histoire du progrès « non è per Lucrezio che la tragica storia dell'infelicità degli uomini » ; A. C. KELLER (« Lucretius and the idea of progress », *Class. Journ.*, 46 [1951], pp. 185 ss.) pense au progrès retracé par Lucrèce comme à un phénomène le plus souvent positif, du moment que — grâce à lui — les hommes peuvent satisfaire leurs besoins naturels et nécessaires ; pour B. FARRINGTON (« Vita prior in Lucretius », *Hermathena*, 81 (1953), pp. 59 ss.) il faut partager l'« histoire » de Lucrèce en deux sections (BAYET, *Lucrèce*, etc., pp. 96 s. y voit aussi deux sections): la première, relative aux temps archaïques, de laquelle Lucrèce est spirituellement proche ; la deuxième, déterminée par la naissance de l'activité politique, des lois, des villes, vis à vis de laquelle Lucrèce serait en position polémique (mais l'interprétation de Farrington dépend d'idées préconçues, malheureusement trop courantes, selon lesquelles Lucrèce serait un révolutionnaire vis-à-vis de l'ordre constitué). Pour R. MONDOLFO (*La comprensione del soggetto umano nell'antichità classica*, Firenze, 1958, p. 705), dans la conclusion du Vᵉ livre, « l'ammirazione entusiastica prevale sull'esigenza epicurea dell'*ataraxia*, e ispira un vero inno alla creatività dello spirito umano, generatore della cultura » ; au contraire, pour E. PARATORE (*Lucreti « De rerum natura » locos praecipue notabiles collegit et illustravit* H. PARATORE, *commentariolo instruxit* H. PIZZANI, Roma, 1960, p. 422), à la *culpa naturae*, avec l'histoire de la civilisation, s'ajoute une nouvelle *culpa*, celle des hommes (Rour GRILLI, *la posizione*, etc., p. 10 & ; « Epicuro nello sviluppo della civiltà umana non vede, in fondo, un progresso reale, un ascendere dal bisogno materiale alla contemplazione del divino, ma un progressivo deterioramento, un vero e proprio regresso, un continuo allontanamento dalla natura e perciò dal vero benessere dell'homo. ») Outre l'apport général de A. KROKIEWICZ (« Et genus humanum... », *Filomata*, 150 [1961], pp. 45 ss.) il faut rappeler les apports de J. P. BORLE (« Progrès ou déclin de l'humanité ? La conception de Lucrèce (*De rerum natura*, V 801-1457 », *Mus. Helv.*, 19, (1962), pp. 162 ss.) polémique envers Merlan : il voit un contraste, chez Lucrèce, entre le sociologue, enthousiasmé par le spectacle du progrès humain, et le moraliste qui formule un jugement de condamnation) et de C. R. BEYE (« Lucretius and progress », *Class. Journ.*, 58 [1963], pp. 160 ss.), qui découvre une opposition entre le « pessimisme » de Lucrèce et l'« optimisme » d'Épicure : dans sa description de l'histoire humaine, Lucrèce aurait placé l'accent sur les détails les plus sombres. L. PERELLI (« La storia dell'umanità nel V libro di Lucrezio », *Atti Acc. Scienze Torino. Classe Sc. mor. stor. filol.*, 101 [1966-67], pp. 117 ss.) consacre une ample étude au morceau : pour lui c'est le pessimis-

ture du IIe livre semble avoir été un véritable préambule par rapport au
V^e livre dans son complexe, à part la section centrale — vv. 416-771 —,
empruntée probablement d'une section de la Lettre à Pythoclès. À vrai
dire, même le concept de la caducité du monde (sur lequel le poète revient fréquemment dans tout le poème) devait trouver un précédent — en
plus d'autres sources[13] — dans un passage de cette Lettre (cf. 88-89).
Mais à l'intérieur de cette histoire « cosmique » Lucrèce a inséré le thème
des âges : exemplairement dans le IIe livre ; dans un plan syntagmatique
dans le Ve. Le tout placé dans une « structuration » essentiellement analogue : dans le IIe, comme dans le Ve, outre le concept de la mortalité du
monde et le motif des âges, paraît aussi la polémique contre la foi dans
l'intervention divine (2,1090 ss. ; 5,1161 ss.) et la conscience de proclamer
au destinataire une vérité inouïe (2,1023 ss. ; 5,97 ss.). Ce sont là de sur-
prenantes analogies structurelles qui montrent qu'on doit considérer la clô-
ture du IIe livre comme un « noyau » générateur par rapport au Ve livre tout
entier. La source principale de ce dernier, même à un niveau embryon-
naire, semble avoir été Lucrèce lui-même, avec la « nouvelle » disposition
de matériaux culturels et littéraires qui précède. Introduits dans le circuit
du monde de Lucrèce, ces matériaux, grâce à l'*ars* combinatoire du poète,
se sont posés selon des structures tout à fait nouvelles. Et cette nouveauté
ne regarde pas seulement la façon de réaliser le signifiant (= le *pattern*
traditionnel) : le signifié même est nouveau, nouvelle est aussi l'idéologie
qui l'accompagne.

Il est connu que toute œuvre littéraire vit dans une tension dialectique avec son destinataire : elle est l'expression d'un milieu culturel et po-

---

me du poète qui détermine quelques déviations par rapport à la ligne tracée par le maître.
L. EDELSTEIN (*The idea of progress in classical antiquity*, Baltimore, 1967) voit un contraste entre l'épicurisme orthodoxe et de nouveaux courants qui acceptaient l'idée de progrès :
les incertitudes de Lucrèce dériveraient alors du fait qu'il n'a pas su concilier les deux ten-
dences ; contraste personnel — entre le savant et le moraliste — voit au contraire M. RUCH
(« Lucrèce et le problème de la civilisation. *De rerum natura*, chant V », *Les Étud. Class.*,
37 [1969], pp. 272 ss.). Des points de contact avec Philod. de Gad. sont suggérés par J. C.
FREDOUILLE, « Lucrèce et le 'double progrès contrastant' », *Pallas*, 19 (1972), pp. 11 ss.,
tandis que quelques comparaisons et affinités entre Lucrèce et Sénèque sont examinées par
F. MORGANTE (« Il progresso umano in Lucrezio e Seneca », *Riv. Cult. Class. Med.*, 1974,
pp. 3 ss.) : pour les deux auteurs la conquête du progrès matériel ne s'est pas accompagnée
d'un affinement moral. P. H. SCHRIJVERS (« La pensée de Lucrèce sur l'origine de la vie
(*De rerum natura* V 780-820), *Mnemosyne*, 27 (1974), pp. 245 ss.) dirige son attention
sur les vv. 780-820, en les examinant surtout dans leur dimension artistique. Citons encore
deux études qui retrouvent chez le poète, dans une certaine mesure, des qualités d'historien :
C. F. MULLETT, « Lucretius in Clio's chariot », *Journ. of the History of Ideas*, 19 (1958),
pp. 307 ss., et E. J. KENNEY, « The historical imagination of Lucretius », *Greece and Rome*,
19 (1972), pp. 12 ss. En outre, sur les rapports entre la description de Lucrèce et la science moderne, cf. au moins P. BRIEN, La génération des êtres vivants dans la philosophie
épicurienne », *Rev. de Synthèse*, 89 (1968), pp. 307 ss., et P. CASINI, « Zoogonia e trasformi-
smo nella fisica epicurea », *Giorn. crit. filo. ital.*, 42 (1963), pp. 178 ss. Pour une vue d'ensemble, cf. la dissertation de K. WESTPHALEN, *Die Kulturentstehungslehre des Lukrez*,
München, 1957 (mais à consulter avec précaution).

[13] Sur le concept de « fin du monde », cf. la bibliographie chez SPOERRI, *o.c.*, p. 107,
n. 10. F. SOLMSEN, « Epicurus and cosmological heresies », *Amer. Journ. Philol.*, 72 (1951),
pp. 1 ss., indique, spécialement en rapport avec les vv. 235-416, comme source principale,
les réponses polémiques d'Épicure à l'Académie.

litique déterminé et elle est dirigée aussi vers un type déterminé de lecteurs (on ne peut pas imaginer une œuvre, quelque lyrique et subjective
qu'elle soit, privée de ce contexte). Or, pour le lecteur cultivé de l'époque, l'application du thème traditionnel des âges dans le poème de Lucrèce devait sans aucun doute apparaître nouvelle. Et ce peut-être, non
tellement à cause du contenu (on a vu que, essentiellement, les différents
âges supposés par la version mythique chez Lucrèce sont reduits à deux),
mais plutôt à cause de la forme, de la façon inhabituelle dont le poète
en avait traité (qu'on se souvienne surtout du contenu narratif du Ve
livre). Enfin, le fait de considérer le déclin moral de l'âge actuel (malgré
le progrès technique) n'était pas en soi nouveau: mais nouveau était l'art
combinatoire du poète dans l'emploi du *pattern* (= schéma fondamental).
Non seulement cela, mais Lucrèce semble aussi avoir rempli une *fonction
idéologique* précise. Il existe, dans les passages examinés, me semble-t-il,
des «intrusions d'auteur» qui contribuent en quelque sorte à délinéer la dimension socio-sémiologique du signe littéraire. Les différentes expressions
du poète relatives à la crise sociale et politique devaient paraître claires
au lecteur de l'époque. Déjà aux vv.5,1120 ss. sont décrits avec compassion ces hommes désireux de puissance et de richesse, qui sont terrassés
ensuite par l'œuvre de l'envie. Il est vrai, toutefois, que ce passage peut
être considéré comme une version de la capitale VIIe maxime d'Épicure,
de même que le reflet des maximes XVII («L'homme juste est bien tranquille, l'homme injuste est plein de la plus grande inquiétude») et XXV
se constate en 5,1151 ss.: *Inde metus maculat poenarum praemia vitae./
Circumretit enim vis atque iniuria quemque/atque, unde exortast, ad eum
plerumque revertit,/nec facilest placidam ac pacatam degere vitam/qui
violat factis communia foedera pacis.* Celui qui viole les pactes de paix
communs ne peut donc espérer vivre une existence tranquille. Dans le sillage de l'enseignement du maître, alors, Lucrèce réprouve ceux qui cher-
chent le pouvoir, ceux qui violent l'ordre constitué et aussi, condamne
plusieurs fois la guerre (vv.999 s.; 1435), surtout aux vv.1297 ss., morceau
aux teintes terrifiantes, où, le poète décrit avec des accents sombres les
plus atroces techniques de guerre[14]. Il est clair que tout cela devait être,

---

[14] Le morceau sur les techniques de guerre a éveillé, sous divers aspects, l'interrêt
de plusieurs savants: quelques parallèles sont déjà signalés dans le bref apport de R. B.
ONIANS, «Lucretius V, 1308-1340», *Class. Rev.*, 1930, pp. 169 s.; on trouve une information
plus importante, avec un bagage de nombreuses comparaisons, chez E.L.B. MEURIG DAVIES,
«Elephant Tactics: Amm. Marc. 25, 1, 14; Sil. 9, 581-3; Lucretius 2, 537-9, *Class. Quart.*,
45 (1951), pp. 153 ss., tandis que F. C. BOURNE («Military arts and Lucretius' madness»,
Class. Bull, 33 [1956], p. 3) cherche à défendre le poète de l'accusation de folie mentale
(qu'on lui a dressée à cause du caractère extrêmement surréaliste du morceau) en montrant
la cohérence de Lucrèce avec l'épistémologie d'Épicure; K. L. MCKAY («Animals in War
and ἰσονομία, *Amer. Journ. Philol.*, 85 (1964), pp. 124 ss.) pense que les spectacles du cir-
que ont inspiré la scène de Lucrèce, (mais en ces sens cf. déjà l'anthologie de Lucrèce de
Perelli, Torino, 1962. p. 227); R. MINADEO aperçoit une intention morale chez le poète
(«Three textual problems in Lucretius», *Class. Journ.*, 63 [1968], pp. 241 ss.): Lucrèce aurait voulu mettre en relief l'absurdité d'une industrie humaine orientée vers la destruction.
Enfin, outre les pages exemplaires que SCHIJVERS (*Horror ac divina voluptas*, Amsterdam,
1970, pp. 29 ss.) consacre à l'argument, nous citons aussi C. F. SAYLOR («Man, animal,
and the bestial in Lucretius», *Class. Journ.*, 67 [1972], pp. 306 ss.), qui croit que, comme

explicitement ou *in nuce*, déjà en Épicure et, pour cela, on serait tenté de refuser à ces passages toute fonction idéologique. Mais encore une fois, c'est l'*ars* combinatoire du poète qui confère une connotation idéologique aux morceaux en apparence neutres: il insère les remarques d'Épicure dans ses structures temporelles. Par conséquent, la théorie anodine du maître s'est changée en *commentaire* du poète. C'est ainsi que la critique de ceux qui recherchent pouvoir et qui brisent l'ordre constitué devient profondément idéologique, du fait qu'elle est insérée dans un contexte diachronique précis, celui qui expose les étapes de la fondation de l'État de droit[15]. Il est clair qu'en lisant ces passages à la lumière de ce contexte, la position de Lucrèce devait refléter celle des gens respectueux de la légalité, des défenseurs de l'ancienne tradition aristocratique. Qu'on relise le passage relatif à l'expulsion des rois (vv. 1136 ss.):

Ergo regibus occisis subversa iacebat
pristina maiestas soliorum et sceptra superba,
et capitis summi praeclarum insigne cruentum
sub pedibus volgi magnum lugebat honorem;
nam cupide conculcatur nimis ante metutum.
Res itaque ad summam faecem turbasque redibat,
imperium sibi cum ac summatum quisque petebat.

À part l'expression *sub pedibus volgi*, qu'on pourrait entendre avec une nuance méprisante, on peut remarquer surtout les deux derniers vers: l'État parvient au comble du désordre lorsque sévit la lutte, où chacun est engagé, pour le pouvoir suprême. Nous croyons que tous ces éléments devaient être suffisamment clairs pour le lecteur du temps, qui apercevait en eux une dénonciation voilée, bien que discrète, de la guerre civile, de la violation de l'ordre constitué, de l'ambition personnelle, de la course au pouvoir individuel au détriment du gouvernement légal de la république. Et le lecteur avisé devait discerner une autre intrusion idéologique, plus nuancée même, dans la conclusion du IIe livre que nous avons considérée comme le préambule du Ve. Là le *pattern* des âges avait été appliqué en ce qui concerne le signifiant, d'une manière essentiellement fidèle à la tradition: deux âges opposés, emblématiquement (et donc sans structures temporelles), entre eux. Mais la fonction idéologique, qui au Ve livre était exercée par les mêmes structures temporelles (l'insertion de quelques axiomes d'Épicure comme commentaire à des situations précises narrées dans le

---

Esope, Lucrèce utilise la représentation du comportement des animaux pour éclairer quelques aspects de la nature humaine; cf. aussi S. R. WEST, «Problems with lions. Lucretius and Plutarch», *Philologus*, 119 (1975), pp. 150 s.

[15] D'autre part R. MUELLER (*Lukrez V 1101 ff. und die Stellung der epikureischen Philosophie zum Staat und zu den Gesetzen*, dans *Die Krise der griechischen Polis*, ed. by O. VON JUREWICZ et H. KUCH, Berlin, 1969) a bien démontré qu'Épicure aussi avait une position loin d'être négative envers les lois, l'état respectueux de la légalité et l'ordre constitué. La thèse de Müller s'oppose clairement à ceux qui, à partir de Farrington, veulent voir à tout prix des éléments de révolution sociale et de subversion dans la phisolophie d'Épicure (cf. par ex. K. LESNIAK, «Epikureizm jako doktryna socjologiczna», *Mysl Filozoficzma*, 1 (1956), pp. 85 ss.). Quant à la position de Lucrèce, A. GRILLI («Miscellanea latina», *Rend. Ist. Lomb.*, 97 [1963], pp. 119 s.) y voit une attitude nettement favorable à la monarchie des premiers rois, tandis que la démocratie n'est considérée que comme l'ochlocratie.

temps), est réalisée au IIᵉ par la façon d'opposer, exemplairement, les âges: le paysan se souvient des temps anciens où la terre dans son exubérance produisait d'elle-même abondamment, tandis que maintenant elle arrive à peine à produire, après un travail exténuant, quelques fruits misérables. Mais la terre — avait dit le poète — est désormais fatiguée (cf. v.1150 *Iamque adeo fracta est aetas, effetaque tellus*) et le paysan ne s'aperçoit pas (vv.1173 s). que peu à peu tout est destiné à s'user et à tomber en ruine. Si dans le Vᵉ livre Lucrèce semble avoir pris position devant la crise socio-politique, il semble avoir exprimé ici d'une manière tout à fait claire le motif allégué par les classes aristocratiques de l'époque (hostiles à l'exploitation agricole intensive) pour expliquer la crise agricole: la terre ne produit plus et l'économie agricole est par conséquent dans une situation précaire, non parce que le système est mauvais (travail esclavagiste, diffusion de la grande propriété foncière, décadence de la petite propriété même terrienne), mais parce que la terre est fatiguée[16]. Le fait n'échappait pas aux destinataires de l'œuvre, qui voyaient reflétée, dans des formes littéraires très fines, leur « vision du monde[17] ».

---

[16] Un savant soviétique, SERGEENKO (*Vestnik Drevnej Istorii*, 1953, pp. 65 ss.) a étudié la diffusion d'une théorie qui cherchait à expliquer les conditions précaires de l'agriculture par l'épuisement progressif du sol, las de produire. Cette théorie s'était imposée sous l'influence des classes dirigeantes et aristocratiques dans le but de masquer les causes réelles et profondes de la crise agricole, comme l'économie de la grande propriété foncière et esclavagiste et la limitation drastique du travail libre. Pour plus de détails sur cette théorie « aristocratique » et pour la bibliographie qui s'y rapporte, nous renvoyons à notre « Lucano e la crisi agraria del I secolo dell'impero », *Boll. St. Lat.*, 4 (1974), pp. 22 ss. (nous rappelons seulement la polémique engagée par Columelle, dans le préambule du premier livre de son ouvrage, contre cette théorie aristocratique ; pour un survol d'ensemble des différentes théories cf. R. MARTIN, *Recherches sur les agronomes latins*, Paris, 1971).

[17] La position philo-aristocratique de Lucrèce, que nous avons soutenue, peut probablement soulever quelques discussions. Pourtant, certaines allusions du poète nous semblent suffisamment claires. Des passages comme le morceau relatif à l'usage de la navigation, qui peuvent sembler critiques envers la classe dirigeante (vv.999 ss.), ne font que souligner l'urgence d'atteindre la modération, l'équilibre, même dans la gestion du pouvoir. D'autre côté, Lucrèce donne une importance fondamentale à la naissance des lois, qui sont, justement, la base de l'ordre constitué : elles marquent le passage d'un état d'anarchie à un état de tranquilité : *Nam genus humanum, defessum vi colere aevom,/ex inimicitiis languebat ; quo magis ipsum/sponte qua cecidit sub leges artaque iura* (vv.1145 ss.). Avec la naissance des lois disparaît le droit du plus fort et la paix est assurée ; toute subversion de l'ordre ne peut donc que ramener dans un état d'anarchie dangereuse ; le respect de l'ordre et des lois est une garantie pour l'ataraxie du sage (en somme, il serait difficile d'imaginer un épicurien qui poursuivrait l'idéal de l'ataraxie et, en même temps, chercherait à bouleverser cet ordre social qui en constitue le fondement): « Les lois ont été promulguées pour les sages, et cela non pas pour qu'ils ne commettent pas d'injustice, mais pour qu'ils ne la subissent pas ». (fr. 101 Bignone = Stob., *Flor.* 43, 139). Et, en dernière analyse, les vv.1129 s. de Lucrèce *(ut satius multo iam sit parere quietum/quam regere imperio res velle et regna tenere)* ne sont-ils pas une invitation discrète à se tenir en repos et à ne pas troubler la chose publique, spécialement en un temps 'inique pour la patrie' ? Qu'on n'oublie pas, non plus que, dans le célèbre éloge d'Athènes au préambule du VIᵉ livre, parmi les plus grands titres de gloire de la ville, il y a la promulgation des lois (VI 3 *et recreaverunt vitam legesque rogarunt*) (nous renvoyons à l'étude documentée, déjà citée, de R. Müller, qui sur la base d'une controverse précise menée contre Ermarque et Colotès, démontre l'existence d'une position de l'épicurisme officiel qu'est bien loin d'être négative envers l'État). Non seulement cela, mais A. MOMIGLIANO (*Secondo contributo alla storia degli studi classici*, Roma, 1960, pp. 375 ss.) a clairement démontré l'inexistence d'un épicurisme « démocratique » :

En somme, comme d'habitude, nous avons retrouvé la présence d'un « modèle culturel », d'un *pattern* chez Lucrèce: le motif des âges. Ce schéma de base, centré sur l'opposition des âges, est traité, dans la tradition culturelle et littéraire, d'une manière toujours emblématique: deux ou plusieurs moments, isolément considérés, s'opposent (d'une façon « exemplaire », dirions-nous). Lucrèce s'en tient à ce module traditionnel dans la conclusion du IIᵉ livre (que j'ai considéré comme un préambule du Vᵉ livre); mais au Vᵉ, il introduit une nouveauté essentielle, dans l'emploi de ce schéma (qui est un signifiant): il le dispose dans un plan syntagmatique le long d'une narration. On a tenté de déterminer les structures grammaticales de cette « narration », l'alternance significative de l'aspect verbal. Mais ce n'est pas seulement le signifiant qui est modifié par la structure particulière du poème de Lucrèce: une signification idéologique me paraît s'y ajoutés, qui semble appliquer aux schémas traditionnels les conceptions de la « vision du monde » aristocratique (et en ce sens le modèle « culturel » peut être considéré aussi comme un modèle « historique »), soit par leur application au *pattern* traditionnel (IIᵉ livre), soit par les « intrusions idéologiques » de l'auteur le long de la dimension syntagmatique et linéaire de la « narration » singulière du Vᵉ livre.

Carmelo SALEMME,
Université de Calabre.

---

ce sont là des pages dignes de foi qu'on ne peut pas, me semble-t-il, ignorer: cf., par ex., p. 387: « the Epicureans were sympatetic to a State founded upon consent, as the Roman aristocratic Republic was ». Momigliano arrive à cette conclusion: « We should like to believe that the *Vita Borgiana* of Lucretius is reliable in saying: « cum T. Pomponio Attico, Cicerone, M. Bruto et C. Cassio coniunctissime vixit », « même s'il ajoute par la suite: « All those people certainly read their Lucretius, but the *Vita Borgiana* is no evidence of it. » Enfin, même la forme poétique employée par Lucrèce est déjà un clair indice de la destination élitiste du poème (dédié — et non par hasard — à la *Memmi clara propago*). Et Cicéron devait bien s'être aperçu de tout cela, puisqu'il condamnait d'un côté les écrivains épicuriens comme *mali verborum interpretes* (*ad fam.* 15,19,2), il admirait le poème de Lucrèce, malgré l'indubitable divergence doctrinaire, (pour le jugement positif contenu en *ad Quint. fr.* 2,9,3 cf. J. TRENCSÉNYI-WALDAPFEL, « Cicéron et Lucrèce », *Acta ant. Acad. Hung.*, 6 (1958), pp. 355 ss.; P. BOYANCÉ, *Lucrezio e l'epicureismo*, tr. it., Brescia 1970, pp. 34 s.), au point d'en soigner la publication (dans le *Chronicon* de Jérôme *emendare= edere*: cf. E. PARATORE, *« Emendo »* in *Suetonio-Donato* e in S. *Gerolamo*, dans *Ricerche di biografia lucreziana*, Roma, 1964, pp. 135 ss.), et d'évoquer, dans une commune adhésion aux modèles archaïques et traditionnels (spécialement Ennius: cf. R. WRESHNIOK, *De Cicerone Lucretioque Ennii imitatoribus* &, Breslau, 1907) des expressions et des modules stylistiques (cf. les remarques équilibrées de A. RONCONI, *Osservazioni sulla lingua del « Somnium Scipionis »*, dans *Interpretazioni grammaticali*, Padova, 1958, pp. 45 ss.): et l'admiration pour un écrivain transparaissait dans les allusions (cf. à ce sujet les pages définitives de A. TRAINA, « Lucrezio e la « congiura del silenzio », *Studi Vallot*, Venezia, 1972, pp. 159 ss.).

Notre hypothèse d'un Lucrèce partisan d'aristocrates, respectueux des lois et essentiellement conservateur (comme nous l'avons déjà soutenu ailleurs cf. « Funzioni e grandezze variabili nell'inno a Venere di Lucrezio », *Boll. St. Lat.*, 7 (1977), pp. 3 ss.: « Structure narrative nel preludio lucreziano », *Giorn. ital. filol.*, 9 [1978], pp. 150 ss., peut paraître peu convaincante à ces savants qui préfèrent retrouver dans le poème une citation à la subversion sociale. À notre avis, toutefois, une discussion sur le problème reste toujours utile, au moins pour tempérer quelques conclusions, peut-être trop tranchantes, formulées par les uns ou par les autres (la réalité est toujours « nuancée »). De toute façon, notre principale intention, ici comme ailleurs, est l'étude de l'utilisation que le poète fait des structures sémiologiques, littéraires ou non: leur application subséquente au point de vue sociologique pourrait susciter des divergences, mais ne devrait pas compromettre notre but principal.

III. — *Merged Horizons*
Hermeneutes et philologues en interaction

Horace's Soracte Ode (C.I, 9)

Vidēs ut āltā∥stēt niuē cāndidūm
Sōrāctē nēc iām∥sūstineānt ōnūs
    sīluaē labōrāntēs gelūquē
      ∥flūmina cōnstitērint acūtō.

dīssōluē frigūs∥ligna sūpēr focō   5
lārgē repōnēns∥ātque benigniūs
    dēprōmē quādrimūm Sābinā,
      ō Thāliārchē, merūm diōtā.

pērmittē diuīs∥cētera, quī simūl
strāuērē uēntōs∥aēquorē feruidō   10
    dēproēliāntis, nēc cupréssi
      ñec uēterēs agitāntūr ōrni.

quīd sīt futūrūm∥crās, fuge quaērere, et
quēm Fōrs diērūm∥çūmque dābit, lucrō
    ādpōne, nēc dūlcis amōrēs   15
      spērne puēr nēque tū chōreās,

dōnēc uirēntī∥cānitiēs abēst
mōrōsa. nūnc ēt∥cāmpus ēt āreaē
    lēnēsque sūb nōctēm susūrri
      cōmpositā repetāntūr hōrā,   20

nūnc ēt latēntis∥prōditōr intumō
grātus puēllaē∥risūs ab āngulō
    pignūsque dēreptūm lacērtis
      āut digitō mālē pērtinācī.

                *   *   *

You see how deep the snow is lying
on white Soracte, and how the sagging woods
can no longer bear its weight and the sharp frost
has stopped the rivers.

Thaw out the cold. Heap up a load of logs
on the hearth and be more generous,

Thaliarchus, in drawing off the four year old wine
from its two-handled Sabine jar.

Leave everything else to the gods. The moment
they still the winds brawling
on the boiling sea, the cypresses stop waving
and the old ash trees.

Don't try to find out what's goint to happen tomorrow.
Whatever sort of day chance brings you chalk it up
on the credit side, and don't look down on the pleasures of love and
    dancing
while you're a young man,

while the cantankerous grey spares
your dark head: now is the time for the training fields,
for the squares, for soft whispering before nightfall
at the time arranged,

and what you've been waiting for, the girl laughing
in her secret corner, giving herself away,
and the memento torn off her arm or finger
without much resistance.

(translated by David West)

*   *   *

Vois-tu comme, sous l'épaisse neige qui le blanchit, se dresse le Soracte, comme ploient sous leur fardeau les forêts surchargées et comme le gel pénétrant arrête les rivières?

Dissipe le froid en mettant largement du bois dans le foyer et sois plus généreux, Thaliarque, à puiser dans une cruche de Sabine du vin de quatre ans.

Abandonne aux dieux le reste: dès qu'ils ont abattu les vents qui se livraient combat sur la mer bouillonnante, ni les cyprès ni les ormes antiques ne bougent plus.

Ce que sera demain, évite de te le demander et le jour, quel qu'il soit, que te donnera le Sort, fais-en ton profit; ne méprise pas les douces amours, enfant, ni les danses non plus, tant que ton âge vert est loin de la blancheur bougonne. C'est maintenant qu'il te faut aller au Champ de Mars et sur les places et vers les tendres chuchotements, le soir à l'heure du rendez-vous,

c'est maintenant qu'il te faut retrouver le rire charmant de ton amie, qui la trahit du coin où elle se cache, et le gage dérobé à son bras ou à son doigt qui résiste bien mal!

(Traduction par Pierre Grimal)

Horace's Soracte Ode (I.9)

The Philological Aspects

The philologist's goal, as far as concerns us here, is first to *explain* a particular poem by setting it in its literrary, social, historical, and linguistic contexts; then, secondly, as a critic, to throw light on its aesthetic value, if possible, by a variety of strategies, perhaps by defending its "consistency," as Professor Quinn has argued, whether this be psychological or logical, or by pointing to the poetic tensions produced by its skilful use of antitheses, the tack adopted by Professor Pöschl.

As Quinn pointed out, this is the ninth ode in the first book and it is written in the predominant metre of the collection Alcaics, unlike the first eight which are written in different and less favoured metres. The choice is significant, since Horace seems to have picked Alcaeus as his *persona*, almost thinking of himself as the Augustan version of the engaged soldier-poet. He therefore begins with an echo of Alcaeus, which was fortunately quoted in part by Athenaeus:

ὔει μὲν ὁ Ζεῦς, ἐκ δ' ὀράνω μέγας
χείμων, πεπάγαισιν δ' ὑδάτων ῥόαι . . .
κάββαλλε τὸν χείμων', ἐπὶ μὲν τίθεις
πῦρ, ἐν δὲ κέρναις οἶνον ἀφειδέως
μέλιχρον, αὐτὰρ ἀμφὶ κόρσᾳ
μόλθακον ἀμφι⟨βάλων⟩ γνόφαλλον

The language of Horace's model for the opening stanzas is the matter-of-fact, simple, stark language characteristic of Lesbian lyric: Zeus is raining and there is a great storm coming out of the sky.

As Tenny Frank once perceptively observed, it is Horace's practice to start a poem from a motto, as it were, by verbally echoing a familiar poem written in a familiar metre that his sophisticated Roman audience would recognize.

So far, so good. But here two possible philological interpretations of the poem come into question. Is this an essentially literary poem, based on Alcaeus, with a little local colour thrown in through the reference to Soracte, whose modern name is Monte Soratte. This is a hill, height 2,400 feet, situated about twenty miles north of Rome; it is visible from the Gianicolo and the Pincio, from much of the Campagna, and from Tivoli, but not from Horace's Sabine farm. (This might help to locate

Horace in this imaginary, or real, setting as a guest of Thaliarchus, who, though presumably young, is so hospitable that he performs the functions of heaping wood on the fire and of pouring the wine, functions that would normally be performed by a slave.) Alternatively, is the poem, as Professor Quinn would argue, a poem based on an experience which is then structured by literary reminiscences of a complex Greek tradition which provides the formal framework, but in no way militates against the reality of the occasion and the philosophical advice which it prompts (then or later) in the poet's mind? As evidence of this latter view, one might cite the simple conversational tone, *vides ut alta*, whether one takes this as a statement in the indicative or, more naturally, as a question — but in either case recognizing the possibility of its representing the imperative mode. This introduces, as Professor Colaclides noted, the question, important for the formalist and the phenomenologist, of the verbal mood and its ramifications. Is the first stanza a description of a static scene, as indicated by the three important verbs *stet, constiterint*, and *(nec) sustineant*? It would seem so and this stasis is then broken, as Colaclides insisted, by the very peremptory *dissolve frigus*, counterbalancing all that preceded it. (Horace's creative, almost surrealistic, translation or adaptation of Alcaeus' κάββαλε τὸν χείμωνα — "overcome the winter" is worth noticing.) The dynamic here counterbalances neatly the static, just as other elements in the poem will be given their appropriate contrasts and antitheses. Some of these are unmistakeable and they are accentuated by the careful interplay of consonants and vowels in, for example, *dissolve, deprome, reponens*. One obvious contrast is to be found in the humane (and human) adverbs *large* and *benignius* which are set in opposition to the cold immobility of nature in the first stanza *(geluque/flumina constiterint acuto)* ; another is the juxtaposition of Greek and Latin elements in the lines *deprome quadrimum Sabina, / o Thaliarche, merum diota* (Greek and Italian names, *quadri-* and *di-*, etc.)

Are these contrasts, these sudden movements, likely to destroy the "consistency" of the poem that a critic such as Quinn desiderates? No, since Quinn would cite the abrupt contrast where in the first stanza the two persons in the poem, the poet and his much younger host, are clearly outside the house, looking at snow-laden Soracte directly (since Roman villas had no picture windows), and in the second they have moved, or are about to move, inside the house. In building a consistency one has to exploit such oblique clues in order to come up with the correct answers.

Consistency in a poem is not injured by contrasts, as Professor Segal observed. In the second stanza, for instance, we find ourselves in a fictive *locus*, partly real, partly imaginary, between Greek and Latin, between a pastoral and a hostile landscape, between the cold wintry outdoors and the warm indoors.

Admittedly the elements are heterogeneous and this may detract from the harmony of the poem. Particularly noticeable in this respect is Horace's treatment of locale in these central stanzas. We move from the land, from the earthbound landscape of trees and forests to a more violent seascape, where winds battle on seething waves. As soon as the gods put these winds to rest, we are told — then we expect some positive action, but, on the contrary, the reader is offered two negatives. This is a shift not only from sea to land, from winds and ocean to cypresses and ash-trees, but also from positive to negative statements. This is then repeated in an interesting structure of antithetical imperatives: *permitte* (positive) tells us to leave *all* other things (beyond making ourselves comfortable now) to the gods, but it is followed by a negative imperative in stanza four, *fuge*, "do not seek." This structure is paralleled by the juxtaposition of the positive imperative *adpone* with another negative imperative *nec ... sperne*. All this creates an elaborate pattern in these two stanzas of alternation between positive exhortations and negative commands. This is reinforced by the parallelism between *nec cupressi, nec veteres* and *nec dulcis amores ... neque tu choreas.*

Wherever the action is taking place, we are moving from a violent landscape of winds and sea to a *terra firma* characterized by death and age: cypresses have funereal associations and the ashtrees are old *(veteres)*. It is perhaps a *geistige Landschaft*, which has to do with the ages of man as well as the times of the seasons. The word *cetera*, usually an insignificant word, in line 9 is here important, leading as it does to the first two lines of the fourth stanza. Here we temporarily leave the specific visual impressions for some abstract non-visual reflections: *quid sit futurum cras fuge quaerere* — do not seek to enquire what will happen tomorrow.

The mood changes again in the next line with a vivid adjective, *dulcis*. There is a sudden shift from the inside suggested by the previous stanza, the comforting fire and decent wine, to a threatening external world, which has its associations also in the world of passion. In *aequore fervido*, the adjective *fervidus* might hint at the passions of love. *Aequor*, as Professor Quinn reminds us, is any level surface, not just the sea as here, and so contributes to the metaphor in *deproeliantis* of the winds battling to the finish, suggesting in turn reflections on old age and death and the wisdom of not thinking about the future. Then, in the commercial metaphor of *adpone lucrum*, Horace moves us into an urban world, the world of the inner city, to be alluled to again in the last stanza.

Dulcis amores (line 15) contrasts sharply with the harsh general advice of the two previous lines as well as with the images of the cold outside, the suggestions of death and old age implicit in *cupressi* and *veteres orni*.

Again, if *puer* alludes to the theme of old age and youth, as Quinn suggested, the *tu* used in addressing him brings Horace's *persona*, if not himself in person, into the poem. The second person pronoun reminds us that there is an *ego* who is vitally engaged here.

Now in these last stanzas, according to John Sullivan, Horace is presenting himself as old in order to contrast his declining years with those of a lucky and very young man. I have been fortunate in living this long, he suggests, and I want you, my generous friend, you, Thaliarchus, while your age is still green and your head has no cantankerous white hair on it, to gather you rosebuds, *carpe diem*. You need the *piazze*, the Campus Martius, all the activities of a healthy young man, not least the flirtations and the soft murmurings at nightfall. In this last stanza, the complex syntax seems to be telling us something about the content, about the joys and the uncertainty of the hunt, about the pretences, the feigned violence and coyness involved in courtship.

Professor Pöschl would stress once more the basic antitheses in the poem. The first is that between the home with its good fire and generous amounts of wine and the hard winter outside. (Thaliarchus is heading a small symposium.) The second contrast is between the storms, not necessarily real but representing all the sorrows that harass us, and our consolations, since storms do not last forever. The third antithesis is between old age and youth — live for the moment. If winter is bad, the storms are worse, and old age is unavoidable. Yet the healing forces are strongest: fire, wine, the consoling thought that bad things pass. Even when temperamental old age comes *(canities morosa)*, still there are joys. Horace, or at least the *persona poetae*, forgets everything except the happy moments which he advises the young man to enjoy. This is philosophy in action, and the joys of wine in action. The poet sees mainly the wonderful scene at the end, the Epicurean moment: everything else, winters, sorrows, are gone, as he recollects a happy scene form his youth. This last stanza, in a wonderful crescendo, opposes a quiet opposition to the first stanza, where everything is at a standstill.

The connection of images cannot be mistaken: winter and the frozen trees prepare us for the aged ashtrees and the sad cypresses. *Canities* has connections with *candidus*; *virenti* is connected with the trees; winter, the gnome Horace adopted from Alcaeus, has metaphorical links to youth and age. These powerfully connected images guarantee the unity of the poem.

Synopsis by

J. P. SULLIVAN,
University of California,
Santa Barbara.

Horace's Soracte Ode (I,9)

The Hermeneutic Response

In one sense hermeneutics can never oppose itself to philology, especially if the latter means the affectionate care for the word and if the word is experienced as the announcing and making manifest of something. Some of the detail and the direction of what the classicists have said on the Soracte Ode may be taken in this sense. Since philosophy shares its *philia* with philology, I hope it will be taken in the spirit of Socrates' "ardent quarrel" (Rep. 607b-e), if I open up a dispute with the aim of philology and with the notion of aesthetic criticism.

The goal of philology is explanation, according to Professor Sullivan, and explanation is accomplished by setting the work into its setting. Moreover, setting the work in its setting means locating it in a setting presupposed and recognized by the poet and his contemporaries. The goal is to effect an interpretation that understands all the aspects and parts of the whole and whole in the parts, and when explanation succeeds it overcomes the strangeness of the work in its unexplained condition. In this way the poem is necessarily objectified, and anything that is not reducible to its time will remain unexplained. In practice this means that the philologue treats the poem as though it "stated things" and "as though the mode of it were expository" despite the fact that the poem "follows entirely different patterns," as Professor Quinn says. (Compare Professor Pöschl's remarks on paraphrase in his symposium paper.) Accordingly, a total, unified, consistent, prose exposition would constitute the primary exercise of philological science. The object then assimilated and known, philology would go on to the next work, and would only complete itself ultimately when all the texts of all the classical works in critical editions were provided with proper philological explanations. This activity takes place within academic research institutions, universities, journals, and societies.

Now in addition to the philological aspects, there is the question of the aesthetic value of the philological object, which belongs to the critical function according to Professor Sullivan. The object will have an aesthetic value if it exhibits consistency, whether defined as psychological, logical, or rhetorical (antitheses) in nature. Unity, we could say, is the crucial mark of aesthetic judgment as completeness in the sense of exhaustiveness is for philological investigation.

You may surmise from the critical remarks on historicism and formalism advanced in my symposium paper, that I think they can also be brought to bear on the above characterization, and they correspond roughly in terms of the historicistic orientation of philology and the formalist orientation of aesthetics. Hermeneutics, on the other hand, is discussion in the sense of *Er-orterung*, as elucidation of the *Ort*, the place or what I have called the semantic site established by the poetic work. Rather than a psychological or logical conception, hermeneutics demands an ontological conception of the work, that focuses not upon the unity of the alleged aesthetic object but upon the way that the poem violates ordinary language and experience, that is, disrupts and de-familiarizes them by its peculiar spacing and timing, and thus renders accessible some meaning of Being.

Hermeneutic categories of interpretation are simply any ones that assist us in making room for the articulate listening to what the work has to say. Approaching the *Soracte Ode*, we seek an elucidation that allows us to see something new but that also may allow us to see what we have already seen and heard in ways that make its import newly felt. Above all this approach makes no pretense at securing a complete and definitive interpretation, because such is neither necessary nor possible, indeed the very notion of it conceals the concealment that belongs to all interpretation whatsoever.

The overall movement of the ode procedes from the great breadth and height of Earth and non-human nature to focus on a worldly center and on human moment and detail. The poem opens up and reveals a conflict and a juncture between Earth and World, establishes a semantic site that through its peculiar wording and time-design, juxtaposes each and so lets Earth appear *as* Earth and World *as* World. In the first stanza we behold the Earth, set forth for our vision as mountains, snowy woods and rivers, in the mode of coldness, dead weight, and immobility. This is external nature as the inhospitable, the bitter, the frigid. Nature here is named Soracte, around which the other mentioned beings (woods, rivers, snow, trees) are arranged. This proper name makes earth, as Stevens says, "both familiar and yet an aberration."

In the second stanza, we move inside, to the setting up of a world, especially to house and interior hearth, that is, to the place where the earthly things (woods, growth, clay, matters) are converted into worldly uses — logs (once standing hard) for burning on the fire, clay (once frozen ground) for containing and pouring out wine, itself the (once fragile, perishable) product of vinticulture that warms body and spirit. It is to take up and savor these world-building uses that Thaliarchus is summoned to this place, to abide and linger in this richly familiar world. The poem shows up World in relation to Earth and Earth in relation to World, by revealing the place and weight of the usable things and of the life that transpires with them, and implicitly the role of craft and art in securing this place. Such a place must have its space and its time and these are invoked not merely in a symbolic way but as the space and time of human world-making, by reference to the *quadrimum*, the four year old wine, that is to temporality, and to spatiality be reference to the *diota*, the two-handled jar, which also transacts, if I may amend Professor Colaclides' terms, as the Latin years and the Greek space.

The third stanza bids the ephebe leave the larger landscape (its space and width), and the manyness of things *(cetera)* to the gods in favor of some single thing and some single moment of pleasure, as the later verses make clear. But this bidding can't occur until the parameters of space and time are more broadly drawn. Hence the speaker invokes the churning violence of the sea that contrasts the worldly warmth and peace of the second stanza. That sea displays an unworldly uninhabitable space, no human-scale container or interior place, just as the cypresses and ancient ashes signal another boundary difference from world when they suggest an uninhabitable time, the stillness of death.

The summons in the imperative mood is the key speech act of poem. It opens the second *(dissolue...)* and third stanzas *(permitte...)* as it does the fourth *(fuge quaerere)*, and it also recurs in the final line of the same stanza *(sperne...neque)*. Each of these summons bids Thaliarchus, to put out of his mind the poem of the life-time (birth to death) and as well as the poem of destiny that articulates and poetically measures the Augustan Age. For the latter is what the gods and the divine caesars look after. This bidding appeals on the basis of the speaker's *auctoritas* — both authority and authorship — instructing the young Thaliarchus on what he should not to think on as a prelude to pointing out what he should give himself to instead. The poem sets forth the summons *as* summons, in its concreteness and covertness, by showing how this summons belongs to a world, and displaying its poetic import. A signal facet is the multivalent way in which the speaker says so much more than he intends to say. When he says in the fourth stanza, don't consider, don't question or concern yourself with this larger view of things, the speaker by that token considers it and so places and highlights the life moments in relation to the larger circuit of life-time and community-time. According to Professors Quinn and Pöschl, the speaker is the poet or his persona, or as Pöschl summates: "Horace forgets everything except the happy moment which he advises the young man to enjoy; everything else, winters, sorrows, are gone..." But if the saying of the poem shows *both* to us, recollecting the need for forgetfulness, such an interpretation becomes untenable, despite the intention of the speaker or even of Horace himself. While this showing may not be the intended speaking of the speaker, it is no less the saying of the poem, and one that endows the arriving of the 'moment' with poetic charge. In the opening of the fourth stanza, *quid sit futuram cras, fuge quaerere*, a philosophical maxim gains imperative force. As such it breaks with the particularity of the landscape of death in the prior stanza and counterposes the particulars of the verses and stanzas to follow, as Professor Segal notes. But beyond this, the line dramatically violates its own formulation and prescription by considering what is not to be considered, and so shows the difference between speaking and saying.

The fifth stanza sings the time of the now as a time of youth, the time of athletic training in the bloom of physical strength, and of yielding to absorption in the immediate intrigues and impulses of love. Yet with the saying of the *nunc*, is somehow said the not-now and no longer and never-to-come of the senior speaker's own life. Yet further we could say, only the singing of the poem shows youth, for the young man does not know his own youth, and perhaps more unexpectedly the song reveals age *as* age.

The sixth stanza concludes the overall poetic shift from great breadth to close-up focus on the particular seductitive moment, the girl and her finger. The effect is to show up the Earth/World in a new guise, for here is not only the world as defined by the conventions of dress and manner, which domesticate nature, but here is also the upsurging of unconventional nature of the Earth in nature's other season of warmth. Yet without ever resolving the unresolvable tension between the human seasons and the natural seasons. Earth and World can draw close in intimacy but can never match and coincide. The poem calls upon us to witness this truth:

> Vides ut alta stet niue candidum
> Soracte
>
> Look how Soracte stands up sheer
> Under white snow

and so we see it rising candidly in words on the white page...

When I noted that the poetic work disrupts ordinary language, even when it employs colloquial and vernacular speech, it must be noted that all such disruption happens intertextually. That is, the text interweaves with other poems of Horace and his contemporaries, the Alcaeus precedent, and the philosophical texts of Epicureanism, the political text of the Augustan ecumene, and with Roman culture which as Graeco-Latin is intertextual and interlinear throughout. Suc intertextuality opens forward in time however 'unintentionally', for example, to the tradition of the European lyric as late as Trakl and Stevens, just as that of Vergil looks not only to the texts of Homer but also to those of Dante and Herman Broch. This *Wirkungsgeschichte* or history of consequence and effect, is the broad territory of hermeneutics, and the ceaseless topic of discussion.

The overall movement of the poem is from great breadth of earth and nature to focus on a worldly center and on human moment and detail. The poem opens up and reveals a conflict between Earth and World, establishes a semantic site that through its peculiar words and time-design, juxtaposes each.

To sum up!

In the *first* stanza we behold, see (*vides*) the Earth, set forth for our vision as mountains, snowy woods and rivers, in the mode of coldness, dead weight, and immobility. This is outside nature as the inhospitable, the bitter exposure of nature.

In the *second* stanza, we move inside, to the setting up of a world, especially to house and interior hearth, that is, to the place where the earthly things (wood, growth, clay, matters) are converted into worldly uses — logs (once standing hard) for burning on the fire, clay (once frozen ground) for containing and pouring out wine, itself the (once fragile, perishable) product of vinticulture that warms body and spirit.

But the poem alone shows up the earth *as* earth, and reveals the place and weight of the usable things and of life as it transpires amidst them, and implicitly the role of craft and art in securing this place.

Space and time are invoked not merely in a symbolic way, but as the space and time of human world-making, by reference to the *quadrimum*, the four-year old wine, that is the temporality, and by reference to the *diota*, the two handled jar, which also relate, to amend Colaclides' terms, as the Latin years and the Greek space.

The *third* stanza leaves the larger landscape (its space and width), and the manyness of things *(cetera)*, and the larger perspective of time to the gods in favor of some single thing and some single moment of pleasure.

In the *fourth* stanza, just as the poet says don't consider, don't concern yourself with this larger view, he by that token considers it and so places and high-lights that moment in relation to a life-time.

The *fifth* stanza sings the time of the now as a time of youth, the time of athletic training in the bloom of physical strength, yielding to absorption in immediate intrigues and the impulses of love. Yet with the saying of the *nunc*, is somehow said the not-now and no longer and never-to-come of the senior speaker's own life. Yet it is only the singing of the poem that shows youth *as* youth, for the young man does not know his own youth, and perhaps more unexpectedly it reveals age *as* age.

The *sixth* stanza concludes the overall poetic shift from great breadth to close up focus on particular, the girl and her finger, the effect is to show the earth-world relation in a new guise, for there is not only the world as defined by conventions of behavior, dress and education, but also the upsurging of nature or the earth in nature's other season of warmth. Yet without ever resolving the unresolvable tension between the human seasons and the natural seasons, since earth and world can draw close in intimacy but never match and conflate.

Michael MURRAY,
Vassar College.

Horace's Soracte Ode (I,9)

Of Interpretation, Philogic and Hermeneutic

Conferences recollected in tranquillity are almost as ambiguous as literary criticism itself, to say nothing of criticsm about criticism. What was immediate and personal in the face-to-face exchange and hospitable atmosphere of post-prandial discussion seems pallid and abstract when those same issues are mediated by typescritps sent from Santa Barbare or Poughkeepsie.

This observation is not meant as nostalgic reflection (though that delightful occasion which brought classicists and hermeneuticists together certainly deserves nostalgia), but as a parable for philology confronted with hermeneutics. The middle term in the first word of my title, Interpretation. Philology as such does not seek to interpret; it seeks to provide the basic explanations — linguistic, historical, cultural — which make interpretation possible. Hermeneutics, in a sense, stands on the other side of interpretation: its concern is the problems, assumptions, mental processes through which one enters into relation with the work of literature. To the philologist *qua* philologist, as Professor Murray points out, philological explanation is a task finite in possibility, even if not finite in achievement: that is, through amassing philological knowledge total explication is possible in time, as each generation adds its bit to what is known about the text.

The hermeneutic stress lies on the non-definitiveness of such explication. This impossibility of ultimate explication lies in the hermeneutic conception of the work: it is not a closed system of references, allusions, and images, but exists at the point of crossing between self and other, the world implied in the poem and the world of the reader. As Professor McCormick indicated in his contribution to the original discussion there is no such thing as "the" poem, only "my" poem. To this Professor Sullivan responded rightly with the concern that such a veiw opened upon an abyss of hopeless subjectivity. Both views are, of course, right. There is a text, in this case, the 24 lines of Latin which constitute Horace, *Odes* 1.9. We can verify the meanings of those lines against other lines by Horace and by his contemporary Latin poets. On the other hand, those lines have their "meaning" only as each reader hears them, construes them, tests them against his or her own knowledge of literature and experience of life, and integrates them in some way into that experience. It is important to recognize the dialectical nature of this process: it is always in the exchange, the meeting, possibly the conflict of two or more frames of reference, that of the work and that of the reader. Here hermeneutics has a valuable contribution to make to the study of literary texts, be they classical or modern.

In his "Outline of the 1819 Lectures" on *Hermeneutik* Schleiermacher wrote,

> Philology has made positive contributions throughout history. But its method of hermeneutics is simply to aggregate observations... [Hermeneutics is] the art of relating discourse [*Reden*] and understanding [*Verstehen*] to each other; discourse, however, being on the outer sphere of thought, requires that one must think of hermeneutics as an art, and thus as philosophical.
>
> — translated by J. Wojcik and R. Haas
> in *New Literary History*, vol. 10, no.
> 1 (Autumn 1978), "Literary Hermeneutics."

Classical critics are not, of course, ignorant of the issue involved in this different view of the relation of thought and language and the "philosophical" dimension of interpreting a text. In general, however, they prefer to ignore the problem (having enough other things to do) or to subordinate it to their proper task, producing an interpretation that takes account of as much in the text as possible.

Ode I.9 is, in one way, a model text for approaching this question because one of its chief concerns is *place*. Interpretation often depends on where the critic locates himself. The philological interpreter stations himself, one might say, on the farther side of the text, between the text and its predecessors (in this case Alcaeus) and its contemporaries and contemporary world (the Sabine farm, Rome, the conventions and techniques of Latin poetry in the Augustan Age). The hermeneutic interpreter places himself on the other side, between the text and the modern world. Whereas the philologist situates himself at the closest possible location to the text, hoping to enter the mind and thought-world of the poet, the hermeneuticist begins with the fundamental *otherness* of the text. This recognition of otherness means that the *Ort*, or what Professor Murray calls the "semantic site" of the poem, lies at a point where the familiar and the alien cross.

If the text were altogether alien, there could be no response, none of the pleasure in recognition and aesthetic enjoyment which forms the first "hermeneutic bridge" to the work. If the work were utterly familiar, there would be none of the expansion of sensibility, discovery, and joy in seeing how a complex structure creates a unified whole and a fresh synthesis of experience. Professor Quinn stressed the importance of "building consistency" in Horace. This frame of reference presupposes great closeness to the text as a harmonious whole. Professor Murray's hermeneutic stance is more distant: his emphasis is on the dissonance in the poem, "they way that the poem violates ordinary language and experience, that is, disrupts and defamiliarizes them by its peculiar spacing and timing, and thus renders accessible some meaning of Being." If one's frame of reference is "some meaning of Being" rather than the autonomy of the text, then the otherness, the alterity, of the text is essential, for it is in the encounter between word and world that the fruitful exchange comes. The passage of the familiar into the alien gives back to us some heightened consciousness of the familiar world — the delight in wine, a warm fire, friends — which appear in an alien, and therefore new, light when framed by the carefully structured sequence of word-pictures which Horace has put before us.

Here, however, as Professor Murray observed, philological criticism and hermeneutics are not at odds, but in fact complement one another. One point of agreement among classicist-interpreters is that the imagery of the poem has a great deal to do with life and death, the contrast between age and youth, symbolized by the snow and the green color, and the contrast between tomorrow's uncertainty and the "now" (*nunc*, 18, 21) of a scene of young lovers' tryst (21-24). Professor Murray's hermeneutic approach essentially repeats the point made about this central aspect of the ode synthesized so skillfully be Professor Sullivan; but he takes a more generalizing and and conceptualizaing attitude toward the material, its relation to the spatiality and temporality which define human life ("World") or, to put is differently, the points where individual experience touches "Being."

Taken at this level of generality, Horace's text enters into an "intertextual" relation with other poems, both of Horace himself, his contemporaries, and predecessors on the one hand, and of his successors in later European lyric on the other. In calling attention to this fact, Professor Murray reminds us indirectly of the hermeneutic view of interpretation as process rather than result.

"Intertextuality," however, is not foreign to philology. One of the first points of Professor Sullivan's account, as of most philological approaches to the Soracte Ode, is its use of a poem by Alcaeus some 600 years earlier. This historical fact is essential for understanding the poem. It indicates that the landscape of the first stanza is not merely a *vécu*, the result of private recollection or even, necessarily, of lived experience, but has a place within a long literary tradition. Horace has not chosen a winter landscape entirely of his own invention. Instead, he has entered a dialogue with an ancient literary tradition of poems about winter, wine, friendship, song. At this point, the philologist reaches for his texts to compile a list of parallels. He might point to the characteristic fusion of Greek and Roman in Augustan poetry.[1] The hermeneuticist, however, might be more interested in the consequence that the "place" of this poem is thereby defined in part as an imaginary place, a place where diverse experiences of winter, the natural rhythms of the world, can meet and be exchanged across centuries. The philologist can helpfully supplement this view with instances of other such imaginative places in the *Odes* (e.g. 1.17 or 1.22) or in contemporary poetry (e.g. Virgil's *Eclogues*).

The historical orientation of philology can be as powerful a means of confronting the "otherness" of the text as the hermeneuticist's "inter-

---

[1] See Gordon WILLIAMS, *Tradition and Originality in Roman Poetry*, Oxford 1968, chapter 5.

textuality." By grasping concretly and generally the differences between the ancient attitude toward life and ours, we confront the uniqueness of both world-systems. This point is excellently made for the medieval world-model in a recent essay by Hans Robert Jauss, "The Alterity and Modernity of Medieval Literature," *New Literary History* 10 (1979) 181-229, especially 191-194. Classicists are probably still resistant to theoretical formulations of the problem, an unfortunate result of the theoretical backwardness of our field, caused in part by the difficult nature of the material and the achievements of nineteenth-century positivistic philology. Yet classicists have contributed some important historical confrontations of differing world-views: one may mention the books of E. R. Doods, Moses Finley, Arnaldo Momigliano, Bruno Snell, Jean-Pierre Vernant.

To return to *Odes* 1.9 and literary interpretation, philology and hermeneutics have different — and potentially complementary — approaches to the *tradition* of interpretation. Philological criticsm seeks, justifiably, a consensus of interpretations, each building on the preceding one, adding, amplifying, correcting. This has been the tradition of classical study from antiquity to the present, and it is a grand and noble tradition. Hermeneutics looks beyond the work of literature itself to the relation of the work to the nature and process of interpretation, to the problematical status of interpretation in general, the recreation, rationalization, and externalization of an experience which begins, at least, as private, affective, internal. It focuses less on the final result of interpretation than on the shifting relations of systems of interpretation as different modes of understanding the "juncture between Earth and World" which each work creates.

Without the primary factual basis of philological explanation, as Professor Murray would agree, the hermeneutic activity is impossible. Without hermeneutic reflection, the philological explication has no means of reaching beyond the historically conditioned status of the poem in its relation to a world of men living two millennia later. The poem thus remains a captive of its own historical circumstances. It is hermeneutically dead, denied contact with the otherness of minds from a different culture. Without hermeneutic reflection, even if not fully articulated, the task of interpretation at any level cannot, as Socrates would say, give an account of itself. Explanation of a text without awareness of the aims of interpretation becomes a mindless, self-justifying activity, a blind groping after facts which are ultimately meaningless because they have no larger context.

Both at the beginning and at the end of his paper Professor Murray stresses the poem's disruption of ordinary language, its "violation" of ordinary language and experience. The classical philologist is likely to work from the other side, from the normative aspect of the language of the poem, its coincidence with the usages of contemporaries as established by parallels drawn from other texts. He is thereby able also to determine the deviations from those norms and from his experience with the literature of his period can assess the significance of those deviations. He can also clear away misunderstandings which our own historically conditioned perspective may put in the way of full appreciation.

A small illustration drawn from the text of Horace can show a possible area of fruitful interaction between philology and hermeneutics. From a philological (stylistic) point of view, the density of nouns and adjectives in the last stanza is remarkable:

> nunc et latentis proditor intimo
> gratus puellae risus ab angulo
>   pignusque dereptum lacertis
>   aut digito male pertinaci. (21-24)
> Now (let there be sought) also the hiding girl's betrayer, pleasing laughter from most inward corner and the pledge snatched from arms or from ill-resisting finger.

There is no verb, but only a characteristically Horatian mosaic of intricately arranged, syntactically and imagistically interpenetrating nominal phrases. The ode ends as abruptly as it began: *Vides ut alta...* (1), *aut digito male pertinaci* (24). The ode opens with a mountain invoked abruptly by a strong verb of sight denoting the presence of a single observer and his companion, the speaker of the ode. It ends with a single "finger" in a complicated interweaving of hands and arms in a gesture which itself has double meanings: play and seriousness, refusal and acquiescence, hesitation and coy delight. The ode itself, then, gives us both the large, expansive vision upon a landscape of a distant mountain and a miniature of interlaced hands where distance is uncertain and vision blurred in the groping of hands.

Both images begin and end with equal arbitrariness. There is no preparation and no gradual fading out. There is as little reason to begin with a mountain as there is to end with the playfull reluctant finger. In the midst of the rhythms of life and death, cold and warmth, frozen river and surging sea, chill forest and crowded piazza, the poem places two discontinuities: the abrupt silence before *vides*, the sharp truncation after *digito male pertinaci*. In its own dialogue between natural rhythm and unnatural discontinuity the poem self-consciously disrupts experience in order to reconstitute it in heightened, symbolic form. In real life we do not begin with the pure vision of the mountain, nor end with the play of hands. A journey or sojourn precedes the first; speech, reflection, hope, love, or sadness follow the second. The arbitrariness of the poem's frame cuts off continuity at both extremes and gives us a discontinuity which is unnatural and false to experience. But that very unnaturalness, that deliberate distortion of reality, is a potent element in the "meaning" of the poem. The silence which frames its beginning and its end intensifies the continuities of nature's rhythms in which we, as mortal creatures, participate. The frame invites us to consider the poem as timeless; the content is nothing it nof a meditation on time.

Philology can show us the consistencies of thought and feeling which give this meditation its depth; hermeneutics opens out the contradictions implicit in the very act of interpretation which make repeated interpretation necessary. From the hermeneutic perspective, then, the contrasts of this last stanza seem to involve larger issues than the "quiet opposition" be-

tween staticity and movement, old age and the serene "Epicurean moment" of youth pointed out by Professor Pöschl.

Ultimately, this is the contradiction between time and eternity. Horace's poem, like his massive white mountain, does not age, but "stands";
but Horace's reader, like the spectator in the poem, will age and die.
The movement from the static mountain which weathers seasonal change
year in year out to the flirtatious play of girl and boy inscribes the poem's
own dialogue between its conditioned existence as the product of a mortal
man living and writing at a specific place and time and its status as a "timeless monument" (*exegi monumentum aere perennius, Odes* 3.30), a dialogue between the modesty and finitude of its moment and its infinity of
aspiration as a work of art. Here the intertextuality of the poem is one
with its own basic, philologically interpreted meaning. From the hermeneutic perspective, both text and intertext participate equally in the wonder
and the problematical status of the work's ever-changing timelessness.

Charles SEGAL,
Brown University.

Horace's Soracte Ode (1,9)

Philosophical Hermeneutics and the Interpretation

What a delightful exercise in postprandial exegesis we had! A pale shadow indeed is John Sullivan's synopsis of an hour's discussion in a half-dozen typed pages. Gone are the lively repartee, the playful concessions, the impassioned defenses. Led by General Quinn, the five formidable philologists made their way line by line, word by word, through the Soracte Ode. One was aware of competing strategies; there were appeals to approach the analysis in specific ways. Quinn, for instance, in his opening remarks called upon his colleagues to work together to "build a consistency" — since that is what "sound" interpretation really must do. Colaclides, assigned the second stanza, focused on the modes of the verbs in the first two stanzas and the contrast between verbs of stasis and verbs of movement. This meant he had to insist on going back to the first word of the Ode to show the progression of modes and meaning in the verbs. Next Quinn and Sullivan observed that the perspective seems to shift from outside to inside, as if the speaker were saying "It's bloody cold out here; let's go inside." Segal then enlarged on the dimensions of the "site" of the poem: it is situated between Latin and Greek, in a landscape partly real and partly imaginary, partly winter and partly pastoral, partly present and partly past. Segal viewed the poem in terms of a progression of sites: first the earthbound landscape of mountain, trees, and river, then the violent scene of wind and a seething sea, then cypresses and ashtrees, and finally a more intimate, inner, recollected scene. Segal noted a turn in the sequence of his stanzas to negative elements of old age and death. Professor Quinn interjected the observation that line 13 refers to tomorrow, while the preceding stanza referred to yesterday; this means that the oppositions need not be thought of as existing in the present but as looking before and after: "As soon as the gods have calmed the battle of the winds on the sea, then you have the absence of movement." To which Colaclides added that the imperative forms of the verbs *permitte*, *fuge*, *adpone*, and *sperne* have a quite different character from *dissolve*, which would actually put something aside.

Was it accidental that Sullivan, who had read a paper on Roman sexuality in Martial, was assigned the stanzas with the happy giggle and the coyly reluctant finger? Sullivan noted that we have the aging man advising the lucky youth that now, now is the time, and he also observed that the form seems to produce the content in the stanza with its resonant images. Finally, Professor Pöschl suggested that three antitheses were at work in the poem: first, between home and winter, second, between storms and consolation, and third, between old age and youth. And he noted that in all three cases there are defenses, even "healing forces," at work: a good fire and large quantity of wine, the consolation that the sorrows of life will pass because we know storms do not last forever (he interprets the storms as not real storms but the storms of life), and most of all one has, along with the *canities morosa*, the welling up of warm memores of love at eventide.

From the vantage point of philosophical hermeneutics, this display of loving interaction with the poem was very interesting and memorable. Equally interesting is the fact that the synopsis presented by Sullivan not only does not recapture this interaction, it passes over it altogether. For he takes it as his taks to assemble the *results* of that doing not the modes and methods by which those results are obtained. I take this to be symptomatic of the positivist tendency to be preoccupied with "valid results" and with "soudness" but to give no sustained consideration to what might be more appropriate modes of relating to the Ode as poem, as art.

Now philosophical hermeneutics is concerned with the processes of interpretive doing. But because Sullivan's summary assembles only the results of that doing, it omits the very thing philosophical hermeneutics finds of crucial importance: how the various interpreters were relating to the poem, what each thought the task of interpretation required, what each was looking for and finding in the poem. What Sullivan shaved away as irrelevant was precisely what would be the object of hermeneutical reflection. What seems beyond question is precisely what is at issue. It is important to ask: what does reading an ode *do* for the reader? Does it make him more knowledgeable about ancient history, about mountains and storms, about verb forms, or is such knowledge a fringe benefit or a prerequisite for the experience of reading the poem? Is the benefit of reading the Ode definable in terms of "aesthetic experience" conceived as a response to its form, its interacting images, its progression of thought, the music of its sound, the delight of recollection?

It is precisely the adequacy of conceiving interpretation either as acquisition of knowledge or as aesthetic response to form which philosophical hermeneutics attempts to question. The validity of the results of scholarly research is not at issue, nor even the loving interaction of classicists with their texts, but their self-understanding of the act of reading. What is at issue is what sort of activity it is to read the text appropriately. Professor Segal rightly points to the contrast in saying that philology precedes interpretation and hermeneutics comes after it. But what is at issue is the claim of philology to be exempt from the philosophical review of its presuppositions. The problem arises when the tendencies to historicism and formalism in philology become full-blown philosophies of interpretation. One's methods and complicated exercises in explication subtly become one's ideology. When one begins to equate historical explication with interpretation per se, when one falls so in love with formalist or structuralist exegesis that one begins to equate them with interpretation, then the trouble starts. However valuable and even indispensible historical, philological, and formal analyses may be, they are radically incomplete as philosophies of interpretation. This is the reason that Professor Murray in his response to Sullivan did not debate the results of philological exegesis but raised the issues of historicism and formalism.

Hermeneutics as philosophy of interpretation calls our attention to the fact that neither philological, nor historical, nor formal analysis treats the text of a poem as work of *art*. Rather it is the object of historical, linguistic, or formal scholarship and could as well be of no artistic value whatever. Furthermore, they leave completely unanswered the matter of how the information they provide can be integrated into a reception of the text *as* art. On this matter, I refer the redear not only to Murray's paper here and his earlier book but specifically to Heidegger's "Der Ursprung des Kunstwerkes" ("The Origin of the Work, of Art"). Heidegger distinguishes the appreciation of the craftsmanship of a work of art from its function as art; a magnificent exercise in craftsmanship may have little merit as art. Heidegger argues that a work of art opens up a world in a perennially fresh way. It brings something into being, and thus it has an ontological function. At its site, it brings together the fourfold of earth and world, mortals and gods. For instance, a Greek temple standing in a valley or on the side of mountain opens up a space in being; it sets up the dimensions of a world. The issue is how to integrate this view of the experience of art with the traditional processes of interpretation.

Of course, one might argue that literary interpreters should not deal with metaphysics: metaphysics lures one into scientifically unsound statements; it causes one to see things in works that really are not there; or it lifts one to dizzying heights of generality where one can be neither right nor wrong. But there are several things wrong with such a view. First, if the character of an artwork is such as to demand that it be taken as art, can one willfully disregard the question of what this means because it is threatening or difficult? Is this an excuse for treating the work as if it were not art? Second, this attitude toward metaphysics is itself an historically and ideologically shaped interpretive stance. The positivist orientation is itself at issue. The question is how adequate to the challenge of understanding art is a positivist way of relating to a text? Or: At what point does one stop relating to the text as a scientific object and start relating to it *as* work of art?

An earlier draft of this present response carried the title "Hermeneutics as Philosophy of Interpretation." It is this theme and its possibilities that I want to place in relief. The argument is that contemporary philosophical hermeneutics defines itself not a system of rules of explication of difficult texts (the earlier and more basic conception) nor as methodological foundation for the humanities and social sciences (the Diltheyan conception, which makes it ancillary to those disciplines) but as philosophy of interpretation. As philosophy of interpretation, it starts all over again, with Socratic ignorantia and asks: What is interpretation? What is interpretive commentary in relation to the moment of interpretive understanding of a text? Is it the function of commentary to explain how a thing is put together? Or where it comes from? Does one "understand" a work of art when he knows how it is put together or where it comes from, or may one understand both of these without experiencing it as work of art? As philosophy of interpretation, hermeneutics focusses critically on the interpreter's act of understanding the text and the act of enabling others to experience it. It focusses on this act not psychologically, however, but phenomenologically. And it is able to ask where interpretation leads necessarily back to subjectivity or does it lead back only to a play of differences? It asks whether interpretation can be conceived in a way that leaves behind the presuppositions of subject-centered thought and even of what has been called "logocentricsm" (issues I cannot go into here).

In a sense, one's philosophy of interpretation is conditioned by one's philosophy of language, of truth, of art, and ultimately of man's place and being-in-the-world. Interpreters today need to think through the implications of this fact. I believe that literary interpreters at present still are at a fairly primitive stage of philosophical self-understanding and reflection about their own interpretive doing and the philosophical presuppositions on which particular modes of doing rest. This deficiency has serious consequences. It causes us to systematically misrepresent to ourselves the nature of our own interpretive activity. A general philosophical ethos of positivism and factuality has bewitched us, and we have been blind to important dimensions of our own interpretive doing. Neither the categories of historicism of formalist aesthetics are adequate to the activity of reading the classics. Most interpreters presuppose a philosophically outdated contemplative model of human knowing which is a variance with the constructive character of interpretive doing as defined in contemporary hermeneutics. Until we see clearly the limitations of scholarly positivism as a philosophy of interpretation, we will be unable to show how our interpretive procedures and activity contribute to appreciative understanding of the classics, and we will have great difficulty in justifying our activity to those who cannot understand our commitment to them.

I should like to close with a remark or two on the hermeneutical significance of the Soracte Ode. I believe it is an excellent illustration of the function of the poem as art and the poet as artist.

Hermeneutically, a fundamental question is what is Horace *doing* when he writes an ode, and specifically this ode? He is *writing*. Writing leaves a trace, and from that trace we can construct a world — and not just any world but the world in which we as human and finite beings must live and die. Writing itself possesses a certain timelessness; Horace in writing the Ode is making war on time.

Time is especially central to this Ode. Professor Segal rightly called it a "meditation on time." Directly or indirectly every image and every verb in the poem is connected with time; the poem is drenched with time. The opening words — "Vides ut alta stet niue candidum/Soracte" — are the exclamation of a man confronted by a more vast dimension of time presented spatially as mountain and snow. The mountain is everpresent, vast, perduring. On it is the snow with its coldness, unopposable power, grandeur, eternity. This image of a mountain covered with snow, with trees weighed down with snow, is a backdrop for everything that comes afterward in the Ode. The crystalline and lifeless whiteness of the snow of the organic green, living, resisting branches is a metaphor of death at war with life. If foreshadows a series of such revagers of life: the natural elements, the sorrows of life, the onset of age; but as Pöschl notes, the healing forces are stronger: fire and wine, the knowledge that this, too, will pass with time, and finally the vivid flashback to love at eventime. Mountain eternity and human time, stasis and notion, yesterday and today — all are dimensions of the human experience of time. And for a brief moment time's power and time's ravages are forgotten in a moment of delighted recollection.

There is one defense against time that the poet does not mention: the Ode itself. It is a weapon against time. Like the aging persona in the poem, the reader too can meditate on the nature of life as a struggle against time. For the poet's advice applies not merely to Thaliarchus but to the reader. The play of the forces in the poem is the play of the forces in every life, and thus the imperatives of the poem are directed to the reader as much as to Thaliarchus. The poem is a meditation on the experience of time in the modality of being human. That modality is quite different from the god's — strictly speaking the gods do not experience time, for they are exempt from death and from necessity, $\alpha\nu\acute{\alpha}\gamma\kappa\eta$. The interplay of earth and world is balanced by the interplay of divine and human. In contrast to the mountain, which is relatively fixed in time, standing changeless from generation to generation, is the cabin, the fire, wine, and love, which belong to the human modality. The gods, living above time, do not experience aging and loss of powers. So Horace advises: *Permitte diuis cetera* — leave other things to the gods and seek only the perfecton in time that is available to human beings. *Quid sit futurum cras, fuge quaerere* — do not inquire, do not reach beyond the day. Seize the now, for now in one's youth is the great "time", and enchanged space in being:

> Nunc et campus et areae
> ...
> Nunc et latentis proditor intumo
> Gratus puellae risus ab angulo.

It is this earth, in this human time that lovers find their moment. Therefore make war on time also by seizing the moment — *carpe diem*.

Hermeneutically, the function of reading parallels that of writing. The poet used writing as a weapon against time, and we find in reading it our own defense against time. Of course the poet could simply have carved *carpe diem* in stone, but this would not have persuaded the reader in the way that the Ode's vivid depiction of the dimensions of human life has done. In writing the Ode he has achieved the permanence of stone, and it is a jewel that can be handed down through time. Ode I, 9 uses the dimensions of writing — absence and presence, play of differences — to become an ontological jewel through which we can open up to ourselves the temporality of this human world in which we take shelter, drink wine, dance our moment, and face the inevitable waning of our powers. The unmentioned defense against time's destructive power is this other human thing, this Ode, which captures an eternal moment and perennial truth in the changelessness of letters scratched on paper.

Richard E. PALMER.
MacMurray College.

Miser Catulle, ... Obdura

Lecture poétique du poème VIII

The tissue of this poem is so delicate that one is almost
afraid of applying to it the scalpel of rational analysis.

Eduard Fraenkel [1]

Man darf wohl aufseufzen bei der Erkenntnis, dass es
eizelnen Menschen gegeben ist, aus dem Wirbel der eigenen
Gefühle die tiefsten Einsichten doch eigentlich mühelos
herauzuholen, zu denen wir anderen uns durch qualvolle
Unsicherheit und rastloses Tasten den Weg zu bahnen
haben.

Sigmund Freud [2]

BUT ET MÉTHODE

Sans tomber dans un jargon hermétique et ésotérique, nous essaie-
rons de suivre le mouvement et le déroulement du texte catullien, en nous
appuyant sur l'observation des signaux qu'il nous adresse, d'en déceler les
sollicitations, d'en montrer le fonctionnement et d'exposer la dimension
de son ouverture particulière au monde. Nous adoptons comme principe
d'opération le cercle herméneutique formulé par Schleiermacher: pour
comprendre l'ensemble d'un texte on doit comprendre ses détails, et les
détails supposent la compréhension de l'ensemble.

Le but de notre interprétation est de donner au lecteur contemporain
une meilleure compréhension de ce poème, ainsi que la satisfaction esthétique maximale, et de susciter des opinions différentes sur l'*ARS INTER-
PRETANDI* qui par la science veut valoriser l'art.

Nous n'aborderons pas l'identification des sources grecques et ro-
maines de notre poème; nous ne discuterons non plus des données biographiques, chronologiques et prosopographiques, ni d'autres réalités brutes
qui se cachent derrière les réalités poétiques. Trop d'experts ont dépensé
leurs énergies intellectuelles à résoudre ces problèmes et à proposer leurs
solutions, toujours parsemées de pudiques « peut-être » et de « probablement » hésitants. Le poète n'a pas cru bon d'indiquer, dans son poème,
la pertinence de ces aspects, et, même si nous pouvions les découvrir,
ils seraient extrinsèques, accesoires, paralittéraires et métatextuels.

---

[1] « Two Poems of Catullus », JRS, 51 (1961), p. 52.
[2] *Gesammelte Werke*, London, 1948, vol. 14, p. 493.

La forme poétique est la seule réalité de l'art. Dans la forme se trouve la textualité du discours, la « littérarité » du texte. La forme, évidemment, n'est pas un simple uniforme, mais une intimité continue avec les faits, les pensées, les sentiments et les émotions exprimés. La partie conceptuelle, le signifié, et la partie linguistique, l'image acoustique ou visuelle, le signifiant, sont indissolubles parce qu'elles jaillissent d'un même élan créateur. Le rapport entre le message et la structure est indissociable. La structure est sens, la structure donne du sens. « La forme ne signifie pas, mais se signifie » (Focillon). Il n'y a pas du contenant, de la forme, détachée du contenu, du fond d'un poème. Entre les deux existe une alliance aussi intime que celle du corps et de l'âme. La matière et la manière sont fondues comme le cuivre et l'étain dans le bronze. L'analyse des idées seules viderait le poème de la poésie. « L'intelligence nage en tenant la poésie hors de l'eau », estime Valéry. Pourrions-nous ajouter que la plénitude lyrique n'exclut pas du tout l'intelligible ?

Donnons maintenant la parole au texte[3] de Catulle.

1 Miser Catulle, ‖ desinas ineptire,
2 et quod vides perisse ‖ perditum ducas.

3 fulsere quondam ‖ candidi tibi soles,
4 cum ventitabas ‖ quo puella ducebat,
5 amata nobis ‖ quantum amabitur nulla.
6 ibi illa multa ‖ tum jocosa fiebant,
7 quae tu volebas ‖ nec puella nolebat.
8 fulsere vere ‖ candidi tibi soles.

9 nunc jam illa non vult : ‖ tu quoque impotens noli,
10 nec quae fugit sectare, ‖ nec miser vive,
11 sed obstinata mente ‖ perfer, obdura.

12 vale, puella. ‖ jam Catullus obdurat,
13 nec te requiret ‖ nec rogabit invitam.

14 at tu dolebis, ‖ cum ‖ rogaberis ‖ nulla.
15 scelesta, vae te ! ‖ quae tibi manet vita ?
16 quis nunc te adibit ? ‖ cui videberis bella ?
17 quem nunc amabis ? ‖ cujus esse diceris ?
18 quem basiabis ? ‖ cui labella mordebis ?

19 at tu, Catulle, ‖ destinatus obdura !

TRADUCTIONS

Bien que nous interprétions ce poème d'après le texte latin, nous croyons bon de joindre quatre traductions (française, anglaise, allemande

---

³ Nous avons repris le texte même du livre *C. Valerii Catulli Carmina*, lectorum in usum edidit G. P. GOOLD, Grotonii Massachussetensium MCMLXXIII. Pour la division du poème, nous avons adopté la partition naturelle et évidente, si bien justifiée par R. P. ROWLAND dans son article « *Miser Catulle :* an Interpretation of the Eight Poem of Catullus », *Greece and Rome*, 13 (1966), pp. 15-21, et par L. A. MORITZ dans « *Miser Catulle :* a Postscript », *ibidem*, pp. 155-157.

et italienne) afin que nos lecteurs qui auraient un peu oublié leur latin puissent suivre notre argumentation. Nous avons préféré aux recréations libres les traductions des philologues latinistes parce que leur but n'était pas de remplacer l'original mais de favoriser sa compéhension. D'ailleurs, les quatre traducteurs sont des latinistes chevronnés; ils ont une connaissance érudite de la langue de départ, et la langue d'arrivée est leur langue maternelle. Ils font preuve de respect pour l'original latin. Ils ont tous une grande sensibilité littéraire, le don de l'écriture et de l'art et ils ont essayé de transmettre aussi fidèlement que possible le message catullien. Évidemment, tous les arguments contre la traduction se résument à un seul: elle n'est pas l'original. Le frisson de l'original ne se retrouve jamais dans la traduction. «The poetry is what gets lost in translation» (Robert Frost). Toute étude du fonctionnement poétique passe obligatoirement par la langue originale. Le texte littéraire ne saurait exister sans la présence constante et impérative de l'auteur original.

Traduction française (du professeur H. Bardon[4]):

Malheureux Catulle, assez de sottises; et ce que tu vois perdu, tiens-le pour bien perdu. Ont brillé pour toi, jadis, des soleils radieux, quand tu t'empressais d'aller où te menait une jeune femme, aimée de nous comme nulle jamais ne sera aimée. En ce temps-là, c'étaient des ébats sans nombre, et tu disais oui et elle ne disais pas non. Ont brillé pour toi, vraiment, des soleils radieux. Maintenant elle dit non. Toi aussi, faible Catulle, dis non; cesse de poursuivre celle qui te fuit, cesse ta vie de misères, mais sans faiblir subis et tiens bon. Adieu, jeune femme. Désormais Catulle tient bon. Il ne t'adressera ni requêtes ni prières: puisque tu n'en veux pas. Mais c'est toi qui gémiras, quand nulle prière n'ira à toi. Perfide, malheur à toi! quelle est la vie qui t'attend? maintenant qui t'abordera? qui te trouvera jolie?, qui, maintenant, aimeras-tu? à qui dira-t-on que tu es? à qui tes baisers? de qui mordilleras-tu les lèvres? Mais toi, Catulle, de l'énergie; tiens bon.

Traduction anglaise (du professeur K. Quinn[5]):

Don't be a fool, my poor Catullus, you must stop it,
and count as lost what you see is lost.
There was a time when the bright sun shone for you:
The girl was leader and you her ready companion,
and you loved her then as none will be loved.
There, there were done those many merry things,
things you wanted, and she was ready enough.
Beyond all doubt the bright sun shone for you.
But now it's No she says. Don't then rage for Yes,
don't chase a girl that runs away. Don't live dejected,
but with hardened heart endure it. You must be firm.
Good-bye, girl, Catullus now is firm.
He'll not run to ask a girl that is unwilling.
You'll be sorry when no man wants you.
Wretched woman! what has life left for you?
Who now will come to you? Who think you pretty?
Whom will you love? Whose will they say you are?

⁴ *Catulli Carmina*, édition-traduction de H. BARDON, Bruxelles, Collection Latomus, 112, 1970, pp. 42-44.
⁵ K. QUINN, *Catullus, an Interpretation*, London, Batsford, 1972, p. 89-91.

Whom will you kiss? Whose lips bite?
Stop, Catullus. You must be resolved. You must be firm.

Traduction allemande (du professeur K. Büchner[6]):

Armer Catull, so lass doch, sie nicht mehr albern,
was du verloren siehst, musst als Verlust nehmen.
Die Zeit war einst, da dir die Sonnen hell strahlten,
sooft du kamest, wo dein Lieb dich hinführte,
geliebt von mir, wie keine wird geliebt werden.
An diesem Ort geschah damals an Spiel vieles,
was du begehrtest und dein Mädchen nicht wehrte.
Es glänzten wahrhaft dir die Sonnen hell strahlend.
Doch jetzt will sie nicht mehr: mach SchluB auch du, Schwächling,
und laufe der nicht nach, die flieht, noch sei elend,
vielmehr ertrag es starren Sinns und lern hart sein.
Leb whohl, Geliebte! Jetzt beweist Catull Härte,
wird nicht dich suchen, nicht dich bitten, dich Spröde.
Doch du wirst leiden, wenn dich keiner wird bitten.
Du Schlimme, weh dir! Welch ein Leben harrt deiner!
Wer kommt nun jetzt zu dir? Wem wirst du nett scheinen?
Wen wirst du jetzt nun lieben? Wessen Lieb heissen?
Wen wirst du küssen? Wem die Lippen wund beissen?
Doch du, Catullus, wanke nicht und lern hart sein!

Traduction italiennene (du professeur E. D'Arbela[7]):

Infelice Catullo, smetti di vaneggiare, e quel che vedi perduto stimalo
veramente perduto. Rifulsero un tempo per te giornate luminose, quando
5   solevi andare dove ti traeva la donna, amata de me quanto nessuna altra
sarà amata. Lí si facevano allora quelle molte dilettevoli follie che tu
volevi e che ella non ricusava. Rifulsero per te giornate davvero luminose.
10 Ora ella non vuol piú; anche tu, o folle, cessa di volere, e non seguire colei
che ti fugge, e non vivere misero, ma con animo ostinato sopporta e tien
duro. Addio, bella mia. Già Catullo tien duro, e non ti cercherà né ti
15 pregherà contro tua voglia. Ma tu ti dorrai, quando non serai pregata.
Sciagurata, guai a te, qual vita ti rimane? chi ora verrà da te? a chi
sembrarai bella? Chi amerai tu ora? Di chi si dirà che tu sei? Chi bacerai?
A chi morderai le labbra? Ma tu, o Catullo, risoluto tien duro.

* * *

IMPORTANCE DU RYTHME ET DES SONORITÉS

Avant d'aborder l'analyse détaillée, selon l'ordre où les faits se déroulent dans le texte (pour mettre en relation les procédés de l'auteur et la
convergence des effets qu'il visait) nous devons spécifiquement insister sur
le mètre et sur les sonorités, parce que les interprétations modernes d'un
poème ancien n'accordent pas toujours l'attention voulue à ces signes très

---

[6]   Karl BÜCHNER, *Die römische Lyrik*, Stuttgart, Reclam, 1976, p. 39.
[7]   Edmondo D'ARBELLA, *Catullo: I Carmi*, édition-traduction, Milano, IEI, 1957,
p. 109.

importants qui nous permettent d'identifier un poème[8]. La littérature,
comme la musique, est un art de l'ouïe. Il y a des poèmes dont le charme
nous pénètre avant que nous en pénétrions le sens. Ainsi le célèbre vers
virgilien: *Ibant obscuri sola sub nocte per umbram*. Mallarmé disait que la
poésie pure, réduite à son principe, n'est plus autre chose que la musique.
L'harmonie des mots et leur musique ébranlent le lecteur. Évidemment,
l'intégration du son et du sens font un tout indivisible. Pour recréer son
mode de transmission originale, le poème devrait être récité ou chanté.
Du moment même que les poètes sont vraiment poètes, leur pensée est
inséparable d'un certain chant. Le vers est d'abord une figure phonique ré-
currente. Mais il n'est jamais uniquement cela. Le vers existe aussi comme
rapport entre le son et le sens, comme une structure phono-sémantique
dans un discours poétique, c'est-à-dire dans l'enchaînement des suites de
phrases organisées.

Dans ce poème, Catulle emploie le senaire (trimètre) ïambique,
plus précisément le cholïambe ou l'ïambe boiteux (ἴαμβος σκάζον ου
χολίαμβος), appelé ainsi parce que l'ïambe final obligatoire est remplacé,
défiguré par un spondée (il traîne sa jambe) de sorte que le mouvement du
vers est interrompu inopinément à l'endroit où le rythme est le plus mar-
qué. La césure est penthémimère, moins souvent hephthémimère. Dans le
texte latin nous avons indiqué cet entrelacement de syllabes brèves et longues ainsi que les césures et les temps forts. Insistons sur le second temps
fort du mètre ïambique. Cela dit, fions-nous à l'instinct du récitant qui ob-
servera des successions homogènes de sommets et de dépressions, semblables à des vagues. En général, les cholïambes ont été traditionnellement
employés par le poète mendiant Hipponax ainsi que par Phoenix, Heron-
das et Callimaque pour exprimer l'ironie et la satire. Conclure de là,
cependant, que tous les poèmes catulliens en ïambes boiteux (8, 22, 31,
37, 39, 44, 59, 60) relèvent de cette veine, constituerait une généralisa-
tion dangereuse, en sachant que Catulle ne s'est pas laissé subjuguer par

---

[8]   Il nous semble que les livres de N. I. HERESCU, *La poésie latine: étude de
structures phoniques*, Paris, Les Belles Lettres, 1960, ainsi que *Golden Latin Artistry* de
L. P. WILKINSON, Cambridge, C.U.P., 1963, ont été passés sous un silence immérité par les
philologues classiques. Pour les points de vue modernes sur l'adéquation du son au sens,
de la lettre à l'idée, voir P. DELBOUILLE, *Poésie et Sonorités*, Paris, Les Belles Lettres,
1961, et son article « Recherches récentes sur les valeurs suggestives des sonorités », dans
Le Vers Français au XX‍e siècle, Paris, Klinscksieck, 1967, ainsi que Claude TATILLON,
Sonorités et Texte poétique, Paris, Didier, 1976 (in « Studia Phonetica » 10). Le problème
est loin d'être tranché. En tout cas, la diffusion de l'imprimerie a dissocié l'alliance consub-
stantielle de la musique et de la parole dans le langage poétique. Pour reconnaître la
structure sonore de ce poème on doit le lire à haute voix d'après les indications données.
Les livres antérieurs classiques: *Die Antike Kunstprosa* d'Eduard NORDEN 1ère édition,
Greifswald, 1898, cinquième réimpression chez Teubner, Stuttgart, 1958, et *Traité de stylistique latine* de Jules MAROUZEAU, Paris, Les Belles Lettres, 1935, 5e tirage, 1970, sont
toujours utilisables. N.B. STANFORD, dans *Hermathena*, 1943, donne un aperçu des opinions
grecques sur l'euphonie. Je ne prétends point donner ici une bibliographie étendue. Homer
F. REBERT, dans son article « OBDURA — a Dramatic Monologue », CIJ, 26 (1930/31),
pp. 287-292 a fait à propos de ce poème quelques observations fines. Nicolas Ruwet, dans
son livre *Langage, musique, poésie* (Éd. du Seuil, 1972) dégage dans la musicalité poétique
une tonalité nouvelle. Voir aussi *Six leçons sur le son et le sens* de Roman JAKOBSON,
publiées en français (Éd. de Minuit, 1976) et traduites en anglais par John MEPHAM (MIT
Press, 1978).

la convention pédantesque qui consistait à lier les mètres à des thèmes traditionnels. Nous pensons avec Bardon[9] que la terminaison brusquée de ces vers est admirablement adaptée au déchirement intérieur du poète et au rythme intérieur du poème. Le caractère dramatique de la pénultième longue dans tout le poème ainsi que l'entrechoquement de deux accents à la fin de vers sont à relever.

Plusieurs critiques, entre autres Eduard Fraenkel, ont remarqué que l'enjambement est totalement absent dans ce poème cholïambique, — ce qui constitue une déviation par rapport à d'autres poèmes semblables de Catulle, — et que cette structure répétée du staccato et du rythme saccadé et la halte finale sont voulues et fonctionnelles, appropriées à la tonalité adamantine du poème qui est jalonné par la récurrence du verbe-thème *obdurare*.

Chez Catulle, *poeta doctus* (et laborieux comme tous les artistes vraiment grands) les traits de versification ne sont évidemment pas de simples artifices phoniques, mais exercent une fonction sémantique. Naturellement, comme chez tout véritable artiste: *ars latet arte sua*, et on doit déceler cet art.

* * *

ANALYSE DÉTAILLÉE

Le poète Catulle commence son monologue dramatique intérieur entre le locuteur et l'interlocuteur Catulle[10] par le mot-clé *miser* qui, dans le contexte de la poésie érotique latine, désigne un malheureux que la passion subjugue. Il termine l'ensemble du poème par le leitmotiv *obdura*. Ces deux mots clefs prennent un relief significatif en raison de leurs positions pertinentes — *miser* ouvre le vers et le poème, et *obdura* les clôt — et par leur répétition d'importance: *miser* aux vers 1 et 10, et *obdurare* dans les vers 11, 12 et 19. Ces deux mots sont comme un rayon médulaire traversant tout le texte. Ils sont un reflet de la pensée essentielle de l'auteur. Leur rôle unificateur du poème est clair: ces deux mots constituent le thème principal. Autour d'eux s'organisent les champs sémantiques. Par leur charge émotionnelle ils annoncent le drame. Dans les

---

[9] H. BARDON, *Explications latines de licence et d'agrégation*, Paris, Vuibert, 1954, p. 23.

[10] Dans sa thèse, *La récurrence lexicale dans l'œuvre de Catulle: étude stylistique*, Liège, Les Belles Lettres, 1976, p. 79, note 46, Janine EVRARD-GILLIS a justement remarqué: «Le poème 8 a un *auteur* qui est Catulle. Le discours est énoncé par quelqu'un qui s'adresse à quelqu'un d'autre et emploie, occasionnellement ici, la première personne: c'est le *locuteur*, distinct évidemment de l'auteur comme tel. D'autre part, l'*interlocuteur* est explicitement nommé: *Miser Catulle*. Mais ce *Miser Catulle*, destinateur du poème, est une réalité de discours, distincte également de Catulle comme auteur et conçue par lui. Il me paraît capital, dans l'analyse d'un poème comme celui-ci, d'opérer nettement ces distinctions.»

deux premiers vers, qui sont comme un prélude, un locuteur imaginaire *(Catulle)* s'adresse à la raison de Catulle et l'encourage à mettre fin à ses sottises. C'est ce que suggère le verbe rare, hapax legomenon catullien, *ineptire* (déraisonner, faire des niaiseries). Ce verbe, fort par sa charge sémantique, est au surplus mis en évidence par sa position privilégiée à la fin du vers rare, composé de quatre mots seulement. Dans une corrélation de subjectivité, avec le subjonctif de supplication *desinas*, Catulle est invité d'une façon tempérée à cesser de s'apitoyer sur son sort d'amant délaissé par une *invita puella*. Pour donner plus de poids à cette exhortation (le subjonctif n'est pas encore un impératif!), le poète dresse un bilan et recourt à l'expression proverbiale: *et quod vides perisse, perditum ducas* (à chose faite point de remède), *write off as lost what is plainly lost*. Après l'exposition du thème, qui n'est pas encore clairement précisé, et l'exhortation à reprendre ses sens, jaillissent impétueusement les souvenirs du passé. Les émotions fléchissent la volonté. Du vers 3 au vers 8 le poète est envahi par le bonheur lumineux du passé. *Fulsere quondam candidi tibi soles*. Chaque mot, porteur du chant, intimement lié aux autres, artistiquement placé dans le déroulement poétique de ce vers à juste titre célèbre, est chargé d'émotion,. *Fulsere*, parfait de majesté, au début du vers et de la phrase, désigne l'éclat et l'ardeur des soleils (au pluriel: *soles*), points d'orgue placés au début et à la fin, et renforcés par leur déterminatif chargé d'affectivité: *candidi* (radieux) au milieu du vers. Le vers *(fulsere ... candidi ... soles)* irradie de toutes parts. Pour accentuer l'individualité de l'expérience du destinataire, le poète intercale *tibi* entre *candidi* et *soles*. Mais *fulsere*, par son aspect de parfait résultatif, exprime une action, hélas, achevée. Cet achèvement est encore renforcé par l'adverbe mélancolique *quondam* (jadis) qui renvoie l'expérience à un passé révolu mais encore ressenti.

Dans les vers 4-7, le poète évoque nostalgiquement, dans des termes suggestifs et voilés, le bonheur passé où le temps et l'espace restent estompés. Le jeux gracieux d'initiatives réciproques est habilement rendu par le parallélisme syntaxique qui s'instaure entre *velle* et *nolle*. Si dans le vers 7 *(quae tu volebas nec puella nolebat)* l'amant semble prendre l'initiative, dans le vers 4 *(cum ventitabas quo puella ducebat)* il semble trotter docilement comme un petit chien derrière sa *puella* dans son *servitium amoris*. L'imparfait fréquentatif *ventitabas*, second hapax legomenon, indique par son aspect verbal que le bonheur s'était répété dans une succession heureuse.

Les vers 4, 6 et 7 sont solidement installés dans la durée des imparfaits langoureux *(ventitabas ... ducebat ... fiebant ... volebas ... nolebat)*. Les vers 4 et 7 présentent un parallélisme syntaxique *(ventitabas ... volebas; puella ducebat ... puella nolebat)*.

Au vers 5 *(amata nobis quantum amabitur nulla)*, le poète qualifie pathétiquement son amour — dans un hyperbolisme cher aux amants — d'unique et d'incomparable[11]. Le datif pluriel *nobis*, au lieu du singulier

---

[11] Observant le parallélisme obvie entre les vers 5 et 14, nous sommes enclin à donner raison à J. EVRARD-GILLIS *(op. cit.*, p. 89) qui affirme que *nulla* ici n'est pas le

mihi, en augmente l'intensité. C'est la seule fois dans ce poème que le «je» est mentionné explicitement. Le pouvoir suggestif des «a» chaleureux ainsi que des «m» et «n», historiquement semi-vocaliques, donne de l'expressivité symbolique au bonheur des amants.

Il semble que le jeu des amants était essentiellement physique d'après le terme *iocosa* (euphémisme pour les jeux corporels et verbaux de la *res venerea*). L'accord complet des volontés des amants est indiqué doublement: au vers 6 par le passif *fiebant*, et au vers 7 par la tournure: *quae tu volebas nec puella nolebat*. Buechner[12] qualifie cette dernière tournure d'«unübersetzbar». La traduction de Bardon «tu disais oui, et elle ne disait pas non» serre d'assez près, par l'art de la litote atténuée, la réserve et la pudeur exprimées par la double négation du latin.

Le vers 8 reprend en refrain le vers 3, lumineux, substituant le confirmatif *vere* au nostalgique *quondam*, fermant ainsi le cercle magique du bonheur vécu et marquant implicitement le désir que les jours de la rêverie mélancolique reviennent. Il y a de grandes chances pour que les douceurs du passé l'envoûtent, que l'admonition du début s'estompe et que la raison fléchisse dans sa faiblesse. La séquence du passé heureux, encadrée par des vers presque identiques (3 et 8), est terminée.

* * *

L'emphatique *nunc* du vers 9 rompt brutalement avec l'évocation du passé voluptueux et on revient sans ambages au présent moins séduisant. Les quatre monosyllabes du premier hémistiche, *nunc iam illa non vult*, résonnent comme des coups de glas. La négation énergique *non vult*, située avant la coupe, provoque la riposte virile de l'amant, blessé dans son amour-propre, et il s'écrie avec un impératif vigoureux NOLI qui est encore davantage mis en évidence par le déterminatif *impotens* (= *sui non potens*) qui exprime son impuissance à dominer la passion. Le présent péremptoire *non vult* et l'impératif ferme et inflexible NOLI s'opposent farouchement au passé des rêveries: *tu volebas ... nec puella nolebat* (vers 7) qui exprimaient l'accord harmonieux de deux volontés. NOLI fait partie de cinq impératifs tranchants (*noli, sectare, vive, perfer, obdura*) qui, par leur martèlement incantatoire, alimentent la fermeté et la résistance de l'amant rejeté. Ces impératifs, à la différence des subjonctifs exhortatifs du début, sont un mode d'action, un ordre en vue de provoquer un résultat. Leur emploi est motivé par un mouvement affectif. Au trottement docile de Catulle derrière sa *puella* (vers 4) s'oppose *nec quae fugit sectare* (cesse de poursuivre celle qui te fuit). Le fréquentatif *sectare*, troi-

---

sujet de *puella*, mais, comme dans le vers 14, la négation forte, relevant de la langue familière, et par conséquent la traduction du vers 5 doit être: «aimée de nous comme *elle* ne sera plus aimée» au lieu de: «aimée de nous comme *aucune autre femme* ne le sera».

[12] «Vom Wesen römischer Lyrik», AU, 2 (1951), p. 7. La traduction de Janine EVRARD-GILLIS, *op. cit.*, p. 78: «que toi tu désirais, qu'elle ne refusait pas» me paraît aussi adéquate. La traduction de Bardon est imprimée ici.

sième hapax legomenon, est pour les gourmets littéraires une réminiscence possible de Sappho, de Théocrite et de Callimaque: τὸν φεύγοντα διώκειν. Mais en comparant le contexte — et le contexte est le dieu de la compréhension et de l'interprétation d'un texte — cette expression est uniquement catullienne parce qu'elle est unique dans son contexte. Les expressions ne se conservent pas seulement dans les livres, mais aussi dans la mémoire et le cœur. Les parallèles littéraires dont nos commentaires des œuvres classiques sont bondés, faussent parfois la jouissance concrète d'un texte poétique et nous amènent à confondre l'*origine* et l'*originalité*. Sans nier «l'intertextualité», c'est-à-dire le fait que tout texte est tissé d'autres textes, il est prudent de scruter d'abord la relation que le mot entretient avec les autres unités linguistiques de l'espace verbal qui le comprend. La belle logique de la recherche des sources (*Qwellenforschung*) est parfois singulièrement fragile, précaire, rigide et — futile.

Les vers 9 à 11, dont l'action est au présent, se trouvent architectoniquement au milieu du poème et forment une clef de voûte, un pivot entre le passé obsédant et le futur incertain. Ce groupe éclaire aussi les deux premiers vers du poème. Alors les ambigus *miser* et *ineptire* deviennent clairs. Le mot clef *miser*, renforcé par *vive* (équivalent emphatique de *esto*) trouve ici par le sens, la structure et la métrique, son entière justification. La prise de position se résume dans la résolution énergique: *obstinata mente perfer, obdura*, phrase célèbre à plusieurs titres. L'allitération de *ob* (*ob*stinata ... *ob*dura), la répétition de la *littera canina* «r» (pe*r*fe*r*, obdu*r*a), la consonne sifflante obstinée dans l'hapax ob*s*tinata, l'intensif *per* dans le nouvel hapax *per*fer, en asyndète avec *obdura*, renforcent davantage par la structure phonosémantique, par *Lautmalerei* et par le rythme, sa détermination pénible. Les spondées lourds de *noli*, *vive* et *obdura* rendent plus pénible la décision de couper court, enfin, avec une vie dominée par la nostalgie et l'obsession. La logique de raison (*mente!*) et la forme poétique sont réunies pour forger ce dur contrat.

* * *

La décision est prise. Le moment de l'adieu a sonné. D'une façon brève et familière l'amoureux constate, cliniquement détaché, qu'il tient bon. Il interpelle la bien-aimée de jadis (vers 4 et 7) de nouveau comme *persona muta*, sans la nommer, en utilisant le vocable pathétique, doux et sonore du langage populaire *puella*, mais sans le déterminatif affectif usuel *mea*.

Dans le jeu des fonctions référentielles, *puella* était, dans les onze premier vers, à la troisième personne (*puella* aux vers 4 et 7, *illa* aux vers 6 et 9). Dans les vers 12 à 18, l'autre moi de Catulle — JE est un autre, disait Rimbaud — et *puella* échangeront leur rôle respectif de distinateur et de destinataire. *Puella* est invoquée dorénavant à la deuxième personne, et Catulle se désigne lui-même à la troisième personne. Une dé-

charge d'émotion replace les acteurs. Mais, en réalité, Catulle, par la dialectique extrêmement subtile du Même et de l'Autre, s'identifie à la *puel-*
la, et s'adressant à elle par cinq pronoms personnels insistants *(te, tu,*
te, tibi, te) pour exprimer des rapports intersubjectifs, il s'adresse au fond
à la partie émotive de lui-même, tandis que la partie rationnelle est maintenant — c'est, du moins, son *wishful thinking* — détachée, loin, une tierce
personne. Catulle se tourne donc maintenant vers cette part de lui-même
à laquelle il vient de dire adieu *(vale, puella)*. Ce sujet, l'auteur lui-même,
se transportant dans son œuvre et vivant à l'intérieur de son propre texte,
sa pensée agissante, réfléchissante et consciente, constate à la troisième
personne du présent qu'il tient bon. De nouveau intervient ce verbe obsédant en position privilégiée : *obdurat*. Trois longues syllabes, *ob* et *du* se
suivant, avec un « r » dur, suggèrent déjà par leur sensation auditive le
courant sous-jacent de signification : il endure, il supporte avec fermeté
ce qui est pénible. *Iam* (désormais) annonce l'avenir. Le locuteur objectif toujours, dans la troisième personne, au vers 13, passe clairement à
l'avenir et précise ses relations futures avec la *puella : nec te requiret nec*
rogabit invitam. S'il n'y avait pas cet *invitam* (contre son gré), on estime-
rait que l'affirmatif *obdurat* (il tient bon) dans le vers précédant avait de
la stabilité. Nous voyons maintenant que cette rupture est conditionnelle :
il ne la cherchera plus, ne sollicitera plus son amour, si cette sollicitation
va à l'encontre de sa volonté. Il a trouvé une échappatoire. *Obdurat*
est donc bien instable.

Au vers 14, le locuteur évoque la perspective de la vie de la *puella*
dans son nouvel avenir — sans Catulle. D'après le verbe *rogabit* du vers
précédent et compte tenu du parallélisme avec le vers cinq *(amata nobis*
quantum amabitur nulla) il est clair que la *puella* ne bénéficiera plus des
sollicitations de *Catulle* — d'autres amants n'entrent pas en ligne de
compte. En s'adressant à elle directement, à la deuxième personne, et en
employant abondamment le vocabulaire érotique populaire, le destinateur
peint l'avenir de la *puella*, séparée de lui-même, sous de sombres couleurs.
De nombreux exégètes, qui ont tenté de rattacher ce texte poétique au contexte biographique de Catulle avec Lesbia-Clodia Metelli, se sont égarés
sur de fausses pistes et ont essayé d'adapter le texte du poème à leurs
hypothèses biographiques. Nous y reviendrons.

Affligé par l'avenir de la *puella* sans lui, il va jusqu'au blasphème
et lui lance cette parole impie : « *Scelesta, vae te !* » Mais, nous savons très
bien ce que valent les malédictions des amants. Ils ne savent pas qui ils
craignent le plus, les maudits ou les maudissants. Nous expliquons le mot
scelesta dans ce contexte comme *scélérate* mais en donnant à ce terme un
sens atténué, comme si l'on reprochait à la personne aimée une peccadille,
un égarement[13]. Les sept questions rhétoriques, saccadées, haletantes et
pressantes que Catulle pose à la *puella* dans la langue familière, l'anapho-

---

[13] Il est instructif de voir comment nos quatre philologues ont traduit ce terme :
Bardon : « perfide » ; Quinn : « wretched woman » ; Büchner : « Du Schlimme » ; D'Arbella :
« sciagurata ».

rique pronom interrogatif, emphatique, en sept itérations insistantes, ainsi que le retour de sonorités semblables à la fin des verbes relèvent des effusions tourmentées et du paroxysme de la passion charnelle de Catulle pour sa *puella*. Les réalités rétrospectives du passé (vers 3-8), par le halo suggestif qui entoure les mots érotiques employés ici, sont transportées, concrètes et intimes, dans leurs dimensions prospectives pour que la *puella* se rende compte que le seul bonheur pour elle est de rester avec Catulle. L'amant renverse les rôles et il fait de sa *puella* la délaissée, alors qu'en réalité c'est lui qui a été rejeté. Nous n'appelons pas ce procédé ironie[14], mais jeu subtil de la psychologie poétique, amoureuse et humaine.

Si nous devions suppléer les réponses à ces questions, nous aurions le texte suivant: «Quelle vie te reste?» Réponse: «Nulle, sans Catulle». «Qui te sollicitera maintenant?» Réponse: «Personne, quand Catulle m'aura abandonnée». «Qui te trouvera jolie?» Réponse: «Personne, après Catulle». «Qui maintenant aimeras-tu?» Réponse: «Personne, après Catulle. «À qui dira-t-on que tu appartiens?» Réponse: «À personne, sauf à Catulle».

Ces réponses explicites et vraiment prosaïques d'un discours scientifique détruiraient toute la poésie implicite de Catulle. Les deux dernières questions d'une sensualité précise («À qui tes baisers?» «De qui mordilleras-tu les lèvres?») cachent mal sa jalousie envers un successeur éventuel. Éliminant l'amant hypothétique de l'avenir, Catulle essaie de recréer son bonheur passé. Usant du subterfuge de la pitié pour la *puella*, il s'aperçoit que la passion le submerge.

* * *

La voix de la raison tenace et impitoyable l'arrache soudainement aux rêveries obsédantes et voluptueuses du passé et de l'avenir et le ramène à la réalité présente. De là le sursaut du vers 19: «Mais toi, Catulle, sois résolu!» Apostrophe qui rattache le dernier vers au permier et au douzième vers, de même que l'hapax *destinatus* rappelle *obstinatus* du vers 11. *At tu*, est repris du vers 14, dans un mélange étrange d'intersubjectivité. L'obsédant OBDURA clôt le poème. La composition circulaire est close. La boucle est bouclée. Le recommencement éternel!

ÉCHOS D'AUTRES LECTURES

Ce poème mémorable a donné lieu à autant de lectures qu'il a eu de lecteurs. Il y a exactement soixante-dix ans, E. P. Morris[15] a vu l'incongruité des vers qui se rapportent au passé par rapport à ceux qui évoquent

---

[14]   IRONIE est un terme dont on use et dont on abuse dans l'interpétation de ce poème. Tout ce qu'on ne peut pas élucider on le déclare *ironique*. Amère ironie!

[15]   «An Interpretation of Catullus VIII», *Transactions of the Connecticut Academy of Arts and Sciences*, New Haven, 15 (1909), pp. 139-151. La citation est à la page 143.

la liaison de Catulle avec sa *puella* (que l'auteur identifie avec Lesbia-Clodia Metelli, l'équation traditionnelle connue). Il dit textuellement :

> Whatever difficulties of interpretation the poem presents are not in the verses themselves, but in the adjustment of them to what is known of the life of Catullus and his relation to Clodia.

C'est là l'erreur fatale de presque tous ceux qui ont analysé ce poème. Au lieu de centrer leur lecture et leur intérêt sur le texte lui-même, au lieu de pénétrer le poème, qu'il parle de lui-même et par lui-même, ils ont essayé de le faire coïncider avec ce que nous pouvons savoir des relations incertaines de Catulle avec Lesbia-Clodia, de l'adapter à la personnalité civique du poète, sur lequel nous ne savons presque rien, de l'ajuster à la datation de poèmes pour lesquels nous n'avons aucun repère chronologique ferme. Le vrai Catulle, nous ne le trouverons que dans sa poésie. Souvent on s'aventure aussi jusqu'à tenter des rapprochements sans pertinence avec d'autres textes de Catulle ou d'autres auteurs, sans aucune référence contextuelle, alors que le poète se donne dans chaque cas une identité nouvelle et particulière. C'est oublier que chaque mot d'un poème doit être replacé dans le contexte imaginaire et émotif propre à *ce* poème. L'« objectivisme historique », et son système positiviste, apanage du dix-neuvième siècle, cet excès de l'explication « érudite » de *realia* sont souvent un obstacle à la compréhension d'une œuvre littéraire. L'historicisme diachronique s'est souvent imposé comme une interprétation littéraire. Le texte poétique a servi uniquement de prétexte à une exploration historicisante.

$$* \quad * \quad *$$

Traitons cela avec un gros bon sens. Si les données historiques et biographiques éclaircissent le texte, elle sont utiles et nécessaires. Chaque œuvre est localisée dans l'espace et datée dans le temps. Derrière une création il y a toujours un créateur et aucune œuvre littéraire n'existe dans un vide historique. Certains critiques modernes, dans leur zèle intempestif, font une autopsie de coroner sur le cadavre du poème au lieu d'exercer la maïeutique littéraire. Il n'y a pas de poésie sans personnalité du poète. Chaque texte est le résultat d'un acte humain ; il s'écrit à travers son auteur. Aucun auteur n'est exempt de *toute* dépendance à l'égard de facteurs extérieurs qui conditionnent son œuvre, quoiqu'elle ne soit pas le produit d'un déterminisme aveugle. Le texte littéraire est un phénomène historique. L'histoire des faits sera nécessairement interrogée si le texte y fait allusion.

D'autre part, adapter le poème d'après le lit de Procuste de la vie d'un poète est une attitude funeste et nuisible. Les confessions des poètes sont toujours fonction de leur art. « Le moi qui écrit n'est pas le moi qui vit, « disait Proust. Écrire, ce n'est pas toujours vivre. C'est peut-être se survivre. En scrutant trop les intentions du poète, l'on court le risque de les fausser. Et le poète se modifie en faisant son œuvre. Dans son article « Qu'est-ce que la poésie[16] ? », Roman Jakobson insiste avec raison sur le fait que l'expérience de la vie exprimée dans l'œuvre littéraire et l'expérience réalisée dans la vie privée sont « deux aspects également vrais, [qui] ne représentent que les significations différentes, ou, pour employer un langage savant, des niveaux sémantiques différents d'un même objet, d'une même expérience. Un cinéaste dirait qu'il s'agit de deux prises distinctes d'une même scène ». Si nous avons surtout insisté, dans cet interlude, sur les aberrations d'historicité et de biographisme outrés, c'est la faute des philologues qui en ont abusé.

*   *   *

E.P. Morris est également loué pour une autre aberration qui s'est perpétuée jusqu'à présent, à savoir que ce poème de Catulle constituerait une présentation *humoristique* de Catulle-amant qui essaierait de toucher le cœur d'une Lesbie inconsistante au moyen d'interpellations, de compliments, de pathétiques et sévères menaces. A. L. Wheeler[17] a suivi les pas de Morris et il pense que l'interpétation de ce dernier « is the only satisfactory one ». Il conçoit le poème comme une petite querelle entre les amants, une plaisanterie littéraire à la manière alexandrine. R. A. Swanson[18] suit la même voie en se concentrant sur l'humour dans la structure, la progression, l'équilibre et la symétrie du poème. M. B. Skinner[19] exprime l'opinion suivant laquelle Catulle emploierait le topos de l'amant insensé comme un commentaire ironique de sa folie. Steele Commager[20] pense qu'il serait stupide de nier l'accent comique mais qu'il serait tout aussi stupide d'affirmer que l'accent comique explique tout. H. Akbar Khan[21] y voit une invitation lancée à Lesbie pour qu'elle joue le jeu avec Catulle, lequel aurait masqué les sentiments forts sous l'humour. Friedrich Klingner[22] y voit une clownerie sublime à cause de l'ïambe boiteux avec lequel le poème est composé et à cause de l'ambiguïté et de l'illogisme des sentiments du poète. Helmut Gugel[23] estime que le poème aurait pu être conçu comme une invective, non pas contre les autres, mais contre soi-même. En s'appuyant sur le style du poème, sur sa structure artistique rigoureuse et sur l'intention du poète de dominer des sentiments excessivement puissants, ce commentateur estime qu'il n'y a aucune raison pour voir en ce poème une énorme raillerie.

---

[16] Cité d'après la traduction française, publiée dans les *Questions de poétique*, Paris, Seuil, 1973, p. 117.
[17] *Catullus and the Tradition of the Ancient Poetry*, Berkeley, University of California Press, 1934, réimpression 1964, pp. 227-230.
[18] « The Humor of Catullus 8 », ClJ, 58 (1963), pp. 193-196.
[19] « Catullus 8: the Comic *Amator* as *Eiron* », ClJ, 66 (1971), pp. 298-305.
[20] « Notes on Some Poems of Catullus », HSPh, 70 (1965), pp. 83-110. Sur *Miser Catulle*, pp. 90-92.
[21] « Style and Meaning in Catullus's Eight Poem », *Latomus*, 27 (1968), pp. 555-574.
[22] *Romische Geisteswelt*[4], München, Ellermann, 1961, pp. 220-225.
[23] « Catull, Carmen 8 », *Athenaeum*, nouvelle série, 45 (1967), pp. 278-293.

Eduard Fraenkel[24] décèle dans ce poème «l'humiliation la plus écrasante, décrite avec une précision minutieuse, du reste acceptée par le poète sans pleurnicherie, comme un acte de la Nature, inévitable». Pour K. Büchner[25] ce poème est un exemple parfait du lyrisme catullien, du débordement spontané d'un mouvement d'âme. Le poète est un spectateur passionné de sa double chute de la résolution à la faiblesse. La lutte acharnée avec sa passion est élevée à la hauteur de la poésie. H. Bardon[26] écrit: «Un cœur qui hésite entre le regret et la décision, un cœur qui choisit, mais avec la peine, et dont le choix est bien peu sûr, voilà ce que nous savons... Tout le poème... dit les élans, les retours, les efforts de l'âme de Catulle en lutte contre elle-même. L'âme de Catulle? Une âme humaine, simplement». O. Weinreich[27] trouve qu'il s'agit là de l'«éruption du désespoir». Enfin, lord Macaulay[28] disait qu'il ne pouvait pas lire ce poème sans pleurer. Cela doit être émouvant quand un Anglais pleure — et il le dit.

CONCLUSION

Hegel nous assure qu'une œuvre d'art et d'autant plus belle que son contenu spirituel est d'une vérité plus profonde. William Faulkner, dans son discours de réception du prix Nobel de littérature se plaignait amèrement du fait que les écrivains d'aujourd'hui, surtout les jeunes, «ont oublié les problèmes du cœur de l'homme en lutte avec lui-même, seul matériau dont on puisse faire une œuvre littéraire qui vaille, l'unique sujet digne de l'écrivain, le seul qui mérite le rude effort et la sueur de l'ouvrier des lettres[29]».

Il y a plus de deux mille ans, le jeune poète romain Catullus Veronensis, réveillant les sources motrices profondes de l'âme et jettant à son œuvre en pâture tous ses sentiments les plus intimes, a bien compris les problèmes perpétuels et immuables de la condition humaine, plus précisément celui que Pascal a formulé: «le cœur a ses raisons que la raison ne connaît point». Catulle a artistiquement exprimé la poésie âpre du cœur humain, les convulsions d'une passion qui par le dictat de la raison devrait mourir dans le cœur et le corps d'un homme. Mais la passion ne meurt pas... D'où l'ambivalence du poète et la catharsis à travers l'exercice poétique.

$$* \quad * \quad *$$

---

[24] *Art. cit.*, p. 53.

[25] *Art. cit.*, p. 8.

[26] *Op. laud.*, (*Explications*), p. 26.

[27] *Catull, Liebesgedichte und sonstige Dichtungen*, Hamburg, Rowolhlt, 1960, p. 175.

[28] *Trevelyan's Life* (II, 448). Il y a trois poèmes catulliens qui ont fait couler des larmes à Macaulay: 8, 76, 88.

[29] *Nobel Lectures (Literature)*, publié par les soins de Hornst Frenz, Amsterdam, Elsevier, 1969, p. 444. «The young man or woman writing today has forgotten the problems of the human heart in conflict with itself which alone can make a good writing because only that is worth writing about, worth the agony and the sweat.»

Nous avons essayé de montrer dans notre interpétation que Catulle a exprimé, d'une façon unique, cette lutte pénible de l'itinéraire charnel. Dans cette optique il est tout à fait compréhensible qu'il y ait des changements dramatiques des états d'âme, des convulsions, des fléchissements, des déchirements et des péripéties: détermination faible et incertaine au début, glissement de la résolution vers la faiblesse extrême à cause des souvenirs des ébats joyeux du passé lumineux, nouvelle résolution plus claire et plus ferme dans un présent indigne d'un *vir*, puis, de nouveau, gouffre d'anémie existentielle en prévision d'un avenir sans *puella*, et sursaut final de la résolution, à l'instigation de la raison froide. La courbe sinueuse, l'incohérence est dans le poème comme dans la vie même. Mais c'est une cohérence parfaite dans l'incohérence. Quoique la cohérence ne soit ni la seule ni la principale condition de la satisfaction esthétique, celle de l'amalgame de la matière et de la manière est ici parfaitement réalisée. La lutte du cœur et de la raison pénètre à travers le tissu délicat du lyrisme catullien. Les paroles les plus humbles, tout à fait quotidiennes, sont mises en valeur, sciemment et consciemment, par ce tisserand dans sa tapisserie, c'est-à-dire dans le tissu verbal continu (*textus* = un tissu, vient de *texere* = tisser). Un seul lien, le sens, court à travers l'organisation formelle du texte, l'ordre des mots, la récurrence lexicale, le dosage des mots longs et brefs, les coupes opérées dans le vers et dans la phrase, l'enchevêtrement de ces deux éléments, le parallélisme continu dans les répétitions, dans les antithèses, dans les assonances et les allitérations, dans les rythmes et les sonorités, dans la manière d'exprimer le domaine du temps (dans les formes verbales) et le domaine de l'espace (dans les groupes nominaux). Tous ces artifices poétiques de l'écriture catullienne, mentionnés à leurs places respectives dans notre analyse détaillée, donnent à ce poème une force performative extraordinaire, polyphoniquement et polysémiquement balancée et harmonisée.

Nous avons essayé, sans admiration béate et sans élans incontrôlés, de décoder, objectivement et minutieusement, outre la fonction communicative, manifeste, actuelle, patente et explicite, la fonction poétique cachée, virtuelle, latente et implicite, l'actualisation, la poéticité de ce texte. Le poème est comme un iceberg: les quatre-cinquièmes restent immergés, et la portion émergée est, dans notre cas, si loin et par son code linguistique et par son état de civilisation (la différence des temps et des esprits) que nous ne pouvons pas la voir clairement. Une des finalités de toute herméneutique est de lutter contre la distance culturelle, contre le système de valeurs sur lequel le texte s'établit[30]. Pour vaincre

---

[30] Dans son article «Qu'est-ce qu'un texte?» «Expliquer et comprendre» (dans *Hermeneutik und Dialektik*, publié en l'honneur de Hans-Georg Gadamer, Tübingen, Mohr, 1970, vol. 2, p. 198) Paul RICOEUR dit: «Expliquer, c'est dégager la structure, c'est-à-dire les relations internes de dépendance qui constituent la statique du texte: interpréter, c'est prendre le chemin de pensée ouvert par le texte, se mettre en route vers l'*orient* du texte. Nous sommes invités ... à chercher, en-deça de l'opération subjective de l'interprétation comme acte *sur* le texte, une opération objective de l'interprétation qui serait l'acte du texte». (C'est l'auteur qui souligne)

cette distance, il faut la connaître afin de mieux l'apprivoiser. Mais notre premier souci était de décrire le texte comme tel, son immanence, l'agencement d'unités linguistiques précises. Ce texte apparemment simple est tellement dense et épais qu'il oppose une grande résistance, et il ne se livre pas du premier coup. On doit le secouer, l'interroger, le jauger, le tâter, l'ausculter, le pénétrer, le scruter et le soupeser avec beaucoup de soin et d'insistance jusqu'à ce qu'il laisse entrevoir ses secrets. Mais il n'est pas seulement important de regarder longuement et minutieusement notre objet littéraire. La façon de regarder est très importante. Comme le poème est d'abord une œuvre d'art verbal, l'art du langage, une réalité linguistique originale, notre premier souci était de percer le secret du recours du poète Catulle aux ressources de la langue latine et du langage en général pour y trouver les valeurs expressives. Nous estimons qu'une approche linguistique du discours littéraire à travers la fonction poétique est un moyen de ne pas sombrer dans un impressionnisme débridé et de permettre l'étude détaillée de fonctionnements démontrables et vérifiables. *Expliquer*, d'après l'étymologie (du latin *explicare*), c'est *déplier*, (sens encore usité du XVIIe siècle) et en dépliant nous découvrons, à travers le langage poétique, une émotion esthétique et la visée du message poétique qui est la somme d'ensembles de signes. Car, dans tous les arts, le triomphe est de forcer la matière à témoigner pour l'esprit.

NUNC CURSU LAMPADA VOBIS TRADO[31]
(Je vous passe la torche maintenant)

Nous sommes convaincus qu'une lecture poétique active ne se répète jamais exactement. Chaque lecteur fait son poème. Mais comme le phénomène littéraire est le rapport du texte et du lecteur, le résultat ne dépend pas que du texte, mais aussi de l'apport du lecteur à ce texte. Le lecteur doit disposer d'outils d'analyse suffisants. Tout lecteur lit un poème en fonction de sa formation culturelle et langagière, de son expérience intellectuelle, de sa sensibilité artistique, de sa capacité en symbiose empathique, de son esprit critique, et de son intuition à la fois sensible et intellectuelle.

En outre, les œuvres poétiques possèdent une plurivalence, c'est-à-dire des possibilités latentes assez variées pour répondre aux besoins et aux goûts de lecteurs nombreux et d'époques différentes. Aucune théorie herméneutique n'a encore réussi à formuler assez clairement l'ensemble des prescriptions interprétatives pour que nous puissions accepter *une* interprétation canonique, unique et normative. L'œuvre classique est justement d'une permanence vitale parce qu'elle se prête toujours à de nou-

---

[31] Dans la course aux flambeaux chez les Grecs, il fallait que la torche restât allumée et qu'on la remît à un autre. Ce que je fais. Je m'inspire aussi du beau vers de Mörike *Auf eine Lampe: Was aber schön ist, selig scheint es in ihm selbst*, dont l'interprétation a fait l'objet d'un échange de lettres entre Émile Steiger et Martin Heidegger (« Ein Briefwechsel mit Martin Heidegger », dans E. STEIGER, *Die Kunst der Interpretation*, Zürich, Atlantis, 1955, pp. 34-48).

velles interprétations, délivre des messages toujours divers, et toujours imprévisibles. Elle est en devenir perpétuel, jamais vraiment finie, jamais définitive. Les classiques sont en re-co-naissance perpétuelle. Chaque bon interprète aussi, en vivant l'œuvre classique, en se faisant docile à sa structure, à son rythme, à ses accents, vit sa nouvelle création. L'interprétation devient une poïétique, une création à la fois réceptive et productive.

Cela dit, nous ne voulons d'aucune manière soutenir la vacuité d'une œuvre poétique, disponible pour un sens quelconque, pour une interprétation quelconque. Toutes les lectures sont possibles uniquement quand l'œuvre n'a aucun sens. Seule la page blanche *(tabula rasa)* se prête à toutes les interprétations que l'on voudra.

En revanche, l'œuvre littéraire finie, livrée au public, continue à vivre à différents niveaux de lecture, à différentes couches de significations. Nous avons centré notre lecture sur le signifiant, où la forme refuse de s'abolir dans le signifié. Mais on peut considérer le signe poétique dans son rapport avec l'univers du discours, où le signifiant s'atténue au profit du signifié. D'où des lectures « plurielles » que nous suggèrent les sciences humaines.

Nous insistons sur la nécessité d'une réinterprétation continuelle et différente d'œuvres littéraires du passé et de la compréhension meilleure de soi-même dans le présent par cette fusion des horizons.

Mr P. McCormick donnera un éclairage différent du nôtre et il commentera notre approche. L'éclairage philosophique — nous l'espérons — va enrichir notre compréhension, notre jouissance (joui-sens) et notre co-naissance de l'organisme infiniment simple et complexe qu'est ce poème.

Mon interpétation terminée, je l'ai envoyée au Professeur Gadamer. Il m'a envoyé en réponse l'article que je suis heureux de publier ici. En lisant la biographie de cet humaniste *(Philosophische Lehrjahre)* on constate qu'en plus de la philosophie (Eros philosophos), son domaine de spécialisation, la philologie classique a été une de ses activités privilégiées. Les nombreuses heures consacrées avec ses savants collègues de Marbourg à la lecture et à l'interprétation des auteurs classiques, ses travaux sur les présocratiques, sur Platon et sur Aristote, ses relations d'amitié avec les spécialistes en études classiques, notamment Paul Friedländer, Werner Jaeger, Wilhelm Kroll, Friedrich Klinger, Karl Reinhardt, Georg Rhode, Günther Zünz témoignent de son grand intérêt pour la *Klassische Philologie*. Il avait même songé à faire sa thèse d'agrégation en philologie classique, mais Martin Heidegger l'orienta vers d'autres rivages. Tout philologue sera heureux d'apprendre que le Professeur Gadamer partage l'avis de Nietzsche, qui soutient qu'un bon philosophe doit être aussi un bon philologue, et que le langage joue un rôle central dans la vie de l'homme.

L'école stoïcienne de Pergame enseignait que les paroles des poètes, spécialement celles d'Homère, avaient un sens caché (ὑπόνοια) et que les philosophes sont appelés à découvrir ce «vrai sens». Pour les anciens, φιλολογεῖν et φιλοσοφεῖν avaient souvent une signification très proche, parfois même identique, par exemple quand Plutarque dans son *Cato Minor* (6,3) déclare que Caton était parfois si absorbé par ses devoirs politiques qu'il n'avait pas le temps de φιλολογεῖν (= philosopher). Faut-il aussi mentioner Cicéron qui dans la préface du *De inventione* dit: *Sapientiam sine eloquentia parum prodesse civitatibus, eloquentiam vero sine sapientia nimium obesse plerumque, prodesse numquam*. Dans le *De officiis* (1,50), il distingue explicitement les animaux *(rationis et orationis expertes)* des hommes qui sont capables de raisonner et de s'exprimer. John Salisbury a dit que l'antiquité nous a légué trois sœurs: Philologiam, Philosophiam, Philokaliam. C'est donc avec raison que les philologues (dicti studiosi) et les philosophes (sapientiae studiosi) unissent ici leurs efforts pour une meilleure compréhésion de l'énoncé (littera) et de la pensée (λόγος) de Catulle. N'oublions pas que «si le poème certes est fait de mots, ces mots, eux ne sont pas faits seulement de lettres, mais de l'être» (G.E. Glancier).

Stéphane KRESIC,
Université d'Ottawa.

Reading and Interpreting Catullus 8

In this paper I want to explore, in a preliminary and quite tentative way, a comparison and contrast between two related but different approaches to a classical text. Each approach, although quite personal and therefore limited in great measure, I will take for purposes of my argument here as representative of one type of possible critical reading of almost any classical or literary artwork whatsoever. The first type, my untutored response to "Miser Catulle", I will call a hermeneutic reading and in part one of this paper I will set out some of its characteristic detail. In part two I will take up a classicist's interpretation of the same poem, in this case that of Professor Kresic, and examine its detail in turn. Finally I will investigate the central similarities and differences between these approaches and hazard some general comments on the roles each of these approaches awards to intentions, history, and language.

1. READING CATULLUS 8

Catullus 8 presents its listeners and readers with a situation. This situation is not a static one like of those scenes which, say, pastorals depict, but a dynamic one which includes different *kinds* of changes. And this dynamic situation often affects us in those moments when we are able to interact imaginatively with it.

The lyric poem of Catullus achieves many of its central effects by detailing, with various strategies, the particulars of these different kinds of changes. I want here to indicate two of these changes only and then say a word about their interaction.

The first of these changes turns on the speaker's activity in the poem. Catullus, we know, is being adressed by an unknown speaker who may well be, although need not be, Catullus himself. This unresolved ambiguity is one of the devices the poem exhibits, a poetic feature which introduces still further movement into the text. The two poles of this ambiguity — Catullus as speaker or someone else as speaker — can reverse several times for the audience in the way in which, for example, figure-ground relationship operate in *Gestalt* illustrations. Moreover, the dynamics of ambiguity can also result in both of two possible interpretations being simultaneously present to the hearer or reader in the way in which, say, two separate perceptual details in an Op Art painting inhibit the visual mechanisms from clearly distinguishing anything more than a continuous vibration between both.

The ambiguous speaker stops addressing Catullus and turns instead to Catullus' friend all the while continuing to refer to Catullus but now in the third person only. Although this change of direction is clearly marked in the poem, here too we find another poetic device particularizing the general shift of attention. I want to refer to this device rather loosely as "distance". And what I have in mind is a difference between the relationships that exists between the speaker and Catullus on the one hand — we must often but not always find ourselves imagining both of them present — and the relationship between the speaker and the woman on the other — many would tend to imagine only the speaker as present. I want to say then that the poem presents the speaker and his interlocutor in importantly different ways depending on the distance between them. In the opening section of the poem the speaker and his interlocutor are both present, whereas in the succeeding section there is some doubt whether the interlocutor is present physically or only imaginatively. Whatever the status however Catullus himself is presented as still on the scene, although in this second section he is not being addressed directly.

A final shift in the speaker's activity concludes the poem as it began, returning the audience's attention to the initial situation. For the ambiguous speaker once again addresses the ever-present Catullus and leaves the unnamed woman to ponder the questions already put to her. And here too we find another poetic device effecting and underlining the new change in the poem's dramatic situation, the familiar device of repetition. Catullus is addressed just as directly as at the poem's inception not in the nominative, as he is later on, but in the vocative case. And again, just as peremptorily as at the poem's inception, the speaker puts an order to Catullus.

One major feature of this poem then is the dynamic role which the speaker plays in three different scenes or tableaux. Although the final scene is a brief echo of the initial one, each tableau exhibits a particular poetic device — whether ambiguity or distance or repetition — which serves to particularize the general change of direction in the speaker's activity.

The second major feature of this poem which I want to comment on turns on the changes in temporal perspective. And again the stress is not on a particular temporal perspective as such but on the shift, the change from one perspective to another.

The poem begins in the present. But already in the opening two lines both the past and the future are already either referred to or implied. Both past and future however are focussed in the present situation which the poem presents, the past as the still present and he future as the not yet present.

After this introduction the poem turns its audience's attention to the past, a time of reciprocation between Catullus and his friend. This period in the past is what has continued to haunt Catullus now in the present. The joy of this time moreover is accentuated strongly by the repetition of almost the same line both at the beginning and at the end of the passage. The effect is to frame the previous experience with the image of the beaming sun, and the neat demarcation of this past experience with the same image suggest an almost timeless quality about that experience which now seems to take on an even mythic kind of presence in the mind of Catullus.

Again however the temporal perspective shifts back to the present in lines 9-12 with the speaker first addressing Catullus and then the woman.

This moment in the present is only an interlude. For the speaker goes on in his address to the woman to predict the future in lines 13 and 14 as well as to imagine that future in a crescendo of ever more graphic details in 11, 14-18.

The poem closes with once again the fullness of the present where Catullus is enjoined to repeat no more in the future his vacillating ways of the past and to remain firm.

In general then the temporal perspective changes even more often than the speaker's activity. But these frequent changes like the speaker's activity are kept in careful order by the same device of returning at the end of the poem to the poem's beginning — the present. Moreover, in the case of the temporal perspective there is a carefully balanced contrast as well. The poem thus moves from the present to the past and back to the present; then from the present to the future and back to the present. And of course the present in which the poem opens and closes, unlike the present in which it pauses towards the middle of its progression, is a comprehensive one which echoes the past and anticipates the future. So much then for the second of the two major kinds of changes in the poem.

One final point now should be added, although briefly. We need to be explicit about how these two movements overlap and reinforce one another. Notice first that each of these movements divides the text according to a different scheme. Moreover each of these schemes accommodates more than one interpretation depending on which way me try to resolves the various ambiguities which the poem deploys. Thus, the speaker's activity divides the poem into three sections, whereas the temporal shift divides the poem into five. But the first division allows alternative enumerations because of the ambiguities which attach to the identity of the speaker, and the second division also allows another schema because of the ambiguities which attach to the notion of the present. Notice further that these two divisions not only overlap but in effect allow of particular alternative subdivisions just because each is dependent to some degree on the other. The first dynamic principle, the speaker's activity, operates largely with the help of shifts in tenses whereas the second dynamic principle, the temporal perspective, operates largely with the help of substitutions for the role of the speaker's interlocutors. So neither movement can finally be divorced from the other although each works its effects in distinct and clearly different ways.

We hear this poem then or we read it and part of our response, I am anxious to suggest here, comprises both an awareness of a particular situation which the poem presents and a sensitivity to the dynamics both of the situation and of the verbal strategies which are deployed in the text as means to effect this sensitivity. The result, sometimes but not necessarily and not always, is an emotional response on the part of the poem's audience and not just an intellectual one. The poem, when it comes to exist as an artwork, not only presents an idea; it can bring about some kind of recognition of values through the emotional involvement of its audience.

2. INTERPRETING CATULLUS 8

In the first part of this paper I tried to outline the major elements in a personal response to the poem of Catullus. It is important now to examine first a representative literary interpretation of this poem, and then to compare and contrast this interpretation with the response which we have already looked at.

Stephen Kresic's reading of Catullus, besides an introduction and a conclusion, comprises four parts of unequal length and importance. The first part presents the Latin text with appropriate metrical notation together with four translations. Part two comprises a brief and general analysis of the meter and rhythm of the poem. Part three, the most important and the longest, is a section by section analysis of the poem in which its various levels are all as if were taken together rather than analysed successively. And the fourth and final part looks briefly at a number of other philological readings of the poem.

Before looking more closely at the major elements of this reading, several aspects of this structure should be noted.

Parts one and two are closely related in that metrical and rhythmic analysis of the Latin poem are an explicitation of the oral features of the poem which are already scored on the printed text. Moreover, parts two and three are also closely related in that the general survey of the poem's meters and rhythms in part two are then woven into the much fuller analysis in part three. Although the analysis in part two is a short one, the analysis is nonetheless centrally important because it provides an opening perspective and indeed sets the tone of the much more detailed reading which follows.

Another general feature of Kresic's reading is his concern both to survey however briefly many of the major previous interpretations without however going into any one of these alternative readings in any detail. In fact Kresic's purpose here is not so much the investigation of other possible readings but the double aim of providing instances of the biographical fallacy in the case of Catullus' poem and, more briefly, indicating several instances of previous interpretations which Kresic would build on in his own reading of the poem.

Both of these general features in Kresic's reading — the cardinal role of the metrical and rhythmic analysis and the clear attempt to categorize most previous readings of the poem as fallacious in a quite definite way — are important guidelines for our understanding the specific character of his interpretation.

To achieve a more perspicuous view of this interpretation, at least for our purposes of comparison and contrast, we need to answer I think the usual kinds of questions we put to such readings. What is the starting point, what are the aims, what are the major methods which are taken into account, and what conclusions are drawn — these familiar questions will do for openers.

The aims of the classical interpretation — to generalize now on what I will assume to be the representative status of Kresic's particular reading for at least one kind of philological interpretation — are to be found both in the introduction and conclusion.

In the latter, there is a contrast drawn between the manifest communicative function of a literary text and its latent poetic function. The classical interpretation would put the accent on the poetic function although it would not neglect the communicative function. More specifically, the aim here is to articulate the poetic modalities of the opposition between reason and passion in the experience of one kind of human love. And this articulation is to be achieved particularly by detailing the linguistic markers which chart the play between rational and emotional consistency and inconsistency. The classical interpretation then does not so much aim at "building consistencies" as at describing the dynamic interplay between consistency and its opposites — call them what you will. This aim finally is pursued inside the general intention of understanding "how this poem is made" with the guiding limitation that no understanding of any literary artwork can be perfectly identical with any other interpretation.

In the introduction, however, these aims are expressed more boldly and still other goals are formulated.

The communicative function is stressed very plainly with the talk about "capturing signals which the text addresses to us". And the poetic function is also considered when Kresic talks metaphorically of "uncovering the poem's solicitations". But more striking are the exclusions which are effected. For it is no part of Kresic's purpose to identify sources nor to expound on biographical details. What is to occupy the center of his interpretation rather is the way in which the poem itself achieves its poetic form. This achievement however is not to be discussed in terms of any artificial distinctions between form and matter, content and style, or "le signifiant" and "le signifié". The interpretation, in short, aims at what we might call an organic rather then a discrete description.

If the starting point is the poem itself and not the author of the audience or the history of the text's reception, and if the aim is an organic interpretation of both the communicative and poetic function of the text, what then are the means Kresic chooses to realize his purpose?

Besides the general importance of the metrical and rhythmic analysis, Kresic uses a variety of techniques in his close examination of detail. Thus, one might discern at least six components in his analysis. A statistical element is drawn upon in places (Catullus uses here 37 verb forms and only 6 substantives; moreover his poem includes 6 *hapax legomena*), and the phonological aspects of the poem already surveyed in a general way are scrutinized in almost every line. A historical view of the development of the Latin language is important at places where, for example, Kresic is anxious to distinguish variations in language levels, the familiar versus the archaic, and so on. Syntactic questions are also prominent, expecially where the carefully balanced use of verb tenses and moods is in evidence. Stylistic issues arise repeatedly, and of course various reflections on semantic questions are also investigated. Most important I think is the concerted effort to examine these distinct issues not in any arbitrary or even systematic order but in just that sequence in which the poem turns our attention to one issue or another. Thus, the methods called upon here are various and their use is repeatedly subordinated to the progression of the text rather than to any other extrinsic criteria.

But what conclusions are reached?

We must answer, I think, that no "conclusions" are reached at all. For the goal of this kind of interpretation is not the propounding of a particular set of theoretical views but the enhancement of readers' appreciation of a particular literary artwork. But what then would count as evidence that such an enhancement has been made possible? Perhaps we could count this kind of evidence as the "conclusion" we are looking for. Kresic himself does not explicit this point in his own interpretation so we need to hazard a suggestion here with some care. After consideration I want to suggest that some evidence for the enhancement of our appreciation of the poem is to be found not just in the extraordinary reminders which this interpretation furnishes of the auditory qualities of this poem but also the muted but repeated concern with disabusing the poem's readers of any unexamined commitment to "building consistencies" indiscriminately. Not all poems sustain this particular kind of rational scrutiny, and often those which do require of their readers a much more laminated notion of "consistency" than classicists so far have been able to fashion. Finally, we need to notice that these two elements reinforce each other. The auditory qualities of the poem refine our somewhat crude notion of consistency, and conversely our inchoate views about consistency enable us nonetheless to integrate both different kinds of auditory features and to harmonize such features with other no less important but non-auditory elements of the literary artwork.

3.   SIMILARITIES AND DIFFERENCES

In this third and final section of my paper, now that the main lines of both a personal response to the poem of Catullus as well as a classical interpretation of the poem are in place, I want to examine the salient similarities and differences between these approaches in order to generate several questions about literary hermeneutics.

A personal response to a literary artwork just as well as a representative classical interpretation share a similar starting point. In both cases this starting point is neither the author's intentions nor the historical context of the work nor the place of the particular artwork in the œuvre of its author nor the influences of one sort or another on the text we have at our disposal. The starting point is the poem.

The aims of these two different kinds of reading however are somewhat different. In the case of the classicist the aim is clearly a species of explanation. An attempt is made in other words to explain just how the text produces certain effects which are taken to be satisfying ones by a tradition of readers. In the case of the hermeneutician explanatory goals are eschewed in the interests of providing some elements in the never finished process of fully describing the artwork. The opposition I am suggesting here between explanation on the one hand and description on the other however must not be exaggerated. For clearly this distinction is hardly water-tight. The classicist undertakes a good deal of description- witness the metrical and rhythmic analysis — which most often is both more detailed and more complete than what the hermeneutician arrives at. And, too, the hermeneutician finds explanatory elements often seeping into his impossible, even incoherent ideal of "pure description" — — witness my own talk earlier of how one kind of ambiguity functions. The distinction I am concerned to urge here then is more one of emphasis and accent than of substance alone. Nonetheless, the difference is there, and we will have to raise the question shortly of what if any significance it has.

The approaches, if we want to argue that the word "methods" is too formal, also differ. In the classicist reading we have the careful and sensitive application to the text of something like a canon of methods ranging from statistical lexicography to all kinds of stylistics. Each method is drawn upon in turn to heighten our responses to the poem just at those places where the poem is taken as it were to solicit such an approach. The hermeneutic reading by contrast leaves us often with the impression of either a remarkable ignorance of the tried and true means at our disposal, especially since the heyday of nineteenth-century philology, for taking one text systematically in hand, or of an amateur quality which often comes close to impressionistic musings and nothing more. Historically at least, these notions are inaccurate. Schleiermacher after all and Dilthey especially and in our own times both Gadamer and Ricoeur are neither ignorant readers nor strictly speaking amateurs. Perhaps initially at any rate we may choose then to characterize this difference in approach as a difference between the cultivated classicist on one side and, say, the sceptical hermeneutician on the other. Both are aware of various methodologies; at their best however one chooses to orchestrate the relevant ones with sympathy and attentiveness, while the other tries to subvert the methodological canon with what is always only a partial return to an ever elusive text.

But what of conclusions? What do the classicist and hermeneutic readings finally offer those who would take up the literary artwork anew? I think the similarities are more important here than they were when we looked at aims and methods. For both classicist and hermeneutic readings, if they may properly be said to conclude to anything at all, would send other readers back to the text with a freshened sensibility. But the in general explanatory aim of the classicist when reasonably well fulfilled would seem to enlarge our grasp of the poem, whereas the descriptive goals of the hermeneutician when reasonably well fulfilled would seem to enlarge our responses to the poem. There is of course a difference here. Description often leaves us with no larger comprehension but a fuller sense of what may seem to some to call for explanation. The effect I would point to then in the hermeneutic as opposed to the classical reading is one of more questions to be taken up than explanations to be integrated into some theoretical whole. In short, the cognitive functions of at least hermeneutic descriptions seem much less important than those of classicist explanations.

We can get a better grasp on the significance of these contrasts, I think, if we step back for a moment from the particular features of these two readings and try to discern a more substantive comparison between them. If we go back over the kinds of reading which I have tried to detail here I think we can note at least three underlying similar concerns.

The first of these shared concerns is the role of intentions. The classicist is rightly chary of letting talk of especially the author's intentions abstract us from the many textual features of the poem. The artwork in short is not to be subordinated to the artist. And of course it is often in the careful explanation of just how a particular artwork achieves its central effects that the classicist with his diverse and well-sharpened tools excels. The hermeneutician shares this suspicion of talk of intentions when an artwork is under discussion. But, although he most often lacks the distinctive skills of the classicist, he would call attention to both the variety of intentions that may be at issue as well as the variety of contexts in which talk of intentions takes place. Thus it may not be sufficient to exclude talk of authors' intentions from the discussion of the artwork when performers' intentions or audiences' intentions or translators' intentions or interpreters' intentions may also require examination in their own terms. Similarly, it may not prove sufficient to exclude talk of some kind of intentions from the interpretive context only when both the descriptive and evaluative context must be considered also. Is Catullus 8 a poem, a representative Catullan poem, a successful poem —

these questions are different ones and each at some point must be dealt with by taking a stand on what difference if any the poet's intentions or at least someone's intentions actually make.

A second shared concern surely is with the poem as occupying some kind of curious space in a complex and still continuing historical process.

Both the classicist and the hermeneutician view the artwork as the result of antecendent influence and the occasion for an infinite number of successive interpretations. Both agree too on the different levels at which this historical element is present, whether in the peculiar position which individual lexical items or even whole turns of phrases occupy or on the much larger levels of literary genre and social structures. And both also insist on the irreducibility of the artwork either to its antecedent influences or to its subsequent place in a changing tradition of interpretation. These are similarities and here again, just as in the case of intentions, I would hold for these similarities being finally more important than differences.

There are some differences however which do require attention. The classicist characteristically excels in situating a work like Catullus 8 inside both literary and interpretive traditions. Part of what it means to be a classicist, some would argue, is precisely to be ever at work on this ceaseless process of recalibrating the trajectory of a text inside its double parameters of source and influence. And here surely is where the hermeneutician needs to set aside his usual generalities and submit himself for once to the often illuminating burden of scholarship. But in turn the hermeneutician sometimes has the merits of his failings to offer the classicist. For we are neither clear about the relevant senses of that slippery term "tradition" nor we are in agreement about just what difference some acceptable gloss on that term can make for, if not our explanation, at least our description of a particular artwork. We recognize that a literary artifact is, in an important sense, the result of a complex past; and yet we also recognize that some literary artifacts are novelties and do not seem comprehensible as an intermittent term of some antecedent evolutionary series. So too we recognize as well that a literary artifact is in an important sense the open set of its endless interpretations; and yet we make room in our speculations for that central feature of any work of art which makes it irreducible to however many readings it continues to occasion. The historicality of a text then remains enigmatic for the hermeneutician, and in his struggles to articulate a coherent and consistent understanding of the historicality of any object whatsoever the classicist may find grounds for hesitations of his own about overly facile talk of tradition and convention.

A third and for now final shared concern among classicists and hermeneuticians is the preoccupation with the literary artwork as a linguistic entity.

Both readers call attention above all to the auditory features of literary artworks, whether the meters and rythms of Catullus' polymetric poems or the cadences and codas of literary prose. Both too focus their concern on syntactic and semantic features of their chosen texts and seek to elucidate whatever poetic effects the text works on its hearers and readers by close attention to these features. And both are also centrally interested in the peculiarities of tropes and figures, of diction and tone, of levels of language as well as of lexical oddities.

Here too however, despite the importance of the shared concern, the small differences need some attention. The classicist is trained through his studies in historical linguistics, numismatics, epigraphy, archaeology, and so on to detect with extraordinary precision the shifts and stresses which individual words undergo in the strains of literary production. And this precision must remain the watchword of any hermeneutician who would take upon himself the readings of classical texts. But what if anything can the hermeneutician offer in return? Perhaps only, as so often in other areas, a somewhat different angle of vision on the language of the poets. More specifically, the hermeneutician can perhaps help substantiate the classicist's well-founded complaint that the communicative function of language is subordinate to the poetic function by criticizing communicative models of language and trying to elaborate in clearer less mysterious terms what Heidegger and Gadamer have chosen to call "the event of language", the happening of language. In the literary artwork then language not inly is used by an author to communicate some content or other; language itself sometimes brings something to pass in, for example, the way linguistic novelty makes its appearance or in the way some previously unattended feature of the world comes finally into speech.

Intentions, history, and language then remain the common concerns of both classicist and hermeneutic readings of texts like Catullus 8, and yet the differences in emphasis and perspective on these shared interests suggest the possibility of a more fruitful interplay between these readings than has usually been the case.

Peter McCORMICK,
University of Ottawa.

A Classical Text — A Hermeneutic Challenge*

Classical texts have always been a favorite theme for literary hermeneutics. Texts in the classic languages that are no longer spoken provide the sharpest possible experience of temporal distance. For there is no mistaking what is required to attain the linguistic and world horizon proper to a text composed in a dead language: one has to make a dead language speak once again in a living way in the present. The illusion of contemporaneity that may lead the careless reader astray when he is dealing with either his own literary tradition or that of some other language with which he is familiar as actually alive and spoken cannot even begin to insinuate itself.

Conversely, however, classical literature possesses a contemporaneity that is difficult to deny. It has this contemporaneous character not merely in the manner of any work of art that we find gripping in an especially vivid fashion; besides that, it has the peculiar type of contemporaneity that accrues to the classic works of literature on account of their effective history *(Wirkungsgeschichte)*. By this I mean the lasting relevance of the classical models for the emergence of the later national literatures and which has its suspenseful upshot in the famous *querelle des ancies et des modernes*. But this abiding relevance holds especially true for the generations of readers and interpreters who have always sought to interpret the works of linguistic artistry from any and every heritage precisely in the way they had been trained to do in relation to the classical texts.

Hermeneutics is the art of interpretation. As practiced art of interpretation it has its own specifically constitutive experience and it does not come up as just one approach among others like the various methods of scholarly research. Rather it is both prior to and superior to all the others in the same way the end is to the means. In turn, the philosophic reflection that attends to hermeneutics as the actually practiced art of interpretation and so can be called 'philosophical hermeneutics', is in competition with neither this practical exercise of interpretation nor that performed in the sciences. Instead it makes that performance the subject matter of its job of giving an account. This does not imply, however, that it only deals with the methods of interpretation elaborated by the sciences. Its chief task is to determine precisely the contribution that the

---

* The German original translated by Fred Lawrence.

methods of the sciences can provide for the experience of any art. These methods stand as means over against the end against which they have to be measured. We can take it as our foremost principle that no art, and that would include poetry as well, is fashioned for the sake of the scholarly researcher.

But this presents us with a genuine problem. No one will deny that there are scholarly methods of interpretation and criticism taught and learned and applied to works of art, whether they be historical, philological, sociological, and psychological methods; but no one in his right senses would want to claim that only the scholar understands art or himself in the light of art. Surely one would sooner claim just the contrary. To be sure, there are quite diverse things and many different hermeneutical levels in terms of which the experience of art may be enacted. But it would be absurd to restrict the adequate comprehension of the work of art to a putatively highest level supposedly established by 'scholarship'.

The fact of the matter is rather that the experiece of art possesses various different degrees of explicitness and awareness; and this in such a way that it is the work of art itself which displays itself as one and the same in and through all these forms of experience. The contribution of technical scholarly methods may be grasped adequately as only bringing specific perspectives to bear on the work of art, for example, by locating it within its more general context of social history, or explaining its linguistic usage in the light of a universal history of language, or casting light on its artistic form in terms of art history or e.g. the aestehtic theory of genre. One would always be prepared to acknowledge that in this manner any given work of art appears in a new and clearer lights, just so it appears in its uniqueness and singularity, which it is as a work of art, and does not disappear into a mere instance or illustration of a general rule.

The art of interpretation or hermeneutics, then, makes use of the most diverse methods, but it is not itself a method. Still less is the theory of this art, philosophical hermeneutics, a method. Whatever might be intended by the expression, "the hermeneutical method," I do not know. All methods of interpretation belong to hermeneutics and either play a role or can be brought into play when it comes to interpreting works of art, such as poems. The task of philosophical hermeneutics is to clarify how this can occur.

I consider it a misunderstanding when Paul Ricoeur in one of his excellent and erudite works opposes the structuralist method to the "hermeneutic method". Structuralist method is just one of the methods of interpretation. When in another context he sets up the psychoanalytic method as an archeology over against the hermeneutic interest as a teleology for the sake of reintegrating both, he does not seem to realize that neither of these methods has a common cognitive objective. When the Mona Lisa becomes an object in the investigation of Freud, Freud is quite aware that, as a psychologist rather than one concerned with art as such, his objective is not the work of art but evidence for a life-history. For myself it seems misleading to specify the methodical usage of structuralist method in terms of distantiation and objectification, since every use of method presupposes the alienation of its object and every 'interpretation' intends the overcoming of this alienation. But it is not restricted to the use of methods. Every strangeness encountered by an interpreter, in order to get hold of something hard to understand, requires from him constantly to distance himself from himself, and to weigh alternate possibilities. Still less can I imagine how a 'classical' philological interpretation is supposed to be contradistinguished from a hermeneutical interpretation. It is subordinated to the task to learn, so read, i.e. to let speak the text; and with all its erudition and methodical versatility, it has a hermeneutical function.

How does this initiation look? When is hermeneutics needed? Why is the art of interpretation called for? Well, obviously in virtue of something apparently unintelligible that breaks down the anticipations of our experience and of our apprehension of the world and of language. Now in a certain sense one will be able to say about any work of art that it has something inaccessible about it — we would prefer to say, something incomprehensible that throws all our expectations overboard. Suddenly we are brought up short, as if under a spell. It makes us need to abide with the work of art, and the more of a purchase on it we are granted, the more of a notion of it do we get, without its ever being completely conceptualized. It just keeps on gaining in presence.

Nevertheless, we ought to make distinctions. It becomes increasingly clear that not only is the work as a whole like a miracle, but that this or that marvelous feature is obscure or, in other words, calls forth a more rigorous discipline of interpretation. To state the matter precisely, it will always be the case that we already have a vague sense of what we are about and in the light of which we critically assess the adequacy of our interpretive attempts. Otherwise, the whole would not be for us the marvel it is.

It is probably correct that each work of art as such always directs a question at us. Why does it grip us? Why do we find it 'beautiful'? What is it that convinces us? Perhaps one would always have to reply that in whatever grips us or convinces us we find something like a confirmation of our sense of ourselves. It grips us, convinces us — that means just the same as: we find it 'beautiful.' In this context, the workd 'beautiful' has nothing whatsoever to do with an aesthetic ideal of style which could be contrasted with the ugly or the 'no longer beautiful'. It simply means rather that by its sheer existence and appearance it is lifted up out of the whole network of pragmatic interests that patterns our everyday experience and expectations. It can even be a minute work of art like the poem by Catullus under discussion here that belongs to a series of similar small gems that each stands out like Rilke's "Dies stand einmal unter Menschen,'' at once confirming us and ratified by us: 'That is the way things are.'

The justification of the well-trained interpreter is the ability to enrich the basic experience of the work of art by his distinguished and refined knowledge of language and meter, of patterns and parallels, and the careful weighing of every structuring moment. Still it would be false to connect determinate preconceptions of consistency and closedness of form with the kind of recognition and confirmation described above. The ideal of classical art has nothing to do with this hermeneutic notion of recognition and confirmation. But although one has to concede that each and every work of art has to it a hermeneutic challenge in the sense sketched above, this challenge is experienced most intensely in cases when the structure seems of itself to offer divergent possible interpretations. One thinks, for example of the way the Greek tragedy took on a certain insolubility for the later thought of the Christian era on account of its underlying notion of fate and in spite of this still maintained a convincing quality. But even examples like the *Hamlet* of Shakespeare or the *Faust* of Goethe or perhaps the novels of Kafka can well illustrate the importance of holding open alternative possible interpretations. As we shall see, even the short poem of Catullus that has been interpreted here from two sides has to be counted among these outstanding cases.

In each of these cases at any rate, polysemy is not an end in itself and above all, it is a hermeneutic quality of the text itself. It only apparently resists understanding. Actually, it issues the first invitation to become understood. This of course does not mean one simply eliminates such polysemy and so renders the whole, as we say, a univocal verse: instead one brings the various possible interpretations into play and lets them play themselves out. This is not a matter of that methodical distantiation which we apply to a text in order to reach scholarly objectivity. Such a procedure of leaving interpretive options open rather insinuates itself spontaneously in the reader's endeavor to understand. To this extent every interpretation has to it the capability of distantiation. There is not a single interpretation that does not weigh alternative possibilities, indeed that does not discover its own ultimate determinacy by means of the very alternative possibilities that seem to be offered in the text.

In the case of the poem by Catullus we have a decisive difficulty for interpretation which is clearly profiled in the scholarship. It is worthwhile to accept this difficulty as a special challenge. Obviously, it underlies also the very choice of this poem of Catullus for an object of interpretation. Where does the special hermeneutic challenge lie in this poem?

I think it does not rest in the determination of the speaker and the one being addressed. I find myself incapable of finding in this poem the least trace of evidence for seeing a speaker other than Catullus, who was distinguished for his self-analytic bent. Of a 'friend' who could be the speaker there is no mention at all. It seems to me an instance of hermeneutically false distantiation and alienation to even leave such a possibility open. For the text is unequivocal. It conjures up that *vere candidi soles* which, together with every discreteness, breathes a unique intimacy and witnesses to an earlier happiness in love that excluded any other. Nor can I acknowledge the in itself correctly observed variation in the temporal poems as a hermeneutic challenge. One understands it at once. So one has to see in verses 1 through 13 a completely unequivocal and unified statement.

I must admit that for me this section of the poem seems to be clearer than even the 'classical' interpreter acknowledges in his outstanding interpretation. To begin with, I cannot perceive any signals of uncertainty in this appeal to himself on the part of the poet. *Impotens* in verse 9, as the *quoque* utterly confirms, is to be construed as paralleling the young woman's rejection. It is a blatant expression of powerlessness: because you no longer have any power over the beloved, give her up. Nor is there any more solid reason in my opinion for reading the *invitam* of verse 13 as a signal of insecurity or of a veiled hopefulness. The meaning, it seems to me, is utterly simple: because she is unwilling, he should neither seek her out nor try to win her back. The rather monolithic posture which characterizes the entire self-address is brought out finally in the text by the self-objectification with which Catullus makes himself steadfast against the young woman.

But right in this build-up to the objective statement of fact, "*Catullus obdurat*," there *is* a signal in the text, indeed the only one that as far as I can see is in evidence there. It points to the trope, the turn correctly indicated and described by Kresic, that begins with verse 14 and is set clearly in relief semantically by the word, "*at*." That is the hermeneutic point about which the poem as a whole revolves and which endows it with its unfading charm. At this point there begins an authentic multivalence of meaning. One is sure of this as soon as one joins Kresic in disregarding all misleading biographical clues for interpretation. Just when the real polysemy of the second part of the poem starts to speak, the general hermeneutic task of bringing statements to living speech has to be exercised in a specific way.

The turnabout is clearly indicated as such in the text: from the one no longer striving for his former beloved to the one no longer being sought after. It is a transition marked by peculiar harshness and introduced by the tough expression "*at*." In its form, it constitutes a genuine digression, as the turn back to the speaker in the concluding verse with its "*at tu*" shows so plainly. How does the speaker so bent on abandoning his beloved arrive at his turn towards the beloved one abandoned by all? Is he the only lover left in the world? Is this the way he sees himself? But in the portrayal of the abandonment of the beloved precisely the opposite happens. The chain of questions, all suggesting the answer, 'No one,' evokes with poignant clarity the young woman loved by other lovers. What is going on here? Does the unreality of the one thing — the abandonment of the beloved — show forth the reality of the other thing — faithlessness? Does the abandonment mean its opposite in the sense that the "*scelesta, vae te!*" would then be well explained: 'Oh, no, you will not be left all alone: I know you'?

But this contradicts the series of rhetorical questions that immediately follows and which can mean nothing other than: Without me you are abandoned. How are we to think about this transition? Does the occurrence of the key trope of the no longer sought after beloved who becomes the abandoned one loved by others arouse compassion which in turn awakens a new temptation? As if it would be up to him to regain all that he has lost?

At any rate the discontinuity between verses 15 and 16 is unmistakeable. Verse 15 would only be continued if the following verses also were to describe the abandonment of the beloved (and at the same time the irreplaceability of the lover, Catullus). That would be like the wish-fulfillment of a dream. But there is no mistaking that a sudden shift towards fantasies of jealousy intrudes itself. Plainly, the reader is intended to understand: the speaker is calling himself back from the temptations of such faces. He is resolute (or rather: he would like to be). That is the trust of the "*destinatus:*" he has to tell himself!

Now what general hermeneutic truth may we draw from this example? We start with the assumption that interpretation always means: to understand something as an answer. To what question or challenge is this poem a response, an answer that not only claims the quality of artistry, but also the magic of multivalent meaning? One can hardly doubt that by the appeal to himself to get free, the force of the enchantment of love is evoked in all its power. There is nothing laughable about the absurd turn-around we have been describing and nothing inconsistent in the incoherence and confusion it bespeaks. Precisely the absurdity of the turn-around and the double-entendre of the fantasies conjured up testify to the inexorable violence of the passion by which the speaker-lover is obsessed.

Granted that after all this one were to say: 'That's the way it is,' then one would have understood.

Hans-Georg GADAMER,
University of Heidelberg.

Achevé d'imprimer à Cap St-Ignace
aux Ateliers Graphiques Marc Veilleux Inc.
en avril 1981.